WORKS ISSUED BY

THE HAKLUYT SOCIETY

SOME RECORDS OF ETHIOPIA
1593–1646

SECOND SERIES
No. CVII

ISSUED FOR 1954

COUNCIL AND OFFICERS

OF

THE HAKLUYT SOCIETY

1954

Historia de Ethiopia a alta, ou Abassia:

Imperio do Abexim, cujo Rey uulgarmente he chamado

Preste Joam.

Trata da natureza da terra, e da gente, que a pouoa; dos Reys, que nella ouue; da Fé, que tiueram, e tem; e do muito, que os Padres da Companhia de IESUS trabalharam polos reduzir a uerdadeira, e sancta Fé da Igreia Romana.

Dedicada à Magestade d'El Rey D. Joam o 4 Nosso senhor.

Composta pelo Padre Manoel de Almeida da Companhia de IESVS, natural de Viseu.

The titlepage of Almeida's manuscript (S.O.A.S. MS 11966)

SOME RECORDS OF ETHIOPIA
1593-1646

Being Extracts from
THE HISTORY OF HIGH ETHIOPIA OR ABASSIA
by Manoel de Almeida

Together with
Bahrey's *HISTORY OF THE GALLA*

Translated and Edited by
C. F. BECKINGHAM
AND
G. W. B. HUNTINGFORD

PRINTED FOR THE HAKLUYT SOCIETY
LONDON
1954

PRINTED IN GREAT BRITAIN BY ROBERT MACLEHOSE AND CO. LTD
THE UNIVERSITY PRESS GLASGOW

PREFACE

The texts translated in this volume consist of thirty-seven chapters from the *History of High Ethiopia or Abassia (Historia de Ethiopia a alta ou Abassia)*, written in Portuguese by the Jesuit Father Manoel de Almeida between 1628 and 1646, and a short *History of the Galla*, written in Ethiopic by an ecclesiastic named Bahrey in 1593. The selections from Almeida's book describe either the country and its inhabitants or the journeys of the Jesuit missionaries attempting to enter or leave it. These chapters are printed in the order in which they occur in the original; the descriptive extracts precede the narratives of travel. As it seemed appropriate to place together two very early accounts of the Galla, one by a European and the other by an African, Bahrey's work has been inserted immediately before Almeida's chapter on the same subject.

Almeida's history was not published in full until this century when it was included in Beccari's collection, *Rerum aethiopicarum scriptores occidentales inediti*. In making this translation, however, we have followed a manuscript in the library of the School of Oriental and African Studies in the University of London (MS 11966), of which Beccari did not know; he used a slightly inferior manuscript in the British Museum (Add. MS 9861) which we have also consulted. The translation of Bahrey is based upon Guidi's edition and his translation into French.

Bahrey and the first of the travel narratives from Almeida are largely concerned with what is now south-west Ethiopia. The complex ethnological and political history of this area is recorded in a number of rather inaccessible books, of which the most important are in Italian; very little information is available in English. We have therefore summarised what is known of the subject in an essay which is printed immediately after the Introduction, for the use of readers who may wish to appreciate more fully the significance of these texts. For convenience of reference our attempts at identifying place-names in north-east Africa are collected in a separate Gazetteer, instead of being given in the footnotes. The full titles of books mentioned in an abbreviated form in the Introduction and notes will be found in the Bibliography, which is no more than a list of such books. The reader requiring a more adequate bibliography is referred to Fumagalli's *Biblio-grafia etiopica* and the supplements by Zanutto, and to the shorter but more recent *Ethiopica & Amharica. A List of Works in the New York Public Library*, by G. F. Black.

We have found it convenient to distinguish between Abyssinia and Ethiopia, using the former name to denote the historic kingdom of the plateau, and the latter, which is the official name of the empire, for the much larger area incorporated in it after the conquests of Menilek II. In the translated texts we have, of course, followed the practice of our authors.

In preparing this volume we have received much assistance from a number of scholars and travellers to all of whom we offer our cordial thanks. We have particular reason to be grateful to Mr T. P. Waldron, of the Department of Spanish and Portuguese Studies in the University of Manchester, who gave much time to discussing the difficulties in Almeida's text and made very many helpful suggestions. On specific questions we have received generous help from Dr L. D. Barnett, C.B., Litt.D., F.B.A., Mr H. R. Beard, Dr A. Cortesão, Mr A. W. Exell, Deputy Keeper of the Department of Botany in the British Museum (Natural History), Dr W. O. Howarth of the Department of Botany in the University of Manchester, Professor H. W. Janson, of the Department of Fine Arts, New York University, the Rev. A. F. Matthew, of Addis Ababa, Professor Dr R. P. G. Pichi-Sermolli, of the Istituto Botanico in the University of Florence, the Rev. J. B. Primrose, I.C.S.(Retd), Dr Virginia Rau, of the Faculty of Letters in the University of Lisbon, Dr Hugh Scott, Sc.D., F.R.S., Dr R. B. Serjeant, Reader in Arabic in the University of London, the Rev. Professor Jean Simon, S.J., Professor of Ethiopic and Coptic in the Pontificio Istituto Biblico, and Mr Alan Villiers, D.S.C. For the great care with which the photographic reproductions have been made we are very much indebted to Miss Sneath, Photographer to the School of Oriental and African Studies. We should also like to express our thanks to Mr J. D. Pearson, Librarian of the School, for permission to reproduce the title-page of Almeida's manuscript and the accompanying map. Finally, we gratefully acknowledge much courteous assistance and a wide variety of useful suggestions which we have received from Mr. R. A. Skelton.

CONTENTS

vii

ILLUSTRATIONS

ILLUSTRATIONS

BIBLIOGRAPHY

THE following list gives further particulars of books which are mentioned elsewhere by the author's name only, or with an abbreviated title.

I. CLASSICAL AUTHORITIES

Cosmas Indicopleustes

Texts: Montfaucon, *Nova Collectio Patrum et Scriptorum Graecorum*, vol. ii, 1706.

E. O. Winstedt, *The Christian Topography of Cosmas Indicopleustes*, Cambridge, 1909.

Translation: J. W. McCrindle, *The Christian Topography of Cosmas*, Hakluyt Society, 1897.

Periplus of the Erythraean Sea

Texts: C. Müller, *Geographi Graeci Minores*, vol. i, Paris, 1855, pp. 257–305.

Hjalmar Frisk, *Le Périple de la Mer Erythrée*, Göteborg, 1927.

Translations: W. Vincent, *The Periplus of the Erythraean Sea, Part I containing an account of the navigation of the ancients from the sea of Suez to the coast of Zanguebar*, London, 1800.

J. W. McCrindle, *The Commerce and Navigation of the Erythraean Sea*, Bombay, 1879.

W. H. Schoff, *The Periplus of the Erythraean Sea*, New York, 1912.

Ptolemy

Texts: C. Nobbe, *C. Ptolemaei Geographia*, Leipzig, 1881.

C. Müller, *Claudii Ptolemaei Geographia*, Paris, 1883–1901.

II. NATIVE SOURCES

1. Ethiopic Inscriptions

Littmann, E. *Deutsche Aksum Expedition*, vol. iv, Berlin, 1913.

Kammerer, A. *Essai sur l'histoire antique de l'Abyssinie*, Paris, 1926.

2. Ethiopic Chronicles

Basset, R. *Études sur l'histoire d'Éthiopie*, Paris, 1881. (Contains the work cited as the 'Paris Chronicle' up to 1729.)

Blundell, H. Weld. *The Royal Chronicle of Abyssinia, 1769–1840*, Cambridge, 1922.

Conti Rossini, C. *Historia Regis Sarṣa Dengel, CSCO*, Scr. Aeth. ser. alt. iii, Paris, 1907.

Conzelman, W. E. *Le Chronique de Galawdewos*, Paris, 1895.

Guidi, Ignazio. *Annales Iohannis I, Iyasu I, Bakāffā, CSCO*, Scr. Aeth. ser. alt. v, 2 parts, Paris, 1903, 1905.

—— *Historia Gentis Galla, CSCO*, Scr. Aeth. ser. alt. iii, Paris, 1907. (In the same volume as Conti Rossini's edition of the history of Sarṣa Dengel.)

—— 'Strofe e brevi testi amarici' [Storia dei Meččā.] *MSOS*, vol. x, 1907, pp. 180–184.

—— *Annales Iyasu II, CSCO*, Scr. Aeth. ser. alt. vi, Paris, 1912.

Pereira, F. M. Esteves. *Historia de Minas*, Lisbon, 1888.

—— *Chronica de Susenyos Rei de Ethiopia*, Lisbon, 1892, 1900.

Perruchon, J. *Histoire des guerres de 'Amda Syon*, Paris, 1887.

—— *Vie de Lalibala*, Paris, 1892.

—— *Les chroniques de Zar'a Ya'eqôb et de Ba'eda Mâryâm*, Paris, 1893.

3. Other Languages

Basset, R. *Histoire de la conquête de l'Abyssinie (XVIe siècle), par Chihab ed-din Ahmed ben 'Abd el-Qader surnommé Arab-Faqih*, Paris, 1897. (The text, French version from Arabic, is referred to as *Futuh* or *Futuh al Habashah*, the notes as Basset, *Conquête*.)

Cerulli, E. *Folk-Literature of the Galla of Southern Abyssinia*, Harvard African Studies, iii, 1922. (Galla texts with translation.)

III. Modern European Works

Abbadie, Antoine d'. 'Sur les Oromo', *Annales de la Société Scientifique de Bruxelles*, vol. iv, 1880, pp. 175 *et seqq.*

—— *Géographie d'Éthiopie*, Paris, 1891.

Alvares, F. *Narrative of the Portuguese Embassy to Abyssinia.* . . . By Father Francisco Alvarez, Hakluyt Society, 1881.

Azaïs, R. P., and Chambard, R. *Cinq années de recherches archéologiques en Éthiopie*, 2 vols., Paris, 1932.

Beccari, C. *Rerum aethiopicarum scriptores occidentales inediti*, 15 vols., Rome, 1905–17. (Vol. I is entitled *Saggi e Documenti*; the series title first appears in vol. ii. The history of Páez occupies vols. ii and iii, of Almeida vols. v–vii, and of Mendes, vols. viii and ix.)

Beke, C. T. 'Abyssinia—being a continuation of Routes in that country', *JRGS*, vol. xiv, 1844, pp. 1–76.

Beke, C. T. 'On the languages and dialects of Abyssinia and the countries to the south', *Proceedings of the Philological Society*, vol. ii, 1845, pp. 89–107.

—— 'A description of the ruins of the Church of Martula Mariam in Abessinia', *Archaeologia*, vol. xxxii, 1847, pp. 38–57.

—— 'An essay on the Nile and its tributaries', *JRGS*, vol. xvii, 1847. (Quoted from reprint, separately paged, pp. 84.)

—— 'Mémoire justificatif en réhabilitation des Pères Pierre Paez et Jérome Lobo', *Bulletin de la Société de Géographie*, Paris, avril-mai 1848. (Quoted from reprint, separately paged, pp. 72.)

Bent, J. Theodore. *The Sacred City of the Ethiopians*, London, 1893.

Bermudes, J. See below, Whiteway, R. S.

Bieber, F. J. *Kaffa, ein altkuschitisches Volkstum in Inner-Afrika*, 2 vols, Vienna, 1920–23.

Blundell, H. Weld. 'Exploration in the Abai Basin, Abyssinia', *GJ*, vol. xxvii, 1906, pp. 529–53.

Borelli, J. *Éthiopie Méridionale*, Paris, 1888.

Bruce, James. *Travels to discover the source of the Nile in the years 1768, 1769, 1770, 1771, 1772 and 1773*, 5 vols., Edinburgh, 1790. (On the frontispiece Bruce is described as 'Lord of Geesh'.)

—— —— Second edition, corrected and enlarged, 7 vols., Edinburgh, 1804.

Bryan, M. A. *The distribution of the Semitic and Cushitic languages of Africa*, International African Institute, London, 1948.

Budge, Sir E. A. Wallis. *History of Ethiopia*, 2 vols., London, 1928.

Burton, Sir Richard F. *First Footsteps in East Africa*, London, 1856.

Castanhoso, M. See below, Whiteway, R. S.

Cecchi, A. *Da Zeila alle frontiere del Caffa*, 3 vols., Rome, 1885.

Cerulli, E. *Etiopia Occidentale*, 2 vols., Rome, 1933.

—— *Etiopi in Palestina*, 2 vols., Rome, 1943, 47.

—— — 'Note su alcune popolazioni Sidama dell'Abissinia meridionale', *Rivista di Studi Orientali*, vol. x, 1925, pp. 597–692.

—— 'Per la toponomastica etiopica', *Oriente Moderno*, vol. viii, 1928, pp. 328–36.

—— — *Studi Etiopici: II. La Lingua e la Storia dei Sidamo*, Rome, 1938.

—— — *Studi Etiopici: La Lingua Caffina*, Rome, 1951.

Cheesman, R. E. *Lake Tana and the Blue Nile*, London, 1936.

Conti Rossini, C. 'Catalogo dei nomi propri di luogo dell'Etiopia, contenuti nei testi gi'iz ed amariña finora pubblicati', *Atti del primo Congresso Geografico Italiano*, vol. ii, 1894, pp. 387–439.

—— *Etiopia e genti d'Etiopia*, Florence, 1937.

Crawford, O. G. S. *The Fung Kingdom of Sennar*, Gloucester, 1951.

Dalgado, S. R. *Glossario Luso-Asiatico*, 2 vols., Coimbra, 1918–21.

Dillmann, C. F. A. *Lexicon linguae aethiopicae*, Leipzig, 1865.

—— *Ueber die Regierung, insbesondere die Kirchenordnung des Königs Zar'a-Jacob*, Abhand. d. Kön. Akad. der Wiss. zu Berlin, 1884, pp. 79. (Published 1885.)

Foot, E. C. *Galla-English and English-Galla Dictionary*, Cambridge, 1913.

Grottanelli, V. L. *Missione di Studio al Lago Tana*, vol. ii, Rome, 1939.

Guida dell' Africa Orientale Italiana (ed. G. Vota), Milan, 1938.

Guidi, Ignazio. *Vocabolario Amarico-Italiano*, Rome, 1901.

Harris, W. Cornwallis. *The Highlands of Aethiopia*, 3 vols., London, 1844.

Hobson-Jobson. A Glossary of Colloquial Anglo-Indian Words. By Sir H. Yule and A. C. Burnell. Second edition, London, 1903.

Krapf, Rev. J. L. *Travels, Researches, and Missionary Labours during an eighteen years' residence in Eastern Africa*, London, 1860.

Le Grand, Joachim. *Voyage historique d'Abissinie du R. P. Jérome Lobo*, Paris, 1728.

Ludolf, Hiob. *Historia Aethiopica*, Frankfurt a. M., 1681.

—— *Lexicon Aethiopico-Latinum*, London, 1661.

Mendes, A. See above, Beccari, C.

Montandon, G. *Au Pays Ghimirra*, Neuchâtel, 1913.

Páez, Pedro. See above, Beccari, C.

Parkyns, Mansfield. *Life in Abyssinia*, London, 1853.

Rassam, Hormuzd. *Narrative of the British Mission to Theodore*, 2 vols., London, 1869.

Rey, Sir C. F. *The Real Abyssinia*, London, 1935.

Routes in Abyssinia, London, 1867. Cmd. 3964. (An official compilation of information on routes in Abyssinia from travellers between 1809 and 1867, by Lt.-Col. A. C. Cooke, Topographical and Statistical Dept., War Office. Referred to as *Routes*.)

Rüppell, E. *Reise in Abyssinien*, 2 vols., Frankfurt a. M., 1838–40.

Salt, H. See below, Valentia, G.

Salviac, Martial de. *Les Galla*, Paris, 1901.

Schweinfurth, G. *Abyssinische Pflanzennamen*, Berlin, 1893.

Scott, Hugh. *Journey to the Gughé Highlands (Southern Ethiopia)*, 1948–9: Biogeographical Research at high altitudes, Proceedings of the Linnean Society of London, Session 1950–51, vol. 163, pt. 2, London, 1952.

Soleillet, P. *Explorations éthiopiennes*, Rouen, 1886.

Telles, B. *Historia geral de Ethiopia a alta*, Coimbra, 1660.

Telles, B. *The Travels of the Jesuits in Ethiopia*, London, 1710. (Translation by John Stevens.)

Thesiger, W. 'The Awash River and the Aussa Sultanate', *GJ*, vol. lxxxv, 1935, pp. 1–23.

Thiene, Gaetano da. *Dizionario della lingua Galla*, Harar, 1939.

Trimingham, J. Spencer. *Islam in Ethiopia*, London, 1952.

Tutschek, K. *Dictionary of the Galla Language*, Munich, 1844.

Urreta, Luis de. *Historia ecclesiastica, politica, natural y moral de los grandes y remotos Reynos de la Etiopia*, Valencia, 1610.

Valentia, George, Lord. *Voyages and Travels to India, Ceylon, the Red Sea, Abyssinia and Egypt*, 3 vols., London, 1811. (The narrative of Salt's journey to Abyssinia is contained in vols. 2 and 3.)

Whiteway, R. S. *The Portuguese Expedition to Abyssinia, 1541–3*, Hakluyt Society, 1902. (Translations of the narratives of Castanhoso and Bermudes.)

B

ABBREVIATIONS

AII	Annales Iyasu II. (Guidi.)*
AJIB	Annales Johannis I, Iyasu I, Bakāffā. (Guidi.)*
BM	British Museum.
BSOAS	Bulletin of the School of Oriental and African Studies, University of London.
CA	Histoire des guerres de 'Amda Syon. (Perruchon.)
CB	Chronique de Ba'eda Mâryâm. (Perruchon.)
CGA	Le canzoni geez-amariña in onore di Re Abissini. (Guidi.)
CM	Historia de Minas. (Pereira.)
CS	Chronica de Susenyos. (Pereira.)
CSCO	Corpus scriptorum christianorum orientalium.
CZ	Chronique de Zar'a Ya'eqôb. (Perruchon.)
DAE	Deutsche Aksum Expedition.
GJ	Geographical Journal.
HGG	Historia Gentis Galla. (Guidi.)
HSD	Historia Regis Sarṣa Dengel. (Conti Rossini.)*
JRGS	Journal of the Royal Geographical Society.
KN	Kebra Nagast.
MSOS	Mitteilungen des Seminars für Orientalische Sprachen.
PC	Paris Chronicle. (Basset.)
PME	Periplus of the Erythraean Sea.
RC	The Royal Chronicle of Abyssinia, 1769–1840. (H. Weld Blundell.)
SOAS	School of Oriental and African Studies, University of London.

* References are to the pages of the French version of the *CSCO* texts.

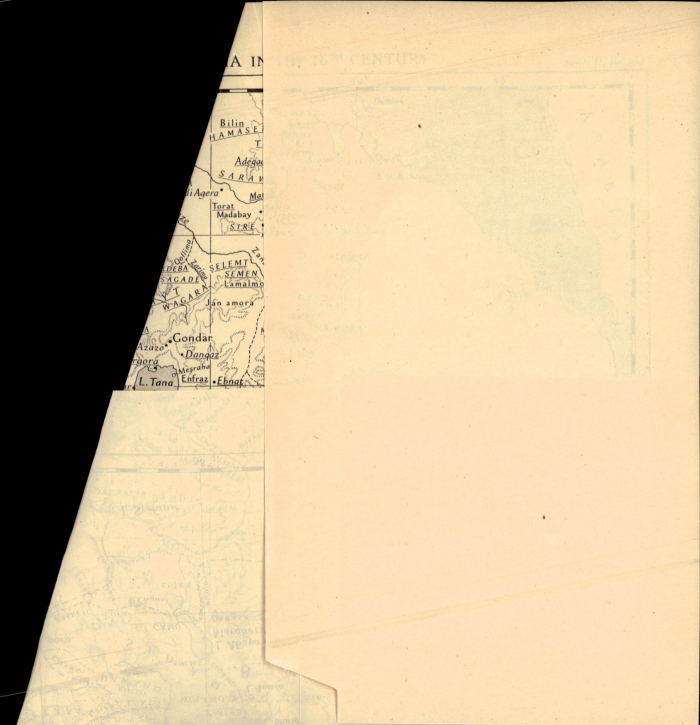

ETHIOP
38

BEJA
"Kingdom of Dequim"   BARYA

Gash   KUNAM
Tak

WAL

Angarab

WALQ

DAMB'Y
bat   Go
Dangal ba

ARABIA

DANAKIL

SOMALI

IFAT

BETAGAR

SHOA
BRITUMA
GALLA

DAWARO

Webi Shabelli

INTRODUCTION

I

The Abyssinian plateau is difficult of access even to its immediate neighbours. Much of it is protected by deserts, tangled, barren hills, equatorial forests or malarial swamps, inhabited by tribes differing profoundly from the Abyssinians and from each other in race, language, religion and culture; it has never been easy and not often safe to travel among them. On the east where the plateau is nearest to the much frequented trade routes of the Indian Ocean and the Red Sea, it rises to an average height of 8,000 feet and a very steep escarpment divides it from an arid coast. The tableland itself is furrowed by deep gorges which are often impassable in the rainy season. It is not surprising that European knowledge of the country should have grown spasmodically and should still be very imperfect, or that its relations with the outside world should have resembled those of a remote archipelago. In some ways, indeed, Abyssinia's history is remarkably like Japan's. In both countries a long period of comparative isolation ended with the arrival of the Portuguese in the sixteenth century; after the navigators and traders came the missionaries of the Society of Jesus to win spectacular but short-lived successes and soon to find themselves proscribed as both empires withdrew into deliberate and almost complete seclusion.

Ever since the time of Prince Henry the Navigator the Portuguese had associated their explorations with missionary work, and this was vigorously stimulated by the foundation of the Jesuits. It was directed not so much to the Moslems, who were usually regarded as unteachable, as to the 'heathens', that is, all who were neither Christians, Moslems nor Jews, and also to the heretical eastern Christian communities, of which the Abyssinians were one. Almeida draws a chronological parallel between the discovery of Abyssinia and the origins of his order, observing that St. Ignatius Loyola was born in 1491, about the time that Pero da

Covilhã, the agent of the Portuguese King John II, reached the country in search of Prester John, that Loyola received the wound that led to his conversion in 1521, the year after the first Portuguese embassy had landed at Massawa, and that Dom Cristovão da Gama disembarked there to assist the Emperor against the Moslems in 1541, the year after the Pope had confirmed the Society's constitutions.[1]

The story of the Jesuit mission has often been told and need not be repeated here. When Almeida himself arrived in 1624, it was already two years since Susneyos, the reigning Emperor, had publicly made his submission to Rome. This triumph, one of the greatest in the Society's annals, had largely been due to the patience, tact and versatility of the Spanish missionary, Pedro Páez, who had died shortly afterwards. Almeida came, therefore, to a country which was nominally converted already. When reading his 'History' it should be remembered that the first part was written under these conditions, but they had been reversed long before it was finished. In the summer of 1632 Susneyos became convinced that there would be incessant revolts unless he permitted the traditional practices of the national church. In spite of the opposition of the Jesuit Patriarch Afonso Mendes, he issued a proclamation restoring the old religion and directing that the churches should again be occupied by the Monophysite clergy. In his personal beliefs he remained a Catholic and not long before his death on September 16th he confessed to a Jesuit, though he died without receiving Extreme Unction. He seems to have intended to permit freedom of conscience to members of both communions, but his son and successor Fasiladas at once excluded the Jesuits from the capital and then sent them to Kolala in Gojam, perhaps thinking, as Almeida conjectured, that they would be a long way from the coast and unable to send for help from India. Soon afterwards he banished them to their headquarters at Fremona in the north. In 1634 he exiled them altogether

[1] Almeida, bk IV, c. 1. The history of these early Portuguese contacts with Abyssinia will be found in two works published by the Hakluyt Society, *Narrative of the Portuguese Embassy to Abyssinia. . . . By Father Francisco Alvarez*, ser. I, no. 64, and *The Portuguese Expedition to Abyssinia in 1541, as narrated by Castanhoso and Bermudez*, ser. II, no. 10.

though a few stayed behind under the protection of local chiefs. The last of them were hanged in 1641.

It is usual for historians to attribute these events to the conduct of the Patriarch, contrasting him with Páez and representing him as an arrogant and stupid bigot.[1] This is unfair. No doubt he was a very different man from Páez but they were both pursuing the same ends in circumstances rendered dissimilar by the Emperor's public conversion just before Páez died and three years before Mendes reached Abyssinia. That the latter was not an irresponsible fanatic is suggested by his petitioning the Viceroy of Portuguese India to allow the rebuilding of Hindu temples in Diu. Remarkable as it was the triumph of Páez had been more apparent than real. The depth and bitterness of the opposition to the Jesuits is shown by the story of the attempt made in 1613–14 by Father Antonio Fernandes and the Emperor's ambassador to travel to Malindi by land, which is translated in this volume (pp. 143 seq.). It failed, and for geographical reasons alone, it would have been very surprising if it had succeeded, but the persons who turned back the embassy were not Moslems or pagan Galla, but Christians and subjects of the Emperor. When the envoys came to Enarya its Christian ruler, who was, Almeida tells us, so loyal a subject that he paid of his own free will a tribute which the Emperor was in no position to exact, was persuaded by a Christian priest to refuse to allow them to proceed through Kafa as they wished and forced them to turn eastward. The independent pagan King of Janjero, on the other hand, received them courteously and sent them on their way. In Kambatta and Alaba they were foiled by the intrigues of a Christian and a representative of the Emperor who preferred Moslems and Galla to the Portuguese as allies. Probably the Jesuits, like many other observers of oriental monarchies, were so impressed by the ruler's arbitrary power over the property and lives of his subjects that they did not see that in some respects his authority was far more limited than that of many contemporary European princes. Their missionary method was to concentrate on making converts among the political and

---

[1] e.g. 'a cruel and intolerant bigot' (Sir Charles Rey, *In the Country of the Blue Nile*, p. 258).

intellectual leaders, hoping that if this were done the common people would follow their example. Susneyos was quickly converted and his emphatic submission to Rome in 1622 made the adherents of the old church into rebels as well as heretics; yet he was unable to suppress the practices to which the Jesuits objected, circumcision, the keeping of the Jewish Sabbath, temporary marriages, the commemoration of Epiphany in a ritual which they interpreted as a second baptism, and others. Formally the most important issue was the Monophysite doctrine, the belief that Christ had only one nature, which the Abyssinians and the Copts of Egypt share with the Jacobites of Syria and the Armenians. The implications of this dogma are not easily explained without the use of the Greek terminology in which it was originally formulated; it need hardly be said that Ethiopic is not a satisfactory language in which to discuss a problem of this kind. Bruce remarks of the words for Nature and Person: 'Neither of them has ever yet been translated into the Abyssinian, so as to be understood to mean the same thing in different places. . . . The two natures in Christ, the two persons, their unity. . . . are all wrapt up in tenfold darkness, and inextricable from amidst the thick clouds of heresy and ignorance of language. Nature is often mistaken for person, and person for nature; the same of the human substance. It is monstrous to hear their reasoning upon it. One would think that every different monk, every time he talks, purposely broaches some new heresy.'[1] It is obvious that the ordinary Abyssinians, like other peoples of similar culture, were more concerned with practice than dogma. The principle 'cujus regio ejus religio' was as familiar to them as it was to the subjects of the Holy Roman Empire. Mansfield Parkyns says: 'I have known instances of their turning Turk for the time of their sojourn in the land of Islam, and returning to their Christianity and bigotry as soon as they set foot in their own country. . . . It is a fact that the Abyssinian is not usually difficult in matters of religion except at home.'[2]

Mention must be made of Bruce's account of these events, for after the expulsion of the Jesuits he was the next important explorer of Abyssinia and his book, eminently read-

[1] Bruce, bk V, ch. 12.   [2] Parkyns, vol. ii, p. 93.

able and written in a language more widely known than
Portuguese and, unlike Almeida's, published in its author's
lifetime, has had immense influence. A Protestant laird,
Bruce was as hostile to the Jesuits as they had been to the
Monophysites. He was often very unfair to them but it can
be said in his excuse that he knew almost nothing of their
writings except for three unsatisfactory works. The first was
the rather absurd and partly incomprehensible Latin translation of Páez's chapter on the source of the Nile by Athan-
asius Kircher, who seems to have had an imperfect knowledge of both Portuguese and Latin; the second was the
Travels of Jeronimo Lobo. They were accessible to him in
Le Grand's French version and Dr Johnson's English translation of Le Grand. Lobo's own text has never been printed,
but if his translators have not done him an injustice he is the
least reliable of the Jesuit writers on Abyssinia. The third
work was an English paraphrase of a compilation made by
the Jesuit Baltasar Telles, who relied principally though not
exclusively on Almeida. Some of Bruce's distortions of
names can be traced to this version of Telles (see p. 148 n. 1,
p. 159 n. 1 and p. 238,) but many of his statements are
merely ludicrous. He alleges that the aim of the Catholic
hierarchy was 'to reduce Abyssinia to a Portuguese government';[1] by no means all the Jesuits in Abyssinia were Portuguese, and from the point of view of the Portuguese authorities it is difficult to think of a more expensive, hazardous and
futile undertaking than this would have been. It is true that
some of the Jesuits wished to introduce Portuguese troops
but only to ensure the success of their mission, and in this
Susneyos supported them, but the scheme was not favoured
by the Holy See. Bruce also charges them with having tam-
pered with the text of Alvares which, he says, 'contains many
things very difficult of belief, which seem to be the work of
the Jesuits.'[2] Alvares's book was published less than a month
after the Pope had confirmed the Jesuit constitutions!
Bruce's most absurd comment, however, is his sinister hint
that Telles 'says not a word' about three Catholic priests who
were stoned to death during the reign of David IV.[3] Even the

---

[1] Bruce, bk III, 'Socinios'.   [2] *Ibid.* 'David III'.
[3] *Ibid.* 'David IV'.

English version of Telles, which Bruce used, was published in 1710, four years before the date he himself gives for David's accession and these executions; the first, the Portuguese edition of Telles appeared in 1660.

Nevertheless Bruce is surely right in contending that the Emperor, though a sincere convert, did not realise all the implications of his submission and expected it to be rewarded with practical help which he never received. Indeed his whole account of this reign is valuable. His prejudices are obvious and easy to discount; his opportunities were unique. His two years' residence in the country, his experience of the Moslem countries with which the Abyssinians have had most contact, his study of their history and his intimate knowledge of their politics, all gave him an understanding of their mentality and of what he quaintly but significantly calls their 'constitution'. He saw the events of 1632 as an Abyssinian 1688, a Glorious Revolution which had preserved national independence, the national church and the constitution from the machinations of an alien hierarchy. When allowances have been made for incongruity, this shows more insight into the character of the native reaction than do those historians who ascribe what happened to theological disagreement or to the tactlessness of the Catholic Patriarch.

II

The life of Almeida was laborious but, except for his journeys to and from Abyssinia, far less adventurous than those of many of his brethren. He was born in the last weeks of 1579 or the first quarter of 1580,[1] the year in which Camões died and in which Philip II united the crowns of Spain and Portugal. His native place was the small cathedral town of Viseu in central Portugal; he speaks of it as a 'noble city' on p. 201. He became a novice in the Society of Jesus in 1594, studied at Coimbra and was sent to India in 1602. He continued his studies at St Paul's College in Goa and professed the final four vows of the Society in 1612. He became a Reader in Holy Scripture and Prefect of Studies at the Col-

[1] The date usually given is 1580. The documents quoted by Beccari, vol. V, pp. v–vi, in his introduction to Almeida's 'History', show that he was seventeen in April, 1597, and twenty-five by December 15th, 1605.

lege and had experience of pastoral work in Salsette. In 1616 he was chosen to lead an abortive mission to Ceylon which the native ruler refused to receive. He returned to Salsette for a while and in 1620 was made Rector and Master of the Novices at the Probationers' House in Goa. Next year he became Rector of the College at Bassein and in 1622 was nominated Visitor to the Abyssinian mission; his brother Jorge, who was also a Jesuit, was to have been one of his three companions had not his bad health prevented it. Almeida's own account of their journey from India to the Emperor's court at Dancaz will be found on pp. 172–190.

They sailed from Bassein on November 28th, 1622, in company with a fleet which was protecting a convoy. The warships temporarily left them at Daman to shadow Dutch ships which had been sighted heading for Goa. Tired of waiting at Daman they chartered a native boat to take them to Gogha. They narrowly escaped pirates by taking refuge in the Purna river and, as the pirate vessel was waiting for them at the river mouth, they disembarked and went overland to Bagwa, taking care to avoid Surat with its English factors. From Bagwa they crossed the Gulf of Cambay to Gogha. They had intended to go thence by land to Diu, where they could find a ship bound for Suakin, but the roads across Kathiawar were too dangerous, being infested by marauding Rajputs. They were forced to wait for the fleet after all and it finally brought them to Diu two months after they had left Bassein. Here there were difficulties with the secular authorities, who were not always sympathetic to the Society. At last, on March 24th, 1623, they sailed in an overloaded ship with a Hindu captain. The monsoon wind failed them, a very strange circumstance, and although they sighted Socotra they were not able to anchor there. They next tried to reach Qishn, which belonged to the same Sultan as Socotra, as it still does; he was normally friendly to the Portuguese. Failing in this too the ship was forced to shelter off Dhufar, which was subject to the Sultan of Shihr, an unfriendly princeling owing allegiance to the Turkish Pasha in the Yemen. The Jesuits had the appalling experience of spending the whole summer, from May 18th to October 16th, in a small ship off south Arabia, living on rice, brackish water and a little fish, hiding whenever Arabs from the land came aboard and in constant alarm at reports that their presence had been discovered, or that Dutch or Turkish ships were approaching. It is not surprising that they suffered severely from skin disease. When at last they left the wind was not strong and they were slow to reach the entrance to the Red Sea. They passed through at night, choosing the channel between Perim and the African side; though it was shallower and more dangerous to navigation there was less risk of their meeting Turkish ships. The voyage up the Red Sea was difficult and when the wind dropped they spent ten or twelve days sailing about twenty-four miles through the maze of islands, reefs and shoals. Not until December 4th, fifty days after leaving Dhufar and over eight months since their embarkation, were they able to go ashore and pay their respects to the Pasha at Suakin.

They were well received for the Abyssinian Emperor was on friendly terms with the Pasha and was an energetic soldier whom it was not wise to offend; in these circumstances a bribe was a sufficient inducement for him to let them pass. They hired a small native boat and sailed for Massawa on December 21st. The voyage lasted sixteen days as they cast anchor every night. At Massawa the Pasha's representative caused them no more than minor annoyance and on January 16th, 1624, they began their journey inland. A day and a half later they met an escort sent from the village of Zalot which the Emperor had given to the Society for such purposes. Early in February they reached the headquarters of the mission at Fremona and at the end of the month three of them, including Almeida, left again for Ganeta Jesus, the modern Azazo, the Jesuit residency nearest to the imperial court, then at Dancaz. The journey took them twenty days and almost as soon as they arrived they were summoned to the Emperor's presence and welcomed with great cordiality. Almeida himself then went on to the camp of the Emperor's brother, Ras Se'ela Krestos, Viceroy of Gojam and the most ardent of the Catholic party at court. Almeida brought him letters from the General of the Jesuits and from the Visitor and the Provincial of India. He then returned to Dancaz and assisted the Superior of the mission, Antonio Fernandes, until the rains began when he withdrew to Gorgora and devoted himself to studying Amharic which is, as he tells us (p. 57), the most useful of the Abyssinian vernaculars. A year after his arrival he laid down the office of Visitor and was then sent to Damot where the Viceroy had asked for a Jesuit priest. He travelled by way of Kolala in Gojam and was received with enthusiasm at his destination. When in 1625 the Patriarch Afonso Mendes reached Abyssinia Almeida went as far as Kambilgē Maryam, north of Gondar, to meet him and then accompanied him on a tour of Wagara. They spent forty-three days there and never slept in the same place twice except on Sundays, when they did not travel, to avoid offending Abyssinian susceptibilities. After assisting the Patriarch to say mass each morning Almeida used to preach to the assembled crowd on the basic Catholic dogmas. 'I always tried', he says, 'to bring in some story in praise of the Virgin Our Lady, for the people of Ethiopia are very devoted to Our Lady and the friars had put it into their heads that we were enemies of her whom we keep as the apple of our eyes and in our inmost hearts.' Later in the day the Patriarch used to confirm while Almeida baptised; he baptised 1585 children during this tour.[1]

Almeida's later years in Abyssinia were spent mostly at Gorgora and it was there in 1628 that the earlier part of his 'History' was written. When in 1632 the Emperor decided to permit again the traditional practices of the Abyssinian church Almeida was one of three priests sent by the Patriarch to try to dissuade him. The attempt failed and after the accession of Fasiladas he and the other Jesuits of the capital were banished, first to Kolala and then to Fremona. On their way north they were robbed and pelted with stones. They arrived in April, 1633, and it was decided to send someone to India to inform the authorities of what had happened. Manoel Barradas was chosen for this task, and three others were sent with him, Damião Calaça, Giuseppe Giroco, who was ill and needed medical attention, and Almeida himself, who had been directed by the Provincial at Goa a year before to take the first convenient opportunity of returning. His journey lasted longer than when he had come and was even

[1] Almeida, bk IX, c. 17.

more dangerous. The Jesuits had not received the Emperor's permission to leave; he had only relegated them to Fremona, and so they dared not travel to Massawa by the ordinary and shortest way. Instead, they crossed the Bur peninsula, struck the coast at Arafali and then followed it for some thirty miles under the July sun over sand and rocks to Massawa. The permit to sail from there had already cost them a payment of 400 patacas[1] to the Pasha of Suakin, but he had died in the meantime and his successor asked for the same sum again; his deputy at Massawa added something for himself, and the priests, who had already been robbed of their more valuable possessions, were obliged to borrow another 600 patacas from Hindu merchants, repayable in Diu. They sailed on August 19th, 1633, the four European Jesuits, two Indian chaplains to the Patriarch, five or six Hindus and fourteen young Abyssinians. They left the Red Sea on the 29th and entered Aden harbour on the 31st. It was known that they were coming and the governor hoped to secure for himself part of the treasure he assumed they were taking away from Abyssinia. Their property was seized and, except for Giroco who was too ill to make the journey, they were taken to his residence outside Aden. Their baggage was ransacked in vain and the disappointed governor ordered that, whatever the risk to his life, Giroco should be brought to him as well. Finding that he too carried no gold he seized the young Abyssinians, who were constrained by 'hunger, blows and torture' to profess Islam, though some of them were later ransomed by the Jesuits. The lives of the priests were constantly threatened and it was six months before they were able to leave. Some of the time they spent at Khanfar, which they found most unhealthy, and for about three weeks they were at Lahej. The governor agreed to accept a ransom of 1200 patacas, which, again, was advanced by the Hindus. Barradas and the two chaplains left first in a small boat bound for Muscat, in the hope of picking up a ship for India before the rains began. They were disappointed, for it took them forty days to reach Muscat and there they had to remain until the September monsoon. Almeida, Calaça and Giroco sailed soon afterwards but the wind dropped and they

[1] See note on p. 44.

were forced to spend two and a half months at Qishn. Giroco
died at sea. Almeida and Calaça arrived in India in mid-
September.

The remainder of Almeida's life was passed in India.
He became Rector of St Paul's College, Provincial and
Assessor to the Holy Office. He died at Goa on May 10th,
1646.

III

For the translator Almeida is an unrewarding author. His
style, except for passages reminiscent of pulpit oratory, is at
once colloquial and pedestrian. We have not thought proper
to disguise the ambiguities caused by his indiscriminate pro-
nouns, repetitive vocabulary, sagging syntax and occasional
anacoluthon. It is probable that much of the work was
dictated, perhaps in haste, certainly by a very busy man,
and its composition was spread over not less than fifteen
years. Part at least of Book I was written at Gorgora in 1628
(pp. 9, 26). Book II was also written in Abyssinia; there is a
marginal note saying so in the British Museum manuscript
of Book III, chapter 1. Book III, chapter 17, refers to a
reigning Emperor who can only be Susneyos but he is mentioned in the past tense in Book IV, chapter 25 (p. 137). Yet
Book VII, chapter 14 was written in August, 1632 (p. 150),
when he was still alive. The latest date in the 'History' is 1643
and the Patriarch Mendes, writing to the General of the Jesuits
on January 4th, 1646, speaks of it as a completed work and says
that a copy is being sent to Portugal.

This copy has been lost. Three manuscripts are now known.
One is in Lisbon but it is very incorrect and of no value for
establishing the text. The others are in London, one in the
British Museum (Add. MS 9861) and the other in the Library
of the School of Oriental and African Studies (MS 11966).
Both these came from William Marsden's collection and seem
to have been in the archives at Goa at some time. Beccari's
edition, which is the only complete printed text, is based on
the British Museum manuscript and includes a reproduction
of the accompanying map. The second manuscript, which we
have followed in this translation, was first described by Sir

Denison Ross in 1922.[1] He concluded from his examination that it represented a corrected version of the manuscript used by Beccari and we have found no reason to disagree with him. The differences are not considerable except for one additional chapter, Book VI, chapter 17, which is translated from an Ethiopic chronicle; the omission of this chapter from the other manuscript is clearly an error and was noticed by Beccari. Where divergences exist the School manuscript is superior. It is also accompanied by a map, which is more legible than the one in the British Museum; it is reproduced for the first time in this volume (p. xcvii). The School manuscript incorporates the corrections written in the margins or between the lines of the other copy, includes a few further alterations and is more liberally and more carefully punctuated. In consequence we have occasionally been able to improve on Beccari's text. We have commented on any such passages in the notes and have recorded any differences between the two manuscripts, both revised in autograph, other than insignificant changes in spelling and accentuation.

The School manuscript includes a dedication to King John IV of Portugal, a preface and a note on the use of the map. Sir Denison Ross published the texts of the dedication and the preface and a translation of the preface which, however, contains some mistakes.[2] The note on the map has never been published; a translation will be found on p. xciii seq below.

John IV became King of Portugal in 1640, after a coup d'état which brought to an end the union of the Portuguese and Spanish crowns. His house was favourably disposed to the Jesuits and Almeida's dedication reveals their hope that he would assist them to regain their position in Abyssinia. 'Your Majesty', he writes, 'has every title to the history of Ethiopia. Omitting other older titles, the King Dom João the Third of happy memory restored the Abyssinian empire, took it out of the power of the Moors of Adel and granted it to the Emperor Gladios or Claudius. He could with complete justice have taken at least a third of it for himself (for that is what the Emperor David, father of Gladios, offered him when he sent to ask his help), but he did not covet the temporal advantage, only the spiritual, which had also been

---

[1] *BSOAS*, vol. ii, pt 3, pp. 513–538.   [2] *Ibid*. vol. ii, pt. 4, pp. 783–804.

promised, namely, that the Abyssinians should submit to the holy apostolic faith and abandon the Alexandrian errors. So may the Most Serene Dom João the Third have the glory, title and renown of liberator of Ethiopia from the hands of the Moors. The Most Serene Dom João the Fourth shall have the other more glorious titles of Restorer of the holy Catholic faith and Destroyer and Extirpator of heresy in that vast and far-spreading empire. The Most Serene Dom João the Third conceded that empire to the King of the country. The Most Serene Dom João the Fourth shall grant it to the King of Heaven, subjugate it to his Vicar, the Pope of Rome, and deliver it from the cruel captivity of the Egyptian Pharaoh, I mean, of the schismatic Alexandrian Patriarch.'

The preface explains why he wrote his 'History' and the use he made of Páez's work on the same subject, and apologises for the inconsistencies caused by the changes that took place while it was being written. The most important passages are these.

'I particularly want it to be known that Father Pero Paez, of whom I shall later have much to say, began to write the History of Ethiopia. The Superiors in India sent him what Father Frei Luis Urreta[1] had published in Valencia a little while before, so that he should refute the great number of errors and lies that Ioão Baltezar[1] had put into that author's head. Father Pero Paez did so, but as his chief aim was refutation he did not make his history as coherent and orderly as was desirable. Besides, as he was a Castilian he had not a perfect command of the Portuguese language, in which he wrote; for he had largely forgotten Spanish, not having used it for many years, though often using Arabic, Turkish, Amharic and the other language, the language of the books of Ethiopia, which he had learnt.[2] For these reasons the Superior, who was then Father Antonio Fernandez, with the concurrence of the other Fathers at the assembly we held at Gorgorra at the beginning of the year one thousand six hundred and twenty-six, charged me to describe that Chris-

[1] See p. 5, n. 2.
[2] Ross misunderstood the phrase 'e da outra dos livros de Ethiopia' which he translated 'the other languages of the books about Ethiopia'. Almeida refers to Ethiopic, sometimes called Ge'ez, which is still the liturgical language. In his time it was the literary language of Abyssinia.

c

tian state for the service of God and in order to make it
widely known.[1] This I did, but I had many things to do and
they compelled me to spend almost all my time in long
journeys. Since then, during these years in India, I have not
been without responsibilities. More particularly when I saw
how badly Ethiopia fulfilled her great promise and became
a squalid ruin, I took no pleasure in writing and not merely
delayed but began to forget the work.

'However an order from our Very Reverend Father General
Mutio Vitteleschi written in a letter of the 15th of December,
1639, compelled me to continue it. . . .

'Under this injunction I applied myself to the work with
determination. As I say, I have profited greatly by what
Father Pero Paez wrote; in the historical part I have added
certain things which time has brought to light and I have
supplemented it with everything that has happened since
the Father's death. These events have been so many and so
various that in the space of twenty years they have surpassed
all those of many centuries past. . . .

' Now that the beams of the holy faith of Rome have
illumined them (i.e. the Abyssinians), they have been so soon
blinded by the great brilliance of the light that one almost
loses hope of their ever seeing it again with open eyes. It
must be apparent that such great and varied deformities cannot well be depicted in an even style. We shall not depict
them as they are unless we depict a chimaera, not fictitious
or imaginary but real, so that the whole world may know
that this nation is the strangest monstrosity that Africa, the
mother of monsters, has bred in her remote and savage
jungles. . . .

'I want to give one warning lest the reader should be
annoyed by the differences there are from time to time in
expressions and ways of speaking, some of which presuppose
that I am in Ethiopia, others that I am outside it. That is
what happened; I began the work there and came to finish it
in India. So in the earlier books I speak as one inside the

---

[1] 'Father Antonio called me up among the many padres who happened to
be present' (Ross). The name Fernandez is abbreviated to 'f'ez'. Ross
ignored the apostrophe indicating abbreviation and seems to have taken
the word for a verb. Even if it were, his would still be an indefensible translation.

country, but not so in the later books; then I speak as one in India.'

We have translated in full the first book of the 'History' which is a general description of the country, its divisions, topographical features, climate, vegetation, resources and the manners and customs of the people. The remaining books are mainly historical in content and are arranged chronologically, with digressions of which the longest are concerned with the doctrines and practices of the Abyssinian church. The narrative becomes detailed with the arrival of the Portuguese, and lengthy extracts translated from the Abyssinian court chronicles are included. The story is brought down to the expulsion of the Jesuits by Fasiladas in 1633 and ends with accounts of the martyrdom of the last members of the Society remaining in Abyssinia and with eulogies of those who died in India up to 1643. Our second extract is a chapter describing the mountain of Amba Geshen where possible claimants to the throne used to be confined; it has been rendered familiar, though not accurately described, by Johnson's *Rasselas*.

The third extract is a brief description of a church in Gojam and this is followed by a translation of a short account of the Galla written by an Abyssinian named Bahrey. This document was printed in the 'Corpus Scriptorum Christianorum orientalium, scriptores aethiopici,' series altera, vol. III, with a translation into French by Guidi, under the title 'Historia Gentis Galla'. The Ethiopic text is written on the first three folios of a manuscript in the British Museum (MS Orient. 534).[1] Wright in his catalogue dates the work 'about 1582' (it can in fact be dated from internal evidence to 1593) and describes it as written 'in an old hand'.[2] There is no heading, and the title, *Zenahu la galla*, 'History of the Galla', is taken from the first line of the text. There are no chapter numbers in the manuscript, but a space of about one inch is left between the last word of a chapter and the first word of the next. The chapter numbers and the word *kefl*, 'division' or 'chapter', which occur in the printed text have been added

---

[1] The title on the back of the volume is 'Mazmura Krestos or Psalterium Christi', which occupies the rest of the book.

[2] *Catalogue of Ethiopic Manuscripts in the British Museum* (1877), p. 184.

by Guidi. An inaccurate text with a German translation were published by A. W. Schleicher, in 1893,[1] and there is a not very satisfactory version in Budge's *History of Ethiopia*.[2] None of these elucidates the subject matter,[3] and Guidi's edition is not easily accessible. The document is important because it contains a contemporary and first-hand account of the Galla invasion of Ethiopia, giving a series of datable events; and because it provides us with an early and detailed account of the age-set system of the Galla people.

Of the author, Bahrey, nothing is known beyond what he tells us in his text. He was an ecclesiastic, apparently a monk, whose home was in Gamo, a district in the south of Ethiopia where Christianity flourished from an early time; and his home there was looted by the Galla. From the chronological clues which he gives the date of his book may be put at 1593, when he was perhaps an old man, as the last paragraph of Chapter 18 suggests. There is some reason to think that Almeida may have known his book (see p. 139). His own description of the Galla follows immediately.

The other three extracts are travel narratives. The first describes one of the most remarkable of all the Jesuit journeys in Africa, undertaken in 1613–14 by Father Antonio Fernandes and an Abyssinian ambassador in an attempt to reach Malindi by land. The circumstances that resulted in the despatch of this mission were as follows.

The Abyssinians had been immensely impressed by the efficiency and the equipment of the small Portuguese force that came to their assistance in 1540 under the command of Dom Cristovão da Gama, especially by the artillery which enabled them to capture mountain fastnesses that had previously been impregnable.[4] Susneyos always hoped that the favour he showed to the Jesuits would enable him to secure

---

[1] *Geschichte der Galla* (Berlin, 1893).

[2] Vol. ii.

[3] With the exception, that is, of Schleicher's, whose notes, however, are not very illuminating, and are characterised by an apparent unwillingness to accept what the author says, as evidenced by his alteration of 'west' to 'east' in the first chapter.

[4] A chronicler of the late eighteenth century, describing the introduction of guns that 'shook the foundations of Gojam' says that nothing like them had been seen since the weapons that were sent to Claudius (*Royal Chronicle*, pp. 363–4).

the help of another contingent from the Portuguese in India. In January, 1611, Pope Paul V sent him a letter congratulating him on his accession, praising him for his zeal for the Catholic faith and raising his hopes by the following sentence: 'As you asked, we have commended the present need of your Kingdom to our very dear son in Christ Philip, Catholic and mighty King of the Spains, who, we hope, will out of his abundant magnanimity and zeal for the Christian faith, give you effective help; we have commanded our Apostolic Nuncio, who is with His Catholic Majesty, to solicit diligently what you ask.' What happened when the Emperor received this letter is best told in Almeida's own words. 'This reached the Emperor at a time when he could not reply during the same monsoon, because the ships in the Strait[1] had left for India, but it gave him extraordinarily great pleasure. He had for some time strongly desired to send an ambassador to Rome and Portugal, and had not done so only because of the difficulty of getting out of Ethiopia and through the Turks. This letter enhanced his desire so much that he decided to send the ambassador to Nareâ[2] to try to reach the coast of Melinde from there. He discussed this with the Fathers and asked that one of them should consent to accompany the ambassador, so that he should be better received in Europe.[3] They deliberated about it and each one suggested himself for the dangerous journey. Father Antonio Fernandez was chosen, a choice at which the Emperor expressed much satisfaction. He knew well the Father's great prudence and virtue and his burning zeal for the reduction of Ethiopia; besides, as he had been at the court for some years, he would be able to give a good account of it and of the empire. Then the Emperor informed the Father of all he intended by this embassy and entrusted to him certain private matters which could not be included in the letters. He and his brother Cellâ Christôs, Viceroy of Gojam, who alone shared this secret, both swore before Fathers Pero Paez and Antonio Fernandes to obey the Roman Pontiff in all things and

[1] i.e. the Strait of Mecca, a common Portuguese name for the Red Sea.

[2] Enarya.

[3] He may have remembered that Matthew, the envoy sent by the Empress Helena about a hundred years before, had been very badly treated by some of the Portuguese officials.

accept a Patriarch from him. They opened their hearts with such moving words that they clearly showed their burning desire to see Ethiopia wholly reduced to obedience to the holy Apostolic See. Then they named as ambassador Fecur Egzy, a man of noble birth and of great prudence and courage who had already embraced the holy faith of Rome. He showed himself, as he always did, so eager to exalt and augment it that the name Fecur Egzy, which means Beloved of God,[1] fitted him well. While the Emperor was despatching the ambassador and having the letters he was to carry written out, Father Antonio Fernandes prepared himself for this perilous and difficult journey with most fervent prayers. He offered for its success as many masses as could be said in the time and the Fathers of this mission offered many more, for the undertaking was in the service and to the glory of God Our Lord, and the Father, the ambassador and all those who were going with them were exposing themselves to evident peril on long and unknown roads among Cafres, Moors and other savage nations.'[2]

They carried five letters, three from the Emperor, which were addressed to the Pope, the King of Spain and Portugal, and the Viceroy of Portuguese India, and two from Ras Se'ela Krestos, to the Pope and the King. The Emperor's letter to the Pope read:

'May the Emperor Seltan Çagued's letter come with the peace of Christ Jesu the good shepherd to the holy Roman Pope Paul the 5th, head and shepherd of the universal Church. We have received, holy and beloved father, your letter of January 611 [sic], full of that love which inflamed the kindly father when he received the prodigal son upon his return; but we received it at a time when we could not reply because the ships of India had left. We therefore decided to send it by another road, which we hope in God will be opened; we have therefore sent Father Antonio Fernandez of the Society of Jesus, who has been at our court for some time, and our ambassador Fecur Egzy, earnestly desiring Your Holiness to take notice of how, by the teaching of the Fathers of the Society who reside in our empire, we have

[1] Ethiopic *Fequr Egzi'e*, 'Beloved of the Lord'.
[2] Almeida, bk VII, ch. 12.

understood the true faith of the seat of the blessed St Peter. We have decided to embrace it and to render obedience to Your Holiness as to the head of the universal Church, and henceforth to govern ourselves by your Patriarch. But to enable us to render this obedience publicly it is necessary for us to have the help of Dom Philippe the mighty King of Portugal, because without it we cannot possibly render it in this way. We therefore humbly ask Your Holiness, since you have written to us saying that you have ordered your Apostolic Nuncio, who is with His Catholic Majesty, diligently to urge our petition, that you should now do so with all haste so that our empire may have help in our time and in your happy reign, and a good opportunity may not be lost. Since too you are the father of all Catholic Kings may you number us among them, and as you pray to God for them before the most holy bodies of the Apostles, may you do so for this your humble son. Written in our court of Dambeâ on the 31st of January, 1613.'

The request for Portuguese help was made more explicitly in the letter to King Philip. The relevant passage is as follows:

'To enable us to render publicly this obedience to the seat of St Peter and to receive a Patriarch from there, it is necessary for us to have the help of a thousand Portuguese from Your Majesty, without which we cannot render it publicly. When they come they must take the port of Maçuâ in the strait of the Red Sea and I shall give them the coast lands and help them to hold them; for the rest we refer you to the Father and to our ambassador.'

To the Viceroy at Goa he was more explicit still. 'Since we cannot make this decision of ours public without having as many as a thousand Portuguese here, we desire you to send them to us as quickly as possible, for we have learnt from a letter of the King our brother that you would please him in this, and you would give us great satisfaction. When they come they must take the port of Maçuâ in the strait of the Red Sea, and I shall give them the coast lands and help them to hold them. It is necessary that five hundred Portuguese should remain there beside the thousand we wish to have with us, and that workmen, especially armourers and builders, should come with them; for everything else we refer you to Father Antonio Fernandez and to our ambassador.'

The Ras's two letters are similar. He tells the Pope as much as the Emperor tells the King, and the King as much as the Emperor tells the Viceroy. To them both he stresses the need for acting quickly, during the lifetime of Susneyos, as otherwise a great opportunity would be lost. It is not surprising that when he was arrested in Alaba Fernandes thought fit to destroy these letters. Almeida is no doubt right in saying that had they been discovered they would have cost him his life.[1]

The ambassador's home was in Gojam and he went there first to settle his domestic affairs before leaving. Fernandes followed him in March, 1613, and stayed for a time at the Jesuit residency at Kolala, which was in charge of Francisco Antonio de Angelis, in whose company he had come to Abyssinia nine years before. He waited there until he knew that the Ras had returned to his camp at Wambarma, and then he and the ambassador went to take leave of him. They were accompanied by ten Portuguese, four of whom wished to go with them to India; the others were to turn back in Enarya. Se'ela Krestos had procured guides for them from the heathen tribes through which the first part of their route lay, but their troubles began before they had even reached the Nile. They were forced to send back for help, but the knowledge that they had done so and the fear of the Ras induced the tribesmen to change their minds. It is not possible to determine exactly the path they followed on their dangerous journey from Wambarma to Enarya; the problem is discussed in a special excursus on pp. 213–217. Enarya was then still Christian and tributary to the Emperor but the leading ecclesiastic was very suspicious of the embassy. Fernandes tried to conciliate him but the local ruler refused to allow them to continue in the direction they had intended, that is, through Kafa. Whatever his motive may have been, it is likely that they owed their lives to his refusal, and the route to which they were diverted, dangerous as it was, offered at least as much prospect of success as that they had originally proposed to follow. He compelled them to turn eastwards and try to reach the Somali coast in the neighbour-

[1] The text of these five letters is given by Almeida, *loc. cit.*

hood of Mogadishu, by crossing the Omo, traversing Kambatta and Bali and then descending the Webi Shabelle. They therefore found themselves travelling through what were then the southern boundaries of the empire, a region not again described at first hand by a European until the nineteenth century. From Enarya they made their way to the little, pagan kingdom of Janjero. Almeida, who knew Fernandes well, gives a description of it which is of great historical and anthropological interest, for very few explorers visited it before it was conquered by Menilek in the late nineteenth century. Even they crossed its borders surreptitiously and left again in haste in fear of being forced to drink boiling water; Fernandes is the only European known to have been received at the court of one of its independent kings.

When they resumed their journey they crossed the Omo into Kambatta. Here they were detained because of the intrigues of a representative of the Emperor whom Almeida calls Manquer. Like the churchman of Enarya he guessed correctly that the object of the embassy was to bring Portuguese troops into the country, and he persuaded the governor not to allow it to proceed without reference to Susneyos. This, of course, took time, the more so as the messengers were arrested on their way and kept prisoners for three months; they then returned to Kambatta and others were sent who succeeded in reaching Dambya. The reply arrived in Kambatta in June, 1614, and the embassy was then able to proceed to Alaba. The local ruler was a Moslem and when he had talked with Manquer, who followed them a few days later, he imprisoned them all, including even the Emperor's envoy, and confiscated their possessions. Their lives were in imminent danger and it was at this juncture that Fernandes burnt his letters, to save being burnt himself, as Almeida remarks. Some of the Moslem chiefs, however, protested and the ruler was induced to send back Fernandes and the ambassador, taking care that they should not pass through Kambatta, as he was afraid that the governor might help them to reach the coast another way. Manquer persuaded him to detain the three Portuguese who were still with the embassy so that they could fight in his army. Fernandes and the ambassador made their way back across the Awash and through what was largely Galla territory into Shoa. As soon as they could they wrote to the Emperor telling him what had happened and offering to make another attempt. They were, however, ordered to return to court, for, as Almeida says, there was no other route less dangerous than the one they had tried. Their travels had lasted a year and seven months.

After this Fernandes spent much of his time at Dancaz. He was Superior of the mission for some years and acted as interpreter when Almeida himself was first received at court. After the arrival of the Patriarch he became his Vicar-General and remained in Abyssinia until the exile of the Jesuits in 1634. He was then about sixty-four and enfeebled by overwork and constant austerities. He arrived in Diu after having been fifty-two days at sea; Almeida, who had only just arrived himself, says that if the voyage had lasted another four days Fernandes would have died. He had to be carried ashore and taken to the Jesuit college in a palanquin. The 'History' concludes with some of Almeida's personal recollections of Fernandes, who died at Goa in 1641. A few passages from them may be of interest.

'When he spoke of the long and difficult roads that he travelled, as bound by obedience and on the orders of the Emperor Seltan Çagued, when endeavouring to reach the Melinde coast by land . . . he used to say that in the depths of that vast and savage wilderness he thought of himself as an ant in a great meadow; countless people were crossing it in all directions, the anthill was in the middle and he was going along with the grain of wheat or millet he carried, without stopping, or pausing or turning aside because of the traffic, without fear of being trodden upon or crushed, and without regarding the purposes of the travellers but only his own. I think that the Father had this attitude not only on that journey, but throughout his life. For whatever happened, come what might, in good times and bad, we never saw him change, stop in what he intended to do or spare himself and give less than the usual time to his spiritual exercises and the holy labours and occupations he had undertaken. . . .

'The Enemy of all good suffered deeply from the war that the venerable Father waged upon him and tried to distress him many times in Ethiopia and in these last years in St

Paul's College. He used to cover the wall of his cell with blots and stains as if he had spat there, and continued this kind of insult for a long while. But the Father avenged himself ... saying that these stains were signs of others upon his soul of which he did not know. He used to make it the occasion for a most strict examination of his conscience, and sometimes made general confessions of his whole life. The Devil raged so much at this that at one time he rained blows upon him; he was so bruised that for some days he could move only with difficulty. . . .

' He was so thin that he seemed no more than skin and bones. His constitution was weak and his strength very limited, yet he never lacked strength enough for the longest journeys and the roughest roads, nor for the discipline he gave himself every day when he arose, nor for fasting in Lent, Advent, on Fridays and Saturdays throughout the year, for a fortnight before the Assumption of the Virgin Our Lady, and for as many days before the feast of the Archangel St Michael in September. These were fasts with the strictness and rigours of Ethiopia, where fish is rarely found and eggs, butter and milk foods are not allowed, so that he often kept the fasts on nothing but *apas*[1] and lentils, not breaking it until sunset in Lent and until four o'clock in the afternoon at other times, and yet, despite all this austerity, making long journeys which sometimes lasted for whole months at a time. In the middle of them he used to be attacked by spasms of severe pain to which he was subject. All he used to do was to press his hand on the place that hurt, which was usually his side or stomach, and go on without a sigh or groan. I saw him do it as I was walking with him; when I asked him what was wrong he used to answer that it was nothing.'

Fernandes was the author of several devotional and theological works while he was in Abyssinia. He revised the Ethiopic missal and manual of doctrine, translated part of the Roman Ritual, compiled a handbook on cases of conscience for the use of native priests and, at the Emperor's request, a treatise on the Creation, and wrote a life of the Virgin and a polemic against the errors of the Abyssinian church. This last was subsequently published. He took it back to India with him and there translated it into Ethiopic

[1] See p. 46, n. 2.

with the help of some Abyssinian Catholics who had accompanied the Jesuits into exile. The Pope sent Ethiopic types from Italy and the book was printed at St Paul's College in 1642, with the aim of sending copies to Abyssinia. It is in Ethiopic and Latin and is entitled *Magseph assetat, id est, Flagellum Mendaciorum*. It is extremely rare but there is a copy in the Biblioteca Nacional in Lisbon.[1]

Little need be said of the other two extracts. The first is Almeida's account of his own journey from Bassein to Dancaz. The second describes attempts to use two new routes. Juan de Velasco, a Spaniard, and Jeronimo Lobo, a Portuguese, tried to do what Fernandes had tried to do, but starting from the coast instead of from Abyssinia. This was a failure, as Almeida recounts very briefly; a more detailed narrative is given in Lobo's own *Travels*. Two other Portuguese, Francisco Machado and Bernardo Pereira, tried to cross the Moslem kingdom of Adel or Zeila. This ended in their imprisonment and execution in Aussa. The Provincial at Goa had been invited by Susneyos to send priests by this route, but, says Almeida, the Emperor's secretary wrote 'Zeila' when he should have written 'Dancalia', that is, the country of the Danakil. It was by the latter route that the Patriarch Mendes, accompanied by Velasco, Lobo and four others, reached Abyssinia in 1625, after landing at the little harbour of Beilul near Assab.

It has never been the practice of the Hakluyt Society to burden the texts it publishes with exhaustive commentaries. Such a commentary on the extracts printed in this volume would be a work of encyclopaedic dimensions. We have attempted to identify places, persons, Ethiopian words, quotations, etc., and to correct any important mistakes. We have also tried, by quoting from and referring to the writings of other travellers in Ethiopia to establish the reliability of the Jesuits and their place in the history of the exploration of north-east Africa. As we have seen, Almeida was able to use the manuscript work left by Páez and did not himself leave Abyssinia till the summer of 1633. More detailed than the histories of Páez and Mendes and more reliable than Lobo's

[1] More correctly *Maqsafta hasetāt*, 'the Scourge of Liars'. We are indebted to Dr Virginia Rau for verifying that there is a copy of this book in Lisbon, and for checking the title, which is often misquoted.

Travels, his book is a compendium of the knowledge acquired by the Jesuits. After their expulsion there ensued a period of well over a hundred years during which the only considerable additions to European knowledge of the country were made by Ludolf at second hand from his native informant Gregory, and by the brief, though essentially truthful account of his own travels by Poncet.[1] Modern exploration began with Bruce, who was violently prejudiced against the Jesuits and who wrote when their fortunes were at their lowest ebb; they were suppressed by the Pope in 1773, two years after he had left Gondar. It is one of the ironies of the history of exploration that the Jesuits were disbelieved by Bruce and Bruce was disbelieved by his contemporaries, yet if parallel passages from their works are quoted side by side, as is sometimes done in this volume, it is evident that both were essentially truthful.

Some of our identifications of place names are only tentative while there are a few about which we can offer no suggestion at all. The historical geography of Ethiopia is peculiarly difficult and, except for the erudite notes to René Basset's translation of an Arabic chronicle of the Moslem invasions, has received very little attention. Even the topography of much of this area of some 400,000 square miles is imperfectly known.[2] More than sixty languages and dialects, belonging to several distinct linguistic families, are spoken within the borders of Ethiopia. Some of the inhabitants are nomads and there has been much disturbance of the settled, agricultural population in the last four centuries. The Somali and Galla invasions of the sixteenth century and the Agau wars of Almeida's own time entailed the displacement of fugitives and the settlement of the conquerors on their land. In the last years of the nineteenth century Menilek II consolidated his conquests by establishing colonies of Amhara in his new territories. Even when such migrants did not take the names of their native villages with them, as they sometimes did, they did not always adopt the existing names of their new homes, which they might not be able to pronounce.

[1] Printed in *The Red Sea and Adjacent Countries at the close of the Seventeenth Century*, Hakluyt Society, ser. II, no. 100.
[2] 'Though Mt. Damōta is shown on map NB.37/1 as only 7,644 feet . . . the height is, in fact, to be taken as 10,400 feet' (Hugh Scott, *Journey to the Gughé Highlands*, p. 109).

If the old inhabitants were not entirely dispossessed both names might survive to the confusion of cartography. When travelling in Agaumeder Cheesman found that villages often had both Agau and Amhara names, and sometimes a third, negro name as well.[1] Moreover, comparatively few sites in Ethiopia have a long record of continuous habitation. What Almeida calls a town was often only a temporary encampment, the name of which may well survive to this day and denote a settlement in the same district, but not necessarily in the same place. Cheesman, describing his journey from Wambarma to the Nile, remarks: 'These negro tribes are semi-nomadic and settle in a district for a few years . . . before the ground becomes exhausted they move off to pastures new, taking the name of their village with them, a custom that may be convenient for themselves, but that has distinct disadvantages in map-making.'[2] There is often confusion between the name of a district and of its chief village and travellers have sometimes confused the name of a headman with one or the other; Cheesman records at least three examples of this.[3] One should also bear in mind the possibility that, in regions where travellers did not know the local language, they may have been misled into recording what were not place names at all. It is well known that 'I don't know' in sundry African languages has not infrequently been written on the map. More elusive mistakes are made when a guide, knowing what his employer wants, invents names sooner than admit his ignorance or try to explain that some particular feature, however much it may seem worthy of a name to the geographer, has not been given one by the local population.

In translating Almeida and Bahrey we have retained their spellings, even their variant spellings of native words and proper names, except for well-known countries, European towns and classical or Biblical personal names; there is nothing to be gained by keeping Almeida's 'Lixboa' (Lisbon) or 'Salomão' (Solomon) and Bahrey's ' Fars' (Persia) would be misleading, as it is Persia and not the province of Fars that he means. In this introduction and in our own notes and appendices we have used standard English forms for place

---

[1] Cheesman, *Lake Tana and the Blue Nile*, p. 326.
[2] *Ibid.*, p. 353.   [3] *Ibid.*, pp. 340, 344–5, 354.

names, when these exist. Portuguese personal names were erratically spelt in Almeida's time and we have preserved his vagaries, but we ourselves have observed the rules adopted by the Portuguese and Brazilian academies; the familiar patronymic ending of surnames is therefore written with *ES* and not *EZ* when the person concerned was Portuguese. These are the forms in which the names will normally be found in modern Portuguese books. As this is not a philological work we have not thought it necessary to disfigure its pages with the multiplicity of diacritical marks that must be used if the native spelling of Ethiopian names is to be represented unambiguously. Moreover, these spellings vary greatly; the same writer will use different forms on the same page and certain letters have long ceased to represent distinct sounds; nor have European scholars yet devised a system that has been generally accepted. When quoting native spellings, therefore, we have not distinguished between the varieties of *H* and *S* though we have indicated long *A* and long *E* in the usual way when desirable. The system we have used is explained in detail in a note at the end of this Introduction.

The Jesuits, of course, spelt Ethiopian proper names and words more or less phonetically and had no system for transliterating the Ethiopic characters. Readers interested in identifying these names and words may like to be reminded of a few relevant features of Portuguese pronunciation in the seventeenth century. *C* was soft, that is, was pronounced *S* before *E* and *I*; otherwise it was hard (*K*) unless written with a cedilla. The manuscripts are, however, very erratic in the use of this sign; it is often omitted in error and as often inserted when it is redundant. *CH* in Almeida's time had the sound it usually has in modern English. *G* like *C* was hard except before *E* and *I*; it then had the same sound as *J*, which was the normal sound of English *J*; the modern Portuguese pronunciation of *CH* and *J* as *SH* and *ZH* did not become general until the eighteenth century. At the end of words, however, *J* was sometimes merely *Y*; thus the name of the lake usually written Zway is spelt by Almeida 'Zoaj'. *NH*, then as now, was the Spanish *Ñ* and French or Italian *GN*. *QH* which occurs occasionally, is an impossible combination of letters in Portuguese; the *Q* seems to be used by Almeida to indicate that the *H* is an aspirate, which it never is in Portuguese. Thus 'Janqhoj' is to be pronounced 'Janhoy'. Had there been no *q* his readers would probably have said 'Janyoy'. *X* represented a number of sounds as it still does, but in the spelling of foreign names was always equivalent to English *SH*; so the Portuguese wrote the title of the ruler of Persia 'Xá', and Almeida explains that he writes 'Accum' instead of the more usual 'Axum' so as not to misrepresent the pronunciation, which is 'Aksum', not 'Ashum'. The circumflex accent is used freely but in the spelling of foreign names its significance is not always certain. Sometimes it indicates the stressed syllable; sometimes it seems merely to mean that the vowel is to be given its full, that is, approximately its 'continental' value, and not slurred into an indeterminate sound or omitted altogether, as often happens to unstressed vowels in Portuguese. The grave and acute accents are also used on foreign names, but it is possible that, sometimes at least, they are only badly written circumflexes. The manuscripts are hopelessly inconsistent in the accentuation of African names.

Note on Transliteration

In the absence of a universally accepted system of transliteration of Ethiopic, we have adopted the following scheme:

ሀ, ሐ, ኀ	Represented by H	ተ	Represented by T
		ጠ	Represented by Ṭ
		ጨ, ች	Represented by Č
ሠ, ሰ	Represented by S	ቀ	Represented by Q
ጸ	Represented by Ṣ	ከ	Represented by K
ሸ	Represented by Š	ኸ	Represented by Ḳ
ዘ	Represented by Z	ጰ, ፐ	Represented by P
ፀ	Represented by Ṣ		
ዠ, ፚ, ጀ	Represented by J	እ	Represented by ' followed by the appropriate vowel; the breathing is omitted when initial.
		ዐ	Represented by ' followed by the appropriate vowel.

(Other characters present no difficulties for practical purposes.)

This system has been followed, we hope, consistently, where it has been necessary to transliterate. Well-known names like Massawa, Shoa, Amhara, Tana, Gojam, are spelt according to the common English practice, except in the translation of Almeida's 'History', where the original spelling is retained.

THE ETHNOLOGY AND HISTORY OF
SOUTH-WEST ETHIOPIA

§ I. THE PRE-GALLA PEOPLES OF S.W. ETHIOPIA

1. *Ethnology*

South-Western Ethiopia, the country that lies south of
the river Abay and west of the head-waters of the Webi
Shabelle, was occupied before the Galla invasion by peoples
of Hamitic stock who may be referred to as Sidama, and represent one of the waves of Europoid immigrants known as
Hamites or Kushites.[1] The first inhabitants of north-east
Africa seem to have been negroes,[2] who were gradually
expelled or absorbed by the Hamitic populations that followed them. That there was contact between the two races
is clear from the negroid physical characters of many of the
inhabitants of Ethiopia; and in fact there still remain a
number of tribes on the Abyssinian-Sudan border which may
be taken to represent the original negro population, and are
known collectively as Shangalla, a name derived from the
Amharic word for 'negro'. These negro peoples include some
of the tribes of Dar Fung, and others extending as far south
as the Konso between Lake Chamo and Lake Stefanie.

The Hamites seem to have entered north-east Africa in
three main waves which may be distinguished thus: (A) The
Proto- or A-Hamites, perhaps represented to-day by the
Nera or 'Barya' and the Badena or Kunama of Eritrea,
though both the ethnic and the linguistic position of these
people is very uncertain. (B) The Early or B-Hamites, represented by the peoples of the northern zone (Beja), central
zone (Agau), and south-western zone (Sidama). (C) The Later
or C-Hamites, represented by the peoples of the eastern zone

[1] Kushite is the term preferred by Italian anthropologists; but since Kush
was the ancient Egyptian name for the northern Sudan, it seems best to reserve this term for the Egyptian province, and keep Hamite for the peoples
of N.E. Africa.

[2] That is, without taking account of any forerunners of 'Bushman' or
other primitive stocks.

1

(Galla, Somali, Afar or Danakil, and Saho). During the later periods of the Hamitic movement there came yet another wave of immigration, this time of Semitic peoples from south-west Arabia, the ancestors of the present Semitic-speaking Abyssinians.

Within the Sidama[1] zone, the subject of this essay, there are further sub-divisions. While each of the principal Hamitic zones referred to in the last paragraph has its own general characteristics, within the zones there are many local divergences, and from such analysis as the material so far available has allowed, it seems that the Sidama languages fall into the following groups: (A) Sidamo, Darasa, Hadiya, Kambatta, Tambaro, Alaba. (B) Wolamo, Gofa, Kullo, Konta, Zala, Kuera or Baditu, Haruro, Kucha, Gamo. (C) Chara. (D) Basketo, Zaise, Doko. (E) The Gonga group: Kafa, Shinasha, Bosha or Garo, Mao or Anfilo, Sheka or Mocha. (F) The Gimira group: Shako, Benesho, She or Dizu, Kaba, Nao, Mazhi or Maji. (G) Yamma or Janjero. It will be noted that while the term *Sidama* is used to cover all the south-western peoples, the form *Sidamo* occurs as the name of a single tribe. The explanation is that as far back as the sixteenth century the Galla made use of the word because it was the name of one of the more important peoples through whose country their invasion route lay. They established some sort of a centre at Wolabo about 40 miles east of Lake Margherita, and according to the evidence of Bahrey, the form *Sidama* was the word used by the Galla for 'Christians'. The tribal name thus came in time to acquire the meaning of 'stranger', 'one who is not a Galla', while for the Sidama the word *Galo* came to mean 'stranger' in the sense of 'one who is not a Moslem,' for they had long been in contact with Moslems from the Red Sea coast.

Till the time of the Galla occupation of the land between the Abay and Gojeb rivers, the whole of the area seems

[1] The name Sidama, which occurs in sixteenth-century Ethiopic literature, is perhaps derived from a western Hamitic stem *sid-*, *sad-*, meaning 'wander', with a suffix *-ama*, and adopted by the Sidama, with a change of final *a* to *o* that can be paralleled in the Sidama languages. The form in *-a* was then taken by the Galla, and applied first to the western Hamites; then to Christians, because many Hamites were of that religion; and finally to the Abyssinians because they also are Christians.

to have been inhabited by Sidama peoples. South of the
Gojeb the distribution of peoples between about A.D. 1000
and 1500 was possibly much as it is now; of the inhabitants of the country north of the Gojeb, however, we can
say little but that the Sidama peoples who lived there
were absorbed or expelled by the Galla, who refer to them
in their traditions as *gabaro*, 'peasant', and describe them as
living in caves and eating fish, probably a gross distortion of
fact.

From an early date, as recorded by Al 'Umari (1345),
whose description was largely repeated by Maqrizi a hundred
years later, it appears that the Sidama countries formed part
of the so-called Empire of Zeila, and were divided between
the states of Hadya, Bali, and possibly Arababni.[1] Islam did
not perhaps succeed in making a very deep impression on the
Sidama, for the rule of the Zeila Moslems was little more than
nominal in this remote region, and some states, like Kafa and
Janjero, successfully resisted all attempts at Moslem domination. But the Sidamo were part of Hadya, and bordered on
the more vigorous state of Bali, which has always been a
corridor leading from the highlands to the riverain areas of
Somalia (the lower parts of the valleys of the Webi Shabelle
and Juba), and there has been a good deal of contact between
the Moslems of Somalia and the peoples of Bali and Dawaro,
resulting in the spread and maintenance of Islamic religion
and culture. This influence was intensified by the emergence
of great religious figures like Sheikh Husain (before 1550),
round whose tomb near the Webi Shabelle some 60 miles
north of Magalo there grew up a religious and cultural centre
comparable to that which developed later at Harar. And
except for the short period of Abyssinian rule, Bali was always
mainly under Moslem control since the establishment of the
'empire of Zeila', thus exerting a strong Moslem influence to
the west of the Webi which spread easily under suitable conditions, and was kept alive by constant intercourse with the
Moslems of Somalia. This, however, did not prevent the kings
of Abyssinia from trying to convert the Sidama to Christianity in spite of their rather tough brand of paganism, or

[1] The remaining states were called Ifat or Awfat, Dawaro, Sharkha, and
Dara.

from claiming some sort of political control over them. 'Amda
Ṣyon I (1312–1342), for instance, claimed to have control of
Wolamo, which is mentioned in the next century in a hymn
of Yeshaq. In the sixteenth century Sarṣa Dengel (Malak
Sagad) made some attempts to introduce Christianity into
Kafa, and Bahrey records that in 1586 he ordered the peoples
of Enarya, Bosha, and Gomar to accept Christianity. In one
of the oldest churches in Kafa, that of St George (Giyorgis)
at Baha, Father Léon des Avenchers found an old wooden
altar, *tabot*, bearing an Ethiopic inscription saying that it was
set up in the reign of Malak Sagad. But there are indications
that Christianity had a hard struggle. Even if it did not die
out, as some traditions suggest, it came very near to extinc-
tion, for Kafa was the seat of a strong cult of the Sky-God of
the Sidama, here called Yero,[1] and since there seems also to
have been in ancient times a goddess equivalent to the Galla
Atete, who became identified with the Virgin Mary under the
name of Astario Maryam, it is probable that there was a
good deal of paganism in such Christian worship as did survive. In Wolamo there existed in Cecchi's day traces of pagan
rites mixed with Christian observances, such as the sacrifice
of bulls at Warata in the ruins of Christian churches,
and the sprinkling of beer on the ground while the priest
muttered in Ethiopic the words 'O Lord Christ have mercy
on me'.

2. *The independent states of Sidama*

The Galla failed to conquer the country that lay to the
west of the chain of lakes that stretches from Lake Rudolf to
Lake Zeway, and it was only after reaching the Gibē region
and forcing their way south-west from there that they were
able to reach the Gojeb and establish a group of five small
kingdoms in the angle between the Gojeb and the Gibē. The
history of these states, except for the early years of Enarya
and Jimma, belongs to the Galla period, and will be examined
later on. Here we may summarize what is known of the
traditional histories of the hitherto unconquered peoples of
the region.

[1] See below, p. 157, n. 1.

(a) Kafa

The most detailed accounts which we possess of any Sidama state relate to the kingdom of Kafa, which till conquered in 1897 by the Abyssinians, was ruled by a king, *tato*, who claimed descent from Solomon and the Queen of Sheba, a claim due to Amharic influence and linked with another tradition that the ancestors of the Kafa spoke Tigre when they arrived and had to learn the Kafa language. The kingship was hereditary, and the king belonged to a family called Bushasho of the Minjo group. His seat was at Bonga hill in the centre of the kingdom, and he had a second seat at Anderacha seven miles to the south-east. The royal burial-place was at Shido hill to the E.N.E. of Anderacha, where the kings were buried in perpendicular shaft-graves 25 feet deep; nobles were buried in shallower gallery-pits. Though the king was, as described by Cerulli, 'semi-divine', there is no evidence that he was put to death when his bodily powers failed, as some people seem to think.[1] Though one of his sons succeeded, it was not necessarily the eldest; and the choice of the successor lay in the hands of a council of seven elders. The king's mother was held in great honour, and had the title of *abet*, 'favoured'; but though she had a certain degree of influence from her position, she had no official powers.

The insignia of the kingship, used before the Abyssinian conquest, are interesting and important. They consisted of twelve objects, many of them made of gold: (1) The king's crown, in the form of a helmet made of gold and silver, with a triple phallus of gold in front; the later form, illustrated by Bieber, is somewhat different from that seen by Cecchi. (2) Golden ear-rings with long hanging chains. (3) A golden armlet. (4) A gold finger-ring. (5) A gold neck-chain. (6) A gold staff. (7) A gold parasol. (8) A green cloak. (9) A golden sword. (10) A golden shield. (11) A two-bladed spear. (12) A drum, *nagarit*. The king's life was hedged about with a good deal of ceremonial, much of it now forgotten; there were many court officers, such as the *atalecho*, whose duty it was to supervise his food and drink. His powers included: (1) The control of the rights and privileges of each section of the

---

[1] Tors Irstam, *The King of Ganda*, p. 143.

Kafa people. (2) The administration of justice, for which purpose he had a tribunal at the foot of Bonga hill, where people could appeal against decisions given in lower courts, for the king was an absolute monarch, with the power of life and death, and of liberty and slavery, over all his people. (3) The settlement in his dominion of people conquered in war, and the control of strangers in the country. (4) The control of the submerged class of hunters called Mancho or Watta, who had a chief of their own called *mancho tato*. (5) The control of relations with other tribes. The king was assisted by a council of elders, the seven members of which had the duty of choosing his successor. The titles of these members were: (i) *gushi rasho*, the chief elder, the head of the Christian Kafa, and commander of the king's slaves (ii) *katami rasho*, the commander of the king's guard. (iii) *adie rasho*, commander of the horse-guards. (iv) *arbash rasho*, who came from the Argepo group. (v) *bonda rasho*, also from the Argepo group. (vi) *arse rasho*, of the Macho group. (vii) *shode rasho*, of the Matto group. Under the king were kinglets or chiefs of the districts called Hinnari, Gonga, Gurabo, and Tejiwo, who were allowed to wear golden armlets as insignia of office. Sub-districts were in charge of lesser chiefs called *rasho*, who were responsible to the king through the kinglets. When members of the Council of elders were away at court performing their duties, their districts were ruled by deputies.

The people were divided into three classes: (i) The Minjo or nobles, to which belonged the royal family Bushasho and the family groups of Argepo, Yirgo, Hiyo, Gonga, Amaro, and Miecho; from this class came all the kinglets and district chiefs. (ii) The commoners, including the groups called Hinnimacho, Hinnakaro, Hinnucho, Osho, and Tura. (iii) The submerged class of Mancho or Watta, the pre-Kafa inhabitants of the country.[1] The Kafa have no *gada* or age-set system like that of the Galla, but they practise circumcision (males at eight weeks, girls between four and twelve months) and infibulation. They are a pastoral people with a somewhat advanced form of agriculture, using a plough which re-

---

[1] There is a short comparative vocabulary of the Mancho language in Cerulli, *La Lingua Caffina* (1951), pp. 11–21.

sembles an Ancient Egyptian New Kingdom type (XVIIIth dynasty). Among the crops they grow are cotton and coffee.

The Minjo are described in tradition as being a people more than human who came out of the rocks and holes in the ground, and were given the land of Kafa by Heqo (God). This tradition of 'coming out of the ground' is found in other parts of Africa, and is possibly one that may be taken almost literally, as indicating that the people once lived in some form of dwelling with its floor below ground level, like the hut-circles found in parts of N.E. Africa. Such an interpretation does not conflict with a possible connexion between the royal family Bushasho and the harbour of Busaso (Bender Kassim) on the north Somali coast which is suggested by a tradition recorded by Cecchi which brings the Minjo to Kafa from the sea-coast. According to this story, there were two brothers named Yakama and Minjo who with their mother left the coast and after two months' travel, during which they lived by hunting, reached the neighbourhood of Kafa. Yakama, tired by the hardships of the journey, rebelled against the tyranny of his mother, who was constantly urging them to go forward, and tried to kill her with his spear. But the wound he inflicted was not mortal, and she recovered through the care of Minjo, whom she blessed, predicting that one day he would rule over Kafa; Yakama, however, she cursed and confined to a mountain called Borru. Continuing the journey, they reached a river called Gum, where the old woman fell ill; before she died, she gave Minjo her bracelet and gold ring. After burying her Minjo washed in the river, and while doing so dropped the bracelet and ring into the water. As he was searching for them, he was captured by the slaves of Matto, the chief of the country, who then lived at Bonga. After being told what Minjo was looking for, Matto put 'medicine' into the water, with the result that the things were found in the belly of a fish. Matto kept them, and Minjo was reduced to the lowly task of cutting grass for Matto's mule. After some years, Matto, leaving his homestead after killing a chicken, was warned by a mysterious voice that he who had eaten the head of the chicken would be raised to the throne. Alarmed by this strange announcement, Matto returned at once, and ordering the women to bring him the chicken's head, learned that it had been given to Minjo to eat. He then called his council together and told the elders what had happened. They declared unanimously that Minjo must be made king, so Matto gave him back the bracelet and ring and set him on the throne, receiving for himself the promise of an office at court.

The Gonga, one of the Minjo family groups, are considered to be the nucleus of the 'true' Kafa, and give as their place of origin Oki Amaro in western Ethiopia somewhere between the Abay and the Dadesa, where they say still live other peoples of the same stock. The Kafa country was anciently inhabited by peoples related to the Gimira group (Group F) who were derived from a wave of Sidama invaders who mixed with Nilotic peoples akin to the modern Anuak. A second Sidama wave impinging on these produced the Kafa; and in pre-Minjo days (Bieber puts the arrival of the Minjo, the second Sidama wave, at about 1390 A.D.) there appear to have been five main political groups in Kafa, those of the Mancho, Nao, She, Benesho, and Mashengo. When the Minjo came, the Mancho, who were primitive hunters with what they call a 'great king' of their own (whence the retention in the Kafa state, from traditional respect, of the *mancho tato*), were driven into the forest; the others were forced into the lands bordering Kafa on the south (Nao, She, and Benesho) and north-west (Mashengo).

We have three lists of the kings of Kafa, two from Bieber (A and B) and one from Cecchi (C). List A contains 19 names up to 1890; B has 15 names; and C, 17 names. All three are derived from oral tradition, for there seems to have been no court historian in Kafa. To each king in List A Bieber has attached a date. Going back to 1775 the lengths of the reigns, if sometimes rather long, are not unreasonable; but for the earlier period, up to 1775, Bieber seems to have taken 35 years as the average length of a reign, and to have varied it at intervals: he gives eight reigns of 35 years, one of 40, one of 33, and one of 32 years. This is too long an interval to be consistent over a period of nearly four hundred years, and the explanation may be that Bieber has left out the names of several kings. Lists B and C give between them some five names which do not seem to occur in List A, and these (unless mere variants of names in List A) may be added to the others and thus make the intervals more reasonable. List B is obviously not in the right order, and the additional names it provides may be added anywhere before 1775. Eleven kings in 385 years give an average of 35 years to a reign, as Bieber discovered, and his arbitrary variations may have been just to break the monotony. If five more names are added, we get an average of 24 years, still rather long, but not impossible; and if we compare this with the average of the kings from 1775 onwards, we find that seven kings in 115 years had an average of nearly 17 years each. Though perhaps still rather high for an average, it is possible. Certain kings in some of the neighbouring states are known to have had long reigns. Gali Sherocho of Kafa reigned from 1870 to 1890; Jawe Oncho of Guma, for at least 38 years; Abba Jifar I of Jimma, for 25 years; and Abba Dula of Guma, for 25 years. The three lists, with Bieber's dating, are:

	List A: Bieber	*List B: Bieber*	*List C: Cecchi*
1390	'The Minjo king'	Minjiloch	Minjo
1425	Girra		Gire
1460	'The Adio king'		Odhe
1495	'The Shadda king'	Shaddi	Sadi
1530	Madi Gafo	Shonge	Madi Gafine
1565	'The Bonga king'	Borrete	Bong-he
1605	Giba Nechocho	Bonge	Giba Nekiok
1640	Gali Gafocho		Gali Ginok
1675	Gali Ginocho	Gali Ginocho	Tan Ginok
1710	Gaki Gaocho	Otti Sheroch	Taki Gaok
1742	Gali Gaocho	Kanechoch	Galli
1775	Shagi Sherocho	Gali Keffoch	Sagi Saro
1795	Beshi Ginocho	Kaye Sheroch	Beshi Gino
1798	Hotti Ginocho	Beshi Sheroch	Oto
1821	Gaha Nerocho	Gali Sheroch	Ganecho
1845	Gawi Nerocho	Haji Ginoch	Gaul Saro
1854	Kaye Sherocho (Kamo)		Kamo
1870	Gali Sherocho		
1890	Gaki Sherocho, deposed in 1897 by Menilek of Abyssinia.		

In the sixteenth century Christianity was introduced through the agency of Sarṣa Dengel of Abyssinia, after the forcible conversion of the Bosha, close neighbours of the

Kafa. The Kafa sometimes claim that they were Christians before this time, but this claim does not seem to be well founded, and is due perhaps to dislike of admitting that they owe it to their enemies the Amaro (Amhara, Abyssinians). The statements concerning the conversion of the Bosha in the *History of Sarṣa Dengel*, together with the evidence afforded by the inscription discovered by Father des Avenchers, seem to indicate that Christianity in Kafa really does date from Sarṣa Dengel's time. In 1567 Sarṣa Dengel was helped in his war against the Bosha by Sepenhi the governor of Enarya. This man became a legendary figure in Kafa under the name of Shipenao; the introduction of Christianity is sometimes attributed to him, and he is regarded as a worker of wonders. According to a traditional account, 'Shipenao of Enarya had his capital at Cheriko on the slopes of Mount Chada. He was a Christian, and the first of his race to make the pilgrimage to Jerusalem, whence he brought the stones used to make the first altar ever set up in any Sidama country. He built churches in Enarya, and made a great expedition into Kafa. To reach it he did not follow the caravan route, but led his troops across country, ignoring all obstacles, building bridges over great rivers, and cutting through impassable mountains. Today there may be seen near Anderacha the great bridge of Gurguto[1] over the river Gicha which Shipenao built in one day, and at Chira is a rocky hill which was split by one stroke of his sword. Entering by the road leading to the west, he founded at Baha the church of St George, and gave to it one of the altar stones from Jerusalem. Then he crossed the Shasha region S.W. of Anderacha and disappeared in the country of the negroes in the west, leaving no trace.'[2] After the Abyssinian conquest in 1897, soldiers who took part in it and had heard local stories about Shipenao identified him with Grañ (who never penetrated so far west); and it is possible that this identification may explain the presence of a 'stone of Grañ' on the bank of the Addio river at Addio, which Bieber mentions in connexion with Shipenao.[3]

Till the middle of the sixteenth century the Abyssinians were the chief enemies of the Kafa, whose kings always

---

[1] A natural arch like a bridge.   [2] Cerulli, *Etiopia Occidentale*, I, p. 196.
[3] *Kaffa*, II, p. 491.

feared the possibility of invasion, though in fact they proved strong enough to maintain their independence against both Abyssinian and Galla, till the former came against them with modern weapons in the nineteenth century. After the sixteenth century their chief enemies were the Galla. This enmity never died out, and was fostered by the nearness of the Galla in the Gibē monarchies; even recently it was inflamed by the part played by Abba Jifar of Enarya when he helped Menilek to conquer Kafa in 1897.

About 1675 Gali Ginocho began to extend his kingdom and brought the small states of She, Benesho, and Mashengo under his rule. These had originally been part of Kafa, but were forced out by the coming of the Minjo and became independent. The Nao, another of the original groups, remained independent till they were included in Kafa in 1867 by Kaye Sherocho. In the last quarter of the eighteenth century the kingdom was enlarged again by Shagi Sherocho, and by the early part of the nineteenth century it extended nearly to the Omo in the south-east and to the junction of the Omo and Dincho in the south; its tributaries included the states of Wolamo (Konta, Kucha, Kullo, Gamo, Gofa, Chara, Tambaro, and Wolamo), as well as many tribes to the west and south.

(b) Enarya

The early history of this state is very obscure. In the time of the Zagwē dynasty of Abyssinia, which came to an end in 1268, it formed part of a small independent kingdom called Damot, which then lay south of Gojam and the Abay; and when Yekuno Amlak the first king of the restored Solomonian dynasty (1268–1283) had been placed on the throne of Abyssinia, he made the king of Damot his viceroy and gave him charge of Enarya. When the war with Grañ broke out in 1527, the ruler of Enarya was a slave from Damot who submitted to the Moslems, and Enarya was thus lost to Abyssinia. From about 1533 it remained under nominal Moslem control till it was invaded by the Galla conqueror Teso about 1570. The result of this invasion was to isolate it from other areas under Moslem control, and part of it was settled by Galla of the Limmu tribe, whence that part of it became known as Limmu-Enarya to distinguish it from the rest of Enarya which for a time continued under nominal Moslem rule. After the Galla conquest, it is said that two Portuguese[1] settled in Enarya. They had come to Abyssinia with Cristovão da Gama who brought help to Galawdewos against Grañ, and were known traditionally as Sigaro and Sapera. The latter married a Galla woman, and perhaps attained some sort of position in Enarya, for the kings in the nineteenth century claimed descent from him, and had as their title not the Galla word *moti*, 'king', but *supera*. In 1567 Sarṣa Dengel visited Enarya, then ruled by a governor appointed by Abyssinia, who was at that time named Sepenhi. This man took part in the king's expedition that year against the Bosha of Garo in south-east Jimma. Sepenhi was a pagan, but he figures (as we have seen) in the legends of both Enarya and Kafa as a Christian champion and a worker of wonders. He was succeeded as governor by Badancho, son of La'asonhi, a pagan who together with the whole population of Enarya was converted to Christianity by Sarṣa Dengel in 1586. Badancho was succeeded by Guamcho, and Guamcho by Emana Krestos, after whom, early in the seventeenth century, Abyssinian control of Enarya gradually ceased.

(c) Jimma

It is possible that Jimma may be the Shimi referred to by Al 'Umari, which would indicate that it existed as a political entity as early as the middle of the fourteenth century. Before the Galla conquest, the western part of the future kingdom consisted of two independent areas: a western inhabited by a number of small tribes of the same stock as the Kafa and apparently ruled on a tribal basis by elected magistrates, each tribe being independent; and a south-eastern called Garo inhabited by the Bosha, a district which is mentioned in a victory song of Yeshaq of Abyssinia about 1412. Between these two areas and Kafa there were many connexions: the Kafa royal family of Bushasho came to Kafa from from Bosha, and many place-names indicate the movement of people from Garo into Kafa. After the Galla conquest part

---

[1] It may be noted that the accounts of Fernandes's journey do not mention these Portuguese.

of south-western Janjero was absorbed into Jimma, so that when that state finally developed into a monarchy it was a composite entity formed from parts of a number of areas previously under different rule. The basis of Jimma was six tribes called Jimma, Gobo, Horo, Rare, Arjo, and Hine; and when these were welded into one under the Galla, the country acquired the name of Jimma Kaka, 'the confederacy of Jimma'. Later still it became known as Jimma Abba Jifar, from the name of its fourteenth king.

The Bosha or Garo in south-east Jimma were attacked in 1567 by Sarṣa Dengel with the help of Sepenhi the governor of Enarya because the father of the chief of Garo had killed many of the soldiers of Galawdewos (d. 1559), and committed many acts of brigandage. At this time Garo was not under Galla control, and it was in fact the last part of Sidama territory that they conquered. At first the Galla invaders did not recognize the existing organization of the local tribes, and brought in their own *gada* system which, when combined later with the kingly office, was considerably modified.

(d) The southern states

The Sidama region now lies south of the Galla states of the Gibē, and is crossed from north to south by the river Omo which divides it into two unequal parts. On the east it is bordered by the Arusi highlands, and on the west by the tribes collectively termed Shangalla or 'negroes' in Amharic. On the south it reaches Lake Chamo. The land may be divided into four geographical regions: (i) Eastern Sidama, comprising the Sidamo, Hadiya, Kambatta, Tambaro, and Alaba peoples. (ii) Southern Sidama, inhabited by the *Ometo* or people of the Omo, who are the Wolamo and a number of small tribal groups. (iii) Northern Sidama, inhabited by the Janjero. (iv) Western Sidama, occupied by the Kafa and associated peoples of whom some account has already been given. To these may be added Guragē the people of which, though basically Sidama, have been heavily overlaid with Tigre stock and speak a language of Semitic type which differs from the Hamitic languages spoken by the rest of the Sidama. Before the war with Grañ the southern Sidama were included in the Moslem states of Hadya, Bali, and possibly

Arababni, though throughout the region Moslem control was only nominal, and Islam never made much headway against the strong local paganism. Nor did the Galla ever succeed in conquering any of these Sidama who, though raided by the Galla, maintained their independence till brought into the Ethiopian empire by Menilek at the end of the nineteenth century.

i. Sidamo

The country of the Sidamo, bordering on if not actually part of the territory of Bali, was a corridor for communication between the coast and the interior. Hence there was a certain amount of Moslem influence on the Sidamo, though today they are nominally Christian. Their history is divided into three periods. (i) In what may be called the 'Bali period' the prevailing foreign influence was Moslem, which introduced in places a veneer of Islamic culture. (ii) The Galla invasion route lay through the Sidamo country, and it was largely due to their resistance that the Galla did not succeed at the start in overrunning the Sidama peoples west of the lakes. One effect of the Galla wars was to put bitter enmity between the Sidamo and the Galla, and even today the Sidamo, according to Galla custom, are *dina* or enemies: payment of blood-money is out of the question in cases of homicide and only retaliation is possible. (iii) In 1604 a certain Dagano paid tribute to Ya'qob of Abyssinia, and he is described in the Chronicle of Susneyos as *garad* of Bali. Dagano is a Sidamo, not a Galla name, and this indicates that the Sidamo considered themselves to be the rightful lords of the land of Bali. The Sidamo seem to have remained largely uninfluenced by Galla institutions, and their system of slavery continued till it was abolished in 1936 by order of Graziani. Both the Sidamo and their southern neighbours the Darasa grow coffee, which is noted in the markets of north-east Africa.

ii. Hadiya

The people of Hadiya call themselves Gudela, but the name by which they are known to the Abyssinians (Hadya) and Galla (Hadiya) is derived from that of the Moslem state of Hadya on which they bordered, or of which they were even a part (for the limits of the Moslem states are not known with any great degree of accuracy). In the time of 'Amda Ṣyon (1312–1342) they were tributary to Abyssinia, but being within the active sphere of Moslem influence and, as it would seem, less independent than the Sidamo, they were largely Moslem in outlook and sympathy; and "Amano", king of Hadiya, sided with Sabr ad din in his war with 'Amda Ṣyon I, who in revenge laid waste Hadiya. The word *amano* is not a name but a title, and the expression 'land of Amano' in a hymn of the time of Zar'a Ya'qob (1434–1468) is thus explained. This king also made war on Hadiya because the Gudela king Mahiko refused to pay the tribute which his father Mehmad had paid. At this period the Hadiya kingdom consisted of eight districts each under a *garad* or sub-chief. Although Hadiya was ravaged under Lebna Dengel by the Abyssinian governor of Bali for non-payment of tribute, its ruler remained faithful enough to his overlord to give asylum to Abyssinian chiefs fleeing from the Moslems who were attacking their country. But in 1532 the ruler submitted to Grañ, and the Moslem conquest of Bali followed within a month or two. After the death of Grañ, Galawdewos sent an army into Hadiya and reconquered it. In 1568 Sarṣa Dengel fought with Aze the *garad* of Hadiya for the usual reason— non-payment of tribute—and defeated him in 1569. According to the *History of Sarṣa Dengel* (p. 47), Aze had 500 horse- men wearing cuirasses, all Moslems; 1700 horses; and number- less warriors carrying shields, 'God alone knew how many'. The last Abyssinian expedition against Hadiya was made in 1604 by Ya'qob; and from then onwards the western penetra- tion of the Galla cut it off from cultural and political inter- course with Abyssinia, as a result of which it slipped into a state of cultural stagnation. Of kings' names we have but few. The title of the first two named in tradition, Ango and his son Ada, was *adil*; later the tributary ruler bore the title of *amano*, and later still, of *garad*. Governors of districts were *garad*, later *koro*, and were appointed by the king. Ordinary people among the Gudela are circumcised; but there is a class of nobles, *kontam*, who are exempt from circumcision. Nominally the people are Moslem, but there is much pagan- ism left; rain-makers, *anjancho*, are important and hereditary.

The Gudela are keen agriculturalists, growing barley, millet, maize, and cotton; they also keep many cattle.

iii. *Kambatta*

The state of Kambatta lies immediately south of Hadiya. The people are of Sidama stock with a small mixture of Abyssinian blood. The first king is said to have come from the east, from the sea, and to have belonged to the Solomonian line of Abyssinia. The king's title appears to have been *adil*. The first mention of Kambatta is in a hymn of Yeshaq (1412–1427). In the reign of Zar'a Ya'qob a few years later, when Mahiko of Hadiya was attacked for not paying tribute, the district of Alaba became independent under a kinglet of its own, but remained vaguely attached to Kambatta. By the seventeenth century Kambatta was still tributary to Abyssinia, according to Fernandes (see below, p. 162). The people of Kambatta were continually fighting the Arusi Galla, who were once actually forced to pay them tribute. Tambaro, the small state south of Kambatta, had an elected ruler, though it is not known how far back this system goes here. A Galla song records that there was a king 'Negita' of the Moslem Tambaro about 1882.

iv. Wolamo

The peoples of southern Sidama are sometimes called *Ometo*, which means 'people of the Omo'; the Wolamo call themselves *Wolamo*, sing. *Wolaito*. This state is first mentioned by name in a record which claims that it was under the control of 'Amda Ṣyon; it also occurs in a hymn of Yeshaq. The kings of Wolamo belonged to three separate dynasties. The first is said to have come from Damot in the time of Yekuno Amlak (1268), and the name of the first king is given as Moti Lami, a title and name which must have crept into tradition after the Galla invasion of Ethiopia, for both these words are Galla, and mean 'king's posterity'. The second dynasty is said to have come from Mount Kucha, a small tribal area next to Wolamo, and is known as the Wolaitamala dynasty. Its rule extended over the tribal areas of Kucha, Gamo, Boroda, and Kullo. There is no indication as to when it was established, but it came to an end about the time of the Galla invasion of the Gibē region. Though Wolamo seems to

E

have been invaded by Moslems during the war with Grañ, it was not under Moslem control. The third dynasty came from 'Tigre', that is, the Tigrean colony at Endageny in Guragē which was founded in the time of 'Amda Ṣyon I. Allowing an average of 27 years to each of the first fourteen kings in the list given by Borelli, the establishment of this dynasty may be placed about the time of the Galla invasion (*c.* 1550–1570). The names of the kings given by Borelli are:

1. Mikael.	8. Sahona.
2. Girma.	9. Ogatto (1761–1800).
3. Gazenja or Gazenya.	10. Amado (1800–1835).
4. Addayo.	11. Damota (1835–1845).
5. Kote.	12. Gobe (1845–1886).
6. Libani	13. Gaga (1886–?1890).
7. Tubi.	14. T'ona (?1890–1893).

The early kings of this dynasty had to repel many raids by the Arusi Galla, and Gazenja became known as the 'Conqueror of the Arusi'. Fortifications were made on the eastern frontier as a defence against the Galla. Ruins of some of them still remain north of Lake Margherita between the rivers Wayo and Bilate, and elsewhere; one, seen by Bottego, had walls 1 kilometre in length and two metres high. By about 1820 Wolamo and most of the other Omo states were tributary to the king of Kafa. In 1893 Wolamo was conquered by Menilek, together with a number of little independent states and tribal areas which were added to it and now form the modern Wolamo. The more important of these were Kullo, Konta, Gofa, and Gamo.

The little state of Kullo was also known locally as Dawaro, because it was colonized by refugees from Dawaro during the war with Grañ; and it was sometimes spoken of as 'Harar' since that famous city was in the state of Dawaro, but there was never any other connexion between Kullo and Harar. Nine names of kings were given to Borelli. The first, Kauka, came 'from the west', and was followed (after a long gap) by:

1. Mahedo.	5. Alao.
2. Adeto.	6. Dagoiye.
3. Dasho.	7. Dada.
4. Sahona.	8. Kanta, ruling in 1887.

The people of Kullo were included in Wolamo for a time during the Wolaitamala dynasty, but they seem to have broken free, perhaps during the early eighteenth century, since the gap in the king-list suggests the period of inclusion in Wolamo, with independence regained under Mahedo. The people are pagans. They grow cereals and cotton.

In Konta, where the ruler's title was *kawa*, there are two versions of the origin of the royal family; one brings it from Gofa (to the south-west), the other from the direction of Shoa (to the north-east); but since the ruler of Gofa also was called *kawa*, the former is perhaps the more likely. About 1600 the king of Konta was a vassal of the king of Kafa. The last king surrendered to Menilek in 1892. The people are mainly pagans, and the headquarters of a spirit-cult called *docho* is among them.[1]

The king of Gofa had the title of *kawa*. The last two kings, Dahoda who was alive in 1887, and Kamma, who was conquered by Menilek in 1893, were of the same line as T'ona of Wolamo, i.e. of Tigrean descent from Guragē. Most of the Gofa are pagans, though there are a few Christians.

Gamo district was raided by Yeshaq of Abyssinia in the early fifteenth century. It was the home of Bahrey, and was raided by the Galla in the sixteenth century. Most of the people are pagans, though there are a few Christians. (See *Gamo* in the Gazetteer.)

The remaining districts of Wolamo are said to have had kings, but it is probable that these were really something more in the nature of tribal chiefs. These lesser components include Zala, east of Gamo; Uba, between Gofa and Zala; Malo, between Gofa and the Omo; Doko, south-west of Malo; Chara and Koisha, west of the Omo from Malo; Kuera or Baditu, east of Lake Chamo; and Kucha, between Gofa and Wolamo proper. Of these, Zala, Malo, Doko, Chara, and Koisha are tribe names; Uba, Kucha, and Kuera being names of districts. The tribes called Mazhi or Maji, Arbore, and Amar, as well as the Burji or Bambala and Konso (of negro stock) are also attached to the modern Wolamo, though before Menilek's conquest they had no political connexion with it.

[1] See p. 157.

v. Janjero

The people of this kingdom call themselves Yamma or Yemma; the name Janjero is an Hamitic word meaning 'baboon' which is applied to them in the forms *janjero* (Galla), *yangaro* (Kafa), *janjor* (Hadiya), and *zenjero* (Amharic). Till 1894 when they were conquered by Menilek they formed an independent state ruled by kings belonging to a family called Mwa which ousted an earlier dynasty called Halmam Gama. The Mwa claim to be of Abyssinian origin, and say that they entered the country from the north, establishing themselves first as lords of a district called Balamo before they dispossessed the Halmam Gama. Claims to an Abyssinian origin are found elsewhere, e.g. among the Konta, and while they may be due in part to a reluctant admiration of Abyssinian power, there may in some cases (as here) perhaps be a basis in fact. An Abyssinian strain may well have been introduced by adventurers unknown to history who made settlements in Janjero and other places during the obscure period of the Abyssinian Middle Ages. But even if there is an Abyssinian element in the royal family, the people have preserved till quite recently a number of primitive customs belonging to the earlier layers of Sidama stock or even to their forerunners; some of these are described below (p. 157).

vi. Guragē

Guragē, lying to the west of the Zeway-Shala group of lakes, is an island of Semitic speech surrounded by Sidama and Galla. Its population is basically of Sidama stock, but has been heavily overlaid by a colonization from Tigre, as well as by later elements from Harar. Marcel Cohen, indeed, has suggested that there may have been an independent settlement of South Arabian peoples in the Zeway region; this, however, requires further investigation.[1] The country is small, and the population not large (a reasonable estimate is probably that of Cecchi, 40,000), yet there is a surprising diversity of languages and religions. The *History of the Macha* extends the kingdom of Damot to Gerawgē in the thirteenth

[1] *Études sur l'Éthiopien méridional*, pp. 49–51.

century; and in the reign of 'Amda Ṣyon I an Abyssinian army under the *azmač* (general) Sebhat left the town of Gur'a in Tigre and settled in Guragē, whence the name, from *Gur'a*, and *gē*, 'country'. This is a more likely explanation than that given by Krapf, who says that it was derived from the word *gura*, 'left', because the country lay to the left when the kings of Abyssinia looked westwards from Entotto near Addis Ababa.[1] That there was a strong settlement of Semitic-speakers in Guragē cannot be doubted, and the modern historian Aleqa Tayye is probably right in assigning it to the days of 'Amda Ṣyon.[2] On the other hand, according to Cecchi, some of the Guragē people claimed descent from Abyssinian refugees who fled from their own country during the war with Grañ, and were ruled by chiefs whose titles were *čimbero*, *bultem*, *tiemo*, *abeye*, *aizeba* and other words. Surrounded by hostile Galla and continually exposed to attack, they sent an embassy to Gondar asking Susneyos (1604–1632) for help, and as a result the *azmač* Sebeate was sent from Tigre. After fulfilling his task of helping the people of Guragē, he settled in the country and made himself king, establishing his headquarters on an island in Lake Zeway. His descendants ruled till Se'ela Sellase, king of Shoa, overthrew the dynasty between 1832 and 1840. Though there may have been a second military immigration from Tigre, there is evidently some confusion here with the earlier movement described by Aleqa Tayye. According to another tradition recorded by Father Azaïs, there was also an immigration of fanatical Moslems from Harar, who had to flee during the war with Grañ, under a supposed brother of Grañ named Abdul Qadir; but this is not confirmed by the *Futuh*, and no Abdul Qadir is known as a brother of Grañ. Guragē is divided into tribal groups, which are not yet known accurately in detail; the main groups seem to be Chaha-Muher, divided into seven sub-tribes known as 'the seven houses of Guragē': Walani, Aymallal, Silte, Gogot, Ulbarag, Endageny, Nurana. Azaïs calls these independent groups; they were often at war with each other, and thus a flourishing slave-market was sustained, for prisoners were sold as slaves.

[1] *Travels*, p. 45.
[2] Quoted by E. Ullendorff in *Africa* (1950), XX, p. 337.

Under Galawdewos, Guragē paid an annual tribute to
Abyssinia made up of gold figures of animals, many hides,
and a thousand head of cattle. In the seventeenth century it
was nominally ruled by governors, šum, appointed by the
king of Abyssinia; but at the same time each independent
tribal group had its own 'king'. In 1875 the country was conquered by Menilek and divided into five nagarit or drum districts (so called from the drums, nagarit, beaten at the instal-
lation of a governor); these districts are Qabena, Walani,
Gadabalo, Abso, and Mokir.

Qabena is a part of Guragē which was set up as an independent slave-trading state by a Moslem from Chaha named
Omar Baksa, who after failing to dominate his own district of
Chaha, managed to oust the weak nominee of Menilek in
Qabena. Cecchi estimated that the population of Qabena
was about 50,000, and that when joined for raiding with its
neighbours Abso and Gedelel could muster some 2000 horsemen and 4000 infantry. These figures are doubtless much
exaggerated, but show that Qabena was considered to be a
formidable enemy. Though there was good grazing here, the
main business of Qabena was slaves. The best came from
Chaha and Ulbarag; trade was maintained with the Galla,
and the peoples of Janjero, Kambatta, Jimma, and Limmu-
Enarya. The prices for slaves in Cecchi's day were reckoned
in copper natter or strips of copper cut from pans and kettles
imported from Zeila and Tajurra, and weighing 432 gr.
According to Cecchi's figures, a fine young virgin in 1880
commanded the highest price, next a beautiful young woman,
and old men and women the lowest.[1] Though Qabena was not
in itself a particularly important place, these details show the
kind of private state that could be set up, given suitable
conditions, by a determined man in Ethiopia less than a
century ago. It is probable that there existed at various
times similar little states, now forgotten, never visited by
Europeans, and of the very existence of which we have no
knowledge.

[1] The value of slaves given by Cecchi, Da Zeila, II, chap. xxx, is as follows; the amounts are stated in numbers of natter: small boy, 20; small girl,
15–20; youth, 26–28; girl, 25; young man, 20–30; beautiful young woman,
40; young woman, 30; ugly young woman, 15–25; fine young virgin, 60–70,
old woman, 6–7; old man, 8–10; strong old man, 20.

§ II. The Galla Invasion

The lowlands of north-east Africa are inhabited today by the Afar, Saho, and Somali. At the time when Aksum first comes into history it is quite clear that the Galla also occupied a good part of the lowlands, especially in what is now British Somaliland and northern Somalia. Their own traditions of origin bring their ancestors from Arabia to Berbera, and Somali traditions are almost unanimous in attributing the cairns and other ruins that are found in many places in Somaliland to the Galla. It is also clear from Somali tradition that the establishment and development of Islam drove the Galla into Abyssinia. The Galla are divided into two main groups called Borana and Bareituma[1] or Barentu, which correspond roughly with the pastoral and agricultural Galla respectively. These two divisions consist of many tribes. The political control of the Galla tribes is based on the periodical election of leaders through an elaborate system of age-sets and age-grades called *gada*, which has survived, though with considerable modification, even in those Galla groups which developed into monarchical states. Under the *gada* system the control of a tribe is in the hands of a man known as Abba Boku, 'father of the sceptre or staff', who is closely associated with the other members of his *gada*, his authority lasting for a period of eight years, the *gada* in power being known as *luba*. At the end of eight years a new *luba* took over, and the Abba Boku retired in favour of a younger man who took the title. In office, his work was assisted by a war leader called Abba Dula, 'father of war', and a ritual expert, *qalu*, who divined by means of the fat of slaughtered animals. Under this system, tribal affairs were in reality controlled by a group of men whose recognized leader was the Abba Boku, while the father of a family had complete authority over his children, including the power of life and death. Descent is patrilineal. The *gada* system is so important that it is necessary to describe it in greater detail; more will be found about it on pp. 205–212.

Though the early home of the Galla was Somaliland, they were not allowed to remain there undisturbed. The growing

---

[1] Written *Baraytuma* in Ethiopic.

strength and consolidation of the Somali, the need for ex-tension of their grazing lands, and the spread of Islam (which was introduced into Somaliland in the latter half of the seventh century) gradually drove a large part of the Galla towards the south-west. This pressure, Cerulli thought, began in the fifteenth century; but it was undoubtedly earlier, and the movement may have begun as far back as the twelfth century, for Yaqut claims the complete islamization of the 'Somali of the Zeila coast' by that time. The Galla thus forced south-westwards were the Borana. The agricultural Bareituma settled on the Harar plateau whence they gradu-ally penetrated into the southern part of Abyssinia. But it is the Borana with whom we are now concerned, for it was they who invaded Ethiopia from the west and occupied much of the south-western part of the country as far north as the Abay. The history of this invasion, written by an ecclesiastic named Bahrey, is printed in this book. When assessing the value of his evidence it must be borne in mind that, although he wrote some sixty or seventy years after the invasion began, he was a native of Gamo, a district close to the in-vasion route and actually raided by the Galla. He writes, therefore, with the authority of one close to the scene of events which may have begun within his lifetime. His first chapter begins with the words: 'The author of this book says, The Galla came from the west and crossed the river of their country which is called Galana, to the frontier of Bali, in the time of the haṣe Wanag Sagad [Lebna Dengel, 1508–1540].' In his edition of the text, Schleicher substituted, quite un-warrantably, the word 'east' for 'west',[1] as it seemed to him quite impossible for a people living (as he thought) to the east of Abyssinia to have entered it from the west. But his emend-ation does not take into account the expulsion of the Galla from Somaliland, and sets aside a plain statement by one who was surely in a better position to know what he was writing. Bahrey's statement, in fact, postulates a south-westerly movement from Somaliland to the region of Lake Rudolf, from the north end of which the Galla were in a position to cross the 'Galana' and thus enter Abyssinia from the west. This Galana is not the Ganale Doria, but one or all of three

---

[1] *Geschichte der Galla*, p. 6.

rivers called Galana. The first is the Galana Dulei which flows into Lake Stefanie; the second is the Galana Sagan which enters the Galana Dulei from the east; and the third is the Galana which enters Lake Margherita. The word *galana* is a Galla word for 'river'; and that called simply Galana is just 'the river', in the same way that the Webi Shabelle has been called, from at least the sixteenth century (and indeed by Bahrey himself) simply 'the Webi', that is, 'the river'. From the north end of Lake Rudolf all three Galanas are on the way to Bali.

It is to be assumed that the Galla settled for a time near Lake Rudolf. Such an assumption helps to explain the presence of certain cultural features among the Nilo-Hamites[1] which can be due only to direct contact. The most important of these is the age-set system which forms the basis of the Masai and Nandi political organization. By 1522 or thereabouts when the Galla began to invade Abyssinia, the ancestors of the Masai-Nandi group had certainly gone from the Lake Rudolf area; but if I am right in attributing a Galla origin to their age-sets, the transmission of this institution to the Nilo-Hamites implies a fairly long period of contact; and since the Galla probably began to leave Somaliland as early as the twelfth century, there was plenty of time for this.

Not only was southern Abyssinia invaded, but another group of Galla went southwards to what is now Kenya Colony, and reached the Tana valley at some period after the arrival of the Bantu Pokomo. These began to settle along the Tana about 1200, and though the date of the arrival of the Galla is not known for certain, it was perhaps less than a century afterwards. The Tanaland Galla, comprising two groups called Barareta and Kofira, are counted as Borana. They were cut off from the rest of the Galla by the westward penetration of the Randile, a nomadic people akin to the Somali and hostile to the Galla, who by 1880 had reached the eastern shores of Lake Rudolf. The Tanaland Galla do not seem to have any clear traditions of their own origin. They

[1] A large group stretching from the southern Sudan to Tanganyika Territory, and including the Bari, Lokoya, and Lotuko in the north; the Toposa, Karamojong, and Turkana in the centre; and the Masai, Suk, and Nandi in the south. See the *Ethnographic Survey of Africa* (Int. African Inst., 1953), East Central Africa, parts VI, VII, and VIII.

say that they came from Tulu (which means no more than 'hill') on the lower Tana between Ngao and Kulesa. There is also a hint that they came from the north or north-west.

In 1527 Degalhan, a general of Lebna Dengel, invaded the lowland kingdom of Adal, and thus began the disastrous war between the Christians of Abyssinia and the Moslems of Adal under Grañ which lasted for fifteen years, and resulted in the ravaging of Abyssinia. It was not till 1569 that the Abyssinians were sufficiently recovered to attempt any measures to check the Galla; and the Moslems themselves lost much of their political influence in southern Ethiopia through exhaustion from war coupled with the effects of the Galla invasion. The condition to which Abyssinia was reduced was such that the Galla were encouraged to pursue their attacks. Bali proper, however, was conquered by Grañ in 1532, and the Sidamo and other peoples of Sidama stock strenuously resisted the Galla, whose area of conquest and effective occupation was restricted by this resistance.

The period when the Galla began to invade Abyssinia was probably a time when the growth and development of the Nilo-Hamitic peoples was exerting pressure on them, so that they had to move somewhere. As to their choice of a new country, we may surmise that (i) the presence of Nilo-Hamites to the north and north-west made an easterly direction the only possible one; (ii) the prospect of better land may have been alluring, for though Turkana was almost certainly a good deal less arid four to five hundred years ago than it is now, it was doubtless not so desirable as the grasslands of southern Ethiopia; (iii) a realization that by going eastwards they would be turning back towards their old homeland may have stimulated their invasion of Abyssinia. From 1522 to 1530 the *luba* or age-set in power was called Melbah: it crossed the Galana. During the next eight-year period under the *luba* called Mudana the Galla reached the Webi Shabelle and the frontier of Bali proper, from which region they made raids into Abyssinian and Sidama territory, returning to their headquarters near the Webi after each raid. Between 1538 and 1546 the *luba* called Kilole invaded the lowlands of Dawaro. We are not certain what exactly is meant by this, but we think it refers to the lowland area between the Webi

Shabelle and the Harar Plateau; the phrase 'the whole of Dawaro' which occurs in the next chapter will then include the Harar Plateau and the country east of the Goreis hills.

It was perhaps during this period that the invasion of Shoa by the Arusi (Arsi) Galla took place. According to tradition this was undertaken by agreement with 'the Moslems of Grañ', and, beginning in Argobba in eastern Shoa, reached the frontiers of Tigre, thus opening the way for infiltration and settlement by the Bareituma tribes.

Between 1546 and 1554 the next *luba*, Bifole, devastated the whole of Dawaro. During the period of Mesle from 1554 to 1562 it is possible that the Galla occupation of the Gibē region began, for Bahrey says that they now for the first time remained in newly conquered territory instead of returning home across the Webi Shabelle after each campaign; a tradition common to all the Galla monarchies of the Gibē puts the Galla occupation at about 1550, that is, eight *buta* before 1800, the *buta* being a festival held at intervals of forty years. By this time the Galla were certainly firmly established up to the Webi Shabelle, and during the *luba* Harmufah between 1562 and 1570 they invaded Amhara, reaching as far as Angot and Begameder. Up to this time the Abyssinians, for reasons which have already been indicated, made no serious attempt to check them. The chief resistance came from the Sidamo and Wolamo, whose lands they never conquered, and the invasion of the Gibē region must therefore have been made from the Webi Shabelle round the north end of Lake Zeway, a distance that would make the old practice of returning to the base after each campaign somewhat arduous and likely to lead to loss of newly-won territory. In 1569 Sarṣa Dengel inflicted upon the Galla their first major defeat; the *Paris Chronicle* calls them the Aze Galla, but gives no hint as to where the defeat took place. But this did not stop their aggression, for between 1570 and 1578 Shoa was devastated by the *luba* called Robale, and although in 1572 the Galla were heavily defeated near Lake Zeway, and again in 1578 at Wayna Dag'a in Begameder, during the next *luba* Birmaje (1578–1586) they were again in the region of Lake Tana and in Damot, while the *luba* Mul'ata raided Gojam (1586–1594).

The main settlement of the Borana in the west was the country south of the Abay, a region extending some 120 miles southward from the Abay, and about 250 miles from east to west. Here lived the Tulama group in the east, the Macha in the west, up to the Dadesa; and, across the Dadesa, the Wallaga and others. It was mainly from the Macha that the Gibē states of Limmu-Enarya, Jimma, Gera, Guma, and Gomma were invaded and peopled; and it was also with some of them that bitter enmity arose and persisted into the last days of the monarchies.

During the advance from the south the Galla reached a place called Wolabo, about 40 miles east of Lake Margherita, where, near 'Mount Wolabo of the Borana', lived the Abba Muda[1] in a land of marvels, where the white cattle yielded so much milk and meat that men neither ploughed nor sowed. But another marvel appeared that was not so pleasant, a strange beast called Likimsa, 'the swallower', that could change its shape, and drove the Galla from their pastoral paradise. The beast, Cerulli thinks, may have been the Somali; but it may equally well have typified a series of defeats inflicted by the Sidamo. Before they reached the Awash, one Assebil, the Abyssinian governor of Shoa who lived in Jibati about 90 miles WSW of Entotto, was told by an old priest named Woreb that the Galla would possess most of Shoa and Amhara for eight generations, after which the Abyssinians would recover the country. This prophecy was followed by the arrival of a body of Galla under Manyaka Moru who defeated the Abyssinians and made them work as farm labourers. A few years later another body of Galla under an old man named Buko Kura came and defeated the first Galla. Both groups were harassed by the two grandsons of Assebil, who raided them from time to time in the hope of recovering their land. One day they captured Buko Kura himself, but were so much impressed by his bearing and venerable aspect that they did not kill him, whereupon Buko Kura and his brother adopted them, and they joined the Galla in raids on the Abyssinians.

During this time the Galla tribes possessed between them

---

[1] Literally 'Father of anointing', the religious head of the Galla, to whom pilgrimages are made at intervals.

only one *boku* or sceptre, the sign of office of the ruling *luba*, and one Abba Boku ruled all the tribes in the area. But now the Macha, who were among the Galla settlers in the Awash region, stole the sceptre and kept it for themselves, which meant that they thereby acquired *gada* and *luba* of their own, with an Abba Boku who was independent of the others. This resulted in a war, which drove the Macha westwards in the direction of the Dadesa, taking the sceptre with them. The Gombichu and others then made a new sceptre of olive wood (the old one is said to have been of iron), crossed the Awash, entered Shoa, and established themselves there, retaining their enmity towards the Macha for stealing the sceptre.

The mid-nineteenth century document called *The History of the Macha*[1] ascribes to the Macha the foundation of the Gibē states. Macha is a group-name covering a number of tribes divided into confederacies called Sadacha, 'three', and Afre, 'four' (Bahrey, chap. i), when allied together against a common enemy. It is from this larger grouping, especially the Afre part of it, that the Gibē states were colonized. The common enemy here was the Sidama population of the region; and according to tradition the Galla were able to subdue one especially ferocious chief only by tempting him with a naked Galla girl who became his wife, and eventually tamed him so that the Galla could catch and kill him. As a result of inter-tribal warfare and of rifts within tribes, the Macha found it necessary to expand their territory. They could go no further west, for in that direction they were held up by the Shangalla or negro tribes along the present Sudan-Abyssinia border, and by the Nilotic Anuak, known in Abyssinia as Yambo. They had therefore to go southwards and came up against the Sidama peoples in the region of the Gibē river system, the land that eventually became the five states of Limmu-Enarya, Jimma, Gera, Guma, and Gomma. As we shall see, several names of supposed early 'kings' in the royal lists of Jimma and Gera are really those of tribes belonging to the Macha confederacy. But in spite of their origin, the Galla inhabitants of the Gibē states frequently fought their Macha kinsmen. This fighting began as early as

[1] *Storia dei regni dei Metča*, ed. Guidi in *MSOS*, X (1906), pp. 182–184. It was written between 1850 and 1860.

about 1700, when the Macha attacked Enarya; and it was intensified in the nineteenth century after the monarchical Galla had become Moslems, the rest of the pastoral Galla remaining pagans.

The economic geography of the western Galla

The country which lies south of the Abay and is now the home of the Macha and other Borana is of an average lower altitude than the Gibē states. Its inhabitants are mainly pastoral. In the Gibē region the Galla developed a system of agriculture combined with cattle-keeping. The states here soon came to form a Galla *bloc* resistant to its pastoral neighbours who still lived in a tribal condition, like the Wallaga, Leka, Nonno, and Gudru; and they were politically distinct from the Sidama peoples to the south and east. In imitation perhaps of the Kafa practice, these states were strongly defended by heavy wooden palisades or dead-hedges which extended for many miles wherever they were considered necessary, broken only by a few gates which were guarded day and night, and were often so low that even an unloaded mule could not enter. Each state had its palisade, and in some places a ditch as well; in addition it was surrounded by a neutral strip, a narrow overgrown and unused area inhabited only by robbers and desperadoes, not very numerous in 1870, but enough to hold up caravans and give shelter to runaway slaves. This strip was known as *moga*, the Galla word for 'boundary'; the gateways were called *kella*, also a Galla word. Within an area covering some 9000 square miles lying to the north of the river Gojeb and to the west of the Gibē, the five Galla kingdoms have an average altitude of 5000–6500 ft above sea-level. In addition to their basic occupation of agriculture and cattle-keeping, they had, till it was suppressed by the Italians, an extensive slave trade.

Limmu-Enarya, the north-eastern state, has a north to south central elevation rising from 5000 to over 6500 ft and covered with forest. The country is well watered. Cereals like barley grow in the upper parts, with millet, maize, potatoes, flax, vegetables, aromatics, cotton, and coffee in the lower and warmer regions. A primitive two-ox plough is used. Zebu cattle, goats, and sheep are kept; and many of the cattle were used in old days to provide gifts for the king and chiefs in order to obtain favours. The population in 1880 was estimated at about 40,000, including slaves, which were one of the chief trading assets. Another product is civet.

Jimma, the south-eastern state, is full of well-cultivated fields, interspersed with wooded pasture and hills with fertile valleys, the land rising from about 5000 ft on the edge to 8000 ft in the centre, the highest part being Kafarsa peak in the Garo range in the south-east (about 10,170 ft). Agriculture in this state was more highly developed than in the others as the result of long contact with traders and others from Shoa and the East Coast. The crops included wheat, barley, coffee, cotton, and aromatics. Like Enarya, Jimma was another centre of the slave trade; an Italian writing in 1880 described the arrival in Shoa of a caravan from Jimma bound for Zeila, with 400 Shangalla slaves of both sexes, mostly young. The trade route ran from Bonga in Kafa through Jimma, and thence by Qabena, Toli (N.E. of Qabena), Anduodi (9 miles S.E. of Entotto), Rogie (18 miles N.E. of Anduodi), Aliu Amba (6 miles S.E. of Ankober), and thence to Aussa in the Danakil lowlands and on to Zeila or Tajurra.[1] Cecchi estimated the population of Jimma in 1880 at between 30,000 and 35,000.

Gera is described by Cecchi as 'a basin surrounded by softly serrated hills with gentle slopes', the centre having an altitude of 6500 ft and less; there is much swamp in the northern hills. In 1880 the population was estimated at between 15,000 and 16,000. Gera also was a flourishing agricultural state, growing the same crops as Jimma, though one of its chief products was maize. Other crops included seven sorts of aromatics, among them ginger and amomum; and a good deal of honey was produced, which before Menilek's conquest was much used to make mead for the king and chiefs who, by custom, alone might drink it openly. There were large numbers of live-stock, and the pastoral *buta* or periodical festival was of much account here.

Guma, a plateau of about 6500 ft in altitude, with a population estimated by Cecchi at about 50,000, was a purely Galla state, whose inhabitants were famous as warriors, the

[1] Cecchi, *Da Zeila*, II, p. 518.

neighbouring Nonno Galla being their hereditary enemies. They were pastoral and agricultural.

Gomma, consisting mainly of a large undulating valley, with a population estimated in 1880 at about 15,000–16,000, produced the same crops as the other states. Guma and Gomma, however, in the nineteenth century were the least productive of the group from a commercial point of view, though conditions changed later; and it is perhaps for this reason that we have no indication that they developed into monarchies before the last quarter of the eighteenth century.

The Gibē states under the Galla

(1) Limmu-Enarya

About 1550–1570 a Galla named Teso overran Enarya, and it is clear that there were two ruling groups in this state: the Abyssinian governors in Enarya, and the Teso dynasty in Limmu-Enarya; these for a time existed side by side. Teso and his son Bofu were pagans, but his grandson Boko became a Moslem. During the seventeenth century Abyssinian authority disappeared, and the Galla dynasty had probably amalgamated with the descendants of the supposed Portuguese Sapera by the time Iyasu I of Abyssinia made his expedition to the Gibē in 1703. The *Paris Chronicle* says, somewhat obscurely, that 'he went to defend the deserts and mountains, for the Gibē and Enarya had suffered great ravages'. It goes on to describe the defeat of the Macha Galla then attacking Enarya, and in this account there appears for the first time a hint of respect for the Galla and an admission of their bravery: hitherto they had been regarded as ferocious savages unworthy of respect or admiration, a reputation which they have generally had among other peoples at most periods of their history. After defeating the Macha, Iyasu paid a friendly visit to Enarya, where he visited the church, and received from the king the gift of a leopard and some horses. This king, whose name is not given, must have belonged to the Teso dynasty; and at this time there evidently were some Christians in the state, though during the rest of the century both Christianity and Islam seem to have died out. Conversion when it was by order (as in this case), is unlikely to be stable, and both religions in the wild and remote parts of Africa have tended to give place to paganism unless constantly reinforced. Islam was re-introduced in the time of the father of Abba Bagibo, the first king known by name in recent times.

Abba Bagibo or Ibsa ('light, not dark') flourished in 1838; Krapf mentions him as being alive in 1840, and Beke in 1843; he is said to have reigned for forty-two years. He is traditionally described as light in colour and like a European, possibly to confirm his supposed Portuguese ancestry, possibly because of it. The tradition incidentally supports the claim that the monarchy in Enarya goes back to the sixteenth century; for although it is sometimes said that the establishment of these Galla monarchies began as late as the eighteenth century, there are in fact indications that in some of the states there were kings at an earlier date. In Enarya we have the facts already related to support this opinion; and in Jimma and Gera the traditional lists of kings given to Cecchi, which at first sight go back some way before the eighteenth century, start with a number of names which are evidently those of tribes or places: Sirba, Raia, Macha, Kako(t), Jimma, the first five in both cases being the same. These tribe-names may perhaps indicate the tribal group from which each ruler came, just as four of the earlier Kafa kings are designated by the name of the group of origin, and not by personal names.

The kingdom of Enarya was hereditary, the successor being normally the eldest son of the chief wife of the king, though when this wife had many sons there might be a war of succession, each son with a band of armed followers trying to kill or expel his brothers. Galla influence appears strongly in the state organization. Under the king, *supera*, there were ministers and officials with Galla titles, such as the Abba Mizan, 'father of scales', the minister of trade and the king's 'Right Hand'; the Abba Dula, the war leader, a title in some states, e.g. Guma, held by the king himself; the Abba Kella, 'father of the gate', who was in charge of the defence system; the Abba Koro and Abba Ganda, 'fathers of the village', who were district governors; and the Abba Funyo, 'father of the cord', the village headman. As regalia the king had a drum and parasol like those of the Kafa king, a gold armlet,

F

and a wooden throne on which he sat to administer justice. Abba Bagibo was noted as an impartial judge and a good soldier. On the other hand, he is described as vain, sensual, irascible, cruel, and superstitious. He had a white bull which slept near his bed, and a tame vulture which wore a collar with a little bell on it. His senior wife came from Kafa and wore a golden armlet to denote her origin. He was succeeded by his third son Abba Gomoli, the last king, who was on the throne in Cecchi's time. Enarya was conquered by Menilek in 1891; Abba Gomoli's son was converted to Christianity, and in 1927 he was known as Fitawrari Gabre Sellase, as well as by his Galla name of Abba Bagibo.

Table of the rulers of Enarya
ENARYA

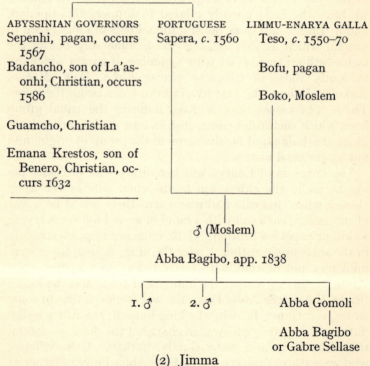

ABYSSINIAN GOVERNORS	PORTUGUESE	LIMMU-ENARYA GALLA
Sepenhi, pagan, occurs 1567	Sapera, c. 1560	Teso, c. 1550–70
Badancho, son of La'as-onhi, Christian, occurs 1586		Bofu, pagan
		Boko, Moslem
Guamcho, Christian		
Emana Krestos, son of Benero, Christian, occurs 1632		

♂ (Moslem)

Abba Bagibo, app. 1838

1. ♂   2. ♂   Abba Gomoli

Abba Bagibo
or Gabre Sellase

(2) Jimma

According to tradition there were 19 kings of Jimma from its establishment up to Cecchi's day. The first eleven are, as we have already suggested, the names of Galla tribes which may indicate the origin of each king thus designated. The list given by Cecchi is:

1. Sirba (Borana).
2. Raia.
3. Macha (Borana).
4. Kakot (=Hakako, Borana).
5. Jimma (Borana).
6. Woju.
7. Kalloti.
8. Jarso (Bareituma).
9. Digo.
10. Horo (Borana).
11. Tulu Horo (='Mount Horo', though possibly a personal name.)

With no. 12 the definite personal names begin:

12. Abba Faro.
13. Abba Magal I.
14. Sanna Abba Jifar I. fl. 1840, son of 13; alive in 1843.
15. Abba Gomoli, reigned one year.
16. Abba Rebo, brother of 15; died 1863.
17. Abba Boka, brother of 14; died 1865.
18. Abba Magal II, son of 17; died 1878.
19. Abba Bulgu ('cannibal') or Abba Jifar II.

The most famous of these kings was Abba Jifar I, who is said to have reigned for 25 years. According to tradition he conquered many small states, which probably means that he made frequent war on all his neighbours; at any rate, his military reputation earned for his state the nickname of Jimma Abba Jifar, under which it figures on some of the older maps. The king of Jimma had by custom three names, those of Abba Jifar I being his own name, *Sanna*, which may not be used for referring to him; his throne-name, which is the name of his war-horse preceded by Abba, i.e. *Abba Jifar*, 'lord of the dappled horse'; and his Moslem name, *Muhammad ibn Daud*, which anyone may mention. The kingdom was hereditary, descending in principle from father to son; but when there was no son a brother could succeed, as in the case of the 16th and 17th kings. The king's wives had the title of *genne*, and were distinguished by the name of their country of origin; thus the wives of Abba Jifar I were called Genne Minjitta, as coming from the Minjo in Kafa; and Genne Sapertiti, as coming from the Sapera, the royal family of Enarya. His mother was known as Genne Gommiti, because she came from Gomma. The family of Abba Jifar claimed descent from a tribe called Badi, in which some of the local Moslems saw, quite unwarrantably, a connexion with the Moslem holy man Ahmad al Badawi who died in Egypt in 1276.

In 1882 Jimma became a member of the Moslem League of Four which was organized by Guma for protection against the Borana; this will be described later. By Cecchi's day, Jimma had become a centre of Islamic learning, its conversion having taken place early in the century. Its prominence among the Moslems of western Ethiopia did not, however, cause any anxiety to either Yohannes or Menilek, for it had been invaded by the governor of Gojam during the youth of Abba Jifar II, who had been forced to pay tribute to Shoa, and the king evidently saw no danger from Jimma. This belief was justified, for when Menilek decided to overthrow the kingdom of Kafa in 1897, he obtained the loyal support of Abba Jifar, whose action caused deep resentment among the people of Kafa, for they had hated the Galla ever since the sixteenth century; and even as late as 1927 could speak to Cerulli of the people of Jimma as 'that uncleanness the Galla'.

(3) Gera

Before the Galla conquest, Gera was inhabited by people of Sidama stock. As in Jimma, there are indications that the monarchy goes back to a period much earlier than the nineteenth century, and the names of the first dozen kings preserved by tradition are in reality those of tribes or places. The list given to Cecchi contains sixteen 'kings' and a queen-regent:

1. Abba Sirba (Borana).	7. Saiyo (Borana).
2. Raia.	8. Bobo (? Bareituma).
3. Macha (Borana).	9. Guragē.
4. Akako (Borana).	10. Gonje or Guneji.
5. Jimma (Borana).	11. Tulu (personal name).
6. Abo (Borana).	12. Bultum.

No. 9 Guragē seems at first sight to be quite out of place here, if it indicates a ruler's place of origin; but Guragē, though not conquered by the Galla, was surrounded by them

and must have numbered many Galla among its inhabitants. Moreover the name of the twelfth king, Bultum, suggests another connexion with Guragē, for Bultem is there a traditional king's name or title. Nos. 10 and 11 figure as one person, Tulu Ganje, in the *History of the Macha* and in Cerulli's *Chronicle of Guma*, and a Tulu Ganje was treacherously killed by Oncho Jilcha of Guma about 1840. This fits in with such chronological indications as we have for Gera, and we may perhaps interpret these four names as referring to one person, 'Tulu Gonje, *bultem*, from Guragē'. Such a person may well have been a Galla, even if he did come from Guragē, and was thus able to start a Galla dynasty in Gera. The rest of the kings are:

13. Abba Boso.
14. Abba Rago I, reigned 15 years.
15. Abba Magal, died 1870.
16. Abba Rago II.
17. Genne Fa, widow of no. 16, regent in 1880.

The dynasty which began with Abba Boso was of Galla stock, and said to have come from somewhere to the E.S.E. of Wolamo, not far from the residence of the Abba Muda. (See note, p. lxxvi.) The queen-regent in Cecchi's day sat on a wooden chair the shape of which recalls the Axumite throne from Adulis described and drawn by Cosmas Indicopleustes.

The most notorious of the kings of Gera was Abba Magal, a cruel man who was suspicious of everybody. He surrounded his house with thick banana plantations in which he hid and listened to the conversation of people who went there, in case anyone should try to plot against him. Near his house he made two cabins in which he confined his personal enemies shackled to heavy logs; in wet and dry weather alike they lay there half naked and starving in a most pitiable state. On his father's death, one of his uncles contested the succession, but was forced to flee, first to Jimma, and then to Limmu-Enarya. From the latter he sent one of his confidential slaves to Gera to collect partisans for a revolt against Abba Magal. The slave, however, being given hospitality by one of his master's friends, dishonoured his daughter, and the trouble that arose in consequence reached the king's ears, thus disclosing the plot. Abba Magal sent presents and an offer of perpetual alliance to Abba Bagibo of Enarya if he would hand over the rebel. This he did, and the unhappy man perished miserably in the stocks at his nephew's house.

(4) Guma

The earliest dynasty in this state of which there is any record is that of the Dagoye, whose last king (the only one named) was called Sarborada. This dynasty was succeeded by one founded by a man whose name is given as Adam, who may have come in about 1770, since his third successor was on the throne in 1841. The story of Adam is that he was a Moslem trader from Tigre who converted the people of Guma to Islam. Tigre does not necessarily mean the northern part of Abyssinia, for as we have seen there was a Tigrean colony in nearby Guragē, and Adam may have come from there. On the other hand, in one version of the story Adam is represented as being at first a savage hunter[1] who lived in the forest of Ebicha Talo between Guma and the Nonno country, and was tamed by sending to him the daughter of Sarborada, in the same way that the Leka Galla tamed the savage Sidama chief; though in this case the result was the overthrow of Sarborada by Adam's sons. Between Adam and the last king, who was deposed about 1900, there seem to have been four monarchs:

> Jilcha Abba Balo, son of Adam, c. 1795.
> Oncho Jilcha, son of Jilcha, c. 1810.
> Jawe Oncho, son of Oncho, fl. 1841, d. 1879.
> Abba Jubir, second son of Jawe, succeeded 1879.
> Abba Fogi, third son of Jawe, deposed c. 1900.

Cecchi gives a list of nine kings from Adam to Abba Jubir; but as Cerulli has pointed out,[2] some of these names cannot represent kings. Cecchi's list is:

1. Adam.
2. Dale Abba Balo.
3. Cholle Abba Boka.
4. Abba Raga Hadi.

---

[1] Galla *adamo* means 'hunting'.
[2] *Folk-literature of the Galla*, p. 160; *Etiopia Occidentale*, II, chapter xxi.

5. Nagesso Abba Jilcha.
6. Abo, remembered for his cruelty.
7. Abba Jilcha.

8. Abba Dula, succeeded in 1854.
9. Abba Jubir, succeeded in 1879.[1]

King Oncho Jilcha fought the states of Jimma, Gomma, and Gera, as well as the Nonno Galla. According to tradition he took to eating human flesh and finally died of drink. His son Jawe Oncho was attacked by Abba Boka of Jimma, because an embassy which he sent to Guma was treated by Jawe with insults. Abba Boka invaded Guma with forty-four horsemen, and made a law that before anointing himself a man must in future kill four Guma men instead of the normal number of two enemy warriors. This small force of forty-four is not merely fable: it indicates the true nature of this kind of warfare, which was carried on by quite small bodies of men on each side. After a time the kings of Guma and Jimma made peace. Later in Jawe's reign Guma was attacked by the Leka Billo tribe of Galla under their leader Garbi Jilo. The Leka crossed Limmu unopposed, defeated the people of Gomma, whose king escaped to Gera, and entered the land of Guma. Being a Thursday evening, the Moslem army of Guma waited till Friday for prayers, whereupon the Leka leader asked scornfully if he was expected to wait till they had drunk coffee also. But while they were waiting, another body of Leka attacked Guma in the rear, and when they finally gave battle on Saturday the men of Guma were defeated.

In 1882 Abba Jubir made war on the Gaba Galla to the north-west of Guma, his particular objective being a place called Hana where the chief was a notorious witch. Not being as successful as he had hoped, Abba Jubir persuaded the kings of Jimma, Enarya, and Gomma to join him in a confederacy which came to be known as the *Arfa Nagadota* or 'league of the four traders' (i.e. Moslems), to counter which

[1] Of these names it may be said that (1) Dale is not a Galla name, and the three words in Galla could mean 'Abba Balo begot'. (2) Cholle Abba Boka may possibly have crept in from confusion with Abba Boka of Jimma. (3) Abba Raga Hadi is unknown. (4) Nagesso Abba Jilcha refers to Jilcha, and *nagesso* may be meant for Amharic *negusa*, 'king'. (5) Abo may be meant for Oncho Jilcha, but Abo is inexplicable. (6) Abba Jilcha may be due to confusion with Oncho Jilcha. (7) Abba Dula, a title, plainly refers to Jawe Oncho.

the pagan Galla formed an *Arfa Oromota*, or 'league of the four Galla' (i.e. pagans), which comprised the tribes Leka Billo, Leka Horda, Nole Kaba, and Hana Gafare.

In their songs, these referred contemptuously to the Moslem Galla as *islama hudu dikatu*, 'the buttock-washing Moslems', in allusion to their ritual ablutions. At first Guma was not very successful in its war with the pagans, for their confederates held back till Abba Diga the elder brother of Abba Jubir had been taken prisoner, when the people of Enarya came to their help. But they were defeated and pursued by the Nole Kaba right into their own country, and the Moslem League asked for an armistice, during which Abba Diga was released. After the armistice Abba Jubir tried to get his allies to renew the agreement, but only Gomma was willing. Abba Jubir then attacked Abba Bulgu of Jimma and sacked his capital in spite of the help given to Abba Bulgu by Enarya and Gomma, though the latter was supposed to be Abba Jubir's ally. In this battle Genne Alima, the sister of Abba Bulgu, was taken prisoner and recovered by her husband Nagau, a Galla of the Leka Billo, who cut off the tail of Abba Jubir's horse while he was chasing them.

Later on, Abba Diga, who because his mother was a Sidama concubine could not be king, tried to increase his power by getting more tribute from the pagan Galla in the Guma sphere of influence, demanding from them a whole year's crop of maize. On their refusal he attacked them, but was defeated, and an invasion of Guma by the pagan Galla was averted only by the bravery of a warrior called Nagari Gana; for in countries where wars could be lost or won by armies of forty or fifty men, acts of individual prowess could still alter the course of a battle. This was the end of the Moslem League, a coalition somewhat unduly magnified in local memory, but deserving of mention in order to show the nature of inter-state politics and of the methods adopted to achieve collective security. Notwithstanding the collapse of the league, Guma remained a stronghold of Islam; and it gave asylum to men exiled from other Galla states for political reasons. It is not certain when it was absorbed into the Ethiopian empire; but Ras Tasama subdued it for Menilek before 1900, since about that time Firisa son of Abba Fogi the last king proclaimed a *jihad* or holy war against the Abyssinians. After some initial success two years were spent in indecisive fighting against Ras Tasama, after which Firisa withdrew to the Shangalla country, disgusted with his lack of results, and gave up the struggle.[1]

(5) Gomma

Less is known of this state than of any of the others. Although it was stated that commercially it was one of the least productive, before the Italian conquest in 1935 it had become the greatest coffee-producer of them all, and much of the coffee that went through the market of Jimma came from Gomma. The original inhabitants of Gomma were of Sidama stock; but although it was invaded by the Galla in the sixteenth century, the kingdom is said to have been founded by a Somali from Mogadishu. This man, Nur Husain, otherwise known as Wariko, was a worker of miracles: he could fly like an eagle, and could change men into animals. He first settled in Kafa, but was forced to flee and took refuge in Gomma, crossing the flooded Gojeb by striking the waters with his staff and dividing them. It is possible, however, that he has been confused with, or perhaps even developed out of, Sheikh Husain, the well-known holy man of Bali, whose tomb is forty miles north of Gimir not far from the Webi Shabelle. To Wariko, however, a tomb has been assigned on the bank of the Dadesa, and Cecchi was told that it was an object of veneration.

The History of the Macha says that the royal dynasty, called Awalni (that is, *awallini*, 'the ancients'), came from Gojam, for which we should perhaps read Gojeb, in view of the tradition (however flimsy) of Nur Husain. Cecchi gives a list of eleven kings; the last was conquered by Menilek in 1886:

1. Nur Husein or Wariko.	7. Abba Rebo, alive in 1843, d.
2. Allaia, son of Nur.	1856.
3. Woda, son of 2.	8. Abba Morke, son of 7.
4. Mijyu, son of 3.	9. Abba Dula, son of 8, d. 1864.
5. Abba Mano, nephew of 1.	10. Abba Jifar.
6. Abba Bagibo, son of 5.	11. Abba Boka, son of 10.

---

[1] Cerulli has published an oral chronicle of Guma in his *Folk-literature*, pp. 148–162 (and cf. also pp. 41–45). Such unwritten records existed in other Gibē kingdoms, but none except this has been collected and published.

§ III. RELATIONS OF THE PAGAN GALLA WITH ABYSSINIA

The Pagan Galla spent the early part of the seventeenth century, from 1605 to 1617, in making raids on Gojam and Begameder, all of which according to the *Paris Chronicle* were defeated by king Susneyos. In 1617 the Galla formed what was known as the Borana League in an attempt to invade Gojam and Begameder with greater success; but Se'ela Krestos, the king's general, defeated them again soon after they had crossed the Abay, and the League collapsed. In 1620 the Wallo Galla were defeated. In 1627 the Galla again invaded Gojam, trying this time to achieve their object by cunning instead of mere strength of numbers. Finding the inhabitants on the alert, they retired in apparent disorder after a little skirmishing, giving out that they were going to raid Enarya. The trick succeeded, and Buko the governor of Gojam dispersed his forces, whereupon the Galla swarmed back across the Abay into Gojam, defeated the few men Buko had been able to recall, and retired with the loot to their own country before the king could get his troops there to give battle.

In 1636 they were defeated by king Fasiladas after another big raid into Gojam; but this did not stop them, for the *Paris Chronicle* records what were probably major attacks in the years 1639, 1643, 1649, 1652, and 1658. In the east, too, the Bareituma were being troublesome to the Abyssinians. Fasiladas had to deal with the Wara Himano in 1661; and the Yeju and Wallo who invaded Amhara were defeated by Iyasu I, who at the time was hunting in western Abyssinia, and had to hurry eastwards to meet them. In 1683 and 1699, however, the tide turned against the Abyssinians, for they were defeated in those years by the Gudru Galla, and in 1709, in the reign of Tewoflos, the Galla invaded Amhara. They looted and burnt the convent of Atronsa Maryam, and threw over a precipice the bones of king Ba'eda Maryam who died in 1478; they also destroyed a celebrated picture of the Mother and Child painted for Ba'eda Maryam by an Italian named Brancaleone.[1]

[1] *Paris Chronicle*, p. 102 (Basset, *Études*, as well as note 108, p. 246, where the story of the picture is told).

In 1719 Bakaffa, the third son of Iyasu I, became king. He had previously been forced, for political reasons, to take refuge among the Bareituma Galla, and had formed many ties with them. It was in his reign that the Galla began to get a foothold in the Abyssinian court, and to play an ever-increasing part in the domestic politics of the country. Bakaffa was largely dominated by his Galla followers: he had in his service a Galla regiment, his Master of the Household was a Galla named Kucho, and towards the end of his reign he was completely surrounded by his Galla guards and accessible to few. His son, Iyasu II (1730–1755), had a Galla wife, a woman of the Yeju tribe among whom Bakaffa had hidden. Iyoas I, the son of Iyasu, who reigned till 1769, naturally favoured the Galla, and spoke nothing but their language. He filled his court with them, gave them official posts, and soon after his accession fell completely under the control of his two maternal uncles. His Abyssinian subjects watched with hatred and fear the growing influence and insolence of the Galla, an influence which has persisted till modern times in spite of continuous enmity between the two peoples.

Throughout the eighteenth century there were minor wars between the kings of Abyssinia and the Borana and Bareituma Galla, especially during the chequered career of king Takla Giyorgis, who lost and regained his throne no less than five times between 1779, the year of his accession, and 1800. In the early part of the nineteenth century king Egwala Ṣyon (1801–1818) owed a good deal to Galla help, for it was owing to the political influence of a group of eastern Galla that he was enabled to retain his throne. None the less, his kingdom was assailed by confederacies of Galla in 1804 and 1808. These attacks were partly due to the machinations of a disgraced *balambaras* (Master of the Horse), a Galla named Asserat, who had begun to seek his revenge by attacking Walda Salomon (who reigned only in the years 1796–1797). Asserat submitted to Takla Giyorgis in 1798, but escaped from captivity and renewed his private war on the king of Abyssinia some years later. He was defeated and sold into slavery from which he managed to escape and took refuge in the west, where he stirred the western Galla into action against Egwala Ṣyon.

By 1837 it had become customary for the king of Shoa to make each year a military expedition against the Macha and other Galla to ensure the collection of tribute; and the lands of those who refused to pay were looted and devastated. Though this may seem to imply that by now the Abyssinians had gained the upper hand, it was not really so, for Krapf remarks that 'the rivers Chacha, Adabai, and Jamma form a natural dyke against the incursions of the Galla from the south, who therefore can never entirely subdue or even over-run the kingdom of Shoa, especially since King Sahela Selassie founded Angolala at a point where the Galla might otherwise have been able to break in.'[1] In fact, it was not till the second half of the nineteenth century that improved weapons (and greater skill in using them) enabled the king of Abyssinia to conquer the independent Galla of southern Ethiopia and bring them more or less under the control of his government; but even today it is doubtful whether he can claim complete control in some of the more remote regions.[2]

[G.W.B.H.]

---

[1] *Travels*, etc., p. 29. Angolala is 12 miles S.W. of Dabra Berhan.

[2] The principal sources for the foregoing introduction are: (A) Native documentary material: R. Basset, *Études sur l'histoire d'Éthiopie* (1882), i.e. the 'Paris Chronicle'; R. Basset, *Histoire de la conquête de l'Abyssinie* (1897), i.e. the 'Futuh al Habashah'; C. Conti Rossini, *Historia Regis Sarṣa Dengel*, CSCO (1907); I. Guidi, *Historia Gentis Galla*, CSCO (1907), a new version of which is given in this book; I. Guidi, 'Storia dei Mečča,' *MSOS*, X (1907), pt. ii, pp. 182–184; H. Weld Blundell, *The Royal Chronicle of Abyssinia* (1922). (B) Traditional material: James Bruce, *Travels* . . . (1790); A. Cecchi, *Da Zeila alle frontiere del Caffa* (1884); J. Borelli, *Éthiopie Méridionale* (1888); F. Bieber, *Kaffa* (1920–23); E. Cerulli, *Folk-literature of the Galla* (1922); E. Cerulli, *Note su alcune popolazioni Sidama* (1925); E. Cerulli, *Etiopia Occidentale* (1932–33). A useful summary of the linguistic situation (though requiring some minor modifications) is given in M. A. Bryan's *Distribution of the Semitic and Cushitic languages of Africa* (1948).

ARABIA

Harar

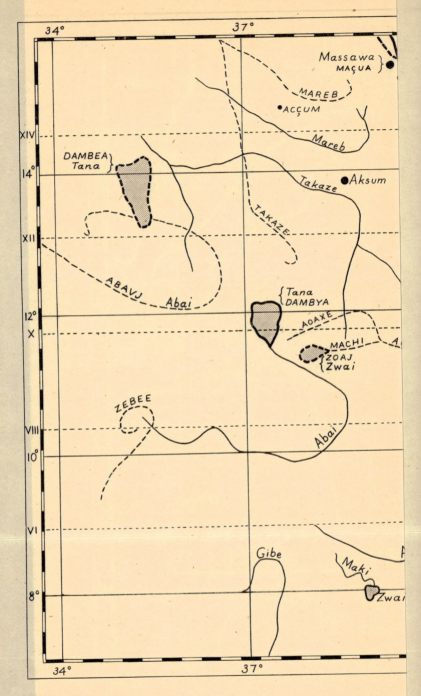

Almeida's map of Ethiopia (S.O.A.S. MS 1196)

ALMEIDA'S REMARKS ON HIS MAP OF ETHIOPIA

There are two versions of this map. The first accompanies the B.M. MS of the 'History' (Add. MS 9861); it has been reproduced by Beccari and others. The second, accompanying the S.O.A.S. MS 11966, is reproduced here for the first time. Almeida's key to the numbers on his map is printed separately on p. xcvii. His note on the map, of which a translation follows, is found only in the S.O.A.S. MS. It was therefore unknown to Beccari and has not previously been translated, nor has the Portuguese text ever been published.

REMARKS NECESSARY FOR THE BETTER UNDERSTANDING OF THIS MAP

Ptolemy's tables and the maps of Hortelio and Gerardo Mercator[1] contain such numerous and remarkable mistakes about Abassia, or the countries belonging to the Abyssinian Empire [sic], commonly called Prester John, that when I was writing the history of Ethiopia I was forced to make this map. In it the kingdoms and territories of this Empire, the mountains and the notable things it contains are accurately shown, all with their gradation and elevation and their distance from the Line and the Pole.

The first and chief mistake of the maps and tables of Hortelio, Gerardo and the rest is that they make the countries belonging to the Abyssinian Empire extend from 22 degrees in the north to 16 or 17 degrees in the south.[2] At this elevation they show Lake Zaire, from which they say the

---

[1] Almeida refers to the *Tabulae geographicae* of Ptolemy, of which many editions were available; to the *Theatrum orbis terrarum* of Ortelius, first published in 1570; and to Mercator's *Atlas*, which, from the edition of 1606 onward, included a general map of Africa by Hondius, superseding that, by Gerard Mercator the younger, in the earlier editions.

[2] The frontiers of the Abyssinian Empire are marked by Hondius; the topographical detail of his map is largely derived from Ortelius and is correctly described by Almeida.

Nile comes.[1] Beside the Lake they show the Kingdom of
Gojam, because they had heard that it rises there. So they
give this Empire from north to south a space of 39 or 40
degrees. From east to west they make it reach from the
shores of the Red Sea to the Rio Negro[2] and the borders of
Congo or Manicongo, which is a space of over 400 leagues.
From this huge bulk, as it were, our famous historian João de
Barros in the 3rd Decade of his Asia in book 4 c. 1 cut off
twenty-six degrees, leaving only fourteen on the east from
the Kingdom of Adea, which he says is the most southerly in
the Empire (and which he places six degrees north of the
Line) to Suaquem, which he puts at nineteen and a third
degrees.

It is not surprising if I take away another four or five degrees from these fourteen, seeing that João de Barros makes
the territories of the Empire reach to the level of Suaquem,
the fact being that they never did extend so far, and in our
own times hardly stretch above Maçua; here three degrees at
least are taken away. On the south too we should take away
one or two, because Adeâ and Cambate, which is still further
south than Adeâ, is [sic] not six, but eight, or at least seven
degrees. Although João de Barros is a most careful writer,
what he asserts in this part is on the word of the Portuguese
who went to Ethiopia with Dom Cristovão da Gama and returned to Portugal.[3] None of them was there for as many
years as we were or passed through the territories of the
Empire so many times, and we do not know that they had an
astrolabe. We did have one and we took the elevation of
Tigrê, Dambeá and Gojam and thereby we estimated the
position of the other kingdoms more accurately.

João de Barros also cuts off the greater part of the breadth
from east to west marked by the maps. Not only does he not
make the boundaries of this Empire extend to Manicongo

---

[1] Ortelius and Hondius show the Nile rising in the Mountains of the
Moon and flowing northwards into a big lake, the southern part of which is
called Zembre, and the northern Zaire. As a river name Zaire means the
Congo.

[2] The Niger, which Almeida elsewhere (p. 33) confuses with the Mareb,
perhaps because Ortelius shows the Niger flowing underground for part of
its course.

[3] Very few of D. Cristovão's companions are known to have returned to
Portugal.

and the Rio Nigro [*sic*], but on the north side which they mark from Suaquem to the Island of Meroe, he gives only a hundred and twenty-five leagues. This is the breadth of the Empire on that side, which is less than the hundred and forty that I give it from the Red Sea coast to Minê, a town situated near the Nile in the bend that it makes to the north after going round nearly the whole of the Kingdom of Gojam, almost opposite the spring where it rises.

João de Barros projects this northern side from Suaquem to the tip of the Island of Meroe, which he says is called Nobâ. Thence he projects the western side to the Kingdom of Adeâ and gives two hundred and fifty leagues to this space. From this Kingdom of Adeâ, which as I said above, he places six degrees north of the Line, he projects the southern side due eastwards to the Kingdom of Adel, the capital of which he calls Arar and says is at an elevation of nine degrees. He gives this space a hundred and eighty leagues. He makes the eastern side a hundred and twenty-two leagues, beginning at the entrance to the Strait and ending at Suaquem. So, adding up the lengths of these four sides surrounding this Prince's state, we can say that they amount to about six hundred and seventy-two leagues.[1] These are the words of João de Barros.

Although I cannot agree with him about the ends of the sides, especially the northern, which he marks from Suaquem to Noba, yet the number of leagues he gives to the boundaries of this Empire is very much in accordance with the truth. I say that the northern side must be reckoned not from Suaquem, but from a little above Maçua, at an elevation of about fourteen degrees, and this space is about a hundred and forty leagues long. As I shall show in a moment it is approximately from the tip of the Island of Meroe, which is not Noba, but the Kingdom of Gojam. Noba or Nubia is a Kingdom that is further to the north beside the Nile stream.

Another very remarkable mistake found in the maps is that they change the names of the Kingdoms and place them a long way from where they really are, and what is worse, they make one Kingdom into many. For example, they mark a Kingdom that they call Tigrai, near the Line, another that

---

[1] The total should be 677; Almeida has copied this arithmetical mistake from Barros.

they call Tigre 10 degrees north of the Line, another, between them, that they call Tigre Mahon, and further on they
mark another they call Barnagasso 14 degrees north of the
Line, making its breadth extend for 130 or 140 leagues from
Macua towards the west.[1] The truth is that there is only one
Kingdom of Tigre and there is not another called Tigrai, but
this name some people pronounce Tigrai (which is closest to the
speech of the natives of the Kingdom) and others Tigre; this
is the way the Amaros [sic], who are the nobility of Ethiopia,
pronounce this name. Tigre Mahon is a little district of the
Kingdom of Tigre which is also called by another name,
Auzen; it is customarily assigned for his maintenance to the
governor whom the Emperor appoints to this Kingdom.
This governor used to be called Tigre Mahon, which means
Prince of Tigre. Barnagasso, or Bahar Nagaes (so it should be
pronounced and written) means Governor of the Sea or of
the coast lands. He does not govern any Kingdom, but two
small districts of which the capital is Debaroa, a place eighteen leagues'[2] distance from Maçua, and his authority does
not extend any further inland. These districts and lands of
the Bahar Nagaes are part of the Kingdom of Tigre.

[1] This is not quite fair; Ortelius and Hondius mark Tigrai, Tigre Mahon
and Barnagasso but not Tigre. Hondius also marks Begameder ('Baga-
midri') in two different places.

[2] The Portuguese league had four *milhas*, or Italian miles of 1480 metres,
and was thus equivalent to 3·2 geographical miles. The degree was variously
estimated as 16⅔, 17½ and 18 leagues. We are indebted to Dr A. Cortesão and
Mr R. A. Skelton for much information on this subject.

0   10

dra
Camara
Haxa

dascra.

Blibele

Terr

quesepode
has d. A...
...del.

Adem

Zeila

Este Rio entra
4 jornadas.

rrele Cáoes
Reino
del agchama
Zeila.

S.

KEY TO NUMBERS ON ALMEIDA'S MAP
(S.O.A.S. MS 11966)

(Notes on some of these names will be found overleaf.)

On the dexter side:

1	Bizam	19	Tres Igreias
2	Asmarâ	20	Oldeba
3	Adegada	21	Lamalmon
4	Debaroâ	22	Arbâtançâ
5	Corbareâ	23	Camby
6	Guele.	24	Dancaz Corte
	Auzen vel Ty-	25	Ganete Jesus
[sic] 7	gre-Mahon	26	Gorgorra Va
8	Cara	27	Gorgorra Noua
9	Sart	28	Debsan Caza
10	Ambâ Salam		do Patriarcha.
11	Ambâ Çanet	29	Anfrâs
12	Camâ	30	Cogâ
13	Assâ	31	Ffagorâ
14	Fremonâ	32	A [sic]
15	Allelo	33	Alatâ
16	Acçum	34	Adaxâ
17	Mascalô	35	Nebessê
18	Maebezo	36	Debra Semonâ
		37	Debra Orc

On the sinister side:

38	Iarâ	47	Alagoa	56	Tābab Mariã
39	Adisalen	48	Ondegê	57	Amba legot
40	Enamorâ	49	Nefacâ	58	Lalibelâ
41	Ligenegus	50	Tancoâ	59	Nefas Mauchâ
42	Debra Selâlo	51	Fonte do Nilo	60	Serra Belza
43	Colelâ	52	Mine	61	Debra Mariam
44	Abolâ	53	Debra Libanos		
45	Sercâ	54	Ambâ Guexen		
46	Nâninâ	55	Ãbâ. Cel		

Nalagoa Illias

Alacoa aque chamão Mar de Dambea ✠

Galila **B**

Mecharaca **G**

Dek **D**

Debra Mariã **E**

Note.—51 should obviously be Mine and 52 Fonte do Nilo.

NOTES ON SOME NAMES ON ALMEIDA'S MAP WHICH ARE NOT INCLUDED IN THE GAZETTEER

(For abbreviations, see p. xix)

1 BIZAM =Dabra Bizan, a convent near Asmara, ND 37/2 Bizen, *HSD* 149 Bizan. 5 CORBAREÂ =Corbaria of *Guida dell' A.O.I.*, map, p. 192, about 11 miles SE of Debarwa; Alvares calls it Coiberia (Hakluyt Soc., 1881, p. 70). 8 CARA is a district shown as Tsera by Markham in the map (opp. p. 231) in his *History of the Abyssinian Expedition*, ND 37/5 Tzetzera, some 35 miles W of Endarta. 9 SART =Saharta, between Endarta and Geralta, *CS* 128 Sahart. 10 AMBA SALAM is in Temben, shown on Markham's map in the Hakluyt Soc. edition of Alvares. 17 MASCALÔ, mentioned by Mendes (Beccari, vol. IX, p. 79) =Ethiopic *masqal*, 'cross;' it was somewhere in Sire. 18 MAEBEZO, mentioned by Mendes (*loc. cit.*, p. 78), who translates it as 'aquam uberum' (*sic*), which suggests Ethiopic *māy bazhu*, 'abundant water.' It was somewhere in Sire. 19 TRES IGREIAS, Portuguese Tres Igrejas, 'three churches;' also somewhere in Sire. 22 ARBÂTANÇÂ =*Arbā'et ensesā*, 'the four animals' of Revelations IV. 6. *AJIB* 165, between Gondar and Lamalmo, to which Almeida's position seems to refer. The name occurs also in Gojam, ND 37/1, as Arvatensa. 23 CAMBY, perhaps Kambilgē Māryām 30 miles NE of Danqaz; perhaps also the same as Kambi in Wagarā of *HSD* 163. 28 DEBSAN =Dabsan of *AJIB* 141, on the E side of Lake Tana between Qaroda and Waynarab (ND 37/4 Uainabar). 30 COGÂ =Qogā of *CS* 62. 31 FFAGORÂ =Fogarā, a district between Dabra Tabor and Lake Tana, *CS* 234, *AJIB* 158 Fogarā. 36 DEBRA SEMONÂ is the monastery of Dabra Ṣemunā in Gojam, *AJIB* 48, *AII* 106. 37 DEBRA ORC =Dabra Warq in Gojam, *HSD* 8, *AJIB* 68, *AII* 106; Amharic *warq*, 'gold.' 39 ADISALEN =Amharic *addis 'ālam*, 'new world.' 40 ENAMORÂ = Ennāmorā in Damot, *AJIB* 13. 41 LIGENEGUS =Lija Negus, a place which seems to have been somewhere S of Sakala. 42 DEBRA SELÂLO =Ṣelālo in Damot, NW of Qolalā, *CS* 12, *HSD* 13, *AJIB* 68. 44 ABOLÂ =Abolā NW of Selālo, *CS* 145 (ND 37/1 Abola Negus). 46 NÂNINÂ =Nāninā in Damot, *HSD* 134. 47 ALAGOA ='the lake', probably the lake called Qurṣ Bāhr in *AJIB* 182 (Quṣr Bāhr 238), in Damot, Cheesman's Kurt Bahr. 48 ONDEGÊ =Wandgē (Agau *wangē*, 'wild boar'), *AJIB* 302, near the SW shore of Lake Tana (ND 37/1 Uendige). 49 NEFACÂ =Nafāšā in Damot, *AJIB* 161. 53 DEBRA LIBANOS is the monastery of Dabra Libanos in Shoa, *CS* 3, *AJIB* 5. 56 TÂBAB MARIÃ =Tadbāba Māryām, 'the sanctuary of Mary', a monastery in Shoa, *CS* 171, *AJIB* 188, *AII* 106. 57 AMBA LEGOT is in Amhara, *RC* 288 Amba Leguat. 58 LALIBELÂ =Lalibalā in Lasta, famous for its rock-hewn churches. 59 NEFAS MAUCHÂ =Nafās Mawčā, *CS* 246, *AII* 244. 60 SERRA BELZA, the mountains of Belesa, S of Samen and W of the Takaze, *CS* 299 Balasā.

NALAGOA ILLIAS ='the islands in the lake' (Tana). B. GALILA is Galilā, *CZ* 28, *AJIB* 86, *AII* 196 (ND 37/4 Ghelila). G. MECHARACA =Mesrāhā, *AJIB* 66, *AII* 151 (ND 37/4 Mitraa). D. DEK = Deq *HSD* 43, Daq *AII* 151 (ND 37/1 Dech). E. DEBRA MARIÃ = Dabra Māryām, in the gulf which forms the southern end of Lake Tana, *AJIB* 121, *PC* 37.

ETHIOPIA AND ITS PEOPLE

From *The History of High Ethiopia or Abassia,*
by Manoel de Almeida, Books I-III

THE HISTORY OF HIGH ETHIOPIA OR ABASSIA

By Manoel de Almeida

BOOK I

CHAPTER 1

The name Prester John

It is so common in Portugal and Europe for the Emperor of the Abyssinians to be called by this name that anyone who undertakes to write the history of Ethiopia and of the Abyssinian empire must necessarily give some explanation of it. Since, however, almost all the historians who have written about this country have argued about this matter and examined and given different explanations and versions of this name, I do not feel myself obliged to stop and repeat what can easily be found in their works. I merely remark that among the rest Father Nicolao Godinho of our Society, in the 5th chapter of his first book on the Abyssinians, treated this question with greater learning and riper judgment than I bring to its consideration.[1] He makes two certain and very well established assertions. The first is that the name Prester or Presbyter John was at first given to a Christian, but Nestorian, emperor, who ruled in the interior of Asia. His ordinary name or title was Jonanam, derived from the prophet Jonah (whom they so name in their language; Europeans have changed it to John in error). This name was common to the rulers of that monarchy as that of Pharaoh was to the Kings of Egypt. They called him Presbyter because of the cross that he always carried aloft before him, as among us Archbishops and Primates do. It is said that when he

[1] The reference is to *De Abassinorum Rebus deque Æthiopiæ Patriarchis Ioanne Nonio Barreto & Andrea Oviedo libri tres: P. Nicolao Godigno . . . auctore*. It was published at Lyons in 1615. Bk I, c. 5, is on the name 'Presbyter Joannes' and includes, besides the two statements mentioned here, the contention of Almeida's third paragraph, that the two Abyssinians who accompanied Alvares invented the derivation from ' Belul Jan'.

3

went to war he took two, one of gold and another of precious stones, signifying by the crosses the Christian religion which he professed, and by the precious material of which they were made that, by so much as precious stones and gold are greater than silver, copper, iron and any other metals, by so much was he greater in power and glory than all the Kings of the world.

The 2nd thing that Father Nicolao Godinho asserts is quite certain. It is that the attribution of this name of the Asiatic emperor to the Emperor of Ethiopia originated in the mistake of Pero de Covilhão. He was sent with a companion (as we shall relate in full below) by King Dom João 2nd of illustrious memory to discover India and the Christian emperor popularly called Prester John, whose fame was then much celebrated in Europe. In Cairo, in Suaqhem and in Adem, which he reached and to which he returned from India, he heard many things told of the Emperor of the Abyssinians, among others that he was a Christian, master of many great kingdoms, and that he was in holy orders and carried a cross in his hand. He was persuaded that he had found him and that this was the Prester John whom his King had sent him to find, and so much he wrote to him from Cairo. This news was welcomed in Portugal and spread throughout Europe and from then until now the Emperor of the Abyssinians has been held and taken to be and has been given the name of, Prester John.[1] The coming to an end of Jonanam's monarchy in Asia contributed to this, in that for many years the name of no Christian emperor in Asia was heard while the fame of this African one resounded daily. So the name of Prester John was confirmed to him and withdrawn from the Asiatic.

In Ethiopia no one has yet had, or will have any suspicion of this for they either do not know that such a name is given

---

[1] The principal source of information on Covilhã's journey is the work of Alvares, who met him in Abyssinia, where he had been detained by successive emperors since his arrival about 1491. His letter to the King of Portugal was written from Cairo and it is not known whether the King ever received it. Almeida is wrong in saying that Covilhã was the first to identify Abyssinia with the country of Prester John. Many fifteenth century writers do so; Bertrandon de la Broquière met Abyssinians at Jerusalem, 'qui sont de la terre du prestre Jehan.'

to their Emperor or, if we tell them, they are amazed and think it strange; there is nothing in their language that corresponds to it nor is there any version of it. In Europe, however, someone may have been influenced by the authority of Çagâ Zà Ab (whom Damião de Goes in the third part of his Chronicle of the King Don Manoel, chapter 60, calls Zagazabo) an ambassador sent thither by King David to the Most Serene Dom João 3rd of Portugal, and by that of Pedro, another Abyssinian, who accompanied Father Francisco Alvares from Ethiopia to Portugal and thence to Italy, where he took the Emperor David's letters to Pope Clement 7th.[1] These two, Çaga Zà Ab, I mean, and Pedro wanted to devise versions of this name in their language. They did so easily among people who had no knowledge of it. They pretended what they liked and said that the name Prester John had been taken from Belul and Jan and that this meant precious Gian and that our people had corrupted Jan into John. All this is fiction that has no justification in fact. Yet the Valencian who imagined that it must be Beldigian and that Belul Jan was not two words but one had still less.[2]

It is certain that the Abyssinians call their Emperor Jan and sometimes they call him Belul also but the one is never joined with the other; among them it would be a solecism and a very barbarous expression if someone were to say 'Belul Jan' or 'Jan Belul'. To each of these two names, in fact, the word 'qhoj' is usually added, which means the same as the word 'my' among us, when it is used to signify love or tender-

[1] Saga Za Ab was the Emperor's representative with the embassy of Dom Rodrigo de Lima while it was in Abyssinia (1520–26) and Alvares has many references to him. When he came to Portugal as ambassador in his turn, Damião de Góis, the celebrated humanist and author of the *Crónica de Dom Manoel*, questioned him about the Abyssinian church. Saga Za Ab wrote a short treatise on the subject and Góis published a Latin version of it. Almeida elsewhere (bk III, c. 5) discusses some of its many errors.

[2] One of Almeida's many allusions to the Spanish Dominican, Luís de Urreta, author of a history of Ethiopia, published at Valencia in 1610. It contains many absurdities and it was to expose them that Páez wrote his own history. Urreta contends that *Beldigian* is a word meaning 'precious object', that it is used as a title in MSS dating from the time of the Queen of Sheba, that many of the Emperors were ordained so that, being celibate, they should not breed more claimants to the throne, that, because they were in communion with the Patriarch of Alexandria, they called priests 'presbyters', and that they therefore came to be addressed as 'Presbyter Beldigian', which Europeans corrupted to 'Preste Juan'. (Urreta, pp. 87–89.)

ness as when one says to a child, as an endearment, 'my sweetheart, my prince, my king.'[1] This is nearly what the Abyssinians mean when they address their King as 'Janqhoj', 'Ianqhoj' or 'Belulqhoj', though this second name is less often used by them than the first. To come to the root from which they were derived, it is this. They say that in the ancient language of Ethiopia 'Jan' means 'elephant', and because this animal is so powerful and terrible compared with the rest, they applied its name to the King as a title of honour and grandeur. So those who call out at the gate of the Emperor's enclosure for him to grant their suits or send someone to hear their complaints at some injustice that has been done to them, they name him by this name if they are Amarâs,[2] shouting at the tops of their voices 'Janqhoj, Janqhoj' until the Emperor sends a servant to see what it is they want. I said 'if they are Amarâs', for if they are Moors they shout 'Cidy, cidy',[3] if Portuguese 'Senhor, senhor', which is the same thing, and if Tigrês 'Adáriê'.[4] Those of other nations and languages also have their own words which are peculiar to themselves.

The name Belul is less common. Properly speaking it means a certain jewel like an ear-ring.[5] Formerly when the electors of the empire chose some prince to be Emperor, because whoever was reigning had died, they used to hand it to a nobleman whose duty it was to go and give the news to the Emperor who had been elected. When he came and gave him the news he put the Belul or trinket in the Emperor's ear, which was a certain and infallible sign that he had been elected. So it came that some people called the Emperor who had been elected by the name of the jewel, calling him 'Belulqhoj', which is as much as to say 'my jewel' or 'my chosen one', that being the sign of his election.

---

[1] *Hoy* is a term used in address; *janhoy* means literally 'O King'.

[2] Almeida forms the plural of African racial and tribal names by adding *s* as if they were Portuguese words. In the Introduction and notes, however, we have used the same forms for singular and plural of these names, in order not to mislead readers about names such as 'Bogos' or 'Kipsikis', of which the singular ends in *s*.

[3] Arabic *saiyidî*, colloquially *sidî*, 'my lord.'

[4] Seems to be Amharic *adarā*, 'master.'

[5] Guidi, *Vocabolario*, gives *belul*, 'the ear-ring given to a newly elected King'; *belulhoy* would therefore mean 'O ear-ring', i.e. 'O chosen one'.

However, as I said, the two words 'Jan' and 'Belul' are never joined together in any way. Usually neither of them is used without the addition of 'qhoj'. Hence it is obvious that there is no foundation whatsoever for the saying that the name Prester John was derived from them, especially since it is certain that Pero de Covilhã, before he entered Ethiopia, wrote from Cairo to the King Dom João 2nd that he had found the Prester John whom His Highness had sent him to seek. He was not inventing this name but applying the name the King had spoken and that he had first heard in Portugal to the Emperor of Ethiopia because he found that he was a Christian, was in holy orders and carried a cross in his hand, which were more or less the indications he had heard of the Prester John of the Indies whom he came to find.

Since we are considering the name Prester John which was bestowed on the Emperor of the Abyssinians in error, it is desirable that we should say briefly that they call the King Nuguç and the Emperor Nuguça nagasta, which is as much as to say King of Kings, the Queen Neguesta and the Empress Negesta neguestát, Queen of Queens. The usual words they use, corresponding to our Highness or Majesty are Áçeguê or by syncope Ácê, stressing the first and last letters strongly. These are not two words but one, for they do not have our distinction between Highness and Majesty, but they have only this word which answers to both of ours. For Highness they do not call the Queen Acê or Áçeguê, but Iteguê. They call the King's sons Habetô whether they are princes or Infantes, if they are males, though this name is now being extended to many who are not sons of a King.[1]

The name Abyssinian, Habex among themselves, they say is Arabic or Turkish, and it means nothing at all.[2] The man who pretended that it meant a free and independent people who had never been subdued by any foreign race was merely

[1] *nugue* is a corruption of *negus*, 'king'; *nuguça nagasta = negusa nagast*, 'king of kings'; *negesta neguestat = negesta negestāt*, 'queen of queens'; *acegue = haṣēgē*, 'his majesty', abbreviated to *haṣē*; *itegue = itēgē*, abbreviated to *itē*, 'queen'; *habeto = abbēto*, or *abbētahon*, which means 'highness' and was applied to princes of the royal family; modern Amharic *abēto*, 'sir'.

[2] The name Habaš is derived from Habashat, the name of a South Arabian people who settled in N.E. Africa and eventually became dominant there. 'Abyssinia' is derived from this through such forms as Abasēnoi, used by Stephanus of Byzantium (c. A.D. 410).

imagining it.[1] There is no one in Ethiopia who knows any such meaning or derivation of the name Habex. Nevertheless if he has some secret basis for it in his Arabic vocabulary he may have the credit for being so well versed in that, but he should know that the Abyssinians have not been so exempt from reversals of fortune that they have not sometimes been subject to foreign masters as will appear below in the course of this history.

CHAPTER 2

What countries and kingdoms are comprised in the Ethiopia which we are considering, and what part of it is controlled by the Emperor of the Abyssinians

Ethiopia is a general term and so includes both eastern and western Ethiopia.[2] The sacred writers call eastern Ethiopia the land of Madian, which is between Arabia and Palestine, beyond the Red Sea. Western Ethiopia includes a large part of Africa because writers use this name for all the land that runs out from Egypt along the Red Sea, and beyond the gateway to this sea, all that extends not merely as far as Cape Goardafuj, but to the Cape of Good Hope, and after doubling that, all the land there is as far as Angola and Cape Verde. We call all the inhabitants of these coasts and of the interior behind them Ethiopians. The geographers, however,

[1] 'The real reason why Ethiopia is called Abassia and the Ethiopians Abyssinians is that that word means a free and independent people (in Arabic, Turkish and the language of the Ethiopians), who had never recognised a foreign king; such is the land of Ethiopia, as we shall relate'(Urreta, p. 4). This is nonsense, but the old national name Ge'ez, which is still applied to the Ethiopic language and which originally meant 'migratory' can also mean 'liberated', 'manumitted' and hence 'free'.

[2] This name, written Ityopyā in Ethiopic, first appears in Abyssinia in the first half of the fourth century in the Greek inscription of Aeizanas, who describes himself as King of the Axŏmites, Hŏmērites, Raeidan and the Aithiopians. After this, the term seems to have been dropped, being replaced by Habashat till the Bible was translated into Ethiopic, a work which was possibly completed by the end of the seventh century. This translation was made from the Septuagint, in which the word occurs both as a territorial and an ethnic name. From this it was eventually adopted as the national name, while Habash(at) became current outside the country.

divide Africa into five parts and restrict the limits of Ethiopia proper, taking from it the part they call in Latin Nigritarum regionem, which we in Portuguese call Cafraria.[1] Nevertheless, even in the geographers' way of speaking Ethiopia includes all that there is from Egypt to Cape Goardafuj and thereafter much further on to Melinde and Mombaça. Authors usually call the part nearest to Egypt Ethiopia supra Egyptum, distinguishing it by this name from eastern Ethiopia, which is the country of the Madianites, lying infra Aegyptum. There is frequent mention of these two provinces and of their kings and inhabitants in the holy scriptures and to them pertains nearly everything that the Valencian historian ascribes to the empire of the Abyssinians.

Yet it is certain that the countries belonging to this empire all lie in western Ethiopia under the torrid zone between the tropic of Cancer and the Equator. When this empire was more extensive it had for its limit on the north a country called Focâj, which faces Suaquem but is not very far from it, and on the south another called Bahargamô. On the east it begins at the shores of the Red Sea, on the west at the banks of the river Nile in the bend that it makes towards Egypt, after encircling the Kingdom of Gojam and making it almost an island. Between these limits that we mentioned from north to south there is probably as much distance as mathematicians would allow to nine degrees; there is perhaps that, and not more, from Focáj to Bahargamo. Suaquem is known to be 18 degrees and I think Bahargamô is about eight degrees north of the line. Although I did not go there I am prompted to say this by the following consideration.

Gorgorâ, where I am writing this history, is a place lying in the middle of the Kingdom of Dambeâ and is thirteen and a half degrees north of the line, as has been found when the sun has sometimes been taken there with the astrolabe. From here to Bahargamo would not be more than 130 or 140 leagues,[2] a large part of which I have travelled at some time

[1] i.e. the country of the Cafres, the name applied by the Portuguese to the pagan negroes.

[2] If Bahargamo is Lake Abaya, his estimate is somewhat in excess of reality, the north end of the lake being about 400 miles, and the south end 450 miles from Gorgora. On his map, however, he makes it about 110 leagues.

when going to the confines of Gojam. The distance of the remainder I knew from having asked persons who had been
there. Though the greater part of this route is to the south,
apart from detours caused by valleys and mountains, which
are numerous, many stages of the journey are made more to
the south-south-east or south-east than due south. I am persuaded, therefore, that from here to Bahargamo the elevation cannot decrease more than five or five and a half degrees,
from thirteen and a half where we are, to eight where I put
Bahargamo. Taking into consideration the windings of the
route and the valleys and mountains, which are numerous,
one may suppose that this would amount to a distance of
250 leagues. I say 'one may suppose' because in this country
there are no leagues corresponding to ours nor are people
in the habit of measuring the distance between places other
than in days of travel. Even there one has no certainty because the travelling days of the Emperor and his camp are
usually very short; those of caravans are a little longer; those
of a man travelling light vary according as each one is in
more or less of a hurry or lingers on the way. So we must
estimate the number of leagues for ourselves and not in
accordance with what they say.

Its greatest breadth is from the shores of the Red Sea to
the banks of the Nile; it is reckoned from Bur to Ombareâ.
Bur is a province of Tigre, the coast of which is washed by
the Red Sea. Ombareà is a district of Gojam near the banks
of the Nile. This width, then, almost all of which I have
covered, might be, in my view, 140 leagues.[1] Between these
limits the kingdoms that Prester John used formerly to control were the following:

Tigré, Angót, Amarâ, Doarô, Fategar, Oggê, Balli, Hadeâ,
Alamalê, Oxelô, Ganz, Beteramorâ, Gurâguê, Buzanâ, Suf-
gamô, Bahargâmo, Cambat, Boxâ, Gumar, Nareâ, Conch,
Dámót, Gojam, Begameder, Dambeâ, Dobâ, Motâ, Auçâ,
Holecâ, Xaoâ, Ifat, Guedem, Ganh, Marrábet, Maûz, Bizamô.

The provinces or states that are less than kingdoms are the
following: Gadanchó, Orijâ, Cagmâ, Margáy, Xercâ, Gamarô,

---

[1] The distance from Mersa Fatma on the coast to the river Dura is
approximately 400 miles; Almeida's measurement of the same distance is
not a bad estimate, in view of the difficult country.

Abexgáj, Talaceon, Ogarâ, Cemen, Calamt, Borâ, Abargalê, Çalaoâ, Çagadê, Holcâit, Mazàgâ.[1]

It will be realised from the distance between the limits and confines of this empire that the whole of it would be smaller than Spain. Its division into kingdoms and provinces should be understood to be like the division of Spain[2] into Portugal,

[1] This list is taken, with slight modifications, from one given by Páez, bk I, c. 1. It was obtained by him from the Emperor's chief secretary; later, in the presence of the Emperor, Páez questioned Ras Se'ela Krestos about it and the Emperor then said that his predecessors had ruled all these territories but that he himself had little control over some of them owing to the Galla invasions. A comparison of this list with the one given in the next chapter will show which these were. Páez gives the same number of kingdoms as Almeida but instead of the last three he has 'Dancalî', 'Cuerâ' and 'Zenyerô', i.e. the Dankali country, Quarā and Janjero; he has one additional province, 'Arench' which is perhaps the district called Ar'ēñ in *HSD*. The Patriarch Mendes in his *Expeditio Aethiopica*, bk I, c. 1, reproduces Almeida's list in the same order, except that he accidentally omits Cagma from the provinces. He then enumerates the more important regions according to their latitude and in order as they occur from east to west. His description may be represented by the following diagram:

```
15  N                                                       T
                                                            i
14            Mazaga          Seguedé                       g
                                                            r
                                                            a
13     Olcait  Lamalmon  Semen  Salent  Abargalé
                                                            A
                                                            n
12     Agaoá   Salaoá   Lastae Montes      Bagamádir        g
       G                                                    o
       o                                                    t
11     j          Holecá         Amará              Guedem
       a
       m
10     á   Bizamó  Gafate  Xaoá  Marrabet  Ifate  Doaró

9          N      Damút         Ganz          Mugár
           a
8          r   Gurague  Hadeá  Alamalé  Ogge  Fategar  Balli
           a
           e
7          a   Cambat  Buzamá  Sugamó    Bargamó  Gomaró
```

Other lists, differing considerably from these, are given by Father Luiz de Azevedo in a letter of 22 July, 1607, to the Provincial at Goa, printed in Beccari, vol. XI, pp. 131–133, and by Ludolf, *Historia Aethiopica*, bk I, c. 3, who procured it from his native informant, Gregory. Almeida's own map is reproduced opposite p. xcvii.

[2] The crowns of Spain and Portugal were united at this time.

Castille, Leon, Granada, Valencia, Toledo, etc. At the same time it should be known that none of these kingdoms had kings of their own when the Emperor controlled them nor have they today. He governed them all through viceroys or governors placed there by his own hand, though in some of them he used not to put strangers, but natives of the same kingdoms, descendants of their former kings. In none of them did they have the title of Kings but of Xumo, which is like Governor.[1] Only some had the title of Kings who were strictly speaking not subjects, though they recognised the Emperor as a superior; the Moorish King of Dancaly still does so today, being so poor in land and power that he may rather be called a goatherd than a King and so does the heathen and very savage and wretched King of Ginzierô. But, as I say, these men are not the Emperor's subjects.

It can be deduced from all this that[2] the whole of lower Ethiopia, or Ethiopia Inferior, which is the interior of the country running from Suaquem to Egypt, now possessed by Moors whom we call Funchos and the Abyssinians Ballous,[3] none of this belongs, or ever has belonged to the empire of the Abyssinian or Prester John. The glorious apostle St Matthew did not reach this country, high Ethiopia, but only what lies between Suaquem and Egypt, and so there is in this country no memory of this holy apostle, nor has any record of him ever been found in a book.[4] When we told them that he had preached and died in Ethiopia they were as surprised at it as at something of which they had never read or heard.

It can also be deduced that it was a very ill-informed man who extended the confines of this empire to the Mountains of the Moon[5] and placed the source of the Nile in them, far be-

---

[1] Amh. *šum*, chief.

[2] Here the B.M. MS has the phrase 'not only the island of Meroe, put by some accurate maps far inside Egypt, but . . .'

[3] The Bellu (Balaw of Abyssinian records) were the original inhabitants of the Agordat region, from which they were displaced by the Beni Amer division of the Beja. Some settled in the plain round Massawa and Arkiko; others occur in the west, such as the Balaw of Asib and Gallabat (*AII*, pp. 119, 120) and beyond Čānqā (*PC*, p. 156). The Funcho are equated by Crawford with the Fung of Sennar.

[4] In the *Ecclesiastical Histories* of Rufinus, bk I, c. 9, and Socrates, bk. I, c. 19, St Matthew is alleged to have been the apostle of Ethiopia.

[5] Urreta, pp. 298–299, where their latitude is given as 16° S. The mistake was a common one; the map of Africa contributed by Hondius to Mercator's

yond the Line and near the Cape of Good Hope. It is certain that the source of the Nile is in the Kingdom of Gojam, the middle of which is twelve degrees north of the Line. No province, kingdom or country subject to this empire reaches, or has at any time reached the Equator, much less the coast of the Indian or Ethiopian Ocean. It is quite certain that this empire has never had an inch of seacoast outside the gateway of the Strait of Meca or Red Sea.

CHAPTER 3

The kingdoms and provinces which at the present time are subject to the Emperor of the Abyssinians: an account of their position is given.

Of the kingdoms I mentioned above those that are subject to the Emperor today are the following: Tigré, Dambeâ, Begameder, Gojam, Amaharâ and part of Xaoâ, Nareâ. The subject provinces are these: Mazagâ, Salemt, Ogarâ, Abargalê, Holcait, Sagadê, Cemen, Calaoâ, Olecâ, Dobâ. So it seems that the Emperor now probably has at most the half of what his predecessors possessed. The Gallas have taken the other half from him since the Emperor Gladios[1] and his successors broke the vow he made to accept and perpetuate the holy faith of Rome in his empire, and since, rejecting the Patriarch Dom João Bermudez[2] and afterwards the Patriarch

Atlas marks them just north of the southern boundary of Abyssinia. The story that they contained the source of the Nile derives from a traveller's tale copied by Ptolemy, from the lost work of Marinus of Tyre. Ptolemy is (except for those who copied him) the only Classical geographer who mentions them; and what he says about them does not support the suggestion that they were in Abyssinia.

[1] Galāwdēwos, or Claudius, 1540–59.

[2] An obscure member of the first Portuguese embassy to Abyssinia, called 'Mestre Joam' by Alvares. He remained behind when D. Rodrigo de Lima returned home and was later sent to Europe by the Emperor to ask for help against the Moslem invaders. In Lisbon he claimed that the head of the Abyssinian church, or Abuna, had consecrated him his successor, that the Emperor had sent him to Rome to convey Abyssinia's submission to the Holy See and that the Pope had then confirmed his consecration by the Abuna and had also consecrated him as Patriarch of Alexandria. It is very

Dom Andre de Oviedo,[1] they obstinately persisted in the errors of Eutyches and Dioscurus.[2]

The position of these kingdoms and provinces is as I shall now indicate here, and I shall begin with the Kingdom of Tigrê, which in ancient times was the foundation and head of *Tigrê* the whole of this monarchy, and is today its best part. Tigre begins at Maçuâ and Arquico which formerly belonged to the same kingdom until in the year 1557 the Turks took possession of this, the only harbour the empire possessed. It goes along the coast of the Red Sea for 10 or 12 leagues in the direction of the Straits as far as Defalô. This too is a harbour in the same kingdom but as the sea has little depth there it is not frequented by boats. All the same, the Turks of Macuâ have it in their power as well and the inhabitants of the coastal lands between Maçuâ and Defalô, who are nearly all Moors, are subject to them. As one goes approximately southwest from Macuâ, almost in the middle of Tigrê, lies Maegogâ or Fremonâ, a place often named in all the letters of the Fathers of our Society of Jesus for some of them have always lived there since the time of the holy Patriarch Dom Andre de Oviedo. Maegogâ is 14 and a half degrees north of the Line. This elevation has often been taken there with the astrolabe. There are as many leagues again in the same direction from Maegogâ to the desert of Sirê or Aldobâ and it is perhaps almost as many to go south-east from Maegogâ to the end of Andertâ. As these are the boundaries of Tigrê I personally consider that its length is about 90 to 100 leagues. Its width may be as much as 50 or 60 where it is broadest, which is from Bur or Agamea to the aforesaid desert of Aldobâ.

Magazá   To its north and north-west are the Ballous, and more to the west the province of Magazâ, whose inhabitants are be-

doubtful whether there was any truth in his claims: neither the law nor the practice of the Abyssinian church permitted the Abuna to choose his own successor, and Almeida himself (bk III, c. 19, not translated in this volume) was puzzled by the fact that the Pope consecrated another man as Patriarch of Ethiopia while Bermudes was still alive. His own account of his adventures was translated by R. S. Whiteway in *The Portuguese Expedition to Abyssinia*, Hakluyt Society, ser. II, no. 10.

[1] A Spanish Jesuit who reached Abyssinia in 1557, was made Patriarch by the Pope in 1562 and died there in 1577.

[2] Noted as exponents of Monophysite doctrines in the fifth century.

tween Ballous and Cafres. The latter also live in those low-lying and very hot countries to the west and south-west.[1] From the point where the eastern border of Tigrê leaves the Red Sea a little below Defalô, abandoning the rest of the coast and shore to the Beduins of the Kingdom of Dancalŷ, it borders on the latter for a little while and then on the Kingdom of Angôt which the Gallas now possess. One corner of the Kingdom of Angót penetrates a long way between Dancaly and Tigrê. Then Angôt spreads out and widens between the deserts of Dancaly and the territories of Doarô and running on south-east of Tigrê, leaves the province of Dobâ, which is *Dobâ* all inhabited by Moors, in the middle between Tigrê and Begameder. It then goes round the Kingdom of Begamedêr behind the Lastâ mountains, inhabited by Agaus of Bega-meder and belonging to that Kingdom.

So on the eastern side a large part of Tigrê borders on the Kingdom of Angót and on the south-eastern on the province of Dobâ, which is inhabited by Moors who are subjects of the empire. Turning southwards it borders on Çalaoâ and Abar- *Calaoâ* gale, provinces lying between Tigrê and Begameder. They *Abargalê* have the province of Cemen on the north, on which also they border in that direction, and Tigrê borders on Cemen on the south and south-west, though the province of Salemt also lies *Salemt* between Tigrê and Cemen almost on the same bearing, be-tween south and south-west.

On the west, as I said, are Mazagâ and certain Cafres. Be-tween west and south-west a corner of Tigrê, which is the desert of Aldobâ, joins the provinces of Holcâit and Sagadê, *Holcait* which properly lie between the province of Ogarâ and the ter- *Segadê* ritories of the Ballous, and one corner of which touches Dambeâ.

These provinces, then, lie to the north-west of Ogarâ; to the *Ogarâ* north of Ogarâ lies part of Tigrê where, coming down from Lamalmôn, one enters the desert of Sirê. The mountains of Cemen lie to the north-east and the low-lying parts of Cemen on the Abargalê side are to the east. Dancaz, which is now part of Dambeâ, lies to the south and other parts of the same Kingdom of Dambeâ to the south-west and west. I have

[1] The full stop after 'south-west' is found only in the S.O.A.S. MS, not in the B.M. MS or in Beccari's text which is therefore unintelligible.

H

Çemen already said that Cemen[1] is between Tigrê, Abargalê, Ogarâ and Salemt. Tigrê and Salemt lie to the north-east and north, Abargalê to the east and south, Ogarâ to the west. Thus we have explained the position of Tigrê and at the same time of the provinces of Dobâ, Çalaoâ, Salemt, which can with good reason be called districts and parts of Tigrê. We have also spoken of the position of Holcâit, Sagadê, Ogarâ, Cemen and Abargalê. Many assert that these provinces formerly belonged to the Kingdom of Begameder, which is continuous with them in Abargalê, and were districts of it. Therefore it used to be said that Begameder was the biggest of all the kingdoms of this empire, a thing that could not be said now, since these provinces or districts have separated from it. I do not define precisely the length and breadth of these provinces or districts for I do not trouble myself with such niceties. In general I should say that, except for Salemt, which is rounder and smaller, the rest are all probably as much as fifteen leagues long and six or seven wide.

Dambeâ Dambeâ borders on and joins with Ogarâ on the northeast, to the east lies Begameder, to the south Gojam, to the west the Agaus of Achafer and Tanqhâ at the Danguel Barr corner and certain Cafres also and some of the Ballous. The greater part of them are really to the north. The Kingdom of Dambeâ lies north-east and south-west, from Ogarâ to Danguel Barr. It is about twenty-four leagues in length. It is probably ten or twelve wide, but if we include the area taken up by the sea or lake which extends beside Dambeâ on the south-east and south and is almost as many leagues across as is the country, then the width of Dambeâ will be almost as great as its length, which is 24 leagues. The centre of Dambeâ is Gorgorrâ. As I said before, we were there for many years. The elevation has been taken with the astrolabe and it has been found at different times that Gorgorrâ is thirteen and a half degrees north of the Line.

---

[1] According to Basset (*Conquête*, p. 455), the name Samen originally meant 'south', but owing to the 'displacement of the centre of the kingdom' it came to mean 'north'. This is confirmed by Ludolf, who says 'My Ethiopian [his teacher Gregory] says it is "north", but it seems to mean the opposite cardinal point, as is evident from the comparison of places' (*Lex. Aethiop.*, col. 125). Dillmann, *Lex. Aethiop.*, col. 334, says that it originally meant 'south' but that the meaning changed to the opposite in later times. In Amharic also, *samēn* has become the word for 'north'.

Between Dambeâ and Begameder are the districts of An- *Anfras* frâs and Darâ which strictly speaking belong to the Kingdom *Darâ* of Begameder, though today they are seperate from it. Anfrâs lies to the east, Darâ to the south-east of Dambeâ.

Gojam lies north-west and south-east and is probably *Gojam* about 50 leagues long. Its width from east to west is probably 32 leagues and is reckoned from one bank of the Nile to the other, for, as I have said, this river rises almost in the centre of Gojam, flows north for 12 or 15 leagues, turns east and enters the Lake of Dambeâ. Until it enters the lake it is flowing all the while through the country of the Gojam Agaus, some of which it leaves on the north-west; it is in- cluded in the length of this kingdom. It is not much, how- ever, and does not exceed six or seven [*sic*]. If we take no account of them we may say that the length of Gojam too is reckoned from one bank of the Nile to another, beginning from Bed on the north-west, where it enters the lake, as far as the projection and bend the river makes to the south, passing beyond Olecâ.[1]

The part of Gojam which we said lay to the north-west, in- habited by Agaus, borders on the Ballous, but some Cafres remain in certain lowlands between. The territories of the Ágaus continue on the western side for they inhabit ten or twelve districts, the best in the whole kingdom and border on Cafres who do not now belong to the empire. So it is with the Ágaus who are on its frontier and most of them are not often subject to the Emperors. Next, turning to the south- west, is the province of the Gongâs, who border on the Ágaus and belong to the empire. Outside it are Cafres on either side of the Nile and some Gongâs[2] too who live on the

[1] Almeida seems to be in some confusion here. From the Little Abay, that is, the Nile before it enters Lake Tana, to the Great Abay between the Walaqa and Jamma rivers on the east is about 130 miles, and from the entry of the Little Abay into the lake due south to the Great Abay about 110 miles. For the first his map gives 55 leagues, and for the second 30. He himself shows the source in the west, and not as the text says, in the centre of Gojam. This region is Agaumeder, his 'country of the Gojam Agaus', the Awiya.

[2] The Gonga stock includes (i) the Kafa, the core of whom were Gonga; (ii) the Bosha or Garo of Jimma; (iii) the Sheka or Mocha; all of these being in the region of the Gojeb river; (iv) the Mao or Anfilo north of the Baro; and (v) the Bworo or Shinasha scattered in about four separate areas north of the Abay between Gubba and the river Dura.

far side. There are also some Gafates mixed with Gallas who inhabit and are masters of, the Kingdom of Bizamô, which was formerly part of the empire. This way lies the route to Nareâ, still a subject kingdom, though it is now divided from the other subject kingdoms. Beyond the Nile, to the south of Gojam, lie some territories of Xaoa, Ganz, Damut, and further to the south-east, east and east-north-east the kingdoms of Amaharâ and Begameder.

Begameder   Passing on, then, to Begameder, it lies east and west, beginning in the Lastâ mountains next to the province of Dobâ; it borders on Dobâ and on part of Tigrê to the north-east, and to the east on the Kingdom of Angôt. After that it comes down between Abargalê and the Kingdom of Amaharâ till it drinks from the river Nile in Darâ, Dábér and other districts. The river Baxilô, which has a great volume of water, flows between it and Amaharâ, separates these kingdoms and goes to join the Nile. The length I mentioned from Lastâ to the Nile may be 60 leagues,[1] the width up to twenty but not more because, as I said above, the provinces of Abargalê, Cemen, Ogará, Seguedê and Olcâit have been separated from this kingdom. If we were to include them in it, its width would be equal to its length. The centre of Begameder is perhaps at an elevation of about 13 degrees.

Amaharâ   The Kingdom of Amaharâ comes next. It lies almost as Begameder does, from east to west for about 40 leagues. To the east is the province of Oifât, to the west Gojam, the Nile dividing the two kingdoms. On the north-east it touches Angôt and then, on the same side and on the north, borders on Begameder, as I said above, being separated from it for a long way by the Baxilô river. On the south side it borders on the Kingdom of Xaoâ and the province of Olecâ. The river Quessan flows between them. It is a big one and goes to join the Nile. The river Gemâ is very big too. It comes from Amaharâ, enters Xaoâ and when it has run its course, it too goes to join the Nile. In general the country of Amaharâ is so mountainous that it has more hills, mountains and ambâs than the rest of the empire, so much so that it is all a chain of very high mountains. The hills and valleys of Amaharâ

[1] The Lasta mountains are about 95 miles from the Abay; Almeida makes the distance 30 leagues on his map, and not 60.

are, however, very fertile in all kinds of food, in honey and horned cattle.

Xaoâ lies to the south-east of Amaharâ. Oifât lies to the *Xaoâ* east of Xaoâ, Fategâr and Oggê to the south-east and south, the Kingdom of Dámót to the south-west, Bizamô to the west, part of Gojam to the north-west, the Nile coming in between and Olecâ being this side of the Nile. Today the Gallas possess the greater part of Xaoâ. Some villages of Abyssinians still exist on a few ambâs.[1]

The province of Olecâ lies between Amaharâ, Xaoâ and *Olecâ* Gojam. The latter kingdom lies to the west, Amaharâ to the north and north-west, Xaoâ surrounds it on the north-east, east, south-east and south. Hitherto it has been subject to the empire, though very near to, and so much infested by the Gallas.

Nareâ is today in the midst of the Gallas and Cafres with- *Nareâ* out a point of contact between it and any kingdom or province still subject to the empire, yet it defends itself from the Gallas, because the people of the kingdom are of great bravery and very intelligent. The Xumo or governor to whom they are subject, is not a stranger nor is he appointed by the Emperor, but is the descendant of their former kings, and sons succeed their fathers as they used to do formerly when they had the title of kings. This kingdom is about eight degrees north of the Line. To the east are the Kingdom of Gingirô, inhabited by heathens who have never been subject to the empire, and the province of the Gurâguês, who are also heathens and Moors. To the north-east is the Kingdom of Bizamó, which today the Gallas and certain Cafres are swallowing up. Through these kingdoms lies the route from Gojam to Nareâ, the Gurágués and the Kingdom of Bizamô. It used to be in the empire. On the north, north-west, west, south-west and south various Cafre countries surround Nareâ.[2] They have never been subject to the Abyssinian empire.

---

[1] This word is explained on p. 37.

[2] These are presumably the tribal areas of Mao, Sheka and the Gimira group (Shako, She, Mazhi, etc.).

CHAPTER 4

The Climate and Characteristics of Ethiopia, winter and summer

As this empire is very large and includes several kingdoms and provinces, so the characteristics of the country vary very considerably. The climate is that prevailing from 8 degrees to 17 North, and though it lies so much in what is usually called the torrid zone, this country is far from being uninhabitable because of great heat. Generally it is as cold as Portugal. The sultriness, the oppressive and moist heat of our summer are not found here; so much is this so that anyone travelling in the full sun and coming to the shade of any trees, even if they are not very bushy or shady, will not notice the heat any more. Still less is it ever felt indoors even if the house is one of the usual sort in the country, which are of one storey and thatched. What is generally feared is the cold. Indeed, that is not usually as great as in our February, but there are some places where it is very extreme, because the ground is very high. This is so in all months of the year, though more so in winter than in summer.[1] It does not prevent there being lowlands where the heat is extraordinary and some are so hot that they are inhabited only by Cafres.

The Abyssinians distinguish between five types of country, to which they give these names: Choquê, Degâ, Oinadegâ, Collâ, Baraqhâ. Choquê means high and extremely cold country, Degâ high and perpetually cold country, Oinadegâ high but temperate country without an excess of cold or heat, Collâ very hot lowlands, Baraqhâ extremely hot desert, like the deserts of Seraoê in Tigrê near the Mareb river and that of Syrê near the Tacazê river and the greater part of the banks of the Nile wheresoever it flows, for its course is mostly between very high mountains.[2]

[1] What is obviously the correct punctuation here is found only in the S.O.A.S. MS.

[2] The climatic zones in Abyssinia are *barahã*, the desert; *quallā*, the hot lowlands; *waynā dag'ā*, the temperate highlands, literally 'highlands of the

The coast lands of this empire, those between Maçuâ and Dancali, extend along the shores of the Red Sea, and their winter is in the months of December and January, as in Portugal. It extends inland for ten or twelve leagues. It is very mild, without being cold, and the rain is not immoderate though it is sufficient to irrigate and fertilise the meadows and cornfields. I spent the greater part of the winter of 1623 to 1624 in the islands of Suaquem and Macuâ, but we never had much rain. When we went inland, however, we had more than we wanted as far as a high place called Asmarâ, two days' travel short of Debaroá. When we arrived there we saw that we had left the clouds and the winter behind. We were not afraid of their reaching us for the people of the country told us that, from there onwards, winter came only from June to the end of September. That is what I experienced afterwards in all the territories of the empire that I went through. So, from Nareâ to Debaroâ or a little further, throughout all the interior, winter is in the same months as on the coast of India from Dio to Cape Comorim. On the Ethiopian coast of the Red Sea it is as in Portugal. The opposite happens on the coast of Arabia for winter prevails along the coast from the gates of the Strait to the Curia Muria islands in June, July, August and September, as on the coast of India. In the interior of Arabia, it is in the months of November, December, January and February, as in Portugal.

As Ethiopia is for the most part high and mountainous there is often hail with very big hailstones,[1] and for the greater part of winter, thunder and lightning, by which many people are killed. I do not know that snow falls in this country except in the Cemen mountains which lie between Tigrê and Ogarâ, and in those of Lástá, belonging to the Kingdom of

grape'; and *degā*, the cold highlands. 'Choque' may be due to a misunderstanding of the name Čoqē applied to the highest part of the Mangestu Mts. (i.e. *mangesta samāyāt*, 'the kingdom of heaven') in central Gojam, of which Cheesman, p. 69, writes, 'the climate is so cold that the Ethiopians cannot live there and seldom cross them.' The word *wurč*, 'frost', is also used of the coldest zone.

[1] Several travellers have been impressed by the violence of hailstorms in Abyssinia. 'The hail lies often upon the top of Amid-amid for hours' (Bruce, bk VI, c. 12). Rassam experienced 'a tremendous hailstorm' at Magdala (vol. II, p. 265). Such hailstorms occur also in many other parts of East Africa.

Begameder. A great deal falls there and the mountain tops, which are high enough to leave the clouds far below, are covered for a large part of the year, as the Alps are said to be, and as we see in Portugal with our Serra de Estrella.[1]

CHAPTER 5

The River Nile: its source and why it rises in the months of August and September[2]

The most notable thing there is in this empire is the source of the Nile, called by the Abyssinians the Abâuy, not because there is anything more remarkable about this source than about any others, but because of the great desire the ancients had to know where it was. I shall not concern myself with passing on what historians, poets and many other authors have said and invented about this source and the rising of the river Nile; the books and what is written in them are better known in Europe than in Ethiopia. However much I were to say about it people would still say they knew more. So I shall say sincerely and truthfully, as an eye-witness, what is really there. Perhaps those who read it may laugh at the amount that has been invented about merely one thing.

In the middle of the Kingdom of Gojam, about twelve degrees north of the Line, is a country called Sacahalâ. It is inhabited by Ágaus, most of them heathens, and some Chris-

---

[1] There has been much discussion about snowfall in Abyssinia. It has been alleged that hailstones lying and glittering in the sun have been mistaken for snow, and Bruce (bk VI, c. 12) states 'Snow was never seen in this country'. But the unnamed king of Aksum whose conquests are recorded in an inscription quoted by Cosmas in the sixth century certainly believed that there was snow in Abyssinia, for he says that the Semēně (peoples of Semēn) inhabit inaccessible mountains covered with snow which lay knee-deep. And Rüppell (vol. I, pp. 356, 402 *et seq.*; vol. II, pp. 14, 243–244, 249, 251) frequently saw snow on the Semen mountains.

[2] This chapter was translated into Italian by Beccari in his first volume, *Saggi e Documenti*, pp. 311–318. Almeida nowhere mentions that he had visited the source of the Nile, as Páez had, but Beccari (*ibid.* p. 309) remarks that Almeida's description is clearer than that given by Páez and differs from it so much that he must have been describing what he had seen himself.

tians, but in name only. The country is mountainous, like the rest of Ethiopia, but there are other districts elsewhere, even very near to this, such that at the base and foot of their mountains these would not be of much account.[1]

Among these mountains, as I say, or hills of Sacahalâ, is a stretch of open country or a plain, not very level, extending for a third of a league. In the centre of this plain is a kind of little lake nearly a stone's throw in diameter. This pool is so full of grass and shrubs and their roots are so entangled that in summer one can walk over them and reach two springs about a stone's throw apart [sic] where one sees clear and limpid water. The people who live near say they are unfathomable and some of them have tested this by putting lances in up to 20 spans without finding the bottom.[2]

The water flows from this pool underground but the course it takes can be told from the grass. First it flows eastwards for a musket shot and then turns to the north.[3] About half a league from the source the water comes to the surface in sufficient quantity to make a not very big stream, but others

[1] An allusion to Urreta who says (pp. 298–299) that the Alps and Pyrenees would appear as 'lowly huts' beside the mountains at the source of the Nile. Bruce (bk VI, c. 12) criticises the Jesuits for ascribing 'fabulous height' to them!

[2] The source, called Gush Abay, is in the district of Sakala, at an altitude of over 9000 ft, a few miles north of Lake Gudera; it has been described by Bruce (bk VI, c. 14), Beke (*JRGS*, vol. XIV, pp. 12–13), and Cheesman (pp. 70 *et seqq.*). Bruce speaks of three springs, each rising in the middle of an artificial mound of turf. These mounds he says were still used by the inhabitants, who were still pagans, for religious rites; he hints that if the Jesuits had really been there they would have referred to 'the idolatry or pagan worship, which prevailed near the source of the Nile'. He found the depth of the principal spring to be 6 ft 4 inches. Beke's description, which is much closer to Almeida's, is not readily accessible and we have therefore reproduced it in full at the end of this chapter. Cheesman (p. 72) calls it 'a deep hole a few inches in diameter full of clear water, but with scarcely enough current to flow'.

[3] 'The Nile . . . runs east for thirty yards, with a very little increase of stream, but perfectly visible, till met by the grassy brink of the land declining from Sacala. This turns it gradually to the N.E. and then due north; and, in the two miles it flows in that direction, the river receives many small contributions' (Bruce). 'The small flow . . . trickles down a small depression, its course marked by a thin line of bright green water-grass and rushes' (Cheesman). He describes its course as 'north-east for about half a mile, after which it curves round and goes north, and by yet another bend flows to the west, passing the spring again at a mile's distance, and finally settles down . . . to a general northerly direction.'

of very great height and the river washes their base though there is nearly always a space between it and the mountains which is in some places half a league, in some a league and in others more. These valleys between Gojam, Begameder and Olecâ are inhabited and produce much cotton,[1] but it is a country of many diseases. In this region the mountain ranges of Gojam are so precipitous as to be frightening, especially those that run from before Adaxâ as far as Nebessê. I sometimes took the path along their summit, and certainly it made one's hair stand on end merely to see those very high cliffs.

In this stretch the Nile stream has many falls which the ancients called cataracts. In some places it hurls itself from rocks and ledges with an astounding roar. Seven or eight leagues after leaving the lake, near a place in Begameder called Alatâ, it falls from so high that some of the water dissolves in the air into something like a fog or fine shower which rises very high and can be seen a long way off.[2] The roar is so great that for a considerable distance around it numbs the hearing. So it may well be that there exist near to Egypt the cataracts so famous in the ancient writers. Even if they are only a little bigger than those of which I speak then certainly either they will cause the country for a league around to be uninhabited, or else the inhabitants will be deafened in a short time.[3]

As it flows among mountains and rocks the river is often very constricted and narrow, so much so that near the same place Alatâ they used to cross it on thick poles placed on both banks of the river on the rocks that are there. The whole of the Emperor's army often crossed by these poles as though by a bridge. Two years ago, in 1626, after stone for making lime had been found in this country, the Emperor ordered a

---

[1] This plant, under the name *tut* (Amharic *ṭiṭ*), is mentioned in the Christian inscription of 'Ēzānā as grown by the people of the lower Takaze.

[2] Cheesman, whose book contains an excellent photograph of the falls, describes them as 600 yards across with a drop of some 150 ft, and says that the native name Tisisat or 'smoke of fire' is derived from 'the resemblance which the mist rising from the big fall bears to smoke, especially in the early morning, when it is visible for a long distance' (p. 227). Bruce, who calls it 'the most magnificent sight that ever I beheld', also speaks of 'a thick fume, or haze' (bk VI, c. 4).

[3] This is the story in Cicero, *Somn. Scip.*, c. 5, and Seneca, *Nat. Quaest.*, bk IV, c. 2.

bridge to be built near there by a craftsman who had come from India with the Patriarch. This has now been done so the whole river which runs very deep there and is confined between rocks, is crossed by a single, not very wide arch.[1]

In places, however, it spreads out so much that it can very easily be forded in summer. It is not so in winter and therefore for the whole of that season the inhabitants of Gojam consider themselves secure from the attacks of the Gallas who live on the far side,[2] in a large part of Xaoa, Damut and Bizamo which they conquered some years ago and which they rule along with many other kingdoms and territories of this empire lying to the south-east and south on the far side of the Nile. In the whole of its course through the lands of this empire the river forms no inhabited or habitable island.[3]

The reason for its floods in August and September, which water the fields of Egypt, is as clear and obvious in this country as is in Portugal the reason for the flooding of the Tagus, Mondego and other rivers in December and January. It is because here the depth of winter comes in the former months, just as it does there in the latter months. It is evident that a river will flood when for over 150 leagues it receives the water that falls in the form of rain on the great countries around, besides what is discharged into it by the big Lake of Dambeâ and what is added by the Tacazée and many other rivers, some of them as big as it is, or not much less, and an almost infinite number of little ones that flood immoderately in winter. I said 150 leagues because that is what is probably comprised in its bend until a little after it leaves the territories of this empire; thus far we know for certain that winter falls in the months I said. From there to Egypt must be more

[1] It is still standing, about a mile below the falls, and is described and illustrated in Cheesman's book (p. 226). Bruce (bk VI, c. 4) describes it as having a single arch 'about twenty-five feet broad', but others have since been added, for Cheesman mentions five. He is evidently wrong in assigning the building of the bridge to the reign of Fasiladas (1631–67); he was misled by a passage in Le Grand's version of Lobo ascribing it to 'Sultan Segued', a name used by both Fasiladas and his father, Susneyos. Almeida elsewhere, bk III, c. 19, calls this 'the first bridge that was seen in Ethiopia'.

[2] Bruce (bk VI, c. 14), however, says Galla 'cross it at all times without difficulty', by swimming or on rafts or inflated skins or by clinging to their horses' tails.

[3] Probably an allusion to Pliny (bk V, c. 10) who speaks of its 'innumerable islands'.

than three hundred leagues if we take account of the windings there usually are in rivers (for the direct route from here till it enters Egypt does not amount to two hundred leagues). They [*sic*]¹ will know whether it is winter or not; I write what I know as an eye-witness.

Appendix to Chapter 5
Beke's Description of the Source of the Nile

'After crossing Mount Jinnit the road was tolerably level, Mount Giesh being to our right hand, till we came to a valley to the left, beyond which, on a gradually rising eminence, is the church of St Michael. We turned off a little way north-eastward into a swampy piece of ground covered with grass and rushes, and surrounded with trees of no great size and brushwood, in about the centre of which a spot was pointed out to me as the source of the Abai. At first it was scarcely distinguishable from the rest of the marsh; but on approaching and inspecting it more closely, a small collection of water about a foot in diameter was visible among the rushes, which could just be reached with the hand when kneeling on a narrow mound of sod which partly surrounds it. From this spot the course of the river was pointed out to me as proceeding south-eastward, north-eastward, and then N. round the church-hill. No water is, however, visible above ground for a considerable distance; and as far as I could see, the course of the river was only marked by a continuation of the swamp along the valley. To the N.N.W. of the principal source another was shown me at about 5 yards distance from it, a patch of dry ground about 2 yards in width being between the two, and the rest being all swamp. I asked for a third source, but was told there was no other. The church is not visible from the spot on account of the intervening trees, but its bearing is about N. 35° E. That of the summit of Mount Giesh is about S. 60° W. On questioning my guides as to the celebration of religious ceremonies here, they scorned the idea of their performing anything of the sort, being

¹ Beccari assumes that this pronoun refers to the inhabitants and trans- ates it 'quelli che abitano colà'. It is more likely to mean those persons, like Urreta, who had never left Europe but presumed to contradict the Jesuit missionaries about Abyssinian geography.

Christians; but they admitted that yearly in the month of Hedar, or Tahsas (about the end of November), after the rainy season, and when the ground is sufficiently dry to allow of it, an ox is slaughtered on the spot by the neighbouring Shum, and its blood is allowed to flow into the spring, its flesh being eaten on the ground. I could not learn that any particular ceremonies accompany this act. Also at the close of the Abyssinian year (the beginning of September), on the eve of St John, sick persons are brought hither and left for seven days, which they say ensures their recovery. Logs of wood have from time to time been laid round the source to serve as a bed for these sick visitants, but they have sunk in the quagmire; still traces of them are visible, and they serve to give a certain degree of solidity to the otherwise unstable soil.' (*JRGS*, xiv. (1844), pp. 12–13.)[1]

CHAPTER 6

The Rivers Zebee, Haoax, Tacazee, Mareb

After the Nile the first three we named are the chief ones there are in this empire. We shall speak of the Mareb too, not because it is big or famous in this country but because people a long way off who invented things about it which they should not have done, have bestowed fame upon it.

People who have crossed it say that the river Zebee is bigger and more copious than the Nile. It rises in a country called Boxâ in the Kingdom of Nareâ, which is the most southerly in this empire. It begins by flowing to the west, but after a few leagues it turns north and encircles the Kingdom of Zingero, making it like a peninsula, as the Nile does Gojam. After leaving this kingdom it flows southwards and some say that it is the river that enters the sea at Mombaça. I shall discuss the Kingdom of Zingeró later; it is small, heathen, and, though it recognises him, is not strictly speaking subject to the Emperor.

[1] Cheesman says that the church of St Michael is dedicated also to 'Zarabruk', and it has been suggested that this name commemorates Bruce, to whom Takla Haymanot II gave the land where the church stood in 1770 (*Lake Tana*, pp. 15, 16). But this word is really the Amharic *zarburuk*, 'blessed seed'.

The River Haoax

The Haoax is nearly equal to the Nile; it rises among the kingdoms of Xaoa, which lies to the north, Oggê, which lies to the south, and Fategar, to the east. It flows north-east and receives the waters of a big river named Machŷ[1] coming from Lake Zoâj which is in the Kingdom of Oggê. After being augmented in this way it goes on to enter the Kingdom of Adel, which we call Zeila, and enters a province called Auçâ Gurrêlê, which was where the blessed martyrs, our Fathers Francisco Machado and Bernardo Pereira remained for some months till the treacherous Moorish King took their lives, undoubtedly because of the rancorous hatred he bore to the Christian name. It is said to rain very little in that country but yet it is fairly fertile because the river Haoax is distributed by the natives in a number of channels and waters their cornfields as the Nile does those of Egypt. Some say they distribute and spread it so that its water is entirely used up there and it flows no further, though others assert that it reaches the sea.

The River Tacazee

The Tacazee is not as big as but is not much smaller than the Nile. Its source is in a country called Axguâguâ at the beginning of the Kingdom of Angót, near Begameder where, at the foot of a high mountain lying to the east, three springs of water burst out with great force within a stone's throw of each other. They all unite and make a big river which flows westwards for some days' journey between the districts of Deqhanâ and Aoage, which lie to the north, and Ebenât and Quinfáz which are to the south. Then with several turns it directs its course northwards between the provinces of Cemen and Abargalê, of which the latter lies to the east and the former to the west. It then goes on to cross the Kingdom of Tigré, leaving the districts of Tembem and Çaná to the east and the province of Çalânt to the West. Then it breaks through the middle of Sirêe, a province of Tigrê, leaving the bigger and richer part of that province to the east and to the west its famous desert, the better part of which, where there

[1] This river does not flow eastwards from Lake Zeway into the Awash, as Almeida thought, but rises about 40 miles south of Addis Ababa and flows into Lake Zeway from the north, having no connection with the Awash.

were many hermits in former times, is called Aldobá. At this point, where it descends a very big slope, the Tacazêe can easily be forded in summer because it grows a little wider. This is the most usual route from Dambeâ to Tigrê.

I sometimes used it and crossed the river. At this place it is nearly a musket shot wide. Where it is deepest it is up to the waist. Below and above it is narrower, being more closely confined to a channel and it has deep pools in which there are many crocodiles and hippopotamuses. Once when I was beside the river in the shade of some trees like very tall and bushy alders,[1] but quite hot because the sun seems to burn in that valley, I saw two of them, apparently a male and a female, go from one pool to another through low water reaching to their knees. They were like big horses. They resembled them about the muzzle but even more about the ears.[2] As for the feet they are short, and the tail much shorter so they look like Canons' mules; the hips are wide; the whole body is wrapped in flesh and has no hair, only naked and very smooth hide. There are many fish in this river. The first time I crossed it the men who accompanied us gave me one of the kind the Latins call 'torpedo'. Many people, and I too, tested its power in a trough of water. I squeezed it in my hand under the water. I felt my hand so weak and powerless that I let it go very hurriedly.

The river passes on to another province called Holcâit, then through some Cafre territories which are very low-lying and hot, and thence it makes its way into the Kingdom of Deqhin, which is inhabited by Moors who are called Ballous here and Funchos on the coast of Suaqhem, as I said above. In the middle of this kingdom it meets and joins the Nile, adding to it its water and its name and losing its own.

Marebo

This river rises in the Kingdom of Tigrê two leagues west of Debaroâ. Its source is between two rocks which are 16 *covados*[3] from each other. It flows over a ledge of rock for a distance of 36 paces. At the end of the ledge it dashes head-

---

[1] *amieiros*. Prof. Pichi-Sermolli considers that a species of *Ficus* is meant.

[2] Beccari reads: 'nas orelhas e coma. Os peês' etc. This would mean 'about the ears and hair. The feet' etc. As Almeida himself says in the next sentence, correctly, that the hippopotamus has no hair, the reading of the S.O.A.S. MS, 'comaos peês,' is preferable. [3] 1 *covado* = 66 cm.

I

long over a high precipice. In summer it has so little water
that it almost all disappears there. When the water does run
over the cliff it flows eastwards. Near Debaroâ a sizable
stream joins it and, increased by that, it leaves the town on
the west and travels on to the south. It proceeds to encircle a
district called Seraoé, leaving it to the north and west and
separating it from the districts of Çamá and Guelà, which lie
to the east, and those of Aça, Haricê, Torat and Sirê which
lie to the south-east and south. About three days' journey
from Debaroâ it washes the base of a mountain on which is
situated the Alleluia monastery.[1] Three or four days' journey
from there it makes its way into the territories of Cafres who,
though they accord some recognition to the Emperor, are not
often subject to him. Here it disappears and goes underground for a considerable distance.[2] The ground above it is
sandy and has little grass though at intervals there are very
bushy and verdant trees.

João Gabriel, who was Captain of the Portuguese[3] for

---

[1] This monastery is described by Almeida (bk II, c. 19) as follows:
'It lies in Tigrê one day's journey from Acçum, situated on a mountain
among high ranges; the Marebo river runs nearby. The ruins of the old
church show that it was one of the best in Ethiopia. It was 132 spans long
and 105 wide. Near to it the ruins or the sites of many round cottages are to
be seen. When the oldest monks were asked about the numbers that there
once were in the monastery, they gave different answers. Some said 1200,
others that they attained 4000. One may suggest that the former were
speaking about those who lived together near the church, and the latter
about those who were living in the district and were subject to the monastery. It is alleged that there used once to be 90 churches dependent on this
monastery and that when the superior went to court on important business,
150 monks on mules accompanied him, every one of whom wore a burnous
over his habit. Of all this nothing is left now but *campi* or mountains *ubi
Troya fuit*. In the middle of the ruined church a quite small round one has
been built, next to which live 10 or 12 monks and there are probably as
many as 20 more in the dependent churches. All the splendours of the
Alleluya monastery have been reduced to this and there is nothing more to
be said about it.'

[2] As the Mareb approaches the Sudan frontier through the lowlands
below 4000 ft it is known as the Gash, and becomes seasonal, disappearing
in the sand west of Kassala.

[3] The small community referred to under this name consisted principally
of the descendants of the soldiers who had come with D. Cristovão da Gama
in 1541. Most of the survivors of his campaign remained in the country and
married Abyssinian women. They and their children retained a sense of
solidarity, chose their own leader or 'Captain' and continued to be a formidable fighting force.

many years and a very truthful and Christian man, averred that when he went that way on a campaign, by digging down to 10 spans at various places in the sandy soil, they came upon a stream of water and not only drank from it but fished in it and ate the fish. A little further on the river bursts out, emerges from the ground and enters the Kingdom of Dequin which belongs to Moorish Ballous, as I said. Because there is little water in their country they distribute what there is in this river and water and fertilise the country with it in such a way that it is all used up in the meadows and cornfields. Even so it is not enough for them and some country is left to be watered. This is what is most probable although some have said the Mareb joins the Tacazeê.

This and no more than this is the truth about the Mareb or Negro river, for the Ariosto or Palmeirim of Ethiopia gives it this name,[1] not because its water is black (he says) but because it flows through negro countries, as if there were any rivers in Ethiopia that ran through white men's country.[2] This, I say, is the whole truth, this and not making it into the source of 3 or 4 lakes, or making it divide into as many arms as Divine Scripture gives to the river that comes from Paradise, and taking some as far as Cape Verde and others to the Melinde coast, and making a pearl and amber fishery with which those of Baharem[3] and Cape Comorim cannot be compared (as indeed they cannot for there is none there). Since the river had run all the time over precious stones it was not surprising that the sea should come to receive it at its mouth with amber, seed-pearls and pearls.[4] All this he

[1] Almeida means to suggest that Urreta was as much a writer of fiction as Francisco de Morais, the author of *Palmeirim de Inglaterra*, 'Palmeirim of England,' a sixteenth century romance of chivalry of the kind ridiculed by Cervantes.

[2] Urreta, p. 311.   [3] Bahrein.

[4] Urreta (pp. 311–313) describes the Negro (the Niger) as passing through four large lakes, one of which is 60 by 30 leagues in area; it then flows between Tonbotu (Timbuctoo) and Melli (the Mandingo empire of Mali) and divides into four branches, all of which reach the west coast of Africa, one being the Senegal. There is no reference to Malindi; perhaps Almeida confused Melli and Melinde. Urreta calls it the richest river in the whole world; the amber fishery is explained by him in the following way. Whales eat a plant growing in the depths of the sea which makes their bodies swell prodigiously. They then seek sweet water which will make them vomit. The Negro being the only river along that coast they congregate at its mouth (Urreta, pp. 314, 315).

says in spite of what really happens in Ethiopia, where they have never seen either a precious stone or a pearl: seed-pearls, yes, for today the Emperor is rich in them, because in the year 1625 he asked me to send for a few from India. With the small handful that I had brought he wears today a richer crown than any of his predecessors ever placed on his head. This should be known and remembered.

CHAPTER 7

The great Lake of Dambeâ which the Abyssinians call a sea

I can be a good witness to what I say about this lake because from my window, at which I am writing this history, I can see almost the whole of it.[1] It lies north-east and south-west, the side on the south-east and south being straighter; I mean that it has fewer bays. The part that ought to go westwards is twisted and turns much to the north-west. So the side which turns north, north-west and west is much longer and has many bays especially near Gorgorrâ, where the water bulges greatly to the north, and the hills of Goârgê and the country of Gorgorrâ project into it. Between this country and Tacucâ the lake inserts an arm or bay which may be two leagues long and one wide, so that I think its southern side may be twenty leagues long and the northern 35. This is going not alongside the lake but keeping a little way away, without turning round the numerous bays it makes. If one were to travel along the edge of the water and follow the windings made by the bays there would be many more leagues on this northern side. The bends on the southern side are not so big but there would still be 30 leagues if one went all the time by the waterside. Where it is widest it may be 12 leagues; usually its width is about 10 or 8. The water is

---

[1] Cheesman (p. 208) describes the view from the ruins of the palace of Susneyos in Gorgora; he looked across over 30 miles of open water and re-cognised Mount Amadamit near the source of the Nile 70 miles away. He comments: 'A more beautiful prospect it is not possible to imagine.'

very limpid, clear and wholesome; it has a great quantity of fish of different kinds. Many rivers fall into it and none leaves it except the Nile which crosses it. In winter the great amount of rainwater makes it rise gradually till the end of August. It then falls, though very slowly, until about the end of December.

It has many islands; there are said to be 21 in all.[1] Some are very big, as is one called Dek which pays the Emperor 300 *calões*[2] of honey as tribute every year and has 400 yokes under cultivation. On seven or eight are monasteries of monks which were formerly very big, though they are now much diminished. Nearly all of them had many lands and churches on the mainland opposite the islands on which they were. There are big monasteries on some peninsulas too. These islands are very hot and all kinds of thorn fruits,[3] citrons and lemons, both Galician and French, grow on them better than anywhere else. Many very good Indian figs are grown and very thick, tall and sweet sugar-canes, so that in thorn fruits Dambeâ and Gojam yield nothing to India.

There are many hippopotamuses in this lake. They come out to graze on land in some of the more level meadows and do great damage to the crops. There are men who live by hunting and killing them.[4] They eat their flesh and from the

---

[1] 'There are forty-five inhabited islands in the lake, if you believe the Abyssinians, who, in every thing, are very great liars. I conceive the number may be about eleven' (Bruce, bk VI, c. 2). Cheesman names 37 islands of which 19 have, or had, or are said to have had churches or monasteries on them. There are, however, more islands now than there were in Almeida's time as the level of the lake has fallen about 6 ft (Cheesman, p. 108). He says that Dek is about 3 miles in diameter and Daga about ¾ mile; no others are of comparable size.

[2] Large earthenware jars.

[3] *fruta de espinho*. Mr A. W. Exell remarks that Almeida seems to use this phrase for 'what we should call Citrus fruits in general (the branchlets are spiny)'.

[4] The Wayto. They are now Moslems and were so by Rassam's time (vol. I, p. 314). They told Cheesman that they had always been Moslems but he remarks that 'it is safe to say that they made the change in comparatively recent times' (p. 93). The fact that Almeida does not call them 'Moors' supports this. Neither an Abyssinian Christian nor an orthodox Moslem would eat hippopotamus flesh. According to Cheesman, p. 93, the hippopotamus is now almost extinct in Lake Tana. The Wayto are a hunting people; elsewhere in Abyssinia similar groups are called Watta; Mancho (Kafa); and Manno (Sidama). The Wayto live on the shores of Lake Tana, and on the banks of the Abay and Takaze. Boys are circumcised at the age

hide they make Alengâs.[1] This is what they call the whips
with which they drive mules and horses, for spurs are not
used in this country. They beat them a great deal and
whip them harder. In general there are no crocodiles[2] so
that the cattle grazing on the turf beside it and all the
people that inhabit its shores and banks drink its water in
safety.

The Abyssinians sail on this lake in tancoas which are a
kind of *almadias* or little boats, not of wood but reeds.[3] A
great quantity of them grow in this country in the marshes
beside this and other, smaller lakes; the reed stems are as
thick as an arm and more than a fathom long. I said 'and of
other, smaller lakes' because in the Kingdom of Gojam there
are many lakes half a league and others over a league long,
and of corresponding width. I have seen five or six of them
and in most of them are many hippopotamuses. In the Kingdom of Oggê which is now inhabited by the Gallas, is one so
big that it has an island in it, on which there was formerly a
very big monastery. It is called Zoâj. The river Mâchy comes
from it as I said above.

of two; no analogous operation is performed on girls. Cerulli quotes from a
writer named Rava (*Al lago Tsana*, Rome, 1913, p. 79) that they may have
numbered some 600 or 700 people (*Folk-literature*, p. 201), though Cohen
suggests about 1000. Their language is a form of Amharic. (Cohen, *Nouvelles
Études d'Éthiopien Méridionale* (Paris, 1939), pp. 358–360).

[1] Amharic *alanga*, 'whip'.

[2] This is confirmed by Bruce (bk VI, c. 2), Rüppell (vol. II, p. 222), and
Cheesman (pp. 156–157), who saw none higher than the lagoon above the
Tisisat falls. Bruce and Cheesman suggest that the water of the lake is too
cold for them.

[3] Amharic *tānkuā*, a reed raft, 'made by first constructing the shell in the
shape of an ordinary stream-lined boat but made entirely of bundles of
reeds bound most ingeniously with narrow strips of the bark of the fig-tree
warka. The whole of the hollow shell is then filled with an oblong collection
of reed bundles bound together and exactly fitting it' (Cheesman, p. 91).
They are made and propelled almost exclusively by Wayto. An *almadia* is a
dug-out canoe or raft. Almeida (bk III, c. 19) says that no other kind of
boat but the *tānkuā* is known in Abyssinia. 'This is quite certain because
they have never had the skill to make them. A few years ago one of their
Abbunas is said to have made a big boat on the Lake or Sea of Dambeâ, but
because it was badly calked and resin had been used instead of pitch, which
he did not find in the country, it went to the bottom on the first voyage he
wanted to make. One of our brothers made a little boat here a few years
ago. Everybody came to see it as a novelty. He calked it with incense. He
made several voyages but did not use it much because there were no
oarsmen.'

CHAPTER 8

Mountains, Valleys and Mountain Ranges of Ethiopia. Description of Lamalmon

The kingdoms that the Gallas acquired from this empire and have held for the last 70 or 80 years, like Ogge, Fategár, Doarô, Bally and others, are said by everyone to be mostly level country with wide open plains. Those, however, that the Emperor now holds, except Dambeâ, the greater part of which is level ground beside the lake and contains fine fields of very rich and fertile soil for a distance of about twenty leagues long and four or five wide, the others, that is Tigrê, Begameder, Gojam, Amarâ and the provinces of Cemen, Ogara, Segadê, Holcâit, Xaoa and Holecâ, nearly all these countries are amazingly mountainous. It is rare to travel one day's journey without meeting mountains so high and rugged as to be frightening. In our own Europe are the renowned Alps and Pyrenees; those who have crossed them assert that in these regions innumerable mountains are found which are higher and more rugged.[1] It certainly does seem an unnatural thing unless either Nature maliciously, or God, by the special judgment of His divine wisdom, as elsewhere in the world He played with other marvels, so here He wanted to make mountains rising above the clouds along with valleys descending to the centre of the earth. As the former have the cold of the 2nd or 3rd regions of the air, so the latter share the fire and heat of hell.

There would be no end if I were to try now to enumerate or describe here all or many of these mountains. In general it is enough to know that there are some which the natives call Ambâs, which stand apart from the rest, very lofty and with perpendicular sides so that they can be climbed with difficulty by one or two paths only. On top they have water and level ground where the inhabitants live as though in a fortress

[1] Bruce (bk V, c. 6) ridicules such statements and remarks: 'It is not the extreme height of the mountains in Abyssinia that occasions surprise, but the number of them, and the extraordinary forms they present to the eye.'

or a city established by God. There are many of them throughout the empire but most in the Kingdom of Amarâ which at
present borders on the Gallas who would have taken possession of it all by now if it were not for these Ambâs or fortresses.
Here is Ambâ Guexen, famous because in former times the
sons of the Emperors were placed there and kept under
guard as we shall relate at greater length further on. In the
same kingdom are Ambâcel and others that are not inferior
to Guexen in the strength and ruggedness of their position.
In Begameder are the mountains of Lâstâ and among them
are many of these Ambâs. There, for the last three years a
rebel and a few people have been withstanding the whole
might of the empire, for the position is such that it seems rash
to consider assaulting it. In Tigre Ambaçanet is similar, but
Dom Christovão da Gama reduced it with four hundred
Portuguese, as we shall recount further on.[1] Other Ambas or
rocks as they call them [sic] are seen and found at every turn
rising from the mountains and often from the level plain,
some higher, some lower, all steep, and some so much so that
they seem to have been hacked and cut away with a pickaxe,
yet they are not highly thought of because of their lack of
water. Nevertheless in a sudden crisis they serve as a refuge
to which the neighbouring people withdraw to escape the
raids of the Gallas and other enemies.

It is wonderful to see such great columns, as it were, which
could well support the roof of this world if it were to fall
down (as Atlas was pretended to have done). Some are like
pyramids, others round at the top and at the base, others are

---

[1] In bk III, c. 9. He there describes it as follows: 'This mountain has about
a league of meadow land on top, though it is not very level, and has sufficient water for many people. Though it has three entrances they are so difficult that it looks as if, given a very small garrison, it would not be possible
to take it by force of arms. All the rest of the way round is very high, precipitous rock, as I have sometimes seen myself. The chief of these entrances
is called Ambâ Çanet, and this name is given to the whole mountain. At the
foot of this entrance was a very strong stone wall, with a gate, and thence
one climbs up for a while by a very narrow and steep path. At the end is
another gate in the rock. The 2nd entrance is called Ambâ Xembat and is
not so difficult, though still very much so. The 3rd is called Ambâ Gadabut
and is incomparably more difficult than the others, for it has no path
except some holes cut in the rock with a pickaxe, where one can climb bare-
foot with difficulty, and the rock falls away in such a manner that the
entrance can easily be defended from above with nothing but stones. It is
perhaps a musket shot from one to the other.'

like towers, others swords and others are of different shapes.[1]
Some are 200 paces high, others 600 and others 1000.

Leaving the Ambâs and rocks let us proceed to the mountains and ranges. The latter usually separate low-lying country from highlands above on a level with the crest of the range. Such are those of Asmarâ as one comes from Macuâ to Debaroâ, those of Senafeê, as one comes from Dancalŷ to Tembem, those of Cemen and Lamalmon as one goes from Tigre to Ogarâ[2] and many others which it is superfluous to name. However, because this last is well known and frequented and I have crossed it five times, I shall stop a little to describe it, so that the others can be judged by it.

Lamalmon[3]

Maegogâ, the district in which is the village or town of Fremonâ, is almost in the centre of the Kingdom of Tigre, about 45 leagues from Macuâ. Anyone coming from there to Dancâz and Dambeâ must cross Lamalmôn, after many other mountains in the desert of Syrê which, though they are high and difficult, seem very mean at the sight of this one.[4] One reaches the foot after crossing a river that runs among other smaller mountains. Those of which I am speak-

[1] 'Some are like pyramids, others like obelisks or prisms, and some, the most extraordinary of all the rest, pyramids pitched upon their points, with their base uppermost' (Bruce, bk V, c. 6).

[2] The characteristics of the mountainous region of Wagara are described in a local saying quoted by Basset, p. 423: 'Of such a kind did God make Wagara that if one enters a house one finds smoke, and on going out there is wind; when one eats corn one has wind in the stomach.'

[3] This difficult region is crossed by a magnificent Italian road cut through the rock in 1936–37.

[4] In bk X, c. 9, Almeida describes his last journey across the mountain in 1633 when he and the other Jesuits were banished to Fremona. Of the desert region north of the pass he says: 'Here begins the desert that extends about twenty-five leagues. . . . A few years ago there was no village at all in the whole of that area. Today there are many near the road. It was settled in order to get rid of the great number of robbers that there used to be in this desert, and to make use of the land for much of it produces food of all kinds in great plenty. Travellers now have a remedy against hunger; robberies, however, there still are, because the inhabitants are either brigands themselves, or else join up with them. If all the rest fail, robbery enough is done every day by the guards of the two customs posts that have been established there. . . . The boldest in these outrages are the Xagnês, people native to the neighbourhood of Maegoga. They were deported from there and came to live near the pass.' The name of these people is perhaps preserved in that of the village of Shahagaanah which Bruce mentions.

ing close in so much that, as the road runs alongside the river, it is necessary to cross it twelve times in one day's journey and another, the Zarimâ, that joins and continues with it, four times more. It is a difficult day's journey for riding animals because of the numerous pebbles of which the bed and banks of the river are full. They are very hard on animals that are unshod, as they all are in this country.[1]

After crossing the rivers of which I spoke you find yourself at the foot of a very high mountain called Dáguçâ which is like the basis and foundation of Lamalmon. This is climbed in half a day, going around it all the time as if in a spiral, along a path often so narrow that it is very frightening. As one goes up the mountain slope a large part of it is over one's head and below are such precipices that if you once stumbled and fell over that side there would be nowhere you could stop. There are many travellers, for the journey is usually made in caravans of many people, because of the robbers that abound, so that a caravan going one way often meets an oncoming one. There are innumerable donkeys and it is common for many of them to be dashed to pieces over the precipices and their loads be lost. The latter generally consist of bars of salt which is the usual merchandise going from Tigrê to Dambeâ and throughout the interior of Ethiopia.

On top of Mount Dáguçâ is a very big piece of level ground over a league round. Here the caravan rests and sleeps because the pack animals are so tired with climbing that they cannot go on the same day and climb Lamalmon. Next day one starts upon a very difficult hill like a bridge or breakwater (this shape fits it better) because it is a ridge of land frighteningly narrow and sharp, especially as it is perpendicular on either side, and both the valleys are so deep that they seem to be not much above hell.

When you have surmounted this hill you find yourself at the foot of an eminence consisting almost entirely of craggy rock; it stands out from the mountain and appears to be a very strong and tall bastion. This is the roughest part of the whole journey because, although Nature has provided some-

[1] 'Travellers themselves suffer much on that stage of the journey for, though the abundance of water gives them some relief, the heat of the sun reflected from both mountains in such a narrow place boils like an oven and it seems to be on fire' (Almeida, bk X, c. 9).

thing like a ladder winding from one side to the other, yet it is so steep that it cannot be climbed without great fatigue. They unload the pack animals because unless they have a place to steady their feet most of them cannot reach the rocks which are like steps, only sometimes two or three *covados*[1] high.

This hill is perhaps 250 to 300 paces high and on the top Nature has made a very level platform which is perhaps half a league round with a diameter of a good musket shot. It has the shape of a chair or stool without arms because the edges of the level piece are the highest part of Lamalmon and it is so sharply cut away that it seems to have been done with a pickaxe; it is all living rock. There is a village at this spot.[2] It has good water which rushes down from the top of the mountain. Here dues are exacted from the merchants on the goods they bring from the sea and from Tigrê. The caravan rests and sleeps because the pack animals are so exhausted by this part of the road that they are fit for no more that day.

From this point almost the whole of Tigrê is discovered and to the east, a chain of very high mountains which are continuous with Lamalmôn; these are the Cemen mountains. To the north-west and north are other similar ones which all form a great bow, in the centre of which the hills and mountains of Tigrê, very high though they really are, yet seem little hayricks or humble shepherds' cottages on a level plain or heath. If the Carthaginians on the summit of the Alps animated their soldiers with the charming and delectable sight of the plains of Lombardy, the sight of these mountains and ranges of Tigre might make any covetous man lose the spirit and will to conquer them, so dry, sterile and forbidding do they look, much worse, indeed, than they really are.

The country of Ogarâ is continuous with Mount Lamalmon at the same height. It is therefore very cold but well supplied with food, wheat and barley. The valleys on the

---

[1] See p. 31 n. 3.

[2] 'Here is a sizable village consisting almost entirely of market women [*sic*]. As dues are paid here, both on the salt that comes from Tigre and on all the cloth and merchandise coming from Macua, the caravans remain here for at least one day and sometimes for many. So the producers of sava, which is what is principally sold here, make a large profit' (Almeida, *loc, cit.*). 'Sava' is native beer; see note on p. 46.

Tigrê side at the foot of Lamalmon and Çemen which, as I said, is continuous with Lamalmon, are what is called collâ, which means hot country. They are very deep and as they have mountains on either side the sun is reflected in them so strongly that they seem to be an oven. Many valleys at the base of mountain ranges in Ethiopia are like this and, as I have mentioned, they are innumerable. Much cotton grows in them and some food crops proper to hot countries like *nachenim*[1] and a certain sort of millet called Zangádá.[2] Some of these regions are such that they are inhabited only by Cafres, and anyone else going there and staying for a few months, usually dies of fevers. So when the Emperor wishes to condemn people to a not very violent death he banishes them to these regions for, unless they escape, few leave them alive.

CHAPTER 9

Mines and minerals: gold, silver, iron, sulphur, saltpetre and salt

Some have written that beyond the Zebê and other rivers the ground was seen to shine so that the mountains seem to be of gold, and other exaggerations of the same kind, which are without foundation.[3] Certainly there is much gold in these regions, especially in the direction of Nareâ and in the countries that are not part of the empire but that are inhabited by Cafres, and adjoin them on the west and southwest. This gold arrives in little grains, which shows that it is found along rivers.[4] There is no other money in this country

[1] Almeida, p. 45 below, identifies this with the Amharic *dāgūsā*, which is usually described as a dwarf millet. Mr Exell considers that *Eleusine Tocussa*, Fresen., is probably meant.

[2] Amharic *zangādā*, *Eleusine multiflora*, Hochst., a small sorghum.

[3] Urreta (bk I, c. 27) has much to say about the immense riches of Abyssinia. He alleges that in some provinces, after rain has fallen, the ground shines with the grains of gold that the rain has washed.

[4] Bruce (bk VIII, c. 3) describes the gold washing done by the negroes 'bordering on Fazuclo' and then says: 'There is no such thing as mines in

except gold, by weight. If so much were not exported over-
seas this country would certainly be rich. However, gold
alone is used for buying clothing from India, carpets, silks
and Meca brocades, and all drugs, pepper, cloves and a
thousand other things that they send for to Maçuâ, Moqhâ,[1]
Iudâ[2] and Egypt in caravans which used to go by land and
stopped five or six years ago, and again the horses of the
Kingdom of Dequin, the natives of which they call Ballous.
The loss of so much gold impoverishes the country especially
as there are no mines, or at least none have been discovered.

Recently one was started in the Tembem district in the
Kingdom of Tigre and some gold from it reached the Emperor but it soon stopped, either because the workman who
allowed the vein to be blocked lacked energy and skill, or because there was none there. Lead and sulphur were taken and
are still taken from the same mine but in a small quantity because, it is generally thought, of the carelessness and lack of
skill of those in charge of the mine. In another district next
to Tigrê and near Lamalmôn, called Salemt, a considerable
quantity of silver was found a few years ago but the vein was
soon lost. That happened because of the stupidity of the
workmen, though some say that these people do not want
there to be such mines in their country in case the fame
of them should arouse the greed of the Turks and other
peoples who might come and make war to get control of
them.

There is no lack of sulphur in Tigre; there is more saltpetre
and with application it would be found more plentifully.
There is plenty of iron in all the kingdoms and in some parts
it is as good as fine steel, but as they do not know how to
temper steel they value it less. Lead too is found in consider-
any part of their country, nor any way of collecting gold but this; nor is
there any gold found in Abyssinia, however confidently this has been
advanced; neither is there gold brought into that kingdom from any other
quarter but this we are now speaking of; notwithstanding all the misrepre-
sentations of the missionaries to make the attempts to subdue this kingdom
appear more lucrative and less ridiculous to European princes.' Gold reefs
occur in Eritrea, Tigre, Amhara and in certain parts of the west—Wallaga,
the Beni Shangul country and Gimira. Alluvial gold comes from Wallaga,
Wanbera and the Harar region. Cheesman (p. 341) calls Wallaga 'the
dreamland of the gold and platinum prospector'.

[1] Mocha, in the Yemen.
[2] Jidda, the port of Mecca.

able quantity but as they do little about it they have very little of it.[1]

Salt is the commonest and most usual merchandise of Ethiopia. They have almost made it into money for in the markets all other things are generally bartered or bought for salt. It is not salt made from sea-water, but the author of nature provided some perpetual and inexhaustible mines of it in the ground. These are on the borders of the Kingdoms of Tigrê and Angot, on the side of Dancalŷ. From these rocks of salt, as it were, they cut with an axe blocks nearly a span long and nearly three inches square on each surface. Everyone carries what he can, men, donkeys and oxen, some to the nearest markets, others to other more distant ones and so it circulates through the whole empire.[2] In the first they give 80 or 100 for a *drime*[3] of gold which is worth a *pataca*,[4] in others inside Tigre they give 50, 60, in Dambeâ 25, 30, in Gojam less, in Nareâ, which is the furthest part of the empire and they do reach so far, they give 6 to 10 when there is plenty. Many blocks are broken on the way and thereby become less valuable, as when broken they are of less use for salting than when whole. It is pitiful to see the roads from Tigrê to Dambeâ all constantly full of people in caravans of

[1] The full extent of Ethiopia's mineral resources is not known. Lead is found in Tigre and iron in Eritrea, Amhara, Shoa and Wallaga; Beke states that large quantities of iron came from 'Gudera', i.e. the Gudru Galla country. Sulphur occurs in the lower Awash region and the Danakil country.

[2] Bars of rock salt, called *amolē* in Amharic, have long been used as currency in Ethiopia. They are often shaped like a whetstone, 10–12 ins. long and $1\frac{1}{2}$–$2\frac{1}{2}$ ins. thick at the widest part. Their value fluctuates. Alone in 1909 gives it as about $\frac{1}{4}$ dollar; Cheesman, p. 184, found that in 1933 it varied between 3 and 5 to a dollar. He says that when a woman goes to market and makes small purchases 'she breaks off a bit of salt and pays with that'. The salt comes from the Danakil country and according to Budge, p. 136, the name is derived from the Amole tribe of the Danakil in whose district there are large deposits of rock salt.

[3] The Arabic *dirham*, itself a corruption of *drachma*. According to an extract from Bruce's notebooks, printed in the second edition of his work as Appendix I to Books VII and VIII, in his time at Gondar it was 40 grains Troy.

[4] An old Castilian silver coin. In his notebooks, *loc. cit.*, Bruce also makes the pataca worth a 'drime' of gold; he says that in ordinary times 72 to 76 'salts' went to the 'wakea', which is Almeida's *oquea* (see p. 85), the equivalent of 10 'drimes'. In bk V, c. 2, however, Bruce gives the rate at Massawa as 16 patacas to the 'wakea' of gold.

a thousand servers (as they call the men who carry it) and 500 donkeys loaded with these blocks so that they are crushed by their burdens, because they are usually far too great. What is worse is that nearly a third of the load is taken from them on the way at different customs posts by way of dues, and many leave it all at the precipices where they fall headlong because the mountains are so rugged and the path so narrow. The donkeys that die or are left exhausted in the desert for the wolves[1] are countless.

CHAPTER 10

Fertility of the country in different kinds of food: its fruits and trees[2]

Generally speaking this country is very fertile, for in some parts it yields two or three crops a year,[3] though the energy and effort the farmers put into cultivating it is not great. In the high and cold country there is plenty of wheat and barley, in the hot country there are grains other than wheat and barley in as great quantity as wheat in our countries. There is millet of many different kinds; they reckon fifteen or twenty. There is the *nâchenim* of India, which they call Daguçâ,[4] there is Tef,[5] a food peculiar to this country and highly esteemed because it grows well and gives adequate nourishment. It is a seed so fine that a grain of mustard might be equal to ten of Tef, though it is rather long but very

[1] There are no wolves in Africa. Almeida may mean the hyaena, the Ethiopic word for which is translated 'lupus' by Ludolf, or the *canis simensis* of Samen, or, most probably, the jackal, which is very common but which he omits from his list of Abyssinian animals, on pp. 51–52.

[2] We are indebted to Mr A. W. Exell, Deputy Keeper of the Department of Botany at the British Museum (Natural History), for much assistance in translating this chapter.

[3] 'At Adowa, and all the neighbourhood, they have three harvests annually' (Bruce, bk V, c. 5).

[4] See p. 42, n. 2.

[5] Amharic *ṭĕf, Eragrostis Tef*, Zucc. Trotter, formerly known as *Eragrostis abyssinica* and *Poa abyssinica*, a grain which forms an important part of the national diet.

thin. There are many chick-peas and beans. There is another
seed they call Nug,[1] from which they extract oil like the
sesame oil of India, but tasting better; it is also used for
painting like linseed oil. The latter is found too, and they
make no use of the flax except for making thin pap in which
they moisten their *apas*.[2] There is mustard, plenty of very
good cabbages of the kind we call garden cabbages and a
vegetable like turnips and dwarf turnips that they call
uxixes and daniches.[3] It bears a flower like saffron and, like
it, this too dyes vermilion and yellow. Its seed is eaten in
other very thin paps, for these are their ordinary food.

Although there is so much food and in such plenty hunger
is common and food is often not to be had. There are many
reasons. One is that they not only eat their food but, in a
beverage like beer which they make (they call it Çalâ)[4] they
drink more than they eat in *apas*. Another reason is the
plague of locusts which in some kingdoms, like Tigrê and
others, is very constant and does not leave a grain of food
and cuts down even the stalk if it is green. Another explanation is the lawlessness with which many troops of soldiers are
always going about the whole country, eating, plundering
and looting everything. They are worse than the locusts for
the latter destroy what is in the fields, but the former what
has been gathered into the houses. Another explanation is
that they do not carry food from one district to another,
from a place where there is some to a place where there is none,
because the roads are difficult and porterage is very costly.

There are many fragrant and medicinal herbs, rue, house-
leek, dill, fennel, wild sweet basil, coriander, onions, garlic
and many purgative herbs from which our Fathers used to

---

[1] Amharic *nug*, an oil-bearing plant, *Guizotia oleifera*, DC, var. *Guizotia
abyssinica* Cass. Mr Exell points out that it belongs to the Compositae and
is not, as Guidi says in his *Vocabolario*, a leguminous plant. Parkyns (vol.
II, p. 72) calls it 'nyhoke' and compares the oil to varnish for its drying
property.

[2] A word of Dravidian origin, Anglo-Indian *hopper*, used for any round,
flat pancake, such as a chapatty. In Abyssinia they are made from un-
leavened *tef* bread.

[3] Amharic *wušiš* and *dennič*, edible roots both of which have been compared with the potato. Bruce (bk VI, c. 12) identifies the 'denitch' with the
Jerusalem artichoke.

[4] Amharic, *ṭallā*, Tigriña *sawā*.

make good pills. There are many that heal wounds; among others there is one they call Amadmagdo[1] that draws out bones that have been broken by a blow and remained inside. Another they call Assazoe[2]; it is so effective against poison that if a snake touches it or comes under its shadow it is as though it were bemused and stunned. If anyone eats the root of this herb he has the same power for many years so that a snake is as though stupefied at his shadow and he can take it in his hand without danger of its biting him. I saw a youth who had eaten this root take snakes, put them round his neck and play with them as if they were eels.

There is much cotton which grows in bushes like Indian cotton.[3] They make much cloth from it, some of it very good and fine. There is much senna, many lemons, Galicians in plenty, very sweet and big citrons, oranges, too, and some lemons like the French kind. In Dambeâ there are many fig-trees and Indian figs, and some of our Portuguese ones also grow in some parts where they have recently been sown.

Ensete[4] is a tree peculiar to this country, so like the Indian fig-tree that they can only be distinguished from very near. The trunk is so thick that two men can with difficulty embrace some of them. When it is cut at the base, 500, 700 and sometimes a thousand grow from the same one. I say cut, because it has no edible fruit. The tree itself is eaten, either sliced and boiled, or crumbled and ground into meal which they put in pits in the ground where it keeps for many years, and is taken out and made into *apas* or pap. In the Nareâ region it is the sustenance of most of the people. The trees

[1] Amharic *amadmãdo*, a plant with whitish leaves (Guidi), resembling marsh-mallow (Baeteman, *Dictionnaire Amarigna-Français*, col. 555). The virtue attributed to it recalls the power of extracting arrows ascribed by Pliny to the herb dittany.

[2] Bruce in the 'Additional articles on Natural History' in his second edition, says: 'In Abyssinia the handling of serpents without harm is known. . . . It [*sic*] is even a shrub the Abyssinians make use of.' He neither names nor describes the plant. Schweinfurth records the Tigriña plant name *waswásso*, which he identifies with a number of grasses.

[3] See p. 26, n. 1.

[4] Amharic *ensat*, the 'wild banana', now called *ensete edulis*, formerly *musa ensete*, which does not bear edible fruit; the root and lower part of the stem are eaten. It is a staple food in parts of S.W. Ethiopia, as in Enarya, Kafa and Guragē. This passage is hardly compatible with the common belief, which Bruce records, that it was introduced by the Galla.

K

grow together thickly like the Indian fig-trees but do not need to be watered. The leaves or leaf-stalks unravel like strikes of thick flax and from them very good and handsome mats are made.

There are good peaches and plenty of them especially in Dambeâ and plenty of very tall and sweet sugar-canes especially in the islands of the sea of Dambeâ, as I have already said; I did not see such good ones in India. Most of them are fruits of the jungle and monkeys [*sic*] except for grapes of which there is no shortage for sacramental wine[1] and to alleviate the fast in Lent, which comes at this time, and compensate for the shortage of fish which is great, at least for those who live at a distance from the Lake of Dambeâ; those who live near it have enough.

Generally speaking there is not much woodland in Ethiopia. In some parts, especially in Gojam, there are forests of trees of various kinds, like wild cedars, *zegbas*,[2] which closely resemble cedars, and other wild and unproductive trees. The anzâ,[3] called in India the *gundeira*, is good timber; it resembles teak and maple but few of them are found growing straight. The whole of this country is well supplied with thorn-bushes and the trees are so tall that where there are many of them together they seem to be groves of pines rather than thorn-bushes; they are used for firewood. There are many tall thickets of bamboo, which resemble those of India in nearly every way. I think, though, that they are different; the reason is that the males and females of the Indian bamboos are together, and in Ethiopia they are not. In a bamboo thicket of a league, and there are such in the hot country, not one female will be found among the males, nor a male among the females; the latter do not grow in the hot, low-lying

---

[1] An earlier Jesuit, Manoel Fernandes, had complained in a letter dated 29 July, 1562, that he and his three companions had been unable to say mass for many days because of the lack of wine, 'because there is none in the country' (Almeida, bk IV, c. 2). Bruce (bk V, c. 12) states that 'excellent strong wine' was made in Dambya but that 'the people themselves are not fond of wine'. Parkyns (vol. I, pp. 209–210) says that only at Aksum and a village in Dambya were grapes grown in sufficient quantity for the making of wine. The sacramental wine used was, he says (p. 96) merely 'an infusion of dried raisins'.

[2] Ethiopic and Amharic *zagbā*, a *Podocarpus*.

[3] Amharic *wānzā*; *cordia abyssinica* R.Br.

country, but in the cold highlands. So they are given different names here; the males are called xemel and the females carcâcâ.[1] The males are never thicker than a man's arm at the wrist; the females attain the thickness of the leg above the knee. They are both used for many purposes; from them are made houses, cross-beams for them, hampers, ladders, food-baskets and a thousand other things.

CHAPTER 11

Domestic and Wild Animals

There are all the domestic animals that there are in Europe, and many more wild ones. There are innumerable dogs, so it seems to have been a malicious joke to say there were none, as João Baltezar[2] did when he gave information and put so much fiction into the head of the man who turned it into good Spanish, if they were not vying with each other to write stories and Don Quixotes. Cats, pigs, sheep, goats, oxen and

[1] Amharic *šimal* and *qarqāha*; the latter is Bruce's 'Kirihaha' or 'Krihaha' which he says (bk VI, c. 19) is an Agau word. In the 'Additional Articles on Natural History', prepared by Murray from Bruce's notes and printed in the second edition of his *Travels*, it is said that the canes of the 'krihaha' are 'of great use in making the roofs of houses, being long, firm and light'. Almeida's remarks are, however, obscure. Dr W. O. Howarth has drawn our attention to the fact that 'all true bamboos have flowers containing both male and female parts'. He suggests that 'certain species of bamboo flower only once in a generation and therefore patches of plants of about the same age might be seeding whilst other patches of, say, younger plants would have no flowers' and that Almeida may have interpreted this phenomenon as sexual segregation. Prof. R. P. G. Pichi-Sermolli writes: 'I think that Almeida interpreted as male bamboo *Oxytenanthera abyssinica* . . . which actually grows in the low lands of the Abyssinian plateau, and is smaller in diameter, while he considered as female bamboo *Arundinaria alpina* . . . which lives in the higher lands.' Dr Hugh Scott has brought to our notice the statement in R. Jeannel, *Hautes Montagnes d'Afrique*, p. 203, that no one has ever seen the African mountain bamboo in flower.

[2] Urreta states in his preface that his convent in Valencia was visited by Juan Baltasar, an Abyssinian knight from Fatagar, who brought with him writings partly in Ethiopic and partly in Italian. He was descended from his namesake, one of the three Wise Men, all of whom had posterity living in Abyssinia. The statement about dogs will be found on p. 254.

cows in great numbers are there, for cattle are the usual form of wealth of these people. There are very big oxen and cows and the horns of the *Gueches*[1] which are big oxen, show that they do not work but are used for slaughter. They are excellent meat. Their skins are the vessels they use most often and by preference for wine as they carry them full or empty on long journeys without danger of breaking them. It is a fine thing to see the great herds of very handsome oxen and cows grazing the meadows, especially in Tigrê and among the Âgaus. The Gafates and Gallas support themselves entirely on their milk and meat, as the Gallas do not sow at all and give milk even to their horses which are made strong with it and with barley.

Donkeys are countless and are hardly used for anything else except draught, though they teach many oxen to pull carts and rich men prefer to use them. The lower classes use she-mules and he-mules as draught animals but there are many good she-mules on which the nobility and the common people generally ride. Even those who have horses do not travel on them, but on their mules and lead the horses with the right hand.[2] They use them only when meeting their enemies and when they have to follow the court and display them. The she-mules are very handsome and walk a long way and very quietly. There are plenty of good horses of high quality; the best are those that come from the Kingdom of Dequim, which belongs to Ballous or Funchos. They are very powerful horses and of a fine breed.[3] Those of Tigrê, too, are good; they are not as a rule as big as the Ballous but are of high quality, very spirited and handsome. They are like the Andalusians of Xeres.[4] There are a great number of nags and they are worth next to nothing. Their saddles are very light, firm and well-made after the style of our jennet and yet the

[1] Amharic *goš*, 'buffalo'.

[2] Cheesman (p. 37), says 'It is rare to see an Ethiopian of any standing riding anything else' but a mule, 'although they own plenty of horses and mount their escort on them.' Cf. Parkyns, vol. II, p. 31; Rassam, vol. I, p. 245.

[3] 'It seems that the strong horses of Dongola, needed for his mail-clad cavalry, passed through Berber on their way to the king of Abyssinia' (Crawford, *Fung Kingdom*, p. 53). Bruce had a Dongola horse of which he thought very highly (bk V, c. 4).

[4] Jerez de la Frontera.

pommels are higher, though the stirrups are all bastard and the leathers very long.[1]

There are many wild elephants and no tame one has ever been seen in this country,[2] but they are greatly surprised by what we tell them about those in India. There are many lions and tigers,[3] and very big ones. They rear some of them from the time when they are very small so that they are tame, though their tameness can never be much trusted. In the year 1630 a peasant killed a lion in our country in Tigrê near Maegogâ; it was eight *covados*, measured from the tail to the neck. The peasant killed it by himself, waiting for it in the meadow with no weapons except two *zargunchos*.[4] The lion was savage and had killed some people and many oxen and cows. They laid a trap for it in a large pit. The peasant saw it coming and said to his younger brother who was with him: 'You take care of yourself and get away in time. I must see what my arm and my *zarguncho* can do ; if they fail me, I have good legs!' After saying this he waited very tranquilly until the lion was within range. He then threw a *zarguncho* and pierced its shoulder. The lion, roaring and bounding, fell into the pit and he finished killing it. Foxes,

[1] The jennet saddle, of Moorish origin, was used by the light Spanish cavalry; it had a high cantle and still higher pommel. To ride *a la jineta* was to ride with very short stirrup leathers. The bastard saddle was intermediate between the jennet and the type used by the mailed cavalry. Almeida means that the Abyssinian saddle is of the jennet pattern, with an even higher pommel, but that the stirrups are of a kind not used with that saddle in Europe. The Abyssinians, like the Galla and Somali, do not insert the foot, but only the big toe into the stirrup.

[2] African elephants were tamed in small numbers in classical times. See G. Jennison, *Animals for Show and Pleasure in Ancient Rome*, pp. 196–198. Parkyns (vol. II, p. 300) records a story that the Abyssinians used to tame them.

[3] There are no tigers in Africa. Early travellers, however, were apt to assume that the two were always found together; thus Tomé Pires, *Suma Oriental*, p. 235, speaks of both in Malacca where tigers only are found. Alvares refers to tigers very frequently and some of the incidents he records show that he had seen an animal which he took to be a tiger, and was not merely repeating hearsay. Bruce (Appendix, 'Hyaena') suggests that this was the hyaena; he remarks that it can hardly have been the leopard as the latter is not common and is not gregarious, as these 'tigers' were. The omission of the hyaena from Almeida's list is otherwise difficult to explain, as it is one of the commonest and most obtrusive of Abyssinian animals. Its stripes may have contributed to the mistake. Bruce is, however, wrong in saying that the leopard is rare.

[4] See p. 76 below, where Almeida explains this word.

wolves,[1] leopards, apes and monkeys are innumerable. There are many wild cats and civet cats; this is the perfume with which they usually scent their clothes.[2] Deer, stags, gazelles, wild goats, hares and rabbits,[3] wild pigs, there are plenty of all these, for the ordinary people are not much given to hunting.

There are many other beasts and wild animals which I am passing over because there is nothing very peculiar about them. I shall end this chapter with two that are half wild and half domesticated. The first is one they call the wild ass, which is not what we call *merû*.[4] It is as big as a good she-mule, sleek, smooth and well-proportioned. It has asses' ears and because of them has earned its name. It is not domesticated though it is easy to tame, but is found only in certain forests beyond the territories now in the possession of the Gallas.[5] What is remarkable about it is the artistry with which Nature has streaked it, for a black stripe runs along to the end of its spine, and from this intersecting stripes or streaks run down to its belly on either side; some are black, some ashen and all astonishingly regular and evenly proportioned in width and length. The most remarkable thing is that these same stripes run across most parts of its body and are more or less wide in proportion to the parts; so those on the neck are narrower than those on the sides, those on the feet are smaller than those on the neck, and those on the tail and muzzle smaller still, and even the ears and lips have theirs in the requisite proportion. It is as though Nature had set herself to adorn and beautify an ass so as to take away the vainglory and abase the pride of the peacock and others who like him make the silks and brocades they wear a display

[1] See p. 45, n. 1.

[2] An extract from the anal glands of *viverra civetta* is the basis of many perfumes. It is collected in Wanbera west of Damot, in Enarya, Jimma, Guma and Gera, and in large quantities in Kafa, where the cats are kept in captivity.

[3] 'I found two kinds of hares . . . in appearance they partake so much of the hare and rabbit that I should be at a loss to decide which of the two they really were' (Parkyns, vol. II, p. 302).

[4] This name was given by the Portuguese to a horned East African animal with a cloven hoof, which was said to have a face resembling a donkey's.

[5] Grévy's zebra is found in open country in Shoa and southern Ethiopia; it is not a forest animal. It is called 'the donkey of the plain' in Amharic.

of vanity. The Emperor sent one of them as a present to a
Baxâ of Suaqhem, from whom a Moor of India bought it for
two thousand Venetians[1] to take it to the Great Mogor.
When I came into Ethiopia I arranged for the Emperor to
send another to our Baxâ who treated us well at Suaqhem;
he took it to the Grand Turk by whom he was said to have
been received and dismissed kindly because of the novelty of
such a present.

The other animal is called here Girâtacachem, which means
thin tail.[2] It is the tallest animal known on earth, for its
height is much more than an elephant's though it is not so fat
or covered with so much flesh. The forelegs are twelve spans
high, the back legs are somewhat less and the neck is in
proportion so that it can graze on the meadow grass on which
it lives. It seems to be the strutio camellus because it is more
like a camel than any other animal.[3] I have heard some men
who say they have passed underneath them on good horses.
The silks of the tail are prized because they are very lustrous
and so bracelets are made from them and worn on the arm;[4]
they are said to be very remedial.

There are almost all the birds and small birds of Europe,
the nightingale, calandra lark, wagtail, sparrow, thrush, sky-
lark and partridge, of which there are three kinds, large and
small, wild jungle fowl, the whole tribe of birds of prey,
eagles, storks, the *guincho*, the sparrow-hawk, harrier, kestrel,
buzzards and ostriches.[5]

[1] i.e. sequins.

[2] Amharic, *jerāt qačin*, 'thin tail'.

[3] *Struthiocamelus* (Pliny) was the ostrich; but this animal is the giraffe.

[4] 'The skin . . . is used by the Arabs for shields, but I am not aware of any
purpose to which it is applied in Abyssinia—probably on account of its
rarity' (Parkyns, vol. II, p. 300).

[5] *guincho, gavião, minhoto, francelho, betardas, emas. Guincho* here pro-
bably means a species of harrier; it can be used as a general term for gulls.
Betardas is the reading of the S.O.A.S. MS. Beccari, following the B.M. MS,
reads *retardas*, which is meaningless. *Ema* now means the emu. The early
Portuguese writers applied it to the rhea in Brazil and the cassowary in
Ceram; Almeida must refer to the ostrich.

CHAPTER 12

The different races inhabiting this Empire

Christians, Moors, Jews[1] and heathens inhabit this country. The latter live chiefly in Gojam, being Agaûs, Gongâs and Gafates and many Gallas to whom the Emperor himself has given much land in Gojam and Dambeâ so that they should help him in his wars against other hostile Galla tribes. There were Jews in Ethiopia from the first. Some of them were converted to the law of Christ Our Lord; others persisted in their blindness and formerly possessed many wide territories, almost the whole Kingdom of Dambeâ and the provinces of Ogarâ and Cemên. This was when the empire was much larger, but since the Gallas have been pressing in upon it, the Emperors have pressed in upon them much more and took Dambeâ and Ogarâ from them by force of arms many years ago. In Cemen, however, they defended themselves with great determination, helped by the position and the ruggedness of their mountains. Many rebels ran away and joined them till the present Emperor Seltan Çegued[2] pressed in upon them in these last years. The majority and the flower of them were killed in various attacks and the remainder surrendered or dispersed in different directions. Many of them received holy baptism but nearly all were still as much Jews as they had been before. There are many of the latter in Dambeâ and in various regions; they live by weaving cloth and by making *zargunchos*, ploughs and other iron articles, for they are great

[1] It is not known when Jews first came to Ethiopia but it is certain that, as Trimingham remarks (p. 20), 'some Jews, probably pre-exilic, did settle in Abyssinia and eventually converted pagan Agao [Agau] groups.' They are called Falasha and are Hamitic speakers, their language being called Kāylā. They practise agriculture and are found mainly in Dambya, Wagara and Samen north of Gondar. Judith, who, according to the chronicles, overthrew the Solomonian dynasty c. A.D. 911, was Queen of the Falasha.

[2] The throne name of Susneyos (1604–32), who 'in his ninth year ... made war on the Falasha Gēdēwon [Gideon] whom he conquered', and 'in his nineteenth year went into Samen, attacked the Falasha and killed Gēdēwon' (*PC*, pp. 129, 130).

smiths.[1] Between the Emperor's kingdoms and the Cafres who live next the Nile outside imperial territory, mingled together with each other are many more of these Jews who are called Faláxâs here.

The Moors live mixed with the Christians throughout the whole empire. They make up nearly a third of the population of Ethiopia, for there is no kingdom in which there are not some, and certain provinces are wholly populated by them. They live by cultivating the land and by trade. They do not allow Christians to come to the sea ports, especially those of Arabia, Moqhâ, Iudâ, Odidâ[2] and the rest, and though the former do come to Maçuâ, the Moors are better received and more welcome there, so that they are left in control of all the important trade of Ethiopia. The great and rich men of this empire all have many of these Moors as their agents, and they carry gold to the sea for them and bring them silks and clothing. As they are not very scrupulous they usually profit by their management of other people's business, so that they get fat and rich on the pickings.

All these Moors are Arabs by race and the Falaxâs or Jews are also of that race. So they both speak their native languages, the Moors Arabic and the Jews Hebrew, though it is very corrupt.[3] They have their Hebrew Bibles and sing the psalms in their synagogues. One may suppose that these Jews, whom the Abyssinians call Faláxâs, which means the

---

[1] Almeida (bk II, c. 25) relates that Zar'a Ya'qob is reported to have killed all the goldsmiths and blacksmiths as sorcerers. 'This is a common saying in Ethiopia, so much so that it is quite usual to suspect nearly all illnesses of coming from sorcerers and to attribute them to the blacksmiths. I think this came about because many of them are so, the majority of them being Jews and addicted to sorcery. Many of them pay for it, as the relatives of those who die kill them, on the suspicion of having caused their deaths by these devilish arts.' It is more likely, however, that this is due to Hamitic influence, for among many of the Hamitic and Nilo-Hamitic peoples of N.E. Africa blacksmiths are regarded with dislike and contempt, in some societies forming a distinct class with which marriage is not allowed. Among the Somali, the Tumal or Blacksmiths are considered to practise magic and witchcraft. Burton (*First Footsteps*, p. 33) confirms what Almeida says about blacksmiths in Ethiopia.

[2] Mocha, Jidda and Hodeida.

[3] Even if this was true in the seventeenth century, it is certainly not so to-day, nor was it in Bruce's time (bk II, c. 6); then, as now, their priests used the Old Testament in Ethiopic.

same as foreigners,[1] came to Ethiopia from the captivity of Shalmaneser, or afterwards when Jerusalem had been destroyed in the time of Titus and Vespasian and the Jews were expelled from Judea. As many of the Abyssinians were also Jews, descendants of those who had come with the son of Queen Sabâ and Solomon, they did not unite with them but rather treated them always as foreigners, while they always lived as such and did not obey the Emperors of this empire except when they could not do otherwise.

The other heathens and Christians have as many different languages as there are kingdoms which we have enumerated in this empire. There are many where there are very different languages even in the same kingdom, especially since the Gallas conquered many kingdoms of the empire, lying to the south-east and south, as Ogê, Fategár, Dámut, Bizamó and others. Their inhabitants have withdrawn to those that the Emperor holds. In some there are many races and different languages, as in Gojam where, within a short distance, are found one village of Dámotes,[2] another of Gafates,[3] another of Xaoâs, another of Zeites,[4] another of Xates, apart from Agaus,[5] Gongâs and others who are more native to the country and were its first inhabitants. Almost all these languages differ very much more from each other, not merely than Portuguese and Castilian, but than these do from French and Italian.[6] One there is indeed which is current and well

---

[1] Ethiopic *falāsi*, 'stranger'; in *HSD* and *CS* the name is written Falāšā.

[2] The people of Damot. See Gazetteer.

[3] See Gazetteer.

[4] The *Futuh* mentions the people of "az-Zait" (p. 224) in connection with Gafat, Damot, Enarya and Jimma. Ludolf's map places 'Zet' N.W. of Guragê and N. of the Gibē. This must refer to the Zeites of the text.

[5] A collective name for the Hamitic peoples of the central zone (see p. 1). They comprise: (i) Bilin or Bogos in the Keren region, who were Coptic Christians until about ninety years ago, but are now largely Moslems: (ii) Khamta of Abargale: (iii) Khamir in Lasta and Waj: (iv) Quara, Kemant and Kayla round the north shores of Lake Tana, the last named being the Falasha: (v) Awiya in Agaumeder, S.W. of Lake Tana and west of Damot.

[6] The Semitic languages of Ethiopia are Tigre, Tigriña and Amharic, with Harari, Argobba and the Guragê dialects outside Abyssinia proper. Ethiopic or Ge'ez is no longer spoken but is the language of the church. Tigre and Tigriña are much closer to Ethiopic than is Amharic. The grouping of the Hamitic languages has been given on pp. l, li.

understood by all noblemen and educated men and that is the Amaharâ language. Hence it is that anyone who knows this language usually finds in all parts many people who can understand him and whom he can understand.

CHAPTER 13

Appearance, Qualities and Dress of the People of Ethiopia

There could not fail to be variations in appearance and in qualities among such different kingdoms and the various races of people inhabiting them, nor can I speak of them all. I shall record the commonest and some that are strange and novel. The Abyssinians generally have well-shaped figures, good height and good facial features, spare bodies (I have seen few fat people), pointed noses and thin lips, so that the people of Europe have the advantage of them in colour but not in other things. The majority of them are black but many are dark brown, which is the colour of which they approve most, and others are ruddy, the colour of copper or brick. There are some who are whitish, but it is a bloodless white. The Ozieros,[1] who are the descendants of the royal house, and of whom there are many, both men and women, generally have large, very handsome eyes. They are brought up to a hard life, without any luxuries, for there are none at all in the country, and so they are very strong and can endure great hunger and thirst. They do not usually eat much, but drink to great excess, whether it is wine or their beer, which they call Çalâ or Saiiâ[2], which is the Tigrê name.

Almost all these people are intelligent and very good-natured. They are not cruel or bloodthirsty, but mild, gentle, kind and so inclined to forgiveness that they readily pardon any injuries. There are not many brawls among them and when there are they rarely strike with sword and *zarguncho* but end them with blows and bamboo strokes. Poison is not

[1] See p. 71.   [2] B.M. MS., *Sallâ*.

used except on the arrows of the Agaus.[1] They are very amenable to reason and justice. In any brawl or quarrel that is not satisfactorily concluded, they choose arbitrators or accept them from the lord of the soil, state their case on both sides and judgment is given. Then the guilty man's punishment most often consists only in asking pardon or, if not that, in making a payment and the brawl is then forgotten as though it had never happened. Among the Tigrês, however, if it happens that by chance someone is killed in a brawl, enmity between the relations of the dead man and the man who killed him lasts for a long time. They call it having blood between them. The dead man's is not washed away without spilling a great deal of the killer's or of his relations' and associates'.

Nevertheless they are ordinarily changeable and inconstant and so today they are with one lord and tomorrow will leave him and take another. They readily swear to any agreement and then break it as if they had not sworn. Hence arise incessant rebellions and most often, if things go badly for the rebel and his followers, they ask the Emperor's pardon and obtain it. They are soon admitted to honourable posts at court, even some who have lapsed into the crime of treason two or three times.

Their clothes are as follows. Less than fifty years ago no one but the King and a close relative or favourite of his was allowed to wear anything but breeches and a piece of cloth with which they cloak themselves,[1] and which is like a cape and at night is used as a sheet and blanket. Usually they have nothing on the bed but a skin which is the mattress underneath them and the piece of cloth of which I am speaking, which is on top and is used as a cloak in the daytime. The bolster is like a small wooden fork on which they rest, not the

---

[1] The Wayto of Lake Tana use poisoned weapons against the hippopotamus (Rüppell, vol. II, p. 223). Parkyns (vol. II, pp. 278–279) says that 'Abyssinians have a great dread of poison; they believe that many of their countrymen have considerable skill in its use. . . . It was . . . described as a powder of light-brownish colour, with which a man could be killed by a small quantity being sprinkled over a bundle of clothes and sent to him, or by its being thrown at him as he passed.'

[2] 'According to strict Abyssinian sumptuary law, no male above eight years of age . . . can wear any covering resembling a shirt over his naked body from the waist upwards, unless that garment . . . is presented to him, in the first instance, by the Sovereign' (Rassam, vol. I, p. 199).

head, which is in mid air, but the neck.[1] Today this is still the ordinary bed of the bigger and better part of the people. It is true that the latter have their *cateres*[2] fastened with leather straps, which are not bad, and they stretch out the skin of which I spoke upon them. However, the richest nobles and princes have a few coverlets of printed calico which come to them from the sea, trimmed with dimity and edged with silk. A man who has two or three of these has his bed in the reception hall, in full view, because the *cateres* are their ordinary seats too.[3] They spread the coverlets in such a way that the fringes of those underneath hang below the upper ones and all can be seen and are on show.

The Emperor has his bed from China, gilded and very handsome, which the Fathers brought him. He has it decorated with rich hangings and with very beautiful screens around it, given him by the Patriarch. On the *catere* are coverlets and blankets from India, from Dio, Cambaya, China and Bengala, and his cushions of velvet and cloth of gold. Beside it are very precious carpets of silk and skin, as well as other very big and beautiful silk ones which usually cover the greater part of the hall and sometimes the whole of it. Ras Cellâ Christôs[4] and Prince Façiladás[5] too have gilded *cateres* from China and silk canopies and hangings with good coverlets.

The breeches and cloths of which I spoke above are the dress of ordinary people today. The richest wear in preference

[1] 'It is about seven or eight inches high, and the part on which the head rests is crescent-shaped. . . . This form of pillow is very necessary to people who, from the custom of having their hair fancifully tressed and arranged and plastered with butter, could not lay their heads on any ordinary one, as they would saturate it with grease, besides seriously deranging their coiffure' (Parkyns, vol. I, p. 359).

[2] The word now means truckle-bed, and is spelt *catre*. The Abyssinian bed is described by Parkyns (vol. I, p. 358) as follows: 'It is a solid framework of wood on four legs. A fresh raw hide is cut into strips, and these are stretched over the frame in and out, one crossing the other about an inch or rather more apart. The whole tightens in drying.'

[3] 'The Emperor now has state chairs covered with velvet and studded with gilt nails, but he rarely sits on them' (Almeida, bk III, c. 4).

[4] Ras Se'ela Krestos, brother of the Emperor Susneyos, Viceroy of Gojam and one of the staunchest supporters of the Jesuits. From the title *Ras* and the first part of the name Dr Johnson coined the name 'Rasselas'.

[5] Fāsiladas, who succeeded his father in 1632, restored the national church and banished the Jesuits.

something like Baniane *cabayas*,[1] not open all the way but only to the waist and held in by tiny buttons. They have small collars and very narrow and long sleeves so they lie on the arm as if they had been folded. They call them *camizas*.[2] They usually make them of Cambaya *bofetás*[3] or of some blue cloths from there that are like fustian. They wear over them pieces of fine local cloth or *bofetás* that they sew in the middle without more ado. Some lords and richer men make these shirts of taffety or satin and damask and wear over them velvet or Meca brocade Turkish *cabayas*. Those who dress in this way do not cloak themselves with pieces of cloth any more than the Turks do. These lords' breeches are Moorish and come down to the foot, narrow and in folds. From the knee downwards they make them of damask and velvet but from there upwards, as they are under the *cabaya*, even the Emperor thinks it a waste of silk. So they make it of linen but it sometimes shows when they sit down. The common people make their breeches of thick cloth of native cotton; those who are better off make them from black or red Cambaya pieces that they call *buckram*.[4] The workmanship of these things is like that of the old slops, as wide at the bottom as at the top and very badly gathered.

Women's dress is something like a smock reaching from the neck till it drags a great deal on the ground. To me it is best represented by a sack with sleeves; I know of nothing else that resembles it more. It is very wide. They tie it at the waist with a sash and it bulges there like a great bosom. They wear or wrap their pieces of cloth over this shirt as they call it, in the way men do. Many women, who have not got so much cloth, go about with either the shirt only or the cloth only. The poorest have no pieces of cloth except dressed ox skins or even skins with the hair on but tanned till they are soft. Many women in Gojam and Dambeâ wear them, even those who are not very poor. In Tigrê, however, they wear

---

[1] A 'surcoat, or long tunic of muslin' (*Hobson-Jobson*).

[2] An Arabic word borrowed by the Abyssinians for a long shirt, Amharic *qamis*.

[3] 'A kind of calico' (*Hobson-Jobson*). The word, in origin a Persian participle meaning 'woven', was still in use in Rüppell's time for a smooth, white cotton stuff (vol. I, p. 282); Amharic *bufetā*, calico or muslin.

[4] *Bocaxim*.

something like shawls of sheep's wool or goat's hair, but so badly tanned and cured that it is more like hair than wool and is a rough hair shirt. Ladies wear the smocks of which I spoke, made from *bofetá* or silk with others of white cloth underneath. They cloak themselves with *bofetas* as the men do, or with silk cloths. As all these are very wide and long they are well wrapped up if not well dressed, for here elegance consists in wearing a great deal of cloth and silk. They do not pay much attention to cut and design.

I have spoken about dress and I must speak about their hair, which is what men and women mostly use for covering their heads and on which they pride themselves highly. They allow it to grow but it does not grow much and as it is curly and fine it is fit for anything and they have many styles of dressing it. Women usually leave loose and lift up the hair that remains on the head. The rest hangs from all parts of the head and over the neck in many little plaits. They soak it in unrefined butter which seems an odd perfume to us. Men, especially youths, are worse about this for they have more styles than women and spend more time in contriving them. Every day and every hour they are arranging them. Now they leave it like a thicket or tangle which makes them horrible, now they make it into little horns, now into ribbons, now into sprays, and so on in as many fashions as idleness teaches them, for as they usually have nothing to do they waste a large part of the day in this.[1] Men of more advanced age, however, and those who are getting old cut or shave their hair and use round, red caps after the fashion of priests; it seems that they copied them from those they saw our Fathers wearing. Rich men have these caps worked for them in silk and gold by Turkish tailors, for there are no others here, and there are very few of them. As the clothes we have mentioned are so simply made, in the ordinary way everyone makes what he wears.

The people who dress best in Ethiopia, who are the Vice-

[1] Parkyns (vol. II, p. 27) observes that Abyssinian hair grows long enough to tress well but is sufficiently woolly to remain set for a long while; he had great difficulty in dressing his own hair in the same way. 'The operation of tressing is a very tedious one, usually occupying an hour or two per head. . . . In both sexes the patterns chosen are various. Some will have only five or seven plaits, while others will prefer as many as thirty or more.'

roys and nobles who are constantly at the Emperor's court, dress in Turkish style. This costume is elaborate and these nobles put on their necks their gold chains which are like what we call skeins with many turns of yarn wound round them. On their arms they put bracelets of the same and their swords which are very large, have scabbards covered with silver. They wear girdles or sashes of very big pieces of gold and so the court, when it is in festival, is brilliant and sumptuous enough.

CHAPTER 14

Communal Customs of the Abyssinians about Circumcision and the Table

All the people of these countries, Jews, Moors, Christians and heathens are circumcised.[1] The first, because their sects command it, the heathens through contact with their neighbours and so that others should not insult them by calling them uncircumcised, and the Christians because, as will be said later, they formerly observed the law of Moses and after they had accepted Christ our Lord's they seem never to have discarded Judaism entirely. So women at the time of menstruation used not to enter their churches and they did not take babies to be baptised for 40 days if male and 80 if female, nor did they baptise them before that time even in case of necessity.[2] It will be apparent from this how many souls have lost Heaven through this error in the course of so many hundreds of years. Today, after they have received the holy Roman faith, one of the things they cannot be persuaded to do is to abandon circumcision. They say they do not do it to keep the law of Moses but only for elegance. Great folly or blindness!

As they ordinarily sit on the ground, the great nobles on

[1] According to Rüppell (vol. II, p. 205), the Wayto of Lake Tana, though nominally Moslems, were not circumcised, but this is no longer so. See p. 35, n. 4.

[2] Parkyns (vol. II, p. 38) was told that Adam and Eve did not receive the Holy Spirit for 40 and 80 days respectively after they had been created. He was also told that a child might be baptised sooner if absolutely necessary.

carpets and the rest on mats, their tables are all low and round. They have neither tablecloths nor napkins on them. They wipe their hands on the *apas* that they eat; the table is full of them in houses where there are plenty. They put the food on them, without using plates, if it is raw or roast meat. If it is a stew of chicken or mutton or their staple fare, which is a kind of thin pap in which they moisten their *apas*, made from the meal of different pulses, such as lentils, chickpeas, linseed and others peculiar to this country, all this comes in bowls of black clay. This is the dinner service of poor and rich so that down to our own times nothing better was seen even on the table of the Emperor himself. Two or three years ago, however, he ordered a dozen silver plates to be made and he sometimes uses them. One Viceroy, the richest man there is in the empire today, has made as many more. The bowls come in covered with Escambiás. That is what they call some things like caps or hats of fine straw, like the straw of the straw hats of the Melinde coast, which they put on top.

Beef they eat raw, calling it Berindô[1] and it is the food they esteem most highly. They put a great deal of salt and pepper on it, if they have the pepper, and the most important people who can have the gall of the animal that is killed, squeeze it by hitting it often on the piece in front of them so the meat should soak it up well; they claim that it gives it a great relish. This is their mustard, though mustard itself is found in the country. They make another more peculiar dish from the soft matter inside certain thin entrails with their salt and pepper.[2] It is a dish for princes and they would not abandon

---

[1] Amharic *berendo*, 'raw meat'. The practice ascribed to them by Bruce of cutting the flesh from the living animal has been denied, or regarded as no more than an occasional possibility, by most travellers. Parkyns (vol. I, p. 376) says that the only animals eaten raw are the cow, certain varieties of gazelle and antelope and, in some districts, the goat. Raw meat banquets are a feature of Ethiopian hospitality; provincial governors and great personages used to entertain up to 3000 or more people at a time to feasts of raw meat. The meat is cut off the animal immediately after it has been killed and is eaten at once. This results in a universal and more or less constant infestation of tapeworms among the Ethiopians who dose themselves periodically with a vermifuge, *kosso* (see p. 98). (Cf. Rey, pp. 109–111.)

[2] 'The "mantay hàmot" or "chogera", is a dish prepared of the tripe and liver cut into small pieces. The contents of the gall-bladder are then squeezed over it, as also a part of the half-digested green matter found in the intestines of the animal' (Parkyns, vol. I, pp. 376–377).

L

it for any other. A Portuguese once had many lords as guests. The marrow of the entrails of a cow that he had killed were not sufficient for the dish. In order to provide for them, he sent early to the yard and had the dish made with the fresh dung that was found there. No one thought it strange at the table but afterwards, when they knew what had happened, the guests considered themselves aggrieved and sued the Portuguese before the Emperor Malaac Sagued. He defended himself on the grounds of the number of guests and by saying that he had mixed it so well that they had not thought it strange at the table. The affair passed off as a joke and the use of the dish was condemned at the time, but it was not therefore banished from the empire or from the imperial table.

Simple as this food seems it is no small labour to prepare it in Ethiopia, primarily because they have no mills to grind the meal. It is all ground by hand and it is women's work; men, even slaves, would not grind at any price. The grindstones are big stones, the lower wide and the upper nearly round and easily handled. A woman grinds every day enough for 40 or 50 *apas*. These have to be made daily because on the second day they are already unfit to eat. Grinding meal and making *apas*, grinding more for the *savâ* or beer they drink (which uses up a great deal of meal) and making that, all this is work that calls for many slave women and plenty of firewood and is very great drudgery. These are the mills about which some-one else said, as a proof of his grandeur, that the Emperor took five hundred of them with his army. It was very much an understatement for he could have said there were three thousand, but it can easily be seen that all this is penury rather than grandeur.

The wine they drink is made from honey. Five or six parts of water and one of honey are put into a pot with a handful of toasted barley which makes it ferment. Afterwards they add some morsels of a certain wood they call Sadô, which draws out the sweetness, and in five or six days it is ready to drink.[1] It has not the taste of our grape wine but its wholesomeness undoubtedly gives it an advantage. These people have one

---

[1] *Sado* is Amharic *ṣaddo*, or *ṭaddo*, the shrub *Rhamnus tsaddo*. Parkyns (vol. I, p. 383) gives a recipe but says nothing of the toasted barley.

great vice which is that they are much addicted to wine. They do not drink while eating[1] but when the table is cleared the *calões* are brought into the house and neighbours or friends assemble. In noblemen's houses and in the Emperor's many guests are always invited. There is no conversation without the wine circulating and being drunk in turns until either they are laid out on the spot or else withdraw so much warmed up that they cannot easily find the door. They achieve this by drinking to such excess that no one knows how they can hold so much. The wine is really very mild and if it were drunk in moderation no harm could be done.

CHAPTER 15

Weddings and Burials

Until our own time weddings among the Abyssinians were of such a kind that there was never true marriage between them, because they married with the tacit or expressed agreement to dissolve it as soon as the husband and wife disagreed with one another.[2] For this reason they used to exchange guarantors with certain rather peculiar and barbarous customs, for these people, who were together like paranymphs, had to be almost eye-witnesses of the consummation of the marriage. The disputes on account of which they used to separate and dissolve the marriage were caused either by one of the married couple's unfaithfulness to the other, or by quarrels

[1] 'The Abyssinians say, you must plant first and then water; nobody, therefore, drinks till they have finished eating' (Bruce, bk VI, c. 3).

[2] This statement concerns the practice of cohabitation when a man and woman decide to live together and separate at will. There is also a civil marriage before a *šum*, with a contract covering the division of property in case of divorce, which can be at the instance of either husband or wife. Marriage with a religious ceremony is indissoluble and is used mainly by better class people (Rey, p. 69). Bruce (bk IV, 'Yasous I') writes as though there were no civil or religious marriages at all. He recalls having been in the company of a lady 'of great quality' and seven men who all had been her husbands. According to Parkyns (vol. II, p. 59), religious marriages are rarely solemnised except between elderly persons who have lived happily for many years after a civil marriage.

between the two of them. When on the point of breaking their faith they were easily reconciled, for if the husband proved to the wife, or she proved to her husband, that adultery had been committed, they were most often reconciled and became friends, provided one of them paid the other out of his or her own property what was adjudged sufficient compensation for the injury. This was possible because usually both husband and wife keep their own property and even the lands they own (especially if they belong to the nobility) wholly separate so that one of them does not interfere with or give orders about the other's. Both are fed and clothed from their own property. They support their servants in the same way so that neither the kitchen nor the table is common to them both. If they eat together they both have brought to the table the food they have provided themselves. When, then, one of them has been found guilty of adultery they easily agree that the guilty party should pay the other some oxen, cows, mules, pieces of cloth, etc.

However, when they disagree and are so disgusted with each other and quarrel so much that they come to hate one another and want to separate entirely, then they appear before the judge. So long as the case is being heard (being verbal, they do not last many days) the woman is in the judge's keeping and in his house with such an immediate and pressing opportunity for licentious conduct with him that even that is not thought strange. The judge gives sentence that as they quarrel and have no affection for each other, she is free from such a husband and he is without obligation to such a wife, and that they can marry again whomsoever they please. This abuse has lasted for so many hundreds of years and was so rooted in this country that it was, and still is today, a great obstacle to the holy faith which has been generally accepted.

They mourn their dead, lamenting loudly and for many days. They begin the lament long before dawn and it lasts until broad daylight, parents, children, relations and friends of the dead man assembling with many female mourners who lament to the sound of the drum, striking together the palms of their hands, beating their breasts and uttering heart-

breaking lamentations in melancholy tones.[1] They bring to
the place of mourning the dead man's horse, if he had one,
his lance, his pennons, if he was a captain, his shield, his
sword, his rich clothing, his gold chains and his necklace and
show each object to everyone saying such things that it is
impossible to keep back one's tears. These seem to be the
lamentations that Holy Scripture says the Jews made for
Jacob and others (Gen. 50, Deuter. 34) and they clearly show
that they inherited them from their fathers and grandfathers.
They bury their dead in churches and the clergy read the
psalms and certain prayers for them.[2] Their possessions are
offered to the churches on their behalf and they give alms to
the clergy and to many poor people for the souls of the dead,
killing and dividing up cattle for them with many *apas* and
much wine and *sava*. This is on the 3rd, 7th, 30th, 40th days
and a year after death.[3] In spite of all this they used to deny
the existence of Purgatory, but they were convinced by this
argument ad hominem.

They have one rather peculiar custom in this connection.
It is that when they hear the news of the death of a relation,
or of a master, or of a son or daughter of a master, they suddenly throw themselves on the ground. Some of them do it in
such a way that they die from it, and others are left maimed
or lame or with broken arms, hands or legs for many months;
I have known and seen many such persons. Those who do not
hurl themselves on the ground like this are thought to have
little affection for the dead or their parents, children or
brothers. The Gafates, instead of throwing themselves on the
ground, give themselves very large wounds in the head and
arms. Generally speaking they all scratch their faces, women
on their husbands' deaths, children on their parents' and

[1] 'Professional singing women frequently attend the funeral meetings of
great people, and sometimes get a handsome present as a reward for their
services; but many go in the hope of getting well fed at the feasting which
takes place after the ceremony' (Parkyns, vol. II, p. 64).

[2] Parkyns (vol. II, p. 61) says that all the psalms, of which the Ethiopic
Bible contains 151, are read together with portions of the New Testament; each priest and *dabtara* has a passage to read and all read at
once.

[3] Parkyns (vol. I, p. 63) states that masses are said for rich men for 40
days after the death, and for poor men on the 3rd, 7th, 12th, 30th and 40th
days, and for everyone on the first anniversary.

others on their friends', so that they are raw and blood flows freely.[1] This is something we used to see every day.

CHAPTER 16

The Women whom the Abyssinian Emperors marry and the ceremonial they observe in receiving and proclaiming them as such.

In the first place one should know that the custom the Emperors of Ethiopia have always followed of having many wives who are held and considered to be legitimate, besides others who had no better title than concubine, is so ancient and inveterate that Menilehec[2] seems to have learnt it from his father Solomon. When they were converted to the faith of Christ our Lord, the people of this country did not abandon many Jewish customs. On the contrary they still keep them today with such obstinacy that it is one of the greatest difficulties that the holy Catholic faith has with them. (As we said above and as we shall say below more fully, bk. 6 ch. 6) they will not abandon circumcision and that on the 8th day; they postpone the baptism of males for 40 days and of females for 80 because they do not come to church until the days of purification are completed, in conformity with the law of Moses, nor do women enter churches at the time of menstruation, nor do men after nocturnal pollution; it is the greatest abomination to talk to them about eating hare or rabbit, etc. So it has happened that till this day they know of no Emperor who has abandoned the custom of having many wives. About the Emperor Onag Sagued, who was at first called David, in whose time Francisco Alvrez came to this country, he said he had not many. Either he was misinformed or if at first he did not have many, because he was a young man, he certainly had many after-

[1] 'The nearer relatives of the dead, both male and female ... rub themselves so severely on the forehead and temples as to abrade the skin completely' (Parkyns, *loc. cit.*).

[2] Menilek, the supposed son of Solomon and the Queen of Sheba.

wards. On the contrary I have sometimes heard from Ras Cellá Christos, brother of the Emperor Seltan Cagued, that he had some heathen wives and that, to please them he had, like his ancestor Solomon, gone so far as to have idols in his palace so that on one side was the church of God and Our Lady the Virgin and on the other the house of the idol.[1]

As for the Emperors' marrying daughters of Moorish and heathen Kings and lords after baptising them first, this was so common that even King Jacobo[2] took the daughter of the Moorish King of Hadeâ in order to marry her, and was treating her as his wife already, but he died before he had gone as far as marrying her. Father Pero Paez who then frequented the court is witness of this.

The women they usually married were daughters of vassals, but of noble families, of which there are many in Tigrê and some other kingdoms, though sometimes they paid no attention to noble birth but only to good character and charm, for they say that the King gains nothing from his wife's noble birth while her great fortune in being chosen to be the Emperor's wife is sufficient nobility for her. When one of these ladies had been chosen, she was summoned to court. There she was placed in the house of one of the Emperor's female relatives so that he could inform himself more closely and positively about her good qualities. As soon as he was satisfied about them she and the Emperor used to go to church one Sunday to hear mass and communicate, for which the whole court was in fête. From the church they both came to the palace where the Abbuna[3] used to bless them. Afterwards the Emperor ate at his own table alone, as he always did, without being seen by anyone. The Queen ate in another house with many ladies and in others a great banquet was

---

[1] Almeida (bk III, c. 7) attributes the disasters of the later years of his reign, the Moslem and Galla invasions, to these sins; he compares Samson and Delilah, Roderic the Goth and Count Julian's daughter, and Henry VIII and Anne Boleyn.

[2] Yā'qob, Malak Sagad II, who reigned for less than a year in 1604.

[3] *Abuna*, the Metropolitan of Ethiopia, who is ordained by the Coptic Patriarch of Alexandria. By an apocryphal canon of the Council of Nicaea, which was accepted until very recently, he must not be a native of Ethiopia. This has, however, been abrogated by a recent agreement and the present Abuna, who succeeded in 1950, is an Ethiopian. The term is also applied to high church dignitaries and holy men,

given to the clergy and Debteras. This is so far as eating is concerned for they all meet to drink always, and this happens every day though on the principal festivals there is more wine and there are more guests. The custom is that many jars of wine are placed in the centre of the imperial hall resting on a kind of not very tall wicker chairs so as to allow the wine to be poured out. The goblets and drinking cups circulate, beginning with the Emperor and the Queen. The rest follow in accordance with their rank. Talking goes on with the drinking, sometimes with the goblet in hand, and stories are told as long as the wine lasts. When that is finished all conversation ceases. In the royal hall, however, it does not usually fail until far into the night, and the party ends only with sleep; sometimes everyone falls down in his place.

The wedding and the bridal feast are then concluded, but the Queen does not yet have the title of Iteguê,[1] which is Her Highness or Majesty. She receives this title some days or months afterwards. When the Emperor wants to give it to her the Queen comes from her house to the palace (for the Queen's house is always separate and in another different enclosure, although next to the Emperor's). She takes her seat next to the Emperor's throne, which is his *catere*, in a rather tall tent. There they robe her in rich clothes. One of the greatest dignitaries of the court then comes on to the dais, stands on a seat as though he were making a proclamation, and says these words in a loud voice: Anagasna danguecerachem,[2] which mean 'We have made our slave to reign'. Everyone present replies with shouts like our 'Vivas'. Thereafter she is honoured as Iteguê.

It is worth noting that as long as the Emperor's mother is alive, if she was Queen and the deceased Emperor's wife, then the wife of the Emperor actually reigning is not called Itegue. The honour always belongs to the old queen, so much so that not only the new Emperor's wives, but he himself, even if he is not her son, calls her mother and behaves to her and honours her as if she really were so.

They never put a crown on her nor has it ever been the

[1] Ethiopic *Itēgē*, 'Her Majesty'.

[2] Amharic *anaggasna dangasrāčin*. Bruce's account (bk V, c. 11) agrees with Almeida's except that he says that the Empress is crowned, which Almeida denies.

custom for any Queen of Ethiopia, nor do the Emperors use a sceptre. Some have said that the cross was the sceptre of the Emperors of Ethiopia, but this was a mistake. Although they used to carry a small cross in the hand,[1] they did not carry it as a sign of empire but as a sign that they were deacons, an order which they all, and most of the lords, entered so as not to remain outside the curtains or chapels, as the laity always do and where they always communicate, but be able to go inside and communicate with the clergy.

It is worth noting here that the Emperor never marries a lady who is of imperial blood or family, whom they call Oizieros.[2] These are all considered to be daughters or sisters of the Emperors, as they are of the blood and lineage of David, even if they are in the tenth or twentieth degree of consanguinity. It may further be remarked that it was a baseless fabrication to say, as one person did, that there were in Ethiopia descendants of the Magian Kings and that the Emperors always married ladies of their race and no others. When they have been asked, the oldest and best informed men of this country have averred that they have never read or heard tell that there were such families in any part of this empire.[3] On the contrary they all aver that they know nothing about the Magian Kings except what is written in St Matthew's Gospel.

The formula of the proclamation: *We have made our slave to reign* will seem strange to any foreigner. In Ethiopia, however, it is so much in use that every time the Emperor bestows an office (which they call Xumete)[4] on anyone, even if it is one of his brothers, the honour is always accompanied by this fly in the ointment: *We have made our slave so-and-so Viceroy or Governor of such and such a Kingdom or of such and such territories.* This is the formula of the proclamation. It is related of one Portuguese that when he received one of these honours from the Emperor and the herald was going to deliver the proclamation, he promised him a great deal of money not to say *our slave* but 'so-and-so' instead. The

---

[1] This fact was of great interest to the Portuguese because it was one of the characteristics ascribed to Prester John by mediaeval writers.
[2] Amharic *wayzaro*, 'Princess,' later extended to any lady of rank.
[3] Urreta, p. 171. Cf. p. 49, n. 2.
[4] Amharic *šumat*, office of the *šum*.

herald did not dare to do it. The reason is that the Emperor considers them all slaves and they are not insulted by it.

CHAPTER 17

Government of the Abyssinian Empire

There is only one King who rules and governs in the countries and kingdoms that we said belonged to this empire. Today he has no King under him since the Moorish King of Dancaly and the heathen King of Gingirô, besides being very petty kings, are not strictly speaking his subjects, though they have due respect for, and give some recognition to such a great and mighty neighbour. He confiscates and grants all the lands as and to whom he chooses, though there are some, chiefly in Tigrê, the lordship and government of which he does not take away from the families and descendants of their first owners.[1] Such are the lands of the Barnagaes,[2] Xumos or governors of Seraoê, Syrê, Tembem and many other places. The office of Cantiba[3] in Dambeâ is of this kind. It never passes from the race and descendants of the former lords who used to own and govern it. But as I say the Emperor takes away these posts from some, and makes changes, and gives them to others of the same families, every two years and sometimes every year, and even every six months.

The worst thing is that these and the other governorships of all his kingdoms and provinces seem to be sold rather than given. No one receives them except by giving for them an amount of gold which is more or less the income and profit

[1] 'All the land is the king's; he gives it to whom he pleases during pleasure, and resumes it when it is his will. . . . By the death of every present owner, his possessions, however long enjoyed, revert to the king, and do not fall to the eldest son. It is by proclamation the possession and property is reconveyed to the heir' (Bruce, bk III, 'Socinios').

[2] Ethiopic *bāhrnagāš*, the title of the governor of northern Abyssinia, literally 'lord of the sea'. His capital was at Debarwa. The office had lost much of its importance by Almeida's time; it finally lapsed in the nineteenth century.

[3] *kantibā*, the title of the rulers of Hamasen, and at one time of Dambya; now an honorary title, given also the the Mayor of Addis Ababa (Baeteman, *Dict.*, col. 705).

the aspirant and applicant hopes to get from them. As there are always many applicants[1] those who give most for them usually receive them. They give much more than they can honestly derive from them, and so as not to be at a loss, they fleece the people, disposing of the lesser offices and the governorships of particular places and territories to those who promise and give most in return for them. So it is all merely an auction. Since these governors are the lords and judges and hold in their hands absolute control over the lives and property of the whole population, generally speaking, they are all plunderers rather than governors.

It is true that, while their government of the kingdom or province lasts, it is possible to appeal from their jurisdiction to the tribunals of the court and to the Emperor, but there are few who dare to appeal. It is as good as declaring themselves enemies of the Governor or Viceroy acto regente, and they are afraid that he may look for some pretended and very plausible pretext to destroy them. When his governorship is taken away from him, or his time is completed, is the time for poor persons to make their complaints about him and for them to be heard on the subject of his injustices to them. All those whose terms of office are coming to an end, either by intercessors or bribes, which are always worth more and can do more than anything else, usually procure from the Emperor an order for the issue of a proclamation to the effect that no one can sue them for anything that they or their servants have done. With this exemption and plenary indulgence all the robberies and acts of violence they have committed against property and against women, married and betrothed, are consigned to oblivion as though they had never been committed. This is the account to which they are called. It is so well established that they do not consider it sinful and this abuse has still not been removed today. Anyone who is shocked by it is told that this has always been the way their country has been governed and that there would be widespread rebellions if any other were introduced.

Under the Emperor there was formerly a dignitary whom they used to call Betêudet,[1] which is equivalent to favourite or confidant, by antonomasia. There were two who had this

---

[1] Amharic *bētwaddad*, 'high chamberlain'.

dignity, one of the left hand and the other of the right. Almost the entire government rested with these two men for the King did not discuss anything with anyone, or give audience or even allow himself to be seen, except by very few people. Those two Beteudetes had everything in their hands. It is now some years since the Emperors have been less muffled and have allowed themselves to be seen by and conversed with by everybody. They then saw that that office was an undesirable one for the two Beteudetes were the kings and the King was one in name only. So they abolished it and created another in its place which they called Ras,[1] which means head, for he who has that position is, under the King, head of all the great men of the empire. He is the chief counsellor and minister both in peace and war, though he applies himself more to the latter and is usually generalissimo in the more important wars.

Under this is another post they call Bellatinoche goitâ,[2] which means master of the servants, because he is like a Mordomo Mor[3] and has the governorship and authority over all the Viceroys, captains, Xumos or governors, and over the Azagês and Ombares, who are the *desembargadors* and *ouvidors*[4] of the empire. In the palace and court there is another whom they call Tecácan[5] Bellatinoche goita, meaning master of the lower servants, or lesser Mordomo Mor, who has control of the ordinary pages, equerries and stable boys, who are very insignificant people and of low degree. As for the Emperor's house servants, I say nothing of their being

---

[1] This office no longer exists. The word is still in use as a title but it is more freely bestowed than it was in Almeida's day.

[2] Amharic *blāttēn gētā*, literally 'master of the pages', the Grand Chamberlain; *blāttēnoč* is the plural.

[3] The head of the Royal household.

[4] *Azage* is Ethiopic *azāzi*, Amharic *azāj*, the title of the four supreme judges of the Emperor's tribunal. *Ombare* is Amharic *wambar*, an appellate judge at provincial capitals or the Emperor's court. In Portugal the *desembargador* was originally a special commissioner appointed to assist the King in the discharge of business of a judicial or semi-judicial kind, such as granting pardons, licences or privileges. The *ouvidor* was a judge of the King's Tribunal who heard appeals from lower courts and acted as a judge of first instance in cases involving persons of a certain status. In their relation to the King and to the lower courts the parallel with Ethiopian practice is close.

[5] Amharic *teqāqen*, 'assistant', lit. 'small'.

Kings' sons, as someone else has pretended they are, for there are none in the empire, but they are not even the sons of ordinary respectable men, but only captive slaves of different races, some Agaus, others Gongâs, others Cafres or Ballous. Yet he often makes these men Xumos and raises them to the greatest offices of the court and this is not thought reprehensible. The Emperor says that he finds that only these men, whom he has in this way created and made from dust and earth, are faithful to him, although not all of them are, but they seem to be more so than others.

Under the great Bellâtinoche goitâ are all the other Viceroys and governors of kingdoms and provinces and the ordinary captains of the Emperor's camp, who are those of the vanguard, the rearguard, the right hand and the left; so they call what we call the right and left wings. There are also the tribunals and magistrates, the chief of whom is the chief of the Azages who seem to correspond to our *desembargadors* though they are not, as among us, divided into those of the palace, of criminal and of civil cases. There are only some of the right hand and some of the left. Under them are the Ombares, which means chairs, because the plaintiff and defendant stand while these men sit in their chairs. To them, if they belong to the court, comes the appeal in any civil or criminal case in the whole empire, and in the first instance, cases from the court or camp, which is the same thing in this empire. They too are of the right and left hand. From them the appeal lies to the Azagês and from them to the King. If the Ombares do not belong to the court then an appeal lies from them to those who do.

No suit is drawn up in writing. They are all begun and finished verbally, and no witnesses are heard except the plaintiff's, so that he is usually successful, since he produces the witnesses he wants. It is true that the defendant can cast suspicion on them, and he does on those he can, but as the case is decided on them only, it gives a great advantage to those who buy them without fear of God for what they ask; there are many to be had, for any purpose, and very cheaply.

The judges order a convicted murderer to be handed over to the relatives, children or wife of the dead man, a custom that like many others, comes down to them from the Jews.

They, if they wish, spare his life in return for goods that he gives them; if not they kill him at their pleasure and by the death they think fit. If it is not established who the murderer was, the inhabitants and neighbours of the place where death occurred are dragged in, and a large quantity of goods is taken from them all, the just man paying for the guilty. Yet it is certain that fear of this punishment prevents many deaths.

CHAPTER 18

Soldiery of the Abyssinians

Generally speaking it can be said that the Abyssinians are good troops; they sit a horse well, are quite strong and healthy and are brought up and inured to toil, enduring hunger and thirst as much as can be imagined, and so they continue in the field for the greater part of the year, suffering all the discomfort and inclemency of sun, cold and rain and with very little food. In war they are reared as children, in war they grow old, for the life of all who are not farmers is war. So that they should follow soldiering and continue to do so the Emperor grants them the lands on which they live and which they enjoy inasmuch as they serve him. As soon as they fail him he gives the lands to others. This and nothing else, is their pay. Hence it arises that the Emperor assembles a large army without much expense.

The arms they use are *zargunchos* which are a kind of half-length lances that have thin hafts and irons that are sometimes narrow, like those of our lances, sometimes broad like halberds but thin so that they can be thrown vigorously against some and manoeuvred against others, in the way they do, brandishing it with one hand only while they manipulate the shield with the other. They make shields of the skin of the wild buffalo, very strong and firm.[1] Every soldier usually

---

[1] 'The shields are round, and nearly a yard in diameter: they are very neatly made of buffalo's hide' (Parkyns, vol. II, p. 17).

carries two *zargunchos*, one of the narrow sort that is thrown in the first encounter with great force so that it pierces mail and shields, and another, broader one with which they continue the fight, as sword and shield are used among us.[1] The men of highest rank have swords but they rarely use them except in peace time for appearance sake. They also carry certain clubs of hard and heavy wood that they call Bolotâs,[2] and their daggers or short swords that they use when they come to close quarters, and to struggling with each other; they also throw them.

The horsemen strike and fight only with short lances in the style of our javelins. Those who have coats of mail, and they are not many, do not trouble themselves with the shield so as to be less encumbered. They do, however, carry some narrow *zargunchos* to throw like darts. Today muskets too are found in this country but there are few who would be able to shoot well with them.

When he musters his forces the Emperor puts into the field thirty to forty thousand soldiers, four or five thousand on horseback and the rest on foot. Of the horses up to one thousand five hundred may be jennets of quality, some of them very handsome and strong, the rest jades and nags. Of these horsemen as many as 700 or 800 wear coats of mail and helmets. All the rest of them, whether on foot or horseback have no arms except what I mentioned above, *zarguncho* and shield. They have more than one thousand five hundred muskets, but not more than 400 or 500 musketeers are found on expeditions and most of them have so little skill that they cannot fire more than once in any action.[3] It cannot be other-

[1] Parkyns (vol. II, p. 21) describes them as 'for the most part very neatly made. . . . Their usual length is 6 feet 6 inches, including the staff. . . . They use, however, lighter ones, principally for throwing. . . . Some of the soldiers, especially horsemen, carry two spears when in action; one of which they throw from a distance, and retain the other in the hand for close encounter.' Bruce (bk VII, c. 5) describes the Shoan cavalry at the Battle of 'Serbraxos' (Sārbākusā, the Serbugsa of ND 37/4 HEK), as each armed with a lance about 10 ft long and two light javelins with shafts of cane, which they threw from a great distance.

[2] Amharic *balotā, bilotā, bolotā*, 'club'. The word occurs in *HSD*, p. 104 (text).

[3] 'I do not imagine that any king of Abyssinia ever commanded 40,000 effective men at any time, or upon any cause whatever, exclusive of his household troops' (Bruce, bk V, c. 11). He estimates the latter at some 8000

wise for gunpowder and balls are so scarce that there are not many who have enough to practise four shots at a target now and again in the year. Some of the grandees do it from time to time but then only upon a rest. As in action against the Gallas and other enemies there is not time to use it, what they have learnt to do with it is of little value to them.

So, as there is not the military discipline of Europe and other countries and the armies and squadrons do not open and close in such order, battles begin and end with the first onset, for one or the other side shows its heels and the other follows up victory. Flight is not much decried because it is a common and everyday thing.

The number of men at arms I mentioned, even if it should be less, makes an excessively big camp because the camp followers and the baggage train amount to many more than the soldiery. The reason is that usually there are more women than men in the camp. Besides the King's being accompanied by the Queen and all or nearly all the ladies who are usually at court, widows, married ladies and even many unmarried ones, and the wives of the chief lords and captains, so that they go to war with their households and families, besides this, every soldier has one or many. The King does not feed them and in Ethiopia there is no biscuit and other food that keeps for many days. They have to make their *apas* every day and for that they must grind meal, which is entirely women's work as I have said. For great men the honey wine they drink goes on being made and there have to be many women to carry it, though many people take it in big horns, as I said above, which travel on baggage oxen. As, however, it is all very quickly used up many women go along with *calões* of honey for making a fresh supply.[1] Besides this there is the great throng of Atârîs[2] who are wine and *sava* tapsters and at the same time merchants selling cloth and other

infantry, 2000 of whom had firelocks. The whole muster of the royal army at Sarbakusa he gives as 'nearly 7000 musketeers, 25,000 foot, armed with lances and shields, and about 7500 horsemen.' Parkyns (vol. II, pp. 23–24) calls them 'exceedingly clumsy' in using firearms and gives an entertaining account of their performance.

[1] According to Bruce (bk VII, c. 5) more than 10,000 women accompanied the royal army to Sarbakusa, this civilian convoy being called *guaz*.

[2] Amharic *ăṭri*, *aṭṭari*, 'beer-seller'.

necessaries. All these people amount to so many that when ten thousand soldiers march, the number in the encampment is usually over thirty thousand souls, and when the Emperor marches with his entire force the whole multitude is over a hundred or a hundred and twenty thousand.

Of these people the Emperor, lords and ladies, captains and many of the soldiers have many tents. They pitch them in a very orderly way which is always the same. The Emperor's tents, four or five very fine tents, are placed in the centre. A handsome open space is left and then on the left hand and on the right, before and behind, follow tents for two churches that he takes with him, those of the Queen and great lords, who all have their allotted places, then those of the captains and soldiers in accordance with the command to which they belong, those from the vanguard in front, and behind those from the rearguard, some of those from the wings on the right and others on the left. When the whole camp has been disposed in the way I describe it occupies a very large meadow and is certainly a splendid sight, especially at night with the great number of fires that are lit.

Most people take no provisions and as for those who do take some, when they are finished, they all live on what they are given and what they take from the places through which they are marching and which they usually leave almost as much ruined and plundered as the Gallas might have done if they had invaded them. This is specially so if the army remains in a district for some days, for there is no solution but for the Emperor or Captain Major to assign certain places to it, which they rob of all kinds of provisions found there. In return for the provisions it usually happens that the inhabitants can only possess themselves in patience and say with holy Job: *Deus dedit, Deus abstulit: sit nomen Domini benedictum* (*Job*, 1, 21). Happy those who should say and do so. This is also the reason why the Gallas easily invade the territories of the empire, and why, on the other hand, the imperial armies cannot far invade those of the Gallas; they do not cultivate at all[1] and have no stock of provisions on

[1] This refers to the Boran, or pastoral Galla, who invaded Ethiopia in the sixteenth century. The Bareituma Galla are agriculturists, though it is not known whether they were so in Almeida's time. Such knowledge as the Portuguese had of the Galla concerned mainly the Boran.

M

which to feed, but live entirely on the milk of their cows. When necessary they easily take them wherever they like, retreat with them and leave the deserted meadows to the imperials, so that in time they are forced to retreat and, if they do not, die of sheer hunger.

The custom of not taking supplies on campaign arises from another which is general throughout this country. It is that the inhabitants of any place are compelled to shelter and give food for one night to all travellers arriving there in the evening. The custom originates in the admirable rule of holy charity which teaches and commands that strangers should be sheltered, and at the same time in the difficulty of transporting provisions in this country, and in the lack of order and government, which means that inns cannot be established. It is a very heavy burden for the poor peasants on whom it all falls. Big companies of men, soldiers and lords bringing many servants come daily to quarter themselves in very small villages. Each one goes into the house he likes best and turns the owner into the street, or occupies it with him. Sometimes it is a widow or a married woman whose husband is away and then by force he gets at not only her food and property but her honour. Nor do those who receive them commonly deserve much in the sight of God as they do it only under compulsion and from fear, so that the wretched and the indigent rarely find anyone to receive them.

I omit to describe the manner in which the Emperor marches with his army because here I find nothing remarkable or that does not exist in other countries. So long as it is going through friendly country, far from enemies, there is no order except that the Fitaurari[1] goes in front. This is what they call the captain of the vanguard, who performs a marshal's duty, chooses the place where the camp is to be, and, when it has been chosen, raises a standard in the centre or on some high ground as a signal that the Emperor's tents are to be pitched there. When this is seen all the rest know their positions and place their tents accordingly. On the way they proceed without any order at all. Only, where the Emperor goes, his

---

[1] Amharic *fītawrāri*, 'general of the advance guard,' the first element being perhaps *fit*, 'front,' but a derivation from *fit*, 'horn,' and *awrāris,* 'rhinoceros,' has been suggested.

shalms or trumpets go in front, which do not sound bad after their fashion, and his kettledrums,[1] of which there are usually three or four pairs, each on its she- or he-mule, and on their cruppers ride the men who beat them. On the right go four or five very strong horses, well caparisoned with trappings of gilded silver, and also one or two of the Emperor's she-mules as reliefs, for he and the rest always ride she-mules. His Highness mounts and dismounts inside his tent. If he alights on the road the men near him surround him and hide him with the cloths that they wear as cloaks. Then they bring him a couch which always travels near at hand, because his habit is to rest on it on rugs and cushions of rich silks. Even at home this is his usual seat and throne.

Near the Emperor travel his Azages and the chief lords who accompany him. On the way he always wears his crown of fine gold with some seed-pearls. Precious stones have never been seen or used in Ethiopia. He also takes his silk umbrella which came to him from India, like those in use there.[2] Those muffling and cloaking curtains by which former Emperors were so enclosed that nobody could see them do not now exist. On the contrary from time to time he gallops his jennet, dismounting from his she-mule to do so, and trampling over the field as I have sometimes seen. When the enemy is near at hand the army proceeds with more order and in closer formation, with closed squadrons; the vanguard does not advance far ahead nor the rearguard fall far behind. The wings proceed in extended formation keeping the Emperor with some of his guards and some lords and ladies in the centre and leaving sufficient ground for the baggage to travel enclosed and safe.

[1] 'Shalms' perhaps refers to the *ambilta*, described by Parkyns (vol. II, p. 48) as 'a set of five or six pipes, or fifes, blown like Pan pipes, except that each performer blows one only, every pipe having a different note.' He compares the sound to that of church bells. Kettledrums are used only by chiefs of very high rank.

[2] The parasol was an essential element in the royal paraphernalia of the Moslem states of Ifat, Dawaro, etc., and a gold parasol was part of the Kafa regalia. Its introduction into Abyssinia thus in all likelihood came from nearer home than India.

CHAPTER 19

Cities, Towns and Buildings of Ethiopia

The Emperor's camp is the royal city and capital of this empire. It deserves the name of city because of the multitude of people and the good order they observe in siting it, particularly at the place to which they retire to spend the winter. This is usually the same although those there have been hitherto have never lasted for many years. The Emperor now retires to one called Dancâz and it is nearly ten years since he chose it. Yet before, this same Emperor in thirteen or fourteen years had five or six other places in each of which he stayed for about two, three or four times. This has always been the custom of this empire. When the Emperor changes these places you will usually see nothing in those he has left but meadows ubi Troia fuit. These changes are made so frequently in the first place because it costs them little to build houses, as I shall explain directly, then because of his different wars, now against one enemy and now against another, and very specially because of lack of firewood. They choose primarily a place near which firewood is found in plenty but as they have no method in cutting down forests and groves the neighbouring hills and valleys are bare in a few years. It is then a question of moving the site to another place where there is firewood. They are amazed to hear that in other parts of the world big cities can remain for many years on the same site without experiencing a remarkable lack of firewood.

Apart from the Emperor's camp there is no settlement in the whole empire that deserves the name of city, or even of town. They are all villages, some larger some smaller, but such that no other name suits them. In some provinces and districts they are so close together that the whole countryside seems to be inhabited. Other territories are less populous and there are many that are solitary and desert. It is evident that they will all be open without a wall or fence. Only those in

Amaharâ and other parts which today border on the Gallas (whose incessant raids ravage the fields so that they cannot be sown) these, I say, situated on Ambâs and high mountains have at the same time some kind of wall of stones without mortar.

Houses are commonly of stone and mud, those of the richest people I mean, for other people make the walls of stakes set very closely and thatched. Only on the coast of Tigrê as far as Debaroâ do they give them a flat roof, but these are normally so low that there are few you do not touch with your head. Most of the houses are round but they make some of them long, as the Emperors' usually were. They call them Sacalâ[1] and this name by antonomasia means the palace of the King and grandees. The round houses, if they are rather big, they call Behetanguç,[2] which means royal house, because Behet is house and Nuguç King. The lords and richest persons arrange their houses with their cross-beams so close together that they serve as a ceiling; to this ceiling they attach and tie braiding of different colours so that they look very well and, for houses of one storey, are pleasant and reasonably commodious. Each lord has six, eight or more of them, in very capacious enclosures, which they make of stones without mortar up to six or seven spans high, above which rise fences very closely set and with plenty of thorns.[3]

The lack of lime that there was in Ethiopia until our times was a great reason for there not being better buildings. However seven years ago an intelligent person from India discovered a kind of fine, light and as it were worm-eaten stone; in the Baroche district of Guzarate he had seen it made into lime or chunambo, as it is called in India, and Nurâ as it is

[1] Ethiopic *saqalā*, originally 'tent' but applied to rectangular houses, which are built of stone in many places, with a thatched roof and a courtyard. In Tigre even cottages may be of stone. Buxton (*Travels in Ethopia*, fig. 69) illustrates one with a flat roof reached by stone steps, on which goats are kept.

[2] Amharic *bēt negus*, literally 'king's house', applied to round, not rectangular houses. (Guidi.)

[3] Cheesman (p. 30) describes the palace of the Governor of Gojam at Debra Markos as divided into courtyards, 'each one surrounded by a high wall of rock blocks laid without mortar, the top protected by branches of stout thorn-scrub woven into the rock.'

called here.[1] The Emperor and grandees valued it highly. Since then, with the help of the Emperor Seltan Cegued and his brother Ras Cella Christôs many very beautiful churches have been built of stone and lime which I shall describe at the proper time. The same Emperor made for himself two palaces, one at Ganeta Jesus, which is one of his pleasances, and another at the Dancâz camp, both very fine and capacious. I must describe them further on in their place when we reach the epoch and the history of this great Emperor. Then some of the grandees copied the Emperor, making houses of stone and lime, as we shall say further on.

CHAPTER 20

Revenue and Tribute of the Abyssinian Empire

I am afraid that in many things I may be thought to have little liking for the Abyssinians whose history I am writing. This is specially so in the matter with which I am now dealing. The reason is the little that used formerly to be known about this country and the fact that things always sound big at a distance. The truth is that I have no little liking for Ethiopia; indeed I do not know of any country in the world, not even Portugal where I was born, for which I have a greater affection than I have for this one. Yet amicus Plato sed magis amica veritas.[2] I cannot, and I never could, speak contrary to what I know, and those who have written about this country have either not come here or, though they have come and stayed for some years, as Father Francisco Alvrez

[1] Ethiopic and Amharic *norā*, 'lime'. *Chunambo*, Anglo-Indian *chunam*, *chinam*, is lime procured by the calcination of sea-shells (Dalgado). Bruce bk V, c. 5) says that lime mortar was used only at Gondar and even there was very bad. Cheesman (pp. 153, 304–305) comments on the scarcity of outcrops of good limestone on the plateau; he mentions a few quarries in Gojam. As a result only the Emperor and nobility could afford to use it; he records (p. 133) that when a commoner used it for building a church on Dek Island in Lake Tana, the neighbours protested that only members of kingly families could use it.

[2] This is the form in which Cervantes (*Don Quixote*, pt ii, c. 51) misquotes a saying from the life of Aristotle by Ammonius, which really mentions Socrates not Plato.

did, have not arrived at understanding the language or gone deeply into things and known them thoroughly. They were guided by what the Abyssinians themselves told them and their exaggerations, even about small things, are known only to someone who deals with them and understands them. I saw fit to make this digression here because if there is any one thing relating to the affairs of Ethiopia about which mistaken belief and opinion contrary to all truth are found in our countries it is this question of its wealth and treasure, for what is related about this is sheer fabrication.

What is certain is that this Emperor who is living today, Seltan Çegued, a prince of great truthfulness, endowed with a thousand gifts of Nature and Grace, implanted in him by God, this lord, I say, has stated many times that none of his predecessors ever had any gold or silver treasure. All that he has, the only one that has hitherto been seen in Ethiopia, is kept in our hands and in our house and never exceeds a thousand or one thousand five hundred oqueas, which is worth ten to fifteen thousand patacas, for every oquea of gold is in this country ten drimes, and every drime is worth about one pataca. Here you have the airy treasures of Mount Amaharâ or Ambá Gexen, for so the Palmeirim of Ethiopia should have called it to be accurate.[1]

Nor does the revenue and tribute which I shall describe directly promise anything better. The kingdom of all others in this empire from which most gold comes is Nareâ. From there none of the former Emperors, so the present one states, ever received as much as Malaac Cegued, who reigned during the years 1563 to 1596. What Malaac Cegued received each year only once amounted to five thousand oqueas, according to some people, for many do not think this is certain. For the rest of the time he did not receive in any one year more than one thousand five hundred, which is fifteen thousand patacas. Our present Emperor too received that amount in certain years but now not more than a thousand oqueas usually reach him. They came to him five years ago when I was in the country of the Damotes and their Viceroy, who was then the

---

[1] Urreta calls Amba Geshen 'Monte Amarà' and states that Prester John kept there a great treasure of jewels. He has much to say about the fabulous wealth of the country.

very Catholic and valiant Bucô, went to seek it through the midst of Gallas and Cafres. But from then till now (because Nareâ is hard pressed by the Gallas and there is dissension among the lords of the kingdom) in all these five years not more than five hundred oqueas came to the Emperor last year. It is hoped, though, that henceforward the thousand, the usual tribute in these days, will not fail.

About one thousand one hundred oqueas of gold come as tribute every year from certain lands in Gojam, though he has often given all or part of these lands to certain lords, like his sons or brothers and they consume this revenue. Three thousand pieces of cloth are raised from the same kingdom, each of which is worth a pataca, and two hundred Bezetes,[1] which are very large, closely woven cotton cloths with the hair of the cotton used as a border as in carpets; each one of them is worth about an oquea. It is said that formerly the same kingdoms used to pay three thousand horses but it must be understood that almost all from that kingdom were, and are still today, nags and jades. This tribute ceased because, when the Gallas became neighbours of the kingdom and habitually made war upon it, King Malaac Çagued thought it best to excuse this tribute so that the inhabitants could defend themselves better against their Galla enemies with these horses. What is added to this by Francisco Alvrez, who saw the tribute come to the court in the time of the Emperor David, and the ceremonies and pomp which he describes, with which the men who brought the tribute made their entry, all this was a trick, like many others that were used in front of him, and his companions, to show something they would recount in foreign countries.[2]

The Emperor does not receive tribute in gold from any other kingdoms of the empire, but the governors whom he appoints to them give him some in return for the governorships he gives them, and so from different governorships called Xumetes in the Kingdom of Tigrê he receives nearly twenty five thousand patacas every year, from the Xumetes of Dambeâ five thousand and from those of Begameder,

[1] Amharic *bezet*, 'cotton prepared by hand for carding' (Guidi), a form of tribute recorded in *CGA* from several places; in Yeshaq's day Gojam paid in mules (*CGA*. 2, 4).

[2] Alvares, pp. 321–322.

Amaharâ, Holecâ and Xaoa too he receives something, though not as much, because these territories are more ravaged by the Gallas. In this kind of revenue former Emperors had a great advantage over those at present, for they had many more and much bigger kingdoms which now partly belong to the Gallas and are partly independent through the Gallas' having pushed in between them and the kingdoms ruled by the Emperor.

He has some customs posts on land, for no Emperor of the Abyssinians has ever had a post on the sea-coast. Formerly they had Maçuâ on the Red Sea, but the Turks have been masters of it for many years now. At the customs posts of which I am speaking merchandise pays some tribute, but the Emperor has given most of them to particular lords along with the lands on which they stand.[1] Lamalmon he has reserved for himself and he probably receives from it the equivalent of one hundred oqueas every year.

The Emperor has some lands like crown lands[2] from which he raises ten or twelve thousand loads of provisions. He also receives a tribute in provisions in the payments of the farmers of Dambeâ, Gojam, Begameder and some other provinces, each man paying about one load. Most of this, however, he has given to different lords. What he receives from Dambeâ, which would be some 10 or 12 thousand loads, he divides

[1] Bruce (bk V, c. 4) passed five such posts between Massawa and Adua. He says the duties were called gifts, 'though they are levied, for the most part, in a very rigorous and rude manner; but they are established by usage in particular spots; and are, in fact, a regality annexed to the estate.' The *Annals of Iyasu I* describe an enquiry held by the king in November 1698 into the duties levied at customs posts from Endarta to Wagara. He was told that there was much extortion, but that in the reigns of his predecessors Susneyos and Fasiladas the regulations were that 'he who carried salt on his shoulders paid no duty, for it was remitted; on each donkey-load of salt, the duty was 1 *amolé*, and on each mule-load 2 *amolé*. This was the duty at the large and distant posts; at smaller and neighbouring posts no duty was levied'. He ordered a revision of the duty, and fixed it at 1 *amolé* on 5 mule-loads of salt, and 1 *amolé* on 8 donkey-loads; those who exacted payment from men carrying salt on their shoulders were to be severely punished. At the same time he issued a list of posts where duty might be levied, and of those which were to be abolished. (*AJIB*, pp. 206–207.)

[2] *reguengos*. The term means either crown lands in general, or strictly, crown lands cultivated by a special kind of tenant at will, called a *reguengueiro*, who usually paid his rent in kind. Almeida applies such terms to Abyssinia with noticeable precision.

among soldiers to whom he has not given lands, gives as alms to the poor and divides among lords and ladies at court who are in need.[1]

One tribute deserves consideration which was imposed in Ethiopia less than 80 years ago. It is that every man who has cows pays one in ten every three years. Since the country has many cattle, mostly horned cattle, this tribute amounts to a great deal for him. He has divided his kingdoms and provinces so that some of them pay this tribute every year. They call it 'burning' because the one in ten that is chosen for the King is touched with fire and its skin burnt with a mark like branding. In reality, though, the name 'burning' suits it much better for other reasons. The men who collect this tribute are usually captains and military men, and the Emperor, in addition to the lands he has given them, usually divides most of these cows among them. In collecting the tribute they use so much violence against the peasants that they ruin and consume them. He receives besides from every weaver weaving cotton cloth one piece of cloth from the Christians and one drime or pataca from the Moors. From this source of revenue he collects in Dambeâ and other neighbouring districts many thousands of pieces of cloth every year. He has the same revenue in other kingdoms but there he has given it to the lords among whom he has divided the lands of these kingdoms.

These are the revenues of the Abyssinian empire. When they are added up it is easy to see that the total amount is quite small, not only in comparison with what is currently reported in the world, but in comparison with what one would expect from so many kingdoms and territories. However, besides what we said, that in a poor country it amounts to more than would be supposed elsewhere, what chiefly makes this King great is that he is lord *in solidum* of all lands that there are in all his kingdoms, so that he can take and give them when and to whom he sees fit. Private persons, great and small, have nothing except by the King's gift and all that they own is by favour *ad tempus*. It is so usual for

[1] Bruce in his notebooks, quoted in his second edition, Appendix I to Books VII and VIII, states that the annual tribute of Agaumeder was about 1000 ounces of gold, of Damot 800, and of Gojam 80 ounces and 70 mules.

the Emperor to exchange, alter and take away the lands each man holds every two or three years, sometimes every year and even many times in the course of the year, that it causes no surprise. Often one man ploughs the soil, another sows it and another reaps. Hence it arises that there is no one who takes good care of the lands he enjoys; there is not even any-one to plant a tree because he knows that he who plants it very rarely gathers the fruit. For the King, however, it is useful that they should all be so dependent upon him. So it comes about that, some from fear that the lands he has given them may be taken away, others in the hope of getting those they have not, all serve him in peace and war and each one gives him presents in accordance with his ability, for usually he who gives more gets more and he who gives less gets less.

CHAPTER 21

Acçum and its Antiquities

In the ecclesiastical histories of the illustrious and learned Cardinal Cæsar Baronio mention is sometimes made of Axum and the Axumites in Ethiopia. This is what I am discussing but I call it Acçum, not Axum, because that is the pronuncia-tion used here by the Abyssinians. The place is so ancient that everyone states that it was the seat and court of Queen Sabâ. Certainly for many generations it was such for the Kings and Emperors of this empire, and even now the Em-peror of the Abyssinians can be crowned nowhere else but in Accum or in a church of Begameder called Mecana Selassê.[1]

Acçum[2] is three leagues distant from Fremonâ and about

[1] Ethiopic makāna sellāsē, '[holy] place of the Trinity.'
[2] This place is first mentioned by name in the *Periplus of the Erythraean Sea* (end of first century A.D.), as the capital of a kingdom which had its port at Adulis (Zula) on the Red Sea. The King of Aksum was converted to Christianity about A.D. 330. For centuries it was 'the sacred city of the Ethiopians' and the Emperors were crowned there. It had ceased to be the capital long before Almeida's time and in the sixteenth and early seven-teenth centuries the Emperor had no fixed residence. Fasiladas, however

forty-five from Macuâ. It is at an elevation of 14 and a half
degrees. It is situated on the edge of very broad meadows in a
gap where they come in between two hills. Today it is a place
with about a hundred inhabitants. Everywhere there ruins
are to be seen, not of walls, towers and splendid palaces, but
of many houses of stone and mud which show that the town
was formerly very large. A church[1] of stone and mud,
thatched, is to be seen there built amid the ruins and walls of
another, ancient one, the walls of which are still visible and
were of stone and mud too (for in no part of Ethiopia is there
any sign or trace that lime has ever at any time been seen
there or any building, large or small, constructed with it) but
very wide apart. From what is visible the church seems to
have had five aisles. It was 220 spans long and 100 wide. It
has a big enclosure wall of stone and mud and inside it a very
handsome courtyard paved with large, well cut stones, ending, on the side where the church is, in a flight of eight or nine
steps, also made of large cut stones. At the top is a platform
of ten or twelve *covados* in the space before the facade and
principal door of the church.

Outside this church's enclosure is another in which five or
six big pedestals of black stone are to be seen. Near at hand
are four columns of the same stone, ten or twelve spans high.
Among them is a seat on which the Emperor sits to be
crowned after having first taken his seat on the pedestals I
mentioned and after various ceremonies have been performed on them.

What is most worth seeing here, a display of presumptuous
grandeur, is many very tall stones like obelisks, needles and

built Gondar which remained the nominal capital until the reign of Theodore II (1855–68).

The chief remains of the ancient Aksumite civilization are: (i) The
obelisks, of which at least 50 are still standing at Aksum, while many more
have fallen. They range from rough monoliths to highly finished represen-
tations of a many-storied castle cut from a single block of stone; the tallest
standing obelisk is 60 ft high and has a maximum frontal width of 8 ft.
7 ins. (ii) Stepped and recessed walls. (iii) Thrones raised on steps with a
(thatched) roof supported by squared stone pillars. (iv) Built-up churches.
(v) Dams. Inscriptions occur in Greek, South Arabian and Ethiopic.

[1] According to tradition, this church was built by Queen Candace after
her conversion. It was burned by Grañ in 1535, and rebuilt by Portuguese
architects. The site was perhaps that of an ancient sun temple. (Cf. Budge,
History of Ethiopia, vol. I, p. 160.)

pyramids. They are in a meadow lying behind the church. I counted some twenty that were standing and seven or eight that have been thrown to the ground and broken into many fragments. The tallest of those standing, if measured by its shadow, is a hundred and four spans. Its width at the base is ten spans. It becomes thinner as it goes up, like a pyramid, but it is not square; it has two sides broader and two narrower, than the other two. It is carved as though in small panels, each of which is like a square of two spans. This is the style of all those that have this carving, which are the taller ones.[1] The rest are rough and unshaped slabs without any carving at all. The shortest are from 30 to 40 spans; the rest are all taller. It can be seen from the fragments of three or four of those that have been overthrown that they were much bigger than the tallest of those now standing, which I said was a hundred and four spans, and some can be seen to have been over two hundred. The old men of this country say that a few years ago, in the time of King Malaac Cegued, and the Viceroy Isaac,[2] who rebelled and brought in the Turks to help him against the Emperor, they overthrew the six or seven that lie on the ground in fragments.

No one can say what was the object of the former Kings who raised them up. It may well be thought that they were like mausoleums erected near their tombs, since this was the object of the Egyptians. It was no doubt from them, through their proximity and the constant communication there was between them, that they learnt about, and that the workmen came to make, these barbarous and monstrous structures. A bombard shot away from this spot is a broad stone not much higher than a man on which a long inscription can be seen. Many Greek and some Latin letters are recognisable but when joined together they do not make words in Greek, Latin, Hebrew or any other known language, and so the meaning of the writing is not discoverable.

[1] See note on p. 90.　　　　[2] Yeshāq. See p. 96, n. 1.

CHAPTER 22

How the Emperors are crowned in this place

This is the way in which the Emperor is crowned here. He arrives at Açcum and encamps in a very big meadow there. When the coronation day arrives he orders his army to be arrayed so that everyone should accompany him with the proper ceremony. The infantry goes in front, divided into different squadrons, the cavalry comes behind them and the Emperor at the end, accompanied by the greatest lords. It is obvious that on such a day they will come out in their richest and best clothes and with the choicest harnesses and trappings for their horses. He approaches this place on the eastern side, and reaches the stone which I said above has an inscription which no one has been able to read for many years. Here the Abuna and all the clergy were awaiting him, all robed and with crosses and thuribles in their hands. When they reach this place the grandees dismount and range themselves in two rows on either side of the road leaving a wide path between which is covered with large, rich carpets. The Emperor too dismounts and walks over the carpets, but he is met and stopped by three maidens whom they call maidens of Sion. Two of them, each taking one end, hold a silken cord across the path. When the Emperor reaches it the third maiden asks him: 'Who are you?' He answers: 'I am the King.' She says: 'You are not.' Then the Emperor walks back three or four steps and returns and the maiden again asks him: 'Whose King are you?' He answers: 'I am King of Israel.' She says: 'You are not our King.' The Emperor walks back again, returns to the same place and the maiden asks him a 3rd time: 'Whose King are you?' Then the Emperor draws his sword and cuts the cord, saying: 'I am King of Sion.' The maiden adds: 'Truly, truly you are King of Sion.' Then everyone present rends the air shouting many times: 'Long live, long live the King of Sion,' all the musical instruments strike up, kettledrums, trumpets and shalms, and the musketeers fire a salvo. The Emperor scatters on the carpets many grains of gold which are picked up by those to whom the privilege belongs by ancient custom. From this place they all go in procession to the first enclosure wall of the church, while the monks, clergy and prebends sing: Benedictus qui venit in nomine Domini, etc.

The first enclosure of the church is the one in which, as I said above, are some seats which were formerly, and still at the time when Father Francisco Alvrez came to this country, twelve very well made stone chairs, as he recounts in his book. Today there are no chairs and the bases or pedestals on which they stood are not as many. The four columns that I mentioned above seem formerly to have supported a vault. In the centre of them they decorate two pedestals with rich cloths and handsome chairs and the ground at the foot is carpeted. The Emperor sits here on one of the two chairs, the Abbuna on the other. At the sides twelve dignitaries, some ecclesiastical, some secular, take their places, six on the right and six on the left. I shall describe them here in the exact words of the book of these ceremonies[1] that is kept in that same church at Acçum. It says as follows:

Elahaquetât,[2] i.e. head of the people; Quelabaz,[3] i.e. counsellor, bringing a little box; Macarê,[4] bringing the oil for anointing the King, in a little gold box, and holy water; Queza Gabez,[5] i.e. treasurer of the church; Lica Diaconât,[6] i.e. Archdeacon, with a silken cord fastened to a stick, goes in front keeping the people at a distance; Arnês[7] carries the um-

[1] Almeida probably took his account from a version of the *Kebra Nagast* (*KN*) or 'Glory of Kings', though if he has quoted correctly it must have been a version differing slightly from that printed by Dillman (*Über die Regierung, etc.*, pp. 18–20) from Bodleian MS no. xxvi, which was given to the Bodleian by Bruce. (*Cat. Codd. MSS Bibl. Bodl.* (Oxford, 1848), p. 68; Budge, *The Queen of Sheba and her only son Menyelek*, p. xxv.)

[2] *Elahaquetât*: *KN* has ''head of the people, that is, *ela'aqaytât*, who brings wild animals, cattle, and poultry''.

[3] *Quelabaz*: *KN* has "*qalabas*, that is, counsellor, who brings a box of perfume, and also wild flowers and fruits, and all kinds of corn except *ṭef*".

[4] *Macarê*: *KN* has "*ma'asarē*, who brings oil for [anointing] the king".

[5] *Queza Gabez*: *KN* has "*qaysa gabaz*". Dillman translates this as 'propst', i.e. provost or prior. In Amharic *gabbaz* means the treasurer of a church.

[6] *Lica Diaconât*: *KN* has "*liqā diyāqonāt*", 'head of the deacons.'

[7] *Arnês*: *KN* has "*arnēs*, that is, *ma'asarē ba'āla harir ṭaṭē*, who brings silk stuffs (?)." The meaning of the definition is not clear, but *harir* means 'silk', and *ba'āla* is the title of an official.

brella or sunshade; Cevâ serguoj,[1] i.e. godfather; De Lamoâ ye Nuguç Hezbaj,[2] i.e. governor of the King's house or people; Raçmecerâ,[3] master of the horse; Decçaf,[4] master of the mules. All these take part in the ceremonies and rites of the coronation. They stand with the objects pertaining to their functions in their hands while they anoint the Emperor, six on the right hand and six on the left, and no one else takes part in this rite. Elahaquetât brings wild and domestic animals that can be eaten, Quelabáz flowers of the field, fruits and all kinds of edible seeds, Cevâ Serguôj brings milk and grape wine, the maidens of Sion bring water, honey wine and fragrant herbs. The man carrying the little box brings in it Mesque, i.e. a confection of perfume. The Queza Gabez and Lica Diaconât stand and hold the altar stone, Raccamaçerá holds the horse by the rein and Decçaf the mule.

The same book goes on to record those who bring presents. From Belenê, which is the country of Amaçem, they bring Torá[5] i.e. jungle cow; from Çegadê, Gox,[6] i.e. buffalo; from Cemen, Hayel,[7] i.e. stag; from Afâ, Agazem,[8] which is like a stag but has twisted horns; from Torát, Iabbedú,[9] which is wild goat; Tigré mohon[10] brings lion and other wild beasts. King Gabra Mascal, on the advice of the priest Iared,[11] added

[1] *Cevâ Serguoj*: *KN* has "*zēwā sarguay*, that is, 'ark (friend) who brings milk and wine."

[2] *De lamoâ ye nuguç hezbaj*: *KN* has "*dalmakay wa negus hezabay*, [that is] *magābē bēt negus* (the last three words meaning "administrator of the king's house")". The title appears to be *dalmakay*; the exact meaning of *hezabay* is obscure. Almeida's transcription *de lamoa* can be explained by supposing that his source had *qaf* instead of *kaf* for the fourth letter of *dalmakay*, and that he misread *qaf* as *wawe* (w), and so produced *lamoa*.

[3] *Raçmeçerâ*: *KN* has "*raq ma'aserā*", a term which means something like 'master of the ceremonies'.

[4] *Decçaf*: *KN* has "*daqqa sâf*, that is, *awfāri*, who brings a horse", while another functionary called *liqā makuāsa* (perhaps the same as the *meskuayh* who is named earlier in the text) brings a mule.

[5] *Torá*: *torā*, a large antelope, *bubalis tora*.   [6] *Gox*: Amharic *goš*, 'buffalo.'

[7] *hayel*: *KN* has "*wālā*, that is, *hayal*", the latter word meaning a large antelope.

[8] *agazem*: *KN* has "*agazan*"; Tigriña *agāzēn*, a kind of antelope.

[9] *iabeddú*: *KN* has "*talē badu*", meaning 'wild goat (*talē*)'. Almeida must have misread *ṭ* as *h*, the Ethiopic letters being somewhat alike.

[10] *Tigre mohon*: *Tegrē makuannen*, 'the governor of Tigre.'

[11] *Iared*: Yārēd the Priest, who is said to have compiled the *Mazgabā Degguā* or 'Treasury of Hymns', lived in the time of king Gabra Masqal (*c.* A.D. 570); the existing work, however, is probably not earlier than the fifteenth century.

to this the ceremony that takes place on Palm Sunday, ordering that the people should bring palm and olive branches, the clergy stand with crosses and thuribles and the cantors sing Benedictus qui venit, etc., and other sequences with different tunes and two in special praise of the King. They sing while going round the place where the coronation ceremonies are performed. Then they bring the Old and New Testaments and read the passages dealing with the Kings and priests and the Psalms of David, etc. Then the people present go once round the place where the royal chair is and throw flowers and perfumes upon it. If there is someone inside the ceremonial area who is not one of those appointed, he is thrown out. A lion and a buffalo are near at hand, tied to columns; the King strikes the lion with his lance; then they release the other animals, tame and wild, and all the birds. The people of the camp kill those they can catch for a feast.

As the King comes to the place where his chair is he throws gold on the carpets. When he sits down they bring two plates of gold and two of silver. On the gold plates are milk and honey wine, on the silver, water and grape wine. They then anoint the King in accordance with custom, sprinkle all the ceremonial objects with water they have from the river Jordan and cut the hair of the King's head as for clergy in the first tonsure. The clergy take up the hairs, the deacons continue to sing at the altar stone with lighted candles and the clergy cense with the thuribles. After going once round the place where the royal chair is, as though in procession, they go towards a stone which stands at the door of the church of Sion, called Meidanitâ Neguestât,[1] i.e. protector of the Kings. They put the hairs on it and light them from the thuribles. Then all the clergy commend the King to God and to Our Lady. They return and tell the King all that they have done. Then they begin to play all the instruments in the camp and the people give loud shouts of joy. Afterwards the King goes to the church and, as he approaches the altar, commends his soul to God and Our Lady. He then returns to the place where he was anointed and stands in the middle of the twelve officers with six on his right hand and six on his

---

[1] *meidanitâ neguestât = madhanit nagast*, 'the salvation of kings;' *KN* has *memheṣana nagast*, 'place of protection of kings.'

N

left. The Abbuna comes to him first, then the priors of the churches, clergy and deacons, each one giving him his blessing. Then the grandees of the camp come to him and in the same way each one gives his blessing. To give a blessing here is to say: 'God give Your Highness a thousand years of life! God cast down all your enemies at your feet!' and invoke other good fortune of the kind. When they finish the King too gives his blessing to them all and then goes to his house accompanied by everybody. So far the Book.[1]

[1] With this account may be compared the following description (*HSD*, pp. 89–91) of the ceremonial reception of Ṣarṣa Dengel at Aksum when he went there to be anointed after defeating Yeshāq the insurgent *bāhrnagāš* in 1580.

'On the 15th of the month of Ter [January] the king set out in the morning for the church at Aksum. The ecclesiastics, priests and deacons, received him with the golden cross, the silver censer, and about twelve parasols, while they displayed hangings of silk. . . . The ecclesiastics, adorned with church ornaments, all the heads of the convents in Sire and in Tigre, wearing albs and chasubles and holding the cross and the censers, sang the hymns of Yared, saying, "Be blessed O King of Israel." In front of these priests stood the Daughters of Sion, in the middle of the road where there is a small obelisk. This obelisk is covered from top to bottom with inscriptions cut by the ancients in Greek letters. The name of this place is Mebtaka Fatl, that is, the cutting of the cord, the significance of which will be made plain by the actions of the King which we shall now describe. This place is on the east of the cathedral of Aksum. The maidens were drawn up on the right and on the left, holding a long cord. There were also two old women who stood with a sword beside these maidens, one on the right and the other on the left. When this puissant and victorious king arrived, mounted on his horse, the old women cried aloud in an arrogant and insolent manner, "Who art thou? Of what family and of what tribe?" The King answered and said to them, "I am the son of David, son of Solomon, son of Ebna Hakim." A second time they questioned him insolently, and he satisfied them by answering, "I am the son of Zar'a Yā'qob, son of Ba'eda Māryām, son of Nā'od." At their third question the King raised his hand and said, "I am Malak Sagad, son of the King Wanāg Sagad, son of Aṣnāf Sagad, son of Admās Sagad." Saying these words, he cut with his sword the cord which the maidens were holding, and thereupon the old women cried aloud, "Truly, truly thou art the King of Sion, the son of David, son of Solomon." Then the priests of Aksum began to chant on one side, and the maidens to applaud on the other side. Thus was he received on entering into the court of the house of the heavenly Sion [a name given to the cathedral of Aksum]. Then he strewed on the ground a large amount of gold, for the men of the law. After this, a magnificent procession was formed: here were the fusiliers, there were the gunners; here were the cavalry, there were the infantry; and all the while the drum Deb Anbasā [the royal drum, "Hyaena and Lion"] was beaten, and the trumpets, horns and flutes, instruments of the Turks and Amhara, were sounded. Then the muskets and cannon were fired, and their noise was like that of thunder. On this day there was great pomp and

BOOK II

CHAPTER 22

The Fortress of Ambâ Guexen: how and upon what the Emperors' sons used to live there, and whether some of their descendants still live there.

The Kingdom of Amaharâ was for many centuries the centre and as it were heart of the whole Abyssinian empire. Now it borders on the Gallas, forming the frontier, and they would have conquered it already if God had not given it natural fortresses which they hold to be impregnable. These are the mountains called Ambâs in this country; they are those which, lofty and steep on all sides, have on top a level space of sufficient size for people to live there. For this, what is needed above all is that they should have perennial springs or pools of water. Now on the borders of this kingdom, on the Xaoa side, lies the Ambâ they call Guixen, among meadows and low-lying, though not very flat country. On the eastern side, two or three musket shots away, are some very high mountains called Habelâ, and others farther off called Ambâ Cel, much stronger than Guixen. On the other sides there are no mountains near Guixen, but only meadows, though not very level ones. It is nearly round, though on top it appears to have the shape of a cross. Going along the edge of the rock it is probably little more than half a league round on top, but one would have to walk for half a day to go round it on foot at the base.[1] Its height is such that a stone thrown from a sling by a strong arm would reach from the bottom to the top with great difficulty. It is precipitous rock all round and in places it turns outward in such a way that it

ceremony such as had never before been seen. Then were precious fabrics stretched on the throne of worked stone which the ancients had made; and on this throne was set the King. The throne is called Manbara Dawit [the throne of David], as the fathers had named it of old.'

[1] In bk III, c. 4, Almeida criticises Alvares for saying that the journey round its base was fifteen days' travel, and states that this must refer to Amba Sel and other mountains near to it.

is impossible to get in. There is only one way in (though once it was entered in another place, as we shall say below) called Macarâquer. The ascent begins with a wide path up to a platform made by the mountain. From there to the top the path is so narrow and steep that it can only be climbed with great labour. Though the cows and oxen of this country climb and jump like goats, they do not go up or down that path unless they have been tied up and dragged with thongs, by which they are lifted bodily. At the top of this ascent is a house where the guards live, built of stone and mud and thatched, as they all are there. In the middle of the plain is a big pool, natural, not artificial, where they wash their clothes. Not far off is another little one from which they drink. It is spring water, but there is so little of it that it does not overflow or make a stream. There are no fish in either of them.

On the whole of this mountain there are no trees except those I shall speak about now. There is a species found in nearly all the high and cold parts of Ethiopia. It is called coço.[1] The wood is hard and red; it is not a very big tree, it might be the size of an olive tree. It is quite bushy and the leaves are long and narrow. It bears a fruit like ears of corn, or like the chestnut flower that we call 'lamps'. In them is a kind of seed as bitter as the whin. Because it is so bitter when drunk it is an excellent medicine with which to kill certain worms that constantly breed in the stomachs of these people. They are like tape-worms but thinner. They are called by the same name as the medicine, coco, or else their name has been given to it. It is thought that they are bred by the raw beef they eat, because those people who never eat it, do not have these worms or need to take medicine. There are also some Zegbas and wild cedars on this mountain, the Zegba being a kind of cedar or cypress too, and a grass or shrub they call Endod[2] which is like jasmine; not in the flower, but in the

---

[1] Amharic *kosso*, a tree from which the Abyssinians make a vermifuge. Grottanelli notes that 'under this name are collected two different products known respectively as *Hagenia abyssinica* Willd. and *Balanites aegyptiaca* Delile. Grabham records *Brayera anthelminthica* with the name of *kosso*' (V. L. Grottanelli, *Missione di studio al Lago Tana*, vol. II, p. 273).

[2] Amharic *endod*, *Pircunia abyssinica*, a plant the ashes of which have a detergent quality and, when dried and pounded, are used for washing clothes.

stem, for it has larger, thicker set leaves. It bears things like clusters of pepper which are used as soap for washing clothes though they cut them badly.

Next to the big pool a kind of hillock rises up, on which are two churches, one called Egzyabeher Ab, God the Father, the other belonging to Our Lady. The Emperor Lalibelâ[1] ordered the first church to be built there in former times, in order to uproot the worship of the Devil by heathens and sorcerers who offered him many oxen and cows in sacrifice underneath a bower of Endod. It is said that the church was very big and beautiful but the Moor Granhe, with whom we shall deal later, burnt it. Afterwards, another small wooden one was made in its place. The church of Our Lady was built more recently. The Emperor Nahod,[2] when imprisoned there, is said to have promised Our Lady the Virgin that he would enlarge and beautify it for her if he succeeded to the empire as he hoped to do. A year later news came to him that he had been chosen and was summoned. He tried to keep the vow he had made and began to build the church of very well cut stone, but he died before finishing it and his son Onag Çagued[3] completed it. It is round and has two rows of stone columns inside. The vault of the chapel rests on the inner ones. The 2nd are 7 covados away from the first. They support the wood of the roof because it is thatched like the rest. The beams that come down from the top of the chapel and are supported on these columns, rest their ends on a round wall which is another 7 covados away from the columns. Granhe's Moors tried to burn this church as they did the other. They set fire to it and the thatch and the beam ends in the porch began to burn, but then the Virgin Our Lady protected her church and stayed the force of the fire which went no further. In memory of this miracle those same pieces of wood with the ends burnt are still there.

Next to these churches live certain monks and Debteras, who are like their canons, beneficed clergy and choristers for

[1] One of the Zagwē kings (c. 1190–1225); he is credited with the construction of the original group of monolithic churches at the place named after him in Lasta.

[2] Nā'od (1495–1508).

[3] Wanāg Sagad, throne name of Lebna Dengel (1508–40).

them.[1] In former times there were as many as 14 monks; there are now said to be six or seven. The Debteras with their wives and children are more numerous. The Emperors' sons and their descendants used to live all over the Ambâ in their cottages of stone and mud, or wood, all of them thatched. Some Emperors promised them a third of the revenues of the empire, but they never gave them anything except some lands that lay nearby, round about Amba Guixen. To cultivate and manage these lands properly on their behalf, collect the revenues and send them what they need for their food and clothing, certain great men live near Guixen who are like their factors and who watch and guard them. Formerly any messages whatsoever that came for the princes, and the letters that came and those the princes themselves wrote, did not pass through without being examined by those men. These guards held the princes in such subjection that they used not to allow them to change their ordinary clothing, which was of cotton cloth. It is related that one of the guards saw a prince dressed with more elegance than custom allowed, and not merely rebuked him but struck him too. It happened that a few years afterwards that same prince was elected to the empire. As soon as he heard the news the guard fled and took refuge, fearing that he would kill him. The new Emperor, however, sent for him and gave him his word that he would do him no harm. He appeared, flung himself on the ground and begged for pardon. He made him rise, had him dressed in rich clothes and gave him a bracelet of gold of great value, saying: 'You performed your duty and your office very well, and served your master faithfully. So, I hope, will you serve me. Go back to the place and the charge you had.'

I have already said above that, from the Emperor Nahod's

---

[1] Ethiopic *dabtarā*, 'tent', used to translate 'the greater and more perfect tabernacle' (*Hebrews*, ix, 11). The secondary and commoner meaning is 'ecclesiastic' (*canonicus*), the origin of which is said to be from the Levites (Ludolf, *Lexicon*, col. 377). The etymology suggested by Dillman is more probable; taking the form *debterā* or *defterā*, he proposed the Greek *diphthera*, 'skin prepared for writing upon.' alluding to the literary attainments of these people, whose duties included performing sacred dances during processions, singing in the choir, composing hymns, and studying the Old and New Testaments and the Civil and Canon Law. They support themselves by writing and transcribing prayers in the form of amulets wrapped in skin and bought by the faithful.

time till now, no Emperor's sons have again been put in Guixen. Now it should be known that daughters were never put in there because no one had a right to the empire through the female line.[1] So the daughters of the men who lived in Amba Guixen used to leave and were married to anybody who wanted them as wives. Ethiopia is full of the descendants of these women, a royal race in the female line, but not much account is taken of them, though the Emperor's women relatives are always honoured, his male relatives not so much. No female Oiziero, however, (for that is what those persons who have royal blood are called) marries an Emperor or any male of the same blood, for they say they are all brothers, even though they are not related except in the tenth or twentieth degree.

Though Kings' sons were not put into Guixen any more, yet those who were there before were guarded with great vigilance till the time of the Emperor Atanef Çagued,[2] that is, the one who was called Glaudios at his baptism and whom we call Claudios, in whose time Dom Christovão da Gama and his men entered Ethiopia. Claudios was careless about having them watched and made light of it, and so most of them came down and went up again when they liked. Only the descendants of the Emperor Hezbinanho[3] are still rigorously watched to this day, because they are more afraid of them. The reason was as follows. The Emperor Zara Jacob[4] had certain disputes with the members of this family and became so angry that he ordered them to be taken from Amba Guixen and exiled to hot lands where there are many diseases. Because only peasants live there it was said as a kind of joke that they were Collâ (so those hot lands are called) Israelites that is to say, he made them peasants and took from them the noble status of Israelites.[5] They were there until, on the death of Zara Jacob his son Beda Mariam[6]

---

[1] 'So much is this so that even if a particular Emperor should have male grandchildren by his daughters, if he has no sons, or male grandchildren by his sons, then the imperial succession must pass to one of the descendants of some former Emperor in the male line' (Almeida, bk II, c. 21).

[2] Aṣnāf Sagad.   [3] Hezba Nāñ, throne name of Takla Māryām (1429–33).

[4] Zar'a Yā'qob, 'the seed of Jacob' (1434–68).

[5] 'So are named those who are descended in the male line from David, Solomon and Menilehec his son, and Queen Sabâ' (Almeida, bk II, c. 21).

[6] Ba'eda Māryām, 'in the hand of Mary' (1468–78).

succeeded to the empire. Because he had pity on them he ordered them to leave their place of exile and return again to Guixen. When they were there he sent three of his servants to visit them with a very affectionate message asking them to forget what his father had done to them because he would remember to treat them kindly in all things. They were so aggrieved that they ignored the kindness the son was doing them and remembered only his father's injury. They rushed upon the Emperor's three servants and killed them cruelly and barbarously. Beda Mariam was inflamed with anger; he assembles [sic] his men and marches to take just vengeance on such an ungrateful race. They lay siege to the Amba and subject it to various assaults and batteries. However, as it is strong and those on top were fighting for their lives, they could not gain an entrance for many days, until some peasants of the country showed them a path at the back of the rock. By this path, though it was full of difficulties, some soldiers climbed up at night, clutching the branches and roots of trees growing there, attacked those on top when they were off their guard, overpowered them and carried them prisoners to the Emperor, who promptly ordered that eighty of the chief of them should have their heads cut off. That is the reason why members of this family are still so much feared today.

So much for Amba Guixen, and there is nothing more to say about it. If it be compared with others in Ethiopia, more than a hundred are to be found that are in every way superior to it. They are higher and steeper and on top they have more water and better fields, for those on this one yield only beans, barley and some wheat, and that in small quantities. Others are much more fertile and productive. The better or worse luck that this one had was to be chosen as the prison and jail of the poor and unhappy princes; this made it famous in Ethiopia and outside it. If this was sufficient for it to be pretended that the Earthly Paradise was there, the author could certainly have pretended with more reason that it was in the Lisbon Limoeiro or the Valencia jail.[1]

[1] Urreta (pp. 97–98) disavows any intention of proving that 'Monte Amarà' as he calls Amba Geshen, was the Earthly Paradise, but he says (p. 99) 'we find in Mount Amarà circumstances and particulars proper to the Earthly Paradise'. The Limoeiro was the Lisbon prison.

Fig 1

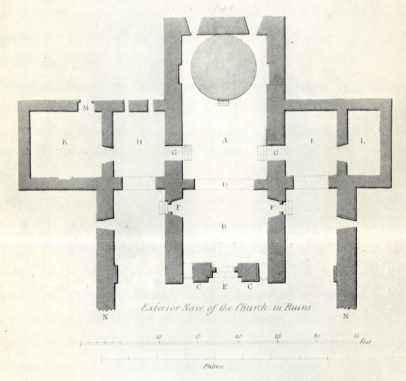

Fig 2

M H G A G I L

K

D

F B F

C E C

Exterior Nave of the Church in Ruins.

N   N

10   15   20   25   30   35
                                              Feet

Palms

Church at Mártula Máriam — Western Elevation and Plan.

Extract from Book III, Chapter 2, describing the Church at Martula Maryam

Almeida recounts how the Empress Helen, wife of Ba'eda Māryām and Regent during the minority of Lebna Dengel, had been a great benefactor of churches. One in particular she built with such generosity that it was the finest church that had ever been seen in the country. 'She sent for the workmen from Egypt; this could not have been done had they not been given very large payments and a great reward, for the work shows that they were masters of their craft. She chose a very suitable site for the church in the heart of Gojam in a district called Nebessêe, which is washed by the Nile; as it bends round, the territories of Begameder, Amahara and Holeca come to drink its water on the other side of the stream. It is very fertile country and in the middle is a hillock rising up like a hummock to a height of two or three lances from the ground, and less than a quarter of a league round. Today it is all clothed and peopled by so many cedars and wild olives or *zambugeiros*[1] that they cover it entirely and number over two thousand. They appear to have been planted there when the building of the church began, because it is the custom in Ethiopia always to surround churches with these tall groves of trees. In the centre of this hill, which has a very level space on top, they built an enclosure wall of stone and mud, square in shape, each side of the wall being probably two hundred fathoms long. The wall had a width of eight spans and a height of over twenty and the mud was so strong that after more than a hundred and thirty years I saw much of one side standing so safe and strong that a strong force of men with pickaxes was needed to demolish it. 'The church was built in the centre of this enclosure. It was made square, not merely the inner building, which was like a

[1] Cf. p. 154, where Almeida calls this tree the *iambugueiro*. In Páez's account of the journey of Fernandes it is identified with the *docoma*, the Amharic *doqmā*.

chapel, for these are made square in nearly all the churches of this country, though they erect a kind of round dome on the inner side at a height of twenty or 30 spans, fixing thick logs next to the four sides from one wall to the other. But this one of which I am speaking had square outer walls between them and the chapel was a space of about twenty-five spans serving as the body of the church, or cloister. I have seen a large part of one side-wall still standing; it and the others might be a hundred and forty or fifty spans long, and fifteen or eighteen high. The floor of the chapel was a platform raised eight or nine spans above the cloisters, so that from them twelve or 15 steps led up to the chapel. When I saw this place the platform was all piled up with fallen stones, but one could see the whole of one side and the way it was made. Both this and the other side of the chapel were 80 spans. In the sides that were standing, and in many very big pieces of stone that were lying on the ground, broad and smooth, could be seen as many varied and different roses as there were stones, each one of them so perfectly done in fine tracery that they looked as if they could not be bettered, I do not say in gold or silver with a burin, but even in wax or painted with brush and pen. That is what I saw; what I heard is that many of these roses were covered over with silver and gold. All the same, I do not think there would have been many, but it is not incredible that there should have been some. It is certain that the church was not only built at great expense, but was adorned and endowed with liberality. It was endowed with the entire district of Nebesse which is very large and productive, and so the monks, clergy and beneficed clergy or canons, Debterás they call them, were very numerous and all had fat prebends.

'The ornaments were very rich. There were some chalices and patens of gold of great weight, and two altar stones of solid gold, one of which weighed 800 oqueas, the other 500. I am a witness of this, for they were saved from the Moors and Gallas and came into the hands of the Emperor Seltan Cegued, who kept them in our house, spending them on restoring this church and on helping others, as we shall say below, in its place. This noble building had one very great fault, which was the light, which as St Ambrose said in his

Exhamero, is prima operis commendatio,[1] the first and greatest merit in the building, when it is present, and the lack of it is the greatest defect there can be. This, however, was not the fault of her who ordered the church to be built, and perhaps not of the workmen, who may have wished to adapt themselves to the country where the churches are all built for bats rather than people. It seems that they were forced to do it for there was nothing for the roof but thatch; so that the water should run off readily the timber work had to be carried up high, and come down from the centre of the chapel over the church and cloisters. All this is joined together without a window or dormer, so it is easy to tell that nothing could be seen without lamps, even at midday in a broad, big church like this. This method of roofing has another disadvantage. It is that as fire and straw are so dangerous together, if there is any quantity of the latter, and fire has to be burning day and night, disasters cannot be avoided. When there are enemies who want to cause damage, a moment destroys the work of many years. So it happened with this, which lasted for very few. It had not been finished for twenty when the Moor Granh[2] invaded Ethiopia. He and his men, on hearing of the riches of this famous temple, hurried to plunder it, and after looting what they found, set fire to it and turned it to ashes. There were some lords who afterwards undertook to restore it, though not to its former splendour. It was not long, however, before the Gallas sacked it again and burnt it. Now a Roman Father of ours is working with the help of the Emperor Seltan Çegued to resurrect from the ashes of this phoenix another improved, and as we hope, more enduring one, for it is of stone and lime, in honour of God and Our Lady the Virgin, whose church it was. It was called Mertolâ Mariam, meaning Mary's lodging.'[3]

---

[1] This saying is not to be found in the *Hexameron* of St Ambrose.

[2] Ahmad ibn Ibrahim al Ghazi, called 'the left-handed' by the Somali, (*grañ* in Amharic), was a Somali in the service of the ruler of Zeila. He was the son-in-law of Mahfuz, the governor of Zeila who fought the Abyssinians for twenty-five years till he was killed by Lebna Dengel in 1517. In 1527-8, in retaliation for an attack on Adal by the Abyssinian general Degalhan, Grañ invaded the country and thus began the war that lasted till his death in 1542. His ravages resulted in the Emperor's appeal to the Portuguese for help and in the expedition of D. Cristovão da Gama.

[3] Beke (*JRGS*, vol. XIV, p. 26), says the church is 'situated on a hill of some

size, on the summit of which a mass of rock forms a natural fortress, the
entrance to the place being at only one point, where there is a door'. The
following description and the accompanying illustration are reprinted from
his article, *A Description of the Ruins of the Church of Martula Mariam in
Abessinia*, published in *Archaeologia*, vol. XXXII (1847), pp. 38–57.

'Whatever may have been the former extent of the building westward,
the only portion now standing is what may be conjectured to be about the
eastern half of the entire structure, the walls of which remain in an almost
perfect state. It consists of five apartments, as shown in Plate V, fig. 2; of
which the centre and principal one (A) is a quadrangular building, the
western end of which (B) resembles a vestibule. This centre apartment is
evidently what Tellez calls "the inner house which was intended for a
chapel". Its length internally, from east to west, is fifty-seven feet six
inches; and as this length is precisely eighty Portuguese palms, which
d'Almeyda says was the extent of one of the walls of the original church, it
is manifest that the new structure was raised precisely on the old foundations. Its breadth inside is thirty palms (21 ft 7 ins). The walls, which are
of the thickness of four palms (2 ft 10½ ins) and rise to the height of forty
palms (28 ft 9 ins) are constructed, as are those throughout the building, of
rough stone and mortar, covered with ashlar. The screen (CC) at the
western extremity of the chapel . . . is a closed wall of the same thickness
and materials as the sides and eastern end. . . .

'Within this chapel, at the distance of twenty-five palms (18 ft) from the
western extremity, is an arch (Plate V, fig. 2, D) of twenty-two palms (15 ft
10 ins) span, and, inclusive of the piers on which it is raised, being about
thirty-five palms (25 ft) from the ground to the crown of the arch. These
piers and the surmounting arch, which is semi-circular, are comprised of
wrought blocks of freestone, three palms (26 ins) in the square, carved, on
the three exposed faces, in panels of fine and elaborate work in relievo, of a
flower-like character. The stone, the grain of which is scarcely perceptible,
is of a light gray colour, and of so excellent a quality. . . .

'The sides of this interior apartment are terminated above by a cornice,
consisting of a broad band, nearly six palms (about 4 ft 6 ins) in depth,
composed of an ornamented roll-moulding, having above it an alternate
series of rectangular panels and projecting blocks, in the form of scroll-
brackets surmounted by human heads; all the surfaces being elaborately
decorated with leaves and flower-like figures. . . .

'The floor of this centre chapel is raised about three feet above the level
of the body of the church and of the side chapels. There are, in all, five entrances to it; one from the centre of the screen (Plate V, fig. 2, E), two from
the aisles (FF), and two from the side chapels (GG). The steps of the first
rise within the thickness of the wall; those from the aisles into the vestibule
were apparently on the outside; whilst to those of the two entrances leading from the front of the high altar, the descent, although now filled up with
rubbish, to the general level of the floor, must have been within the body of
the chapel itself, as otherwise the doorways, which outside—i.e. within the
side chapels— are of the requisite height, would not have sufficient headway within the centre chapel. These two doorways, the lower portions of
which are hidden to the level of the floor, are richly ornamented with
carved stone-work, as also are two niches, one on each side of the high
altar. . . .

'The chief entrance from the nave (Plate V, fig. 1) is a plain Norman door-
way of three square recesses in depth, ascended by as many steps, and sur-

mounted by semi-circular arches, the sides having a simple impost-moulding running all over the jambs. On each side of the doorway is an opening, three palms (26 ins) square, closed towards the outside with a panel, with two mouldings, though scarcely sunk below the surface of the wall. These panels are perforated with small spaces, and have very much the appearance of confessional lattices. . . .

'On each side of the centre chapel is an apartment (Plate V, fig. 2, H & I), twenty-three palms (16 ft 6 ins) in length and fourteen palms (10 ft) in width, open to the aisle, of which it is in fact the continuation, by means of an arch of smaller dimensions than the one in the centre chapel already described, but, like that, ornamented with richly-carved stone-work. These are apparently the side chapels, forming with the principal one the "*three* chapels", which Tellez says the church contained. These side chapels communicate again with two other apartments (K & L) forming the transepts. The one on the right or gospel side, which I am inclined to regard as the "sacristy", likewise mentioned by Tellez, is larger than that on the left or epistle side, and has a door in the external wall (M) leading from the back of the building, by which it may be supposed that the priests entered the church to perform divine service. Into the room in the left transept I could not enter, the door-way between it and the side chapel being blocked up with stones. . . .

'As the church built by order of the Empress Helena was the work of Egyptian architects, and was erected prior to the introduction into Abessinia of the faith of Rome, we may be certain that it was not, as the existing building is, in the form of a Roman cross: in other words, it was without the transepts, and in that case the priests' and deacons' sacristies of the earlier structure will, as is usual in churches built on the Greek model, have occupied the places of the side chapels in the more modern work of Father Bruno.

'Of the roof there exist no vestiges, except one rafter across the principal chapel, and two or three over those on the sides.'

(*Note*.—The circular object shown in the plan above A is a thatched wattle hut built over the remains of the high altar, the door of which was kept locked, and Beke was not allowed to enter it.)

Beke visited the church in October, 1842. The description by Telles, whose book is merely a compilation from the works of Almeida and Páez, will be found on pp. 108–110 of his *Historia geral*. The 'Roman Father of ours' was Bruno Bruni; the church was unfinished when Fāsiladas forced the Jesuits to leave Gojam in 1633. The name Marṭula Māryām means 'Mary's tabernacle'.

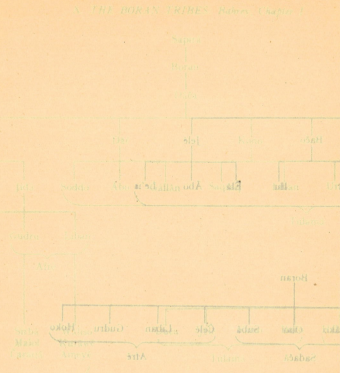

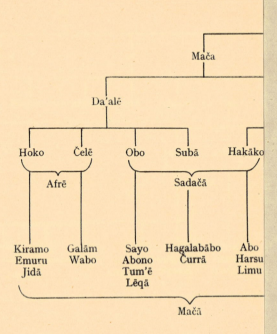

Mača

Da'alē

Hoko   Čelē   Obo   Subā   Hakāko

Afrē   Sadačā

Kiramo   Galām   Sayo   Hagalabābo   Abo
Emuru   Wabo   Abono   Čurrā   Harsu
Jidā   Tum'ē   Limu
                  Lēqā

Mačā

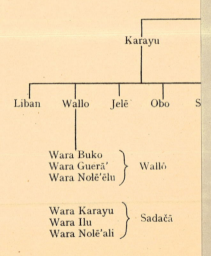

Karayu

Liban   Wallo   Jelē   Obo   S

Wara Buko
Wara Guerā'   } Wallō
Wara Nolē'ēlu

Wara Karayu
Wara Ilu   } Sadačā
Wara Nolē'ali

HISTORY OF THE GALLA

By Bahrey

I have begun to write the history of the Galla in order to make known the number of their tribes, their readiness to kill people, and the brutality of their manners. If anyone should say of my subject, 'Why has he written a history of bad people, just as one would write a history of good people,' I would answer by saying, 'Search in the books, and you will find that the history of Mahamad and the Moslem kings has been written, and they are our enemies in religion. Likewise Giyorgis Walda Amid[1] has written the history of the Persian kings with their childish legends, like those of Afridon and the other kings of Persia, who are now called Sofi.'

CHAPTER I

The author of this book says: The Galla[2] came from the west and crossed the river of their country, which is called Galanā,[3] to the frontier of Bāli, in the time of the Ḥaṣē[4] Wanāg Sagad.

[1] Jirjīs (George) ibn al 'Amīd, generally known as Al Makīn (1205–1273/4). His universal history was translated from Arabic into Ethiopic about 1500. Afridon is Feridun, a legendary King of Persia. Sofi is the 'Sophy' of old English writers, i.e. Safavi, the name of the dynasty that ruled Persia in the sixteenth and seventeenth centuries.

[2] The name *Galla* is of uncertain origin, and the Galla call themselves Oromo, pl. Oromota. The use of *Gāllā* by Bahrey suggests that it may possibly be a Sidama word which gained currency through his work and such writings as the *History of Sarṣa Dengel*. A well-known but apocryphal Moslem derivation is thus recorded by Burton: 'When Ullabu, the [Galla] chief, was summoned by Mohammed to Islamize, the messenger returned to report that "he said *no*"—Kál lá pronounced Gál lá—which impious refusal, said the Prophet, should from that time become the name of the race'. (*First Footsteps in East Africa*, p. 99). In Galla tradition Oromo is said to have been a prominent person in their original homeland of Gellad [in Arabia] whose son crossed the sea to Berbera and founded the Galla nation, which derived its name from the founder's father (Cecchi, *Da Zeila*, vol. II, p. 473). The 'chief Ullabu' of Burton seems due to a confusion with Ulabo or Wolabo, a place west of Harar which became a centre of dispersal for the Galla after their entry into southern Abyssinia.

[3] *galana* = 'river' in Galla. The text has *me'erāb*, 'west.' See p. lxxii.

[4] *'haṣē*, 'his majesty,' is a title of the king of Ethiopia. Wanāg Sagad, 'revered as a lion,' was the throne-name of Lebna Dengel, 1508–1540.

They are two tribes called Baraytumā and Boran.[1] Baray-tumā had six children: the eldest was called Karayu, the second Marawā, the third Itu, the fourth Akaču, the fifth Waranṭiša, the sixth Humbanā.

The father of Boran was called Sapirā. Sapirā[2] begot Dāča; Dāča begot Mačā; Mačā begot Da'alē and Jidā and these two brothers gave birth to numerous tribes. These are the sons of Da'alē: Hoko was the eldest, Čelē the second, Obo the third, and Subā was the fourth. Jidā begot Hakāko his eldest son, Gudru his second, and Liban his third.

Dāča begot the Dāč (whom he called by his own name), Kono, Bačo, and Jelē. These also gave birth to many tribes whose names are these: the children of Bačo are Uru and Ilu; the children of Dāč are Soddo, Ābo, Gāllān; the sons of Kono are Saqsaq, Liban; the sons of Jelē are Ēlā, Ābo, and Le'is; all these are called Tulamā, because they are numerous.[3]

Originally their custom was to set out together to war; but after a long period of time they quarrelled among themselves and separated, as did Abraham and Lot, when their herds became so numerous that they said, 'Let us separate, so that thou goest to the right and I go to the left; or, I go to the right and thou to the left.'[4]

Similarly the two tribes of Da'alē, Čelē and Hoko, and also the two tribes of Jedā (sic), Liban and Gudru, separated from their brothers and formed a confederacy, taking the name of Afrē,[5] in the time of the *luba* which the Boran call Ambisā[6] and the Bartumā Robālē.

Likewise, Hakāko son of Jedā, and the sons of Da'alē,

---

[1] Baraytumā is also written Bartumā by Bahrey; other forms are Barei-tumā and Barentu.

[2] Sapirā may be written here by mistake for Boran. Cf. the last paragraph of this chapter.

[3] This name may be derived from Galla *tulu*, 'swollen'; another form of the name is Tulomā.

[4] Genesis xiii, 9: 'And Abraham said unto Lot ... "Separate thyself, I pray thee, from me: if thou wilt take the left hand, then I will go to the right; or if thou take the right hand, then I will go to the left." '

[5] From Galla *afur*, 'four', i.e. a confederacy of four. This grouping of tribes into confederacies of four and three is a common Galla institution.

[6] The Ethiopic word *'anbasā* ('lion') is sometimes used in Galla in the form *ambesa*, though the proper Galla word is *lenča*. On the word *luba*, 'age-set,' see p. 205.

Ābo and Subā, made a confederacy and were called Sadača,[1] in the time of the *luba* called Birmajē; they also gave birth to numerous tribes. These are their names: The sons of Čelē are Galām, Wabo; the sons of Hoko are Kiramo, Emuru, Jidā; the sons of Liban are Wāliso, Kutāwē, Ameyē; the sons of Gudru are Sirbā, Malol, Čaraqā. The tribe of Hakāko is composed of Ābo, Harsu, Limu; the tribe of Subā is composed of Hagalabābo, Čurrā; the tribe of Ābo [Obo] is composed of Sayo, Abono, Tum'ē, Lēqā. All these when they are allied are called Mača; but when they make war they call themselves Afrē and Sadača; if they are all joined with the Tulamā they are called Sapirā.

Boran, on his side, had twelve[2] children: the eldest Dāča, the second Jelē, the third Kono, the fourth Bačo, which four are called Tulamā; the fifth was Hakāko, the sixth Obo, the seventh Subā, which three are called Sadača; the eighth was called Čelē, the ninth Liban, the tenth Gudru, the eleventh Hoko, and these four are called Afrē.[3]

CHAPTER 2

The Dāwē,[4] who devastated Baṭera Amorā,[5] belonged to the Boran; it has been said that they belong to another group, and an argument in favour of this has been seen in the fact that they have made war on the Boran. But this is a ridiculous theory and quite untrue. Those who are accurately informed declare that when the Boran quit their country, they do not all go, but those who wish to stay do so, and those

[1] From Galla *sadi*, 'three,' i.e. a confederacy of three.

[2] Only eleven are actually named in the text.

[3] This paragraph shows some inconsistency, for Boran is made the father not only of Dāča's sons, but also of three of Dāča's sons, Kono, Bačo, Jelē, and of the sons of Jidā and Da'alē as given earlier in the chapter. The name omitted (see preceding note) may perhaps be that of Dāča's eldest son Dāč. But it must be remembered that Bahrey belonged to a Sidama-speaking people who were hostile to the Galla; and that even to-day European observers have not yet succeeded in getting a consistent picture of the grouping of the Galla tribes. This paragraph seems to have been intended as a summary of the third, fifth and sixth paragraphs of this chapter.

[4] See note to Chapter 16.

[5] See *Beteramora* in Gazetteer.

who wish to leave do so; for they have no ruler who can en-
force his orders, and each man does what seems best to him.
Those of the Boran who stayed came out of their country by
way of Kuērā[1]; that was at the time when Fāsil[2] attacked
them and was killed by them. Then the Dāwē began to make
war on the Christians, and at that time the author of this
history prophesied and said, 'I fear him who killed Fāsil, for
he has tasted Christian blood.' And they devastated the two
districts of Baṭera Amorā and Waj, and it came to pass as he
had foretold, for the spirit of prophecy remains with the
priests. The Dāwē chased this prophet, laid waste his country,
which was called Gamo, and looted all that he possessed. But
let us return to the history of the Baraytumā from which we
have digressed.

CHAPTER 3

Karayu [of the Baraytumā][3] had six children who formed
many powerful tribes: the first was Liban, the second Wallo,
the third Jelē, the fourth Obo, the fifth Subā, the sixth Balā'.
Wallo had six children: Wara[4] Buko, Wara Guerā', Wara
Nolē'elu, who bear the name of Wallo; and Wara Karayu,
Wara Ilu, and Wara Nolē'ali, who are known as Sadačā.
Their separation dates from the time of the murder of
Aboli[5]; but they have now made peace and are leagued
against us.

CHAPTER 4

Marawā Ayā begot Anā, Uru, and Abati; their children and
grandchildren multiplied and formed numerous tribes. They

---

[1] The Koyra or Baditu south of Lake Margherita.

[2] Fāsil rebelled against his brother or cousin Sarṣa Dengel and was defeated in 1567.

[3] This chapter refers to the Baraytumā, not the Boran.

[4] Galla *wara* means 'family'.

[5] This was in 1585, and is referred to again in Chapter 13. The *Paris
Chronicle* tells how the Galla killed Aboli, a Wallo, when he was fighting the
Birmajē *luba* (p. 118).

received their name, each according to his tribe. They have neither king nor master like other peoples, but they obey the *luba* during a period of eight years; at the end of eight years another *luba* is made, and the first gives up his office. They do this at fixed times; and *luba* means 'those who are circumcised at the same time'. As to the law concerning their circumcision, it is thus: when a *luba* is formed,[1] all the Baraytumā and Boran give themselves a collective name, just as the king of Ethiopia's regiments call themselves by names like *Sellus haylē*, 'the Trinity is my strength,' *Badel ṣahāy*, 'the sun in victory,' or *Giyorgis haylē*, 'St George is my strength.'

CHAPTER 5

Thus it was that he who was circumcised when the Galla began to invade the country of Bāli was called Mēlbāh; I know not the name of his father, for no man was able to tell me.

CHAPTER 6

The second *luba* was called Mudanā; his father was called Jebanā. It was he who crossed the river Wabi.[2]

CHAPTER 7

The third *luba* was called Kilolē; he carried war towards the lowlands[3] of Dawāro, and fought with such as the Adal Mabraq, and with the inhabitants of the region.[4]

[1] The text has 'removed', but 'formed' is a better translation, since it is at the formation of a *luba* age-set that the *luba*-name is assumed.

[2] *wabi, webi* means 'river' in Somali, and the word refers here to the Wabi Shabelle, 'leopard river' (Somali *shabel*, 'leopard'). This is an early example of the use of *wabi* without any qualification to denote the Wabi Shabelle.

[3] Ethiopic *quallā*, 'valley, lowlands.'

[4] Guidi suggested *quallānyā*, 'inhabitants,' for the *quallātihā* of the MS. (His note, *HGG*, p. 198, refers to the seventh word of the chapter, but the

CHAPTER 8

The fourth *luba* was called Bifolē; it was he who devastated the whole of Dawāro and began to make war on Faṭagār. He began to enslave the inhabitants, and made of them the slaves called *gabare*.[1] Bifolē also began to drink *kosso*.[2] The first *lubas*, which we have just mentioned, killed people—men and women, horses and mules, leaving alive only the sheep, goats, and cattle; but they had no means of killing the creature which was in their intestines, the tape-worm, which slid down their legs, as in animals.

CHAPTER 9

The fifth *luba* was called Meslē. It was he who killed the Jān Amorā corps and fought against Hamalmāl at Dago;[3] he devastated all the towns and ruled them, remaining there with his troops, whereas previously the Galla, invading from

emendation fits the last word better.) Adal Mabraq seems to be an incomplete form, (due perhaps to a misunderstanding on Bahrey's part), of the name of the *čēwā* or army unit called Ba'adal Mabraq, which *CZ* (p. 45) records as stationed in Dawāro by Zar'a Yā'qob. These *čēwā* formed semi-permanent military colonies in territories conquered by the king of Abyssinia; so this unit may still have been in Dawāro though first stationed there a century before the time of Kilolē.

[1] The literal translation of this passage appears to be: 'He made of them the *agbert* (slaves) which he (Bifolē) called *gabare*.' In Ethiopic, *gabr* means 'slave', but in Galla the word *gabare* which is derived from it means 'servant, cultivator, taxpayer'. Almeida's paraphrase of this passage (p. 139: 'he made the farmers pay him taxes') suggests that the last of these three meanings is the right one here.

[2] Medicine for tape-worm (Galla, *minni*) is made from the leaves of the tree *kosso*, (*Brayera anthelminthica*), an Amharic word, used by the Galla, though they have a name of their own for it, *heto*. (See p. 98, n. 1.)

[3] Hamalmāl was a notable (*abbeto*) who rebelled against Sarṣa Dengel after his coronation on the grounds that he had, through his mother Romāna Warq, a better claim to the throne than Sarṣa Dengel himself. This claim was based on the fact that he was, like Sarṣa Dengel, a grandson of Lebna Dengel, though on his mother's side; Sarṣa Dengel however succeeded his father as king.

the Wabi,[1] had returned there at the end of each campaign. Our king Aṣnāf Sagad[2] fought Meslē, starting from 'Āsā Zanab. And when Nur[3] came down into his country, having done what he did,[4] Meslē met him near Hazalo and killed a very large number of his men. Since the Galla first invaded our country there had been no such slaughter, and the troops of Nur who were killed were more in number than the troops of Awsā [Aussa] which we shall speak of in the proper place.[5] Thus did God avenge on the Moslems the blood of His servants which they had spilt in Waj.[6]

This *luba* Meslē began the custom of riding horses and mules, which the Galla had not done previously, so that he said of the *lubas* which had preceded him, 'Those who travel on two or three legs, I have made them travel on four legs.' He said 'three legs' because they lent on their spears, as men would on their staffs when they were tired.[7]

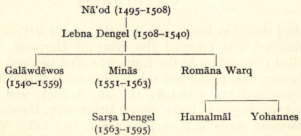

The place called Dago is mentioned in *CZ*, p. 54.

[1] Wabi = Wabi Shabelle. [2] The throne-name of Galāwdēwos (Claudius).

[3] Nur ibn Mujahid, emir of Harar, 1542–1567, was the successor of Ahmad Grañ.

[4] This refers to the death of Galāwdēwos in 1559 at the hands of Nur, who came from Adal in order to kill Galāwdēwos so that he could marry Dulwambara Grañ's widow, who had promised to accept him if he killed Galāwdēwos. Though Nur was successful and married the lady, the death of the king of Ethiopia was followed by a three years' drought (*PC*, p. 113).

[5] No further mention is made of this by Bahrey.

[6] i.e. the battle in which Galāwdēwos was killed.

[7] The date when the Galla began to ride horses (1554–1562) is important because it shows that all their previous movements had been made on foot, and disposes of any idea that they were a nation of horsemen from early times. It would thus appear that the '300,000 horsemen of the Wqlimi [or Wflimi]' mentioned by Mas'udi in the tenth century as going south to Sofala cannot have been Galla, as suggested by Mr G. A. Wainwright, and the Galla cannot have had any influence in the Zimbabwe district at such an early date. (G. A. Wainwright, 'The founders of the Zimbabwe civilization,' *Man* (1949, 80.)

CHAPTER 10

These five *lubas* which we have mentioned exercised power for a period of forty years; their children were not circumcised. Those who were not circumcised abandoned their children both boys and girls, for such is their custom; but after being circumcised they reared the boys, though the girls were still abandoned for two or three years after they had been circumcised.[1]

CHAPTER 11

After these five *lubas* had ruled, the sons of Mēlbāh were circumcised and received the name of Harmufā. Harmufā killed the soldiers of the regiment called Giyorgis Haylē at Qačeno. The Boran call this *luba* Dulu. It was Melbāh who devastated the countries of Gañ, Anguat, and Amharā, and who began to make war on Bagēmeder. Harmufā of the Bartumā made war on Bagēmeder, and killed Wākā the brother of Harbo.[2] Then Harmufā made a wicked statement

---

[1] The statement in this chapter as it stands is far from clear. Almeida refers to the custom (see p. 136), saying that all children born in the first six or seven years after marriage are cast away. It is probable that both accounts are based on a misunderstanding of the facts, and Guidi has a note that 'this barbarous custom is still practised, at least by certain tribes like the Borana, Maraqo (Adiya), Wolamo, and Albaso (Arusi). It is especially when the eldest child is a girl that it is abandoned without pity' (*CSCO*, Scr. Aeth., vol. III, p. 199). That the latter is a Galla custom is confirmed by Cerulli, who speaks of 'the barbarous custom, today almost extinct among the Galla tribes, of abandoning the daughters whom the father considered superfluous' (*Folk-Literature of the Galla of Southern Abyssinia*, p. 127).

This killing of children, it has been suggested, may be due to the Galla custom of not allowing uncircumcised men, though married, to have children. (A. H. J. Prins, *East African Age-Class Systems*, Groningen, 1953, p. 75.) Father Azaïs (p. 209) gives another reason—hunger.

[2] Harbo, who died in 1575, was a rebellious general who revolted against Sarṣa Dengel, with Yeshaq governor of northern Ethiopia.

and said, 'The Sidāmā [Christians] who are clothed in water, I have thrown into the water.'[1]

CHAPTER 12

After eight years Harmufā went out of office and Robālē son of Mudanā was made *luba* in his place; his name has been written in the sixth chapter. It was he who devastated Shoa and began to make war in Gojam. The king of Ethiopia[2] gave battle to him at Zewāy, killed many of his men, and captured many of his cattle; thanks to this booty many people became rich. Robālē killed the *azmāč* Zar'a Yohannes,[3] chief of the dignitaries: may he rest in peace!

In these days were <famous> Soli, Bidāro, Ilālā, in the tribe of Subā of the Boran.[4]

Five years afterwards the Haṣē Sarṣa Dengel attacked the Robālē of the Abaṭi at Waynā Dag'ā and killed them, not sparing one: it is of them that they say not more than ten remained; they alone returned home to carry news of the defeat.[5]

---

[1] The significance of this is not clear. The words in the text are *yelabsu bāhra*, 'clothed (in) the lake,' and Schleicher's interpretation 'who dwelt (by) the lake' gives *labbasa*, 'clothe,' a sense otherwise unknown. The only possible explanation seems to be that of Guidi, who sees in it an allusion either to the Ethiopian custom of baptism by total immersion or to the annual celebration of Our Lord's baptism among the Ethiopians by plunging naked into water. Such customs might well strike the pagan Galla as national characteristics, in the same sort of way that they described Moslems as *Islama hudu dikatu*, 'buttock-washing Moslems,' from their religious ablutions.

[2] Sarṣa Dengel in 1573 (*PC*, p. 117).

[3] Zar'a Yohannes died in 1574 (*PC*, p. 117). *azmāč* = general.

[4] The significance of these words is not known. In Galla, *bidaru* means 'trough' or 'canoe', and *ilala*, 'to see.'

[5] The Abaṭi were a Galla tribe, not Falasha (as Basset says, note 215 to *Paris Chronicle*). 'In his fifteenth year [1578] Sarṣa Dengel fought the Boran in the valley of the Majo [the Mača which flows into the Abay about 50 miles east of Dabra Markos] and defeated them; then he returned to Dambyā where he met the Abaṭi at Waynā Dag'ā and exterminated them all but one' (*PC*, p. 117).

CHAPTER 13

After eight years a new *luba* called Birmajē was created; he was the son of Kilolē who had devastated Dawāro. This Birmajē of the Boran made ox-hide shields of body length,[1] and attacked the Māyā,[2] who are skilled archers, but were beaten because there was no place for their arrows to strike, since the shields were made of stiff ox-hide. Birmajē pressed hard on the *azmāč* Daharagot,[3] commander in chief of the king's army, and killed Zēnāy and his guards. At first Daharagot defeated the Galla many times; but by the will of God, because the sins of the Christians were not expiated, the Galla devastated Ar'eña, the country of which Daharagot was governor, and killed Gāto, Batro, Badlo, 'Āmdo, and other personages.

Two districts became desert, two that used to enrich all poor men who visited them.[4] Birmajē of the Bartumā took the war into Dambyā and killed Aboli of the royal family, Samra 'Ab the bāhrnagāš,[5] and other personages.

[1] The typical Galla shield is circular with a central boss, and a diameter of about ten to thirty inches.

[2] The Māyā, who are mentioned in the *Futuh al Habashah* (fol. 14) and by Bruce (vol. III, p. 251), are described as skilled archers who fought sometimes for the Ethiopians and sometimes for the Moslems. They appear several times in Ethiopian records, and may have been, as Basset suggests, not so much a people as a fighting unit which originally took its name from the district to which its members belonged, for in 1495 we hear of the El-Māyā of Arho in the Danakil country, and in Sarṣa Dengel's time they occur in Waj. According to Basset there is a river Maya near Harar, of which the Amaressa is a tributary. We cannot find this river, but there is near Harar a lake called Haramaya (to which Azaïs and Chambard, *Cinq Années de recherches archéologiques en Éthiopie*, p. 106, refer as Maya), the second element of which may contain the same word. There is also a division of the Galla tribe of Babile, east of Harar, called Wara Maya. Cerulli speaks of the Māyā as 'nomads living on the edge of the Moslem state [of Dawāro]' (*La lingua e la storia di Harar*, p. 18); *AJIB*, p. 54, refers to the Māyā of the *quallā* (lowland) beyond Samēn, and on p. 61 mentions them in connexion with Ebnāt.

[3] Daharagot was a general of Sarṣa Dengel who first appears when summoned by the king with his troops from Waj. Ar'eña would thus seem to have been part of Waj.

[4] The scribe seems to have omitted some words after this sentence.

[5] This was in 1585 (*PC*, p. 118). *Bāhrnagāš* was the title of the governor of Tigre. (See p. 72. n. 2.)

All this befell because our king, Sarṣa Dengel, powerful in his acts and wise in his counsels, was absent; for if he had been in Dambyā, Birmajē would have suffered the fate of Robālē. But that the victory might be gained alternately, God sent the king to Dāmot, far from Dambyā. He was victorious wherever he went, but his generals were defeated because he was not with them.

CHAPTER 14

Birmajē of the Boran surrounded Dāmot, enslaved the men, and carried off the live-stock, for he[1] found the country without saviour or deliverer. At that time 'Āsbo[2] was daj'azmăč, and he, after taking counsel with his brothers, followed the Galla and came to the place where they were busy dividing the booty. The best of his soldiers and cavalry surrounded them with a triple line, that is, with three corps of the advance guard; the Galla took to flight and <many> were killed. Most of them hid in a great cave, whereupon 'Āsbo collected wood and set fire to it at the mouth of the cave. Many of the Galla who tried to escape from the smoke were taken prisoner till they brought back to 'Āsbo the prince royal who had been carried into slavery, together with many prisoners.[3] The heads of the slain were cut off; they were too many to count. After this, until the end of the period of Birmajē, the hand of God was again raised to threaten the Christians, and their sins are not yet expiated. Even if they were defended in the days of Birmajē, the last *luba* which we shall presently mention in its proper place was to ruin them.

[1] Here and in other places the ruling *luba* is personified in the *Abba Boku*, the tribal ruler. It should be remembered that the word *luba* is used by Bahrey in two senses: (1) to denote the age-set, (2) as a synonym for the *Abba Boku* as leader and representative of the age-set.

[2] 'Āsbo was the Ethiopian general who about 1574 rescued Susneyos from captivity among the Galla. Susneyos succeeded Sarṣa Dengel and reigned from 1604 to 1632. *Daj'azmăč* = general in charge of the king's door (*daj* = door), commander in chief.

[3] Guidi suggested as an alternative interpretation: 'till they brought back to the prince royal that which had been looted, together with many prisoners.'

CHAPTER 15

Birmajē then gave up office, and Mul'atā son of Bifolē was made *luba* in his place. He made a *dulāguto* or raid into Gojam. *Dulāguto* signifies a 'war of *guetyā*'.[1] For the Galla give themselves a name at the time when they are circumcised, as we have said at the end of Chapter 4, and they attack a country which none of their predecessors have attacked. If they have killed men or large animals, they shave the whole head, leaving a little hair in the middle of the skull. Those who have not killed men or large animals do not shave themselves, and in consequence they are tormented with lice. That is why they are so eager to kill us.

In those days the Haṣē decided to go into Damot, and while he was on his way there, he learnt that the Galla had attacked the country of Gojam, and that the Queen his mother had gone up to Dabra Abrehām[2] to seek refuge, as well as the princess Tēwodādā the sister of his ancestors king Aṣnāf Sagad and king Admās Sagad,[3] peace be upon them. When the Galla fell upon them suddenly and unexpectedly, all the people of the country were filled with terror, and their troops fled. But the king's eldest son fought valiantly against the Galla who were approaching the place where his mother was, and drove them away, for he was a young man celebrated for his strength. On his return he took his mother by the hand and carried her to a high mountain called Jebalā. The Haṣē, for his part, broke off his journey to Damot and came with speed

---

[1] Galla *dula* = 'war,' 'army'; *gutu*, according to Cerulli, is a method of hair-dressing adopted by the senior group in each *luba*: 'the *gúlā* make an arrangement called *gutú* which consists of several tufts of hair interwoven and twisted around the back of the head' (*Folk-Literature*, p. 170). This is perhaps a clue to the significance of the term *dulaguto*, and explains the presence of the statement which follows about shaving the head. *Dulaguto* may perhaps be translated 'big war'. *Guetyā*, 'laborious,' intended as an Ethiopic rendering, was perhaps suggested by similarity of sound. (There is also a Galla word *gutu*, 'complete.')

[2] Dabra = (1) mountain, (2) monastery, because monasteries are often on mountains.

[3] Aṣnāf Sagad is Galāwdēwos (1540–1559), and Admās Sagad is Minās (1559–1563).

to where the Galla were fighting. He did not act according to the custom of the kings his ancestors who, when making war were in the habit of sending their troops ahead, remaining themselves in the rear with the pick of their cavalry and infantry, praising those who went forward bravely and punishing those who lagged behind. This time, on the contrary, our king put himself at the head of his brave troops and fought stoutly; seeing which, the army threw itself like a pack of wild beasts on the Galla, who were all killed, without any survivors. Most of them fell over a precipice, so that the inhabitants of the country and the labourers killed them wherever they found them. The king ordered the heads of the Galla to be cut off, and Ādorā, a wide place,[1] was filled with them. After this, he brought down the Queen and the princess Tēwodādā from the convent where they were staying and received them with honour. When they saw the number of enemy heads which had been cut off, they were filled with a lively joy, and praised God for having set the spirit of victory on His anointed. The king returned to their owners the cattle which had been taken from them by the Galla.

CHAPTER 16

Then our king decided to set out, for he had done what he had thought of and had accomplished that which he had promised; and he went to Waj to make war on the Galla called Dāwē. It is true that the Galla call them by this name, as if meaning 'those who stay behind'; but the Abyssinians call them Dāwē because of the trouble they have brought to them.[2] The reason for his expedition was his belief that the Galla would await him in battle order and not save themselves by flight; but when he reached the place which he was

---

[1] In the MS the word Ādorā is followed by the letters *zaw'e . . . tu*, with a gap of 15 mm. between the two groups of letters.

[2] There is a Galla word *tā'*, 'remain,' and an Ethiopic word *dawē*, 'sickness, trouble.' It seems that in Bahrey's opinion the name was really of Galla origin, but similar in sound to the Ethiopic word. Conti Rossini has *gawi* for the same people in the *History of Sarṣa Dengel*, p. 144, referring to the same episode.

told was the home of the Galla, he found none. He sought their dwellings without finding them, and since there were neither cattle to carry off nor men to make war upon, he decided to fight the devil instead and snatch from him the souls of the pagans. He therefore sent for the peoples of Enāryā, Bošā, and Gomar, and said to them, 'Become Christians!' and they became Christians and were baptized with Christian baptism.[1]

CHAPTER 17

Mul'atā of the Wara De'ayā[2] having attacked the district of which Rās Walda Krestos was in charge, the latter conquered Mul'atā, recovered the booty which he had taken, and killed a great number of the Galla. He pursued a party of them and drove them over a precipice; and he kept his district safe till the Haṣē came back. On his return, the Haṣē found that the country had been preserved by the readiness of Walda Krestos and the battles which he had fought; and for that reason he made him Rās or head of his house, and set him at the head of the whole kingdom.

CHAPTER 18

Mul'atā of the Boran afflicted the Christians of Dāmot, scattered them, and devastated their country; from his time Shoa and Dāmot were deserts. As to what I have written, that sometimes the Galla were victorious and sometimes the Christians, it is what comes to pass according to the words of the Holy Scripture which say 'Today to thee and tomorrow to another, and the victory is at one time to this one, and another time to that one.'[3] He who is always the vanquisher is the Lord who rules all things. The country submits to

[1] See p. lxi. The word used here is *Krestiyāna*.

[2] This name, in the form Wardai, is now applied to some of the Galla of Tanaland in Kenya.

[3] Possibly a paraphrase, not a quotation, of part of II Samuel xi, 25.

him, Mul'atā, and none remains without submission to him.

When this book was written it was the seventh year of the government of Mul'atā son of Bifolē.[1] They get ready to open the circumcision and investiture of the sons of Meslē; and as to the battles and blood-shedding which will take place in their time, I shall write of them later, if I am still alive; and if I die, others will write their history for me, and that of future *lubas*. But happy is he who dies, for he shall enter into rest!

CHAPTER 19

The wise men often discuss these matters and say, 'How is it that the Galla defeat us, though we are numerous and well supplied with arms?' Some have said that God has allowed it because of our sins; others, that it is because our nation is divided into ten classes, nine of which take no part whatever in war, and make no shame of displaying their fear; only the tenth class makes war and fights to the best of its ability. Now, although we are numerous, those who can fight in war are few in number, and there are many who go not to war.

Of these classes, the first is that of the monks, of whom there are vast numbers. Among them are those who become monks at an early age, drawn thereto by the other monks while they are studying, as indeed was the case with him who has written this history, and others like him. There are also others who become monks because they fear war. A second group is composed of those who are called *dabtarā*,[2] or clerks; they study the holy books and all works relating to the occupations of the clergy; they clap their hands and stamp their feet during divine service, and have no shame for their fear of going to the wars. These people take as their models the levites and priests, namely, the sons of Aaron. The third group is that of the people called Jān Ḥaṣanā and Jān

---

[1] i.e. 1593.

[2] Amharic *dabtarā* = clerk, learned man, cantor. See p. 100.

Ma'āsarē,[1] who look after the administration of justice, and keep themselves from war. The fourth group is formed by those who escort the wives of dignitaries and the princesses; they are vigorous, brave, and strong men who nevertheless do not go to war, for they say, 'We are the protectors of the women.' The fifth group calls itself *Šemāgellē*,[2] 'elders'; they are the lords and hereditary landowners:[3] they share their land with their labourers, and are not ashamed of their fear. The sixth group is that of the labourers[4] in agriculture, who live in the fields and have no thought of taking part in war. The seventh group is composed of those who engage in trade and gain profit thereby. The eighth group is that of the artisans, such as the smiths, scribes, carpenters, and suchlike, who know not the art of war. The ninth group is that of the wandering singers, those who play the *qanda kabaro*[5] and the *baganā*,[6] whose profession is to beg, to collect money. They invoke blessings on those who reward them, flattering them with vain praises and idle panegyrics; while those who refuse to give them presents they curse, though they are not held blameworthy for this, for, as they say, 'This is our custom.' Such people keep themselves as far as possible from war. The tenth group, finally, is composed of those who carry the shield and spear, who can fight, and who follow the steps of their king to war. It is because these are so few in number that our country is ruined.

Among the Galla, on the contrary, these nine classes which we have mentioned do not exist; all men, from small to great, are instructed in warfare, and for this reason they ruin and kill us. Those who say that it is by God's command that they kill us, find their reasons in the fact that the Israelites were conquered and their ruin accomplished at the hands of the kings of Persia and Babylon. If brave warriors gain the victory, they say, who should ask help from God the Exalted and Most High? And if those who are numerous always conquer those who are few, the words of Holy Scripture which say 'One man shall put a thousand to flight, and two shall

---

[1] Lay officials of the royal household.
[2] Amharic *šemāgellē*, 'elder.'   [3] Ethiopic *rest*, 'hereditary estate.'
[4] *gabārāwi*.   [5] A small drum.
[6] A six-stringed lyre.

pursue ten thousand',[1] would be found to be vain. However, you wise men, you can judge if the claim of the first of these arguers is right, or that of the second.

CHAPTER 20

But to return to the affairs of the Galla. They call the small children *muča'*,[2] and those who are older, *ēlmān*;[3] those who are older still are called *guarbā'*,[4] and these are they who begin to take part in warfare. The young men who are not yet circumcised are called *quandalā*;[5] they dress their hair like soldiers, and their style of hairdressing is called *kalalā*;[6] if they kill a man, an elephant, a lion, a rhinoceros, or a buffalo, they shave the heads leaving a patch of hair on the top. But those who have killed neither man nor animal do not shave their heads; in the same way, married men do not shave themselves if they have killed neither man nor animal. In the time of the government of Mul'atā they ate the buffalo and said, 'Since we eat it, it is like an ox, and we ought not to shave our heads when we kill it.' One party said an outrageous thing when they declared, 'Let us not shave our heads when we kill the inhabitants of Shoa and Amhara, for they are but oxen which speak, and cannot fight.'

All the unmarried Galla, be they *luba*, circumcised, or *quandalā*, uncircumcised, are called *qēro*;[7] the *qēro luba*, the circumcised but not married, live in the same house with the *luba*, the circumcised married men; the unmarried *quandalā* live with the other *quandalā* who are married;

---

[1] Deut. xxxii, 30: 'How should one chase a thousand, and two put ten thousand to flight, except their Rock had sold them, and the Lord had shut them up?'

[2] Galla *muča*, 'small child.'

[3] Galla *ilma*, plur. *ilman*, 'son.'

[4] Galla *gurba*, 'youth.'

[5] Galla *qondala*, 'strong young man;' also a *gada*-name (see Appendix I, p. 205).

[6] Galla *kalala* means 'liana'; and Tutschek has 'branches with leaves . . . which are carried before . . . when the warriors return from war or chase' (*Dictionary*, p. 31).

[7] Galla *qero*, 'young unmarried man.'

P

and likewise the *qēro* who is a *gabar* or slave lives with the *gabar*.[1]

A score of men have the duty of building the *saqualā*,[2] the tents; they are called *ajartu*.[3] The Galla also assign to people the duty of killing oxen, and call them *qaltā*;[4] again, two people are appointed to roast and cut up the meat, and they distribute it in pieces equally to all; they are called *wājo*.[5] Likewise five men are chosen to milk the cows of all, and they are called *halabdo*;[6] two have the duty of taking the milk in buckets and giving it to each man in proper proportion; these men are called *ṭehito*;[7] and seven men have the duty of bringing home the herds and searching for strayed animals: they are called *barbādo*.[8]

They also choose from among themselves two men to whom is entrusted the duty of reprimanding and punishing those who have illicit relations with women; these are called *gorsā*,[9] and they take this precaution, not from love of virtue, but so that they may be always alert and ready for war, for 'he who is married studies to please his wife'.[10] Some ten men have also the duty of herding the cattle; they are called *ṭawtu*.[11] Those of them who wish to marry, separate from the others and stay at home: they are called *jelhikā*.[12] The old men are called *melguddo*.[13] The former (the *jelhikā*) do not altogether abstain from fighting, if they are not too feeble, like our brothers Zapo and Ābā Harā.

Nobody has found, as we have, an enemy which takes so

---

[1] This passage seems to mean, in essence, that men are grouped according to whether they are circumcised or uncircumcised, and not according to whether they are married or unmarried.

[2] Galla *saqala*, 'square house,' from Amharic *saqalā*.

[3] Galla *ijartu*, 'builder.'   [4] Galla *qaltu*, 'butcher.'

[5] From Galla *wada*, 'roast.'

[6] From Ethiopic *halaba*, 'to milk'; the word given suggests a borrowed form *halabtu*.

[7] This seems to be the word for 'herdsman' given by Cecchi as *tixitu*, i.e. *tiksitu*, from *tiksu*, 'herd'.

[8] From Galla *barbada*, 'look for.'

[9] Galla *gorsa*, 'one who instructs or warns.'

[10] Cf. 1 Cor. vii, 33: 'He that is married careth for the things that are of the world, how he may please his wife.'

[11] From Galla *toada*, 'inspect cattle.'

[12] This might be an attempt at some such word as '*jellīča*, 'the shame,' accusative singular from *jello* (Cecchi).

[13] Galla *mangudo*, 'old man.'

much trouble to do evil; but at the same time nobody has found, like us, a ruler and king so zealous for doing good. May God guard his servant [Malak Sagad] for a long period of time and for length of days. Thus has written Bāhrey.[1]

[1] Below the last line of the MS, on the dexter side, is written faintly, in larger characters, the word *yamān*, 'right hand.' The distribution of duties, on p. 128, is to be understood as referring to the activities in each village; the 'building of the *Saquala*' would seem to refer to the erection of buildings during *gada* ceremonies.

THE GALLA

From Almeida's *History*, Book IV

THE HISTORY OF HIGH ETHIOPIA OR ABASSIA

By Manoel de Almeida

BOOK IV

CHAPTER 25

A brief Account of the Gallas is given: what race they are, from what countries they came, their customs and habits, and how they conquered and became rulers of the biggest and best part of the Abyssinian Empire.

It should be known that the most southerly territories of this empire are the Kingdom of Cambate, lying due south, the Kingdom of Nareâ to the south-west, and that of Baly to the south east. If we wish to reach the sea-coast from any of these kingdoms and travel due south from Narea or Cambate we must traverse many hundreds of leagues without reaching it, because the land is very vast there and extends to the Cuama rivers and the Cape of Good Hope. Therefore the coast can only be found by going on a line from the north-west straight to the south-east. If we go from these kingdoms it will be found only after travelling over two hundred and fifty or 300 leagues. However, any one who left the Kingdom of Baly and went in the direction I mention would, after less than a hundred leagues, meet the coast and the sea between Cape Darfui, which is nine to ten degrees, and Magadoxo, which is two, at the place the maps call *the Badoẽs*, which is about 7 degrees, continuing along the coast and descending from there to five or four. This stretch of coast is that nearest to the territories of the empire, and indeed at one time belonged to the empire as did the Kingdom of Baly, beyond which in the south-eastern direction, there cannot be more than a hundred leagues, as I was saying. These lands lying between Baly and the sea, the coast of which

133

sailors call 'the desert' is the real home and fatherland of the Gallas.

Thence first came this plague and scourge of God in the days of the Emperor David,[1] who was at first called by his baptismal name, Lebena Danguil, and was also called Onag Çagued afterwards. They emerged at the same time as the Moor Granhe of Adel had invaded and already conquered a large part of the empire. They invaded the Kingdom of Baly, with which they had a common frontier, or of which they were close neighbours. They also invaded the Kingdom of Adel which we call Zeila, bordering on Baly, for the Gallas were the scourge, not only of the Abyssinians, but also of the Moors of Adel. This was either so that they should not be proud about their victories over the Abyssinians, or else so that the Abyssinians should understand that, through Granh and the Moors of Adel, God was punishing them as a loving father, to make them ask for help from the King of Portugal, promise to obey the Roman Pontiff, accept the true faith and abominate the heresies of Eutyches and Dioscurus. (This is what the Emperor Claudius did after the death of Dom Christovão da Gama, for he realised that otherwise the Patriarch Dom João Bermudez would not be willing for the Portuguese to serve him any more, or to help in his wars against the Moor Granhe.) Seeing himself in these straits, since it was essential for him to obtain help, he swore, with deceit in his heart, to obey the Pope of Rome, to acknowledge him as head of the Church, and to abandon the errors of the Alexandrian schismatics. God was so merciful that, at the time, He accepted the oath and gave those few Portuguese who were helping him, courage and strength to destroy many thousands of Moors at the Battle of Ogara against Granhe's Moorish captains, and to kill Granhe himself at the Battle of Oinadegâ.[2] With his death and this victory the Emperor Gladios was left absolute master of his empire.

However, Gladios and his people returned to their vomit or, it would be better to say, dropped their disguises and de-

[1] Dawit II, another name of Lebna Dengel.

[2] This refers to a Waynā dag'ā in Fogara east of Lake Tana where Grañ was killed in 1542.

clared themselves as the heretics they always were. As such they persecuted and expelled from their territories the Patriarch Dom João Bermudez. When he came from Oge, where the camp or court then was, to Debaroâ, God made known to him that the rod and whip which he had first put into the hands of Granhe and the Moors of Adel to punish the obstinacy of the Abyssinians, had now been delivered to the Gallas and that they were to be a crueller scourge and almost the total ruin of that contumacious empire. So the Patriarch, as he came on his way, pronounced many curses on the lands through which he passed, and said many times that there were certain black ants invading the kingdoms and provinces of the empire, destroying and wholly devastating it.

Time showed the truth of this prophecy. Every time that God gave the Abyssinians further instruction and taught them the truth of the holy faith of the Roman Church and the errors of the Alexandrian, which they followed, by the Patriarch Dom Andre de Oviedo, by the five Fathers of the Society who were his companions and by those who entered Ethiopia later, they persisted in their errors and obstinacy. Little by little He began to afflict and punish them by the Gallas, so that when the Emperor Seltan Cegued began to reign, they had made themselves masters of most and the best kingdoms of the empire. They surrounded and encircled the greater part of the territories subject to him, from the Kingdom of Angot, lying nearly east of them, continuing southwards through Doâro, Oifat, Baly, Fategar, Oge, part of Xaoa, Bizamo and Damut, lying to the west of Gojam. To-day they are masters of these kingdoms and of many provinces lying among them which I forbear to name for brevity's sake. If God had not blinded them and willed that certain families or tribes among them should be at war with one another constantly, there would not have been an inch of land in the empire, of which they were not masters. To this end God ordained also that the kingdoms which are today subject should be very mountainous and consist of very steep ranges where the Gallas' cavalry cannot readily make raids, which is the kind of fighting they practise.

Coming now to the history of the Gallas in greater detail,

thousand, but these are mostly picked young men. The same Emperor used therefore to say that the Abyssinians could not possibly withstand their first onslaught. So he used to let them invade the country and steal the cattle and whatever else they found. He used then to wait in the way for them on their return. Their first fury was then broken and they were thinking of reaching their country and securing and preserving the booty with which they were loaded. In this way he often defeated them.

The first of them to leave their own country crossed the river Galenâ and made their first incursion into Baly, a kingdom of the empire, in the time of Onag Çagued. They were two houses or tribes only, as the Abyssinians say, what we call two families or clans, which were Burtumâ and Borem.[1] Burtumâ had six sons, Borem eleven and all these were heads of families, and so were some of their sons. So the clans are now very numerous. They increase greatly because each man has many wives. They have no king or lord, but every eight years they choose one man as consul or governor, whom they call Lobâ[2] and whom they obey. The first thing he does is to assemble the best people he can and make several raids into the territories of the empire, in which he and his soldiers win fame and enrich themselves with much booty. This they call Delâ Gutô, or general muster. They all have the custom of not cutting the hair of their heads so long as they have not killed any enemy in war, or some courageous wild beast such as a tiger or lion. As soon as they do kill it, they shave their heads, leaving on the very top one long lock like a sinay.[3]

The first Lobâ was called Melbâ, the 2nd Mudenâ; he crossed the Obê river, which is in Doarô; the 3rd Lobâ was called Chiloquê;[4] he fought against Doarô and Adel Mabraca. The 4th was called Bifolê; he destroyed the whole of Doarô and began to invade the Kingdom of Fategar which borders

---

[1] Baraytuma and Boran.   [2] luba.

[3] Dalgado derives this word from shenvi, a Konkani and Marathi term applied to the Sarasvati Brahmins. The Rev. J. B. Primrose writes: 'The Shenvis do shave their heads and leave one tuft on top, but practically all Brahmins do so, or rather used to do so. . . . This caste is common on the west coast of India and would be familiar to the Portuguese.'

[4] An error for Kilole.

on Doarô and lies to the west of it. He made many prisoners whom he took as slaves and he made the farmers pay him taxes. He began to drink coço, which is the bitter seed of which we spoke in the first book, which the Abyssinians drink as a purgative to kill and rid their stomachs of certain little worms thinner than tapeworms which breed in there because they eat raw beef. The 5th Lobâ was called Muchâlê;[1] he began to populate the territories of the empire which he conquered and he was the first who rode and taught the Gallas to fight on horseback. He used to say: 'I made men who went on three legs go on four.' He said 'three' because of the *zarguncho* which those on foot sometimes use as a walking-stick.[2]

[1] Meslẽ.

[2] Some of Almeida's statements have evidently been taken from Bahrey, especially in the last two paragraphs, where some of Bahrey's shortest chapters are repeated almost word for word.

(1) THE JOURNEY OF ANTONIO FERNANDES, 1613–14

(*Almeida, Book VII, Chapters 13–19*)

BOOK VII

CHAPTER 13

How Father Antonio Fernandez[1] left for Gojam, and thence for Narea with the Ambassador, and what happened to them till they arrived.

At the beginning of March, 1613, Father Antonio Fernandez left Dambeâ for Gojam. The Viceroy Cella Christôs was there already, and so was the Ambassador Fecur Egzj who had gone ahead to settle the affairs of his household and wife and children, who were living there. The Father reached Collelâ, our residency, where Father Francisco Antonio de Angeles[2] was, and stayed several days, knowing that the Viceroy had gone on a raid. As soon as he knew he had returned he went to look for him at Ombramâ. The Father took with him ten Portuguese, of whom four had offered to accompany him to India, and six as far as Nareâ, where they were to turn back. The Viceroy received the Father with very marked affection and kept him at his camp until the arrival of some Gallas and Xates;[3] he had ordered that they should be sought out to serve the Father as guides as far as Nareâ, since a large part of the route is inhabited by these two peoples. When these guides arrived he pleased them by giving them some pieces of good quality, and promising them better when they should bring him

---

[1] Not to be confused with two other Jesuits of the same name who worked in Abyssinia, or with the explorer of the hinterland of Sofala in the sixteenth century. The latter was not a priest.

[2] A Neapolitan who had come to Abyssinia with Fernandes.

[3] Montandon (p. 202) gives this name to the Shinasha, but the Abyssinian chronicles leave no doubt that the Abyssinians themselves used it with reference to the Gafat. *PC* (p. 24) speaks of the land of Shat, the peoples of which call themselves Gafat, and are pagans.

news that they had accomplished the journey and had taken the Father and Ambassador to Nareâ in safety. On parting from the Father he addressed him with the great fervour and in the spirit one might have expected from a superior of the Society when sending a subordinate on a laborious and difficult mission. He represented to him the importance of the business with which he was entrusted and the difficulties which the Devil would raise up to prevent him from attaining the desired end. He exhorted him to surmount them all with a brave and constant heart, seeing the great glory to God and the gain of so many souls that would follow from the reduction[1] of that empire. He reminded him that amid the greatest toils and dangers he should put his trust in God, being certain and sure that the Lord would not fail to help him, since he had exposed himself to them for His love and since the enterprise was wholly His. He especially urged him to try to conclude the business with the greatest possible speed and despatch so that their intentions could be put into effect during the Emperor's life; if he should die beforehand all would be in vain and the cost and trouble of the journey would be wasted.

At length, so that he should not exhort by words only, but by example too, his eyes filling with tears, he threw himself at the Father's feet to kiss them, believing that he profited greatly by kissing feet which were to walk such long and rough roads for the love of God. The Father hastened to prevent him and raise him up, greatly moved and edified to see the profound humility of such a great prince. The Viceroy then begged the Father most earnestly that when our Lord God took him to Rome he would kiss the feet of His Holiness in his name and bring him a little thread from his clothing, which he would always keep as a very great relic and consider as a treasure of inestimable value. The Viceroy then called the Ambassador and addressed a similar exhortation to him. He parted from him and from the Father with affectionate embraces, showing not merely regret but great envy, for if the distance had allowed, he would have had no greater

[1] i.e. of Abyssinia to obedience to Rome. This word is often used by the Jesuits in this sense. Because of its etymology it was no doubt intended to suggest the 'leading back' of lost sheep to the fold of Christ.

pleasure in life than to go and visit in person the holy places of Rome, kiss the feet of the Vicar of Christ on earth and see the courts of the King of Portugal and of the other kings, princes and potentates of Europe.

The Father and Ambassador left Ombramâ in the middle of April, taking with them some 40 men with shields and *zargunchos*. In two or three days, travelling westwards through the country of the Gongâs, they reached Sinassê,[1] an important town of the heathen Gongâs. In the Viceroy's name they asked for a guard for the remainder of the journey to the Nile. The Gongâs would not provide one, which was as much as to say that they would waylay, plunder and kill them. This they were resolved to do in revenge for one of the chiefs of that country whom the Viceroy had shortly before condemned to death as a criminal. The Ambassador made several applications to them. When he saw that they would not yield he decided to send a message to the Viceroy asking him to send a few companies of soldiers who could ensure their safety in this peril. Nobody, however, was willing to go, for they were all afraid of the journey. Then one of the ten Portuguese travelling with the Father offered to go and set off at full speed to inform the Viceroy of what was happening. The latter was very angry and sent two or three captains with their people to provide a guard for the Father and Ambassador and to punish the Gongâs. They, however, knew that a message had been sent to the Viceroy, and fearing that they would be punished, were now better advised and supplied the guard for which they had been asked. In their company the Father and his companions reached the place where they were to cross the Nile, called Minê, in three days. This crossing is in the bend which the river makes towards the north and Egypt, being nearly opposite its source on a line running east and west. The river has already increased greatly in size[2] and was running very fast at that time. As there was no other way they crossed on a raft of poles

---

[1] The Shinasha are a section of the Gonga group isolated by the Galla invasion. The use of the name for a town probably means no more than that it was a settlement of Shinasha.

[2] i.e. it is a much bigger stream than when it leaves Lake Tana. Almeida does not mean that it was swollen by the rains for this was April, the dry season. Many of the Nile fords are impassable at any other time.

roughly fastened together with gourds among them which helped them to float. Young men swam in front and guided the raft and others pushed it from behind. As this was a slow proceeding and the raft could not hold much baggage or many people they spent a whole day going to and fro across the river.

Next day they sent a man to the Viceroy with the news. The Father ordered that the Portuguese who had been with them and who was now on his way with many soldiers, should be told to turn back as he would not be able to overtake them. From this crossing until they reached Nareâ they always travelled due south. On this route, which is perhaps some fifty leagues, there was no lack of dangers from which God in His goodness delivered them. The first they met on the day they left the river, when they had gone only three leagues. One of the Ambassador's servants, who was coming along a little way behind, took two *apas* from a heathen Gongâ, one of those who live there as subjects of the Gallas. The Gongâ shouted and many others joined him and brought their weapons. This happened near a place where the Gallas used to exact dues from passers by, and they too hurried up both to avenge the injury to the Gongâ and to exact their dues. It was a brawl between armed men and everyone's life was in great danger but the Father, in his prudence and gentleness, gave the Gallas some pieces of slight value, had the Gongâ paid for his *apas*, and so pacified everybody. On the 3rd day after this encounter they had one with a big caravan coming from Nareâ. When they asked the members of the caravan about conditions along the route, they told them that so small a party as theirs was certainly going to its death, because there were numerous Xate and Cafre brigands at certain difficult places through which they would have to go. When they heard this some traders who were travelling with the Father's party turned back. The others, although frightened, went forward, encouraged by the Father and by a Nareâ from the caravan who promised them that, if they paid him for it, he would guide them by devious paths so that they should not meet the brigands. He was promised handsome payment. They went forward and in few days reached the country of the Xates. The men belonging to this nation who were accompanying the Father and Ambassador as guides and guards, finding themselves among their own people, began to demand large bribes and wanted to sell their services for more than they and the guard they provided were worth. Because of this the Ambassador's men closed with them and were prepared to kill them. They let them go, however, and they saw many Xates waiting to plunder them in a defile on a steep mountain. Then they ranged themselves in order; the men with shields formed two little bands, one in front and one behind, and the baggage train was placed in between. The brigands saw the cohesion and determination with which they were marching, were afraid to attack and made off leaving the way clear.

Next day they entered Cafre country and reached a cool stream called the Anquêr. Thinking they had nothing to fear they not only sat down to take a siesta but freed the mules to graze, and they all scattered in different directions. The Cafres, who were watching them, saw they were off their guard, came up, surrounded them, sounded their little trumpets and began an attack. One of the Cafres saw two mules at a distance from the rest and began to drive them into the forest. The Ambassador's people hurried up and ranged themselves in order. Some of them then attacked the man who was driving off the mules and when he fled, brought them back. The rest fought against the Cafres to such purpose that they drove them back for a while. Seeing that the Cafres were slackening in the fight, they spoke to them, said they were the Emperor's messengers and asked to be allowed to go on in peace. The Cafres, who were now hoping for this, came to terms at once, saying they had not recognised them and had attacked thinking they were Gallas; they could pass, and welcome, if they gave them something. They were satisfied with a few blocks of salt[1] and two little caps. At that juncture God brought on the rain which made the Cafres retire to their huts. The travellers took advantage of this and hurried on before those Cafres could send a message to the people of another and larger village nearby.

The same day the Nareâ whom they were taking with them as a guide to the bypaths, led them from the track, through

[1] See p. 44, n. 2.

thick forest which was hard to penetrate, and down a great
slope to a big river called the Malêg. They reached it at night
after much trouble. The worst thing was that when they
looked for the ford and the place where they were to cross the
river the next day, they could not find it. There were some
people who suspected evil things of the guide. They said,
moreover, that on another occasion the same man had offered
to act as guide to a great lord and had done it in such a way as
to lead him among enemies where he and all who were with
him had perished. So some of them began to abuse him and
wanted to lay hands on him but Father Antonio Fernandez,
realising that they would all perish without a guide, called
him, spoke to him kindly and encouraged him, telling him
that failure to find the ford did not matter much, since it was
a dark night and they would find it next day. He saw to it
that he was given a good dinner and reassured him. Nevertheless he instructed four men to watch him very closely,
without his noticing it, so that he should not escape in the
night, which they spent in alarm about this. In the morning
God willed that they should find the ford, cross the river and
leave behind the danger of the robbers who were on the
hither side. The guide went to look for the track which he
found easily. They followed it very happily and reached a
river near which they spent the night with much greater calm
and peace of mind, as they were now a long way from the
Cafres. Next day they entered Nareâ and climbed a steep
mountain called Gancâ, fully inhabited, where the chief
military commander of that kingdom usually lives, since it is
their frontier against many enemies with whom they
are at war.[1] The man there at the time was Abecan.[2] He
received the Father and the Ambassador with great honour
and signs of pleasure, for the Viceroy Cellá Christôs had

---

[1] Bruce, repeating a misprint in the English version of Telles, calls this
place Gonea, and this spelling appears on some nineteenth century maps.
The frontiers of the states of S.W. Ethiopia were crossed only at precise
places and were closely guarded. Soleillet (p. 164) describes the *kella* or gate
in the defences at Abalti, at the northern end of Janjero: 'A passage had
been cut by the hand of man through the living rock, and was closed by a
gate. . . . We found a second gate closed by a thorn barrier and supported
by a forked wooden bar. The defence is formed of a ditch and a thorn
dead-hedge.'

[2] B.M. MS: Abeçan.

states

recommended them strongly and had sent him a handsome present.

CHAPTER 14

The Kingdom of Nareâ and what happened there to Father Antonio Fernandez and the Ambassador Fecur Egzy.

The Kingdom of Nareâ is, as I have said, the most southerly of all those in this empire. At least, coming due south from Maçuâ there is no other in a lower degree of latitude or closer to the Equator. From Maçuâ to Nareâ there are about two hundred leagues and for the greater part of the way one travels in a south-westerly direction, as far as Minê that is, which is a place in Gojam where the Nile is crossed for the 2nd time on the way to Nareâ. Thereafter one travels due south. So, as the centre of Dambeâ lies 13 and a half degrees north and Minê about 12, Nareâ is perhaps eight. This kingdom is not as big as some have said. It seems that they have included in it the territories of the Cafres surrounding it, which extend from Nareâ toward the coast of Melinde, lying to the south-east, and also those which lie toward Angola, which is to the west. It is because of the trade there is with Cafraria that Nareâ has so much gold; it is acquired from the Cafres in exchange for clothing, cows, salt and other goods. What is properly called Nareâ and is subject to its king has, however, an area of 30 or 40 leagues. A considerable quantity of gold is found in it but the greater part comes from outside.[1] The natives of Nareâ are the best in the whole of Ethiopia, as all the Abyssinians admit.[2] They are well-made and not

[1] Páez (Beccari, vol. II, p. 283) says that more gold came from Enarya than from any other part of the empire. Mendes (*ibid.* vol. VIII, p. 35) says explicitly that there are no gold mines, but there are many alluvial deposits ['*granaria*'], namely, the rivers, from which grains of gold are taken in Enarya and other western regions. The gold wealth of Enarya seems to have been grossly exaggerated, and what there was came from alluvial deposits. Beke mentions gold from Sheka and Enarya but the amount exported in his day was not great.

[2] In Beccari's text and in the B.M. MS which he used the stop comes after Ethiopia. We have followed the punctuation of the S.O.A.S. MS. Ludolf (*Historia*, c. 3) says that his informant Gregory praised the Enaryans highly for their honesty.

very black; their features are in no way Cafre; they have thin
lips and pointed noses. They are men of their word and deal
truthfully without the duplicity and dissimulation usual
among the Amarâs. The country is rich in foodstuffs and all
kinds of cattle, mules and horses. They pay gold by weight,
as is done throughout Ethiopia, but small pieces of iron also
circulate as money; they are light and flat, two inches wide
and three long.[1] They were all pagans in the time of the Emperor Malac Sagued. About sixty years ago they were baptised. The faith which was taught them was that held by
Ethiopia, full of the errors of Eutyches and Dioscurus.
Hitherto no Father of our Society has had an opportunity to
go to the country and teach them, both because of the difficulty of the journey and because the Emperor has not
sanctioned it. Now, in August, 1632, when I am writing this
history, the King or Xumo of that kingdom is Emana
Christos, a young man whom I know well, a very good
Catholic, son of Benerô, of whom we shall speak soon.
Emanâ Christôs was in exile from his country and was living
here among the Amarâs, married to a daughter of Ras Cellá
Christos. His father's enemies had killed him by treachery
and made another man Xumo. Those of Benerô's party killed
him and all his minions and then sent for his son Emanâ
Christôs to put him in control of the kingdom or xumete, so
to speak. Since he succeeds by inheritance from father to
sons the ruler of Nareâ is strictly speaking a king, as indeed
his predecessors were. Nevertheless, since he has been subject
to the Emperor he has no longer been called king but Xumo,
which means the same as governor. The Gallas invaded this
empire and made themselves masters of the greater part of it,
yet although they conquered the country lying between
Gojam and Nareâ and placed themselves in between, they
have never been able to prevail against the Nareâs. There are
major wars between them but until the present day the
Nareâs have defended themselves without help from the

---

[1] Páez calls them thin bars about 4 x 1 ins, and says they are called *caera*.
Bruce, in his article on the 'Kuara' tree in his Appendix, says that its fruit
is a red bean which 'seems to have been . . . used for a weight of gold among
the Shangalla (negroes) . . . and by repeated experiments I have found that,
from the time of its being gathered, it varies very little in weight'. This may
perhaps be the origin of the word given by Páez (Amharic, *quārā*).

Emperor. They habitually pay him their tribute out of their native loyalty, the situation being such that if they wanted to free themselves from it, he could hardly go and wage war upon them in the midst of the Gallas, and apart from the Gallas, there are usually many rebels in the kingdoms near his court.

From Gancâ the Father and Ambassador went to Benerô's court, for that is the name of the king or Xumo. They reached it in six days, travelling for the first part of the time through almost uninhabited country, as the Gallas had raided it a few days before. The rest of the journey was through fertile and populous country. Benerô received the Father with kindness, though not with as much honour as he himself wished to show. The reason was that the friar who was his chaplain[1] was very much frightened by the Father's going to that country. He supposed that the Father would stay there and teach our holy faith, so depriving him of the office of chaplain and Vicar General of the Abuna in the country, and of the income he collected which was not small. The Father realised this, visited him, disabused him and asked for his support in persuading Benerô to send them on their way quickly. To secure this he gave the friar a present of *bofetâ*, which undeceived him. Benerô, nevertheless, meant to divine the object of the Father's and Ambassador's journey to India. He was afraid that it was to bring Portuguese into the country. He consulted the grandees of his court and decided that he would not allow the Father to travel by the route he was thinking of using, which was by way of a country called Cafâ that lies to the south of Nareâ, because that seemed to him the most direct route to bring him out on the Melinde coast. Benerô and his people were afraid that if this route were opened up Portuguese would come that way and make themselves masters of his kingdom. So, after

---

[1] *mestre*. This word cannot here mean 'physician' as it sometimes does but must refer to an ecclesiastic of the type described by Almeida (bk III, c. 5) as monks living in the houses of 'grandees' and acting as their confessors on the few occasions when they confessed and as readers of the Scriptures. He also alleges that they baptised their patrons every morning! 'The Devil put the greatest possible indecency into this barbarous custom; so that it should be altogether infernal and of fire rather than of water, both men and women only received it when stripped of their clothes and naked as if they were children eight days old.'

labour, especially after nightfall. They were advancing blindly, without seeing the road, in penetrating rain and cold and through such thick forest that the Father was forced to go on foot; on his mule he could not disentangle himself from the multitude of thorns he encountered.[1] At midnight they stopped under some tall trees to rest and warmed themselves a little at a fire, for they were dead with cold as they travelled. They dined off toasted barley, as they did very regularly, for as they were going through the wilderness no better provisions could have been found for them in Ethiopia nor could people travelling light have carried them.

They put out the fire before dawn so as not to be seen by the Gallas, started on their way and at midday came to some *jambolan*[2] trees. There are many of these in Ethiopia growing by the waterside, but compared with those of India they are like olive-trees. (Yet they are plentiful there as compared with those of Europe, which are properly *iambugueiros*.)[3] The fruit is merely skin and stone. Such are these *jambolans*, yet pinched by hunger, the Ambassador's servants and some of the Father's could not be parted from them. Those who knew the country called out that it was essential to hurry since they were then among the Gallas, but hunger deafened the servants and they would not move a step. When he saw this the Father stopped and went into the forest to fetch them out and make them resume the journey. He found himself among precipices from which God delivered him with danger and toil. When they returned to the road and all assembled they found that one Portuguese was missing. They all felt very sad and many went back to look for him. After a while they heard him shouting in the depths of the forest for he

---

[1] 'I have been astonished at seeing many highways, and even some of those most used, rendered almost impassable by the number of thorns which are allowed to remain spread across them' (Parkyns, vol. I, p. 213). 'In many places also . . . the road . . . was so completely interwoven with thorns, that . . . I found it impossible to ride. Long before we arrived at our destination I had scarcely a rag left to my back or a square inch of whole skin to my body' (*ibid.*, p. 245).

[2] Mr A. W. Exell writes: 'The *jambolan* is an Indian fruit (*Eugenia jambolana* Lam.) known as the 'Black Plum' by Anglo-Indians. Unless these had already been introduced into Abyssinia at that time, the missionary probably saw a similar African species of *Eugenia*.'

[3] A species of wild olive. See also p. 103, n. 1.

had lost his way. They fetched him and in the evening descended a rugged and steep mountain and reached the river Zebeê.

This river carries a greater volume of water than the Nile. At this place it runs in a gorge between cliffs, rushing over boulders and rocks on which the torrent breaks with such fury that the roar is rather frightening. But what frightened them more was the bridge by which they had to cross, which was merely a log long enough to reach from rock to rock across the width of the river, which was no little distance. To look down was to look at hell; when anyone set foot on the log it shook like a green twig. None the less they all crossed over, vying with one another to be first, for the country on one bank belonged to the Gallas, on the other to the Kingdom of Gingerô where they thought themselves safe; fear of the Gallas overcame fear of the bridge. Father Antonio Fernandez, however, did not risk crossing until he had made them cut down one of the trees of which there were plenty there; they laid it beside the first and the bridge was then safer and easier to cross. As soon as they were on the far side they were rid of their fear of the Gallas but there was still one great difficulty; they could find no way to bring the mules across. It was not possible to use the bridge and the river banks were nothing but precipitous rocks. The mules had to sleep on the hither side with two men to keep watch over them, who were sure that if Gallas should come they would be able to reach safety across the bridge. Next day, in the morning God brought to them two men of the country who knew the crossings and, when they had been well paid for it, led them to a place where they were able to cross, although with much trouble.

They left the river, went on a little way and then alighted at a village from which they sent to notify the King of their coming and to ask his permission to come to his court. Because he was busy with magical practices[1] they had to wait there 8 days; when they had permission they left and arrived at the place where he was the same day. They found him, as

[1] 'There are many magicians and witches among the Giangero. The king himself exercises this profession, and several times a month sacrifices, if the Giangero slaves in Gera speak the truth, human victims who are for the most part babies.' (Cecchi, vol. II, p. 355.)

Gingirô means ape or monkey[1] and that is what they are in many ways, in this chiefly: in war, if one of them survives after being wounded, his relatives kill him. If they do not do it his comrades do so without any remission, however much he may cry out and beg for mercy. They say this is done lest it should be said that they have died at the hands of the enemy, a thing they consider to be very dishonourable. This is what happens with apes. When they are wounded, either themselves, or on each other's behalf, they scratch the wound until they pull out the entrails and fall dead.[2] The King also plays the part of an ape on the perch or platform where he sits alone and transacts business. They have an amusing custom that if he happens not to have gone out of his house before sunrise, he does not go out at all, nor does he go up to his perch nor does anyone go in to him on business. The explanation they give for this custom is curious, for they say that two suns cannot endure each other in the world, and since he does not overcome the other by force they think it is not good for him to be second in this rivalry.

When the King dies they wrap his body in rich cloths, kill a cow and put the body in its hide. Then all those who hope to succeed to the Kingdom, his sons or those near to the royal house, from whom the one who seems most suitable is chosen, these, I say, flee from the honour they desire and take refuge from it, seemingly in order that it may follow and pursue them. They betake themselves to the forest and hide as best they can. The electors are very great sorcerers; when they have agreed upon who is to be made King, they go and seek him and the birds gather above the place where he has hidden and reveal him, in particular a bird of prey like an eagle, which they call ybêr, which rises up and then descends

and hot springs. From these there developed a spirit-cult among various peoples, including the Kafa, Kullo and Konta. The spirits were 'specialised' beings which could leave their proper habitations and take up temporary residence in the bodies of certain persons, who formed a priesthood of the spirit that possessed them. Co-existent with the spirit-cult was the worship of a sky god, called *ha'o* in Janjero, and recorded also from the Kafa, Sidamo and Hadiya (Cerulli, *op. cit.*, vol. I, pp. 217–226).

[1] Properly 'baboon'.

[2] We have not been able to trace the origin of this story. Professor H. W. Janson informs us that he does not consider that it can be derived from an ancient or mediaeval source.

uttering loud cries.[1] Then, knowing that he is there, they go
to look for him and find him surrounded by lions, tigers,
snakes and leopards, all of which they bring together with
their sorcery.[2] The one chosen, as soon as he sees they are
seeking him, fights as hard as he can against being taken,
wounding and killing them. Those seeking him put up with
all this at his hands, recover themselves and close with him
till they can secure his hands. In this way they take him as if
by force and he, showing that he can resist no more, accepts
the burden of ruling and the honour they wish to give him.
A rare example of scorn for what the world so greatly desires
and loves if it were not all mere pretence and savagery. On
the way, as they bring along the King they have elected,
there is always a skirmish or a pitched battle. There is in the
Kingdom one family which by immemorial custom has the
right to take the King who has been elected, if they can,
from the hands of the electors who went to seek him, so that
members of this other family should put him in possession of
the Kingdom. For this purpose they join with their friends
and allies, look for a suitable place and there give battle to
the electors and the people on their side. The victors carry off
the King and enthrone him. Those who do this retain his
favour and have the most honourable offices of the court and
Kingdom.

When they have taken the King to the court in this way,
they put him in a tent. On the seventh day after the old

[1] Bruce, misled by a misprint in the English version of Telles, calls this
bird 'Liber'. We have not been able to identify it. It is not possible to say to
what language the word belongs; there is no suitable Amharic bird name
anything like it, although there is an Amharic *yebrā*, meaning 'wild goose'.
Páez says it could lift a kid in its talons. The stories of Harris and Krapf
in the following note suggest that it may have been a vulture, but vultures
are believed to be silent except when fighting over carrion.

[2] Harris, whose account of Janjero was based on hearsay, says (vol. III,
p. 57) that the successor was the man over whom a vulture flew. Krapf
(p. 68) was told by a Guragé priest that the king was chosen by a vulture or
a bee. Cecchi, who collected his information in Gera, says that the claimants
went to an uninhabited area near the Gibē where they lived in huts; the
successor was he to whose hut a lion came, or on the roof of which a swarm
of bees settled (vol. II, p. 356). Cerulli (*Etiopia Occident.*, vol. II, pp. 13–23)
has yet another version; one of the king's sons was chosen by the district
chiefs and taken to an area of bush where a leopard was 'ruler of the
country'; if the leopard approved of him, it settled down nearby; if not, it
killed him.

R

King's death they bring a maggot which they say comes from his nostrils, wrap it in a piece of silk and make the new King kill it, squeezing its head between his teeth. When this has been done they carry the dead King's body to the grave, dragging it along the ground and asking him to bless the fields and lands through which they are taking him. When they reach the place of burial, which is a copse or thicket, the resting place of the Kings of that Kingdom, they dig a pit in the ground and throw him in without closing it or covering it in any way. The body remains there exposed to the rain and the injuries of the weather. On the day he is buried they kill many cows near the grave in such a way that the blood runs into it and reaches the dead body. Afterwards, until another King dies, they kill a cow there every day, doing it in such a way that the blood runs into the pit. It is the slaughterers who benefit for they eat the meat.[1]

A few of them accompany the dead body, most of them stay with the new King and when he kills the maggot of which we spoke, they cheer him loudly and proclaim him King. The celebration ends, like most in the world, in death and mourning among the greatest and best in the Kingdom for the new King immediately summons all the old King's favourites and tells them that since they were so much a part of the dead man that they were not separated from him in life, it is right that they should be with him in death also and should go to the other world to continue in his favour. So he orders them all to be killed at once and chooses others for

---

[1] There is a parallel to this in Ankole in western Uganda. According to Roscoe (*The Banyankole*, p. 53) a white cow, in good condition and with a healthy calf, was killed along with a white sheep. The king's body was laid on the cow-skin, and the sheep-skin, formed into 'a kind of bag was placed on the lower part of the stomach. Some small millet and the remainder of the milk from the cow [some having been previously poured into the king's mouth] was put into the sheep-skin and the cow-skin was folded over all and tightly stitched.'

A parallel to Almeida's account of the maggot also comes from Ankole. Milk was mixed with the fluids that came from the king's decomposing body; this mixture produced maggots, one of which was taken out and declared to be the king reborn. A priest took this maggot to the forest and returned with a lion cub which was said to be the maggot transformed and representing the king. When full grown the cub was released (*op. cit.*, p. 54) The body of the king of Bunyoro was also put into a young bull's hide, after being wrapped in bark-cloth (Roscoe, *The Bakitara*, p. 121).

himself, preferring them to the places and charges that are left vacant.

Meanwhile the houses in which the old King used to live are burnt, and all the furniture and utensils with them. Nothing remains, however rich and valuable it may be, that is not turned to ashes. Again, when any private person dies, they not only burn his houses but also the trees and plants that were near them so that the dead man, who was accustomed to the place, should not return and take pleasure in walking about there. Then the new King at once builds himself a new house and, as I said in the beginning, this is easily done because the material costs little. It is round, 25 or 30 palms in diameter, the walls of posts or pebbles and mud, the ceilings and gutters of logs split and roughly shaped, the ends resting on a pole as a support which has a kind of cartwheel to the edge of which they are joined while their other ends rest on the wall.[1] For the pole of the Gingiro King's house of which we were speaking they go and choose in the forest a straight and not very thick tree. Before felling it, at the foot they cut off the head of a man, the first they find belonging to a certain family in the Kingdom, which is exempt from other tributes of which we shall speak shortly. When the house has been built the King enters with much festivity but before he goes in they kill one of that same family, if the house has only one door, and two if it has two doors. With the blood of these victims they daub the threshold and side-posts of the doors.

A cruel tribute from the poor family that buys freedom and exemption from others at such great cost, though the others must be the heaviest imaginable if they are greater

[1] This is somewhat obscure but the modern Kafa method of placing rafters in position may give a clue to the meaning. (See fig., after Bieber, vol. I, p. 219.)

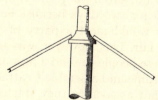

than this one! Whenever the King wants to buy some foreign cloth from the merchants and they agree that 3 or 10 or 30 slaves shall be given for it, all he does is to give orders to his servants who go into the houses and take the sons and daughters of the people living in the country and deliver them to the merchants. He does the same when he wants to make a present of one or more slaves, male or female, to one of the Emperor's servants, or another King, or a neighbouring prince; he orders that the handsomest sons or daughters of any of his subjects should be taken, so long as they do not belong to that family which we said was exempt, and he delivers them as prisoners to anyone he pleases. Such is their submissiveness and the reverence they all have for the King that there is no one who murmurs at this. They have another custom when the new King begins his reign; it is to order a search through the whole Kingdom for every man or woman suffering from leprosy or ringworm; the hospital to which they send them is to make them cross to the other side of the Zebeê and cut off all their heads, so that no such disease should infect other people.

CHAPTER 17

How Father Antonio Fernandez left the Kingdom of Gingirô and reached that of Cambáte

Travelling eastwards from the river Zebeê the Father reached Iangarâ, a place in the Kingdom of Cambat, which was governed by Hamelmal who at that time recognised the Emperor as his overlord. To the left there are people called Gurâguês who do not often obey the Emperor. The Father stayed at Iangarâ for two days because he was told that if they waited they would meet a party of people who were coming there to a fair. This, however, was a subterfuge and a trick to enable these people to send a message to their neighbours in the meantime and assemble to attack and rob them. So it happened that as soon as they started on the journey seven horsemen came up to them, but when they learnt that they were the Emperor's servants they did them no harm. Nevertheless, it was not long before heathen Gurâguês, five on horseback and many others on foot with bows, formed themselves into a company and rushed upon the Father's companions who were only seventeen armed men. They joined battle. Though the Gurâgues were numerous the Father's men were braver and were fighting for their lives; from time to time they drove back the brigands. A young man related to the Ambassador noticed that some of the Guraguês were advancing and were making for the Father. He shouted to those of his companions who were nearer to the Father to go to his help. In his concern for the Father he neglected his own safety and exposed himself in such a way that he was struck by an arrow from which, as it had been poisoned, he died a few days later, to the great grief of all who knew him and loved him for his good qualities. A servant of the wounded man had wanted to avenge his master and was hurling a *zarguncho* at the man who killed him with such determination and at such range that he could not have avoided it. When others of his companions saw it they prevented him from throwing the dart. As they were not in their own country they were afraid that if there were any deaths, a large number of people would join together against them and they would not be able to escape. They simply defended themselves with such courage that the enemy, realising that they could not rob them of their possessions except at great cost to themselves, came to terms and made peace.

CHAPTER 18

The Vexations and Troubles that Father Antonio Fernandez and the Ambassador Fecur Egzy endured in Cambat.

After this encounter the Father, Ambassador and all their company reached the place where Hamelmal, who was then governor of the Kingdom of Cambate, resided. To begin with, when he saw the letters from the Emperor that they brought him, he received them well. However, a servant of the

Emperor's [1] was there at the time; he had come to collect the tribute which Hamelmal used to pay. Either because the grandees of the court, who were enemies of the Fathers and of the Roman faith, had prompted him, or because the Devil had prevailed upon him to oppose and do all the harm he could to the Father and Ambassador, he exerted himself to the utmost to persuade Hamelmal to hinder this journey and not let the Portuguese and his companions proceed by any way. He alleged that they were going for no other purpose than to fetch Portuguese troops who would take possession of the Empire of Ethiopia and force them to change their faith, bartering that of their fathers and grandfathers for that of Rome. He was not satisfied with persuading Hamelmal of this. He laboured to persuade all the people of that country and of the neighbouring districts, Gallas, Moors and Christians. He instilled great fear into them, reminding them that when the Moor Granh had conquered almost the whole of Ethiopia, a few Portuguese had been enough to free it from his hands, because they were very brave and fought with muskets and bombards that struck terror into everyone and killed from a long way off.

Influenced by Manquer's arguments Hamelmal first had the Father, Ambassador and their people closely examined to see whether there was any possibility or trace of lying or falsehood in what they said. He found they were all in agreement and there was nothing on which he could fasten and he would no doubt have allowed them to proceed but for the solicitations of Manquer, who insisted so much and so passionately that he was forced to send a messenger to the Emperor to learn whether he wished those men to go on or not. Having decided on this, he sent one man, Manquer another and the Father one of the Portuguese who were accompanying him to inform the Emperor of all that had happened on his journey. When the messengers had left Manquer planned to seize and get into his own hands all the Father's and Ambassador's possessions, but he was unable to do so, because they deposited them in Hamelmal's keeping. Their great grief was that, when three months had gone and the Emperor's answer was daily expected, the three men who

---

[1] His name was 'Manquer'; see next paragraph.

had been sent to the court returned and said they had not gone past a place only three days' journey away, because they had been arrested and held there all that time. It was necessary to send other messengers and to have patience while wearily awaiting the answer, and in the meanwhile endure the injuries and spitefulness of Manquer and his servants, who wanted nothing so much as to bring about a quarrel with the Ambassador's men so as to have an opportunity to harass them. One day matters came to such a pass that one of the Ambassador's servants, insulted and provoked by one of Manquer's whom he had many times asked to desist, was not only abused but struck and hurt. He then turned upon him and retaliated with such a will that he stretched him out dead. Judgment of the case was referred to Hamelmal whose sentence was that the man who had killed him should die. The Ambassador appealed to the court, alleging that as he was an Ambassador, the Emperor alone could pronounce a capital sentence against one of his servants. The appeal was allowed, though Manquer very much regretted it. He regretted it still more when, a few days afterwards, the murderer broke out of prison and found shelter, leaving Manquer fuming.

Meanwhile the men carrying Hamelmal's message and the news from the Father and Ambassador arrived at the Emperor's court. When he heard it he showed extreme anger and would doubtless have punished Manquer and Hamelmal severely if he had not been so far from Cambat. The fact that Hamelmal, amid so many Galla countries, obeyed him and still accorded him some recognition was rather because he was well-disposed and a vassal of old standing, than because the Empire was strong enough to make him do it if he had wished to revolt. So today Cambate does not pay any tribute nor does the Emperor appoint a governor for that Kingdom; it all belongs to various Galla and Moorish lords who hold and rule it. At the time the Emperor did what he could. He despatched a messenger called Baharô, a man well-known in that region, and with him letters to Hamelmal instructing him to provide the Father and the Ambassador Fecur Egzy with everything they needed to continue their journey out of his revenues. He strongly enjoined upon him to help them

with letters and with his influence and to do all he could to
secure for them the favour of the neighbouring kings and
princes so that they should all grant them free and open
passage through their countries. With this object he sent
rich *cabayas* to Hamelmal and also to a Moor who governed
a country near there which is called Alabâ, the Moor himself
being called Alicô; he was the first person through whose
country the Father and Ambassador had to go when they
left Hamelmal's principality.

The messenger Baharô arrived in Cambate in June, 1614,
with these despatches, so favourable to the Father's and
Ambassador's aims. Hamelmal, aware that such was the
Emperor's wish, considered the matter no further before
giving what he was asked to give, or that seemed necessary
for the journey. Among other things he gave the Ambassador
seven horses because he understood that they were the best
presents that could be offered to the petty kings and princes
of the countries through which they had to pass. Thereupon
the Father and Ambassador resolved to resume their journey,
neither wearied nor disheartened by their past labours or the
long delays, for they had spent more than 14 months so far.
There were, however, some of the Ambassador's servants
who turned back from here. They were afraid of greater
trouble and dangers in the future, when they considered
those through which they had passed hitherto, when travelling nearly all the time through countries subject to the Emperor, which were now at an end. Thenceforward their route
was to be through stranger countries and people who did not
give, and had never given any recognition to the Emperor, or
ever had any knowledge of him.

CHAPTER 19

*How the Father and the Ambassador were arrested in
Alabâ by the Moor Alicô and compelled to return
whence they had come.*

They left Hamelmal and in a day and a half the Father and
the Ambassador reached Alabâ, the country and home of the

Moor Alicô. Manquer had come to him first and sown mis-
chief as usual. The Moor therefore showed himself surly and
not very well-disposed. He received the Emperor's letter and
the *cabayas* that Baharô presented on his behalf, and therefore temporised a little, promised a guide for the journey and
ordered that they should be given two *feridás*.[1] All the same
he delayed matters for two days and on the 3rd Manquer
arrived there. He had escaped from Hamelmal who was keeping him under guard and had promised not to release him
until he knew that the Father had passed beyond Alabâ.

The consequence of the coming and the advice of this devil
was that Alicô at once imprisoned the messenger Baharô and
then the Father and the Ambassador, each in a separate
house, confiscated all the possessions they had brought with
them, the mules on which they had come, the horses Hamelmal had given them and the gold they had for the expenses of
their long journey. It was lucky and great thanks to God that
they did not find the Emperor's letters[2] which the Father
was carrying, which were all tied under the fleshy part of his
arm and escaped. Had they been found Manquer would have
read them, as they were written in Amaharâ, and would have
proved conclusively what he often affirmed on suspicion only,
that this journey and embassy were directed to the arrival of
Portuguese in Ethiopia. Had the Moor known this he would
not have spared their lives, a thing Manquer strongly recommended to him[3] but which he nevertheless did not decide to
do, out of a certain respect and fear which he had for the
Emperor. In short, by God's will, the first time they searched
and felt the Father they did not find them. At the first opportunity he had, when he saw that he was alone, the Father
asked for a light, pretending he wanted to take tobacco, a
thing he never did in his life, but which is so common with the
Moors of Ethiopia that they are smoking it all day long. He
threw the letters on the fire and turned them into dust and
ashes lest they should be the occasion of bringing a like fate
upon himself.

Their imprisonment lasted ten days during which various

[1] Amharic *feridā*, 'young cow or ox.'

[2] For some account of the contents of these letters see pp. xxxvii–xl.

[3] An example of Almeida's carelessness as a writer; he says the opposite
of what he means.

helped them in this way; he permitted them to meet a Galla there. The Emperor's messenger Baharò asked him if he knew another Galla called Amumâ, a great man and a close friend of his. The Galla replied that he was his servant and that his master was near at hand. They promised him a valuable reward if he would go and call him quickly, and they promised Amumâ that they would give him a horse if he would come. The Galla sped on his way. Amumâ came within the hour and with his coming their fears and all danger were at an end. He was a great and powerful man; he assumed responsibility for the Father and Ambassador and all their men and took them under his protection, so none of the Moors of the country dared to take up arms against them.

This Galla took them two days' journey from there to the place where he was staying, where he refreshed them with much milk and beef. Then he took them another three days' journey forward to a place where they had to rest for eight days. When these were past and they wanted to start on their way they met with yet more trials which were perilous enough. The first was from some Gallas who were enemies of another, named Augedem; they, having had news that this man, and not Amumâ, was escorting them, came to look for them and kill them. When they were disabused they abandoned their project. The 2nd was from a great multitude of cattle which were attacked by the fly in the open country they were crossing and which very nearly trampled down and killed them all. The third was from a great number of Gallas who were encamped in a wide plain holding certain festivals for their idols;[1] they strongly urged Amumâ to let go those Christians and hand them over so that they could offer them as a sacrifice.

God delivered them from all and brought them to safety, and afterwards he also saved the three Portuguese who had remained in Alicô's hands. They escaped and fled from him

[1] This suggests Galla initiation ceremonies, during which, according to a text published by Cerulli, the leader of the *qondala* grade 'goes out into the plain, constructs an enclosure upon it, and there proclaims the law . . . and spends fifteen days there' (*Folk-Literature of the Galla*, p. 173). Almeida forgets that he has said (p. 136 above), quite truly, that the Galla have no idols.

to Hamelmal, whom they helped greatly in some attacks on the Gallas. The Emperor and Ras Celá Christôs were very persistent in their efforts to rescue them from captivity. They wrote very earnestly to the Moor Alicô and to Hamelmal pressing them to send them the Portuguese. However, in the period that they were kept there, which was more than a year, one of them died of an illness. The other two arrived safely and the Emperor and Ras showed them many favours for the good service they had rendered them on that journey.

Some will want to know what became of Manquer, the author and cause of such great evils. I reply that divine justice did not forget to punish him as he deserved while still in this life. He had so much influence at court that, in spite of all that he had done, he did not hesitate to present himself there, denying everything he had done. However, Ras Cellâ Christos had him arrested. What he so shamelessly denied was easily proved and he was sentenced to death by all the judges. The Emperor confirmed the sentence and it was about to be executed. It was God's will that, in order to exercise the mercy and patience of Father Antonio Fernandez and for the sake of an example to us, the Father should have been in the camp at the time. He went to the Emperor and asked for his enemy's life. He asked with such sincerity and fervour that the Emperor could do no other than grant it to him. Even so he could not escape from divine justice, though he escaped from the death sentence here. He was banished to a mountain, escaped from his escort, went away to join the Gallas and in less than three months brought many companies of them to attack the Emperor's territories. The people of the country, however, hurried up and took to their weapons; the Gallas fled and this man, who was their guide, fled with them. In his flight he fell and broke his leg so that he could go no further. He lay there till he died three days later, though some say that when the Gallas saw him with his leg broken they killed him off so that he should not suffer for so long. It would be better to say so that the pains of eternal fire should be no longer delayed which that infernal soul had so richly deserved.

land. On this journey God miraculously delivered us from the
Malavares.[1] We came upon two proas almost face to face in
the mouth of the Naçavrim[2] river. They were looting a boat
they had taken and so gave us time to turn round. We turned
back and entered the mouth of a river called Muâçâ.[3] The
tide was out, the river has little water, we were left stranded
and the mouth by which we had entered was nearly waterless.
It was getting dark; the proas arrived but saw that the entrance to the river was dry and ran down to another that had
more water. As soon as the tide began to rise we made our
way to the inlet leading to the great Naçavrim river. We
went up it a considerable distance but that could not have
availed us if the most holy Virgin Our Lady had not favoured
and protected us as she did that night, (the vespers of her
feast of the Ô).[4] The proas returned to the mouth of the
Naçavrim river knowing that we were there. As soon as night
had fallen one of them, the smallest and lightest, made its
way up the river to look for us. The Virgin permitted that it
should mistake the channel, go very much to one side and
strike a shoal where it turned over and stuck.[5] It was midnight. We heard the shout of the Malavares who left the proa
stranded, returned to the river-mouth by land and embarked
on the other proa that had remained there. When morning
came the river was seen to be full of cocoanuts, with which
the proa had been loaded, as well as some shields, bows and
arrows that the ebb tide was leaving up the river. We gave
many thanks to God and the most holy Virgin who had delivered us. Because the proa was still waiting for us at the
bar, we procured small carts there and went by land to

[1] Malabar pirates.

[2] The Purna. 'Below Navsári the Purna is in books of navigation referred
to as the Navsári river' (*Gazetteer of the Bombay Presidency*. Gujarat. Surat
and Broach. vol. II (1877), p. 26).

[3] Presumably one of the many creeks in the marshy country between the
mouths of the Ambika and the Purna, near the town of Masa, with which
the name may be connected. Masa was known to Europeans in Almeida's
time; it is mentioned in Sir W. Foster, *The English Factories in India, 1622–
1623*, p. 220.

[4] The Feast of the Expectation on December 18th.

[5] On the Purna, the *West Coast of India Pilot* (7th edition, 1926, p. 183)
says: 'It is difficult of access, on account of the winding channel among the
sandbanks, in which there is generally a depth of 3 or 4 feet. . . . The river
. . . should not be attempted without local knowledge.'

Bagoâ,[1] passing behind Surrate and leaving word for the commander of the *catur*[2] to go and take us off there as soon as he could safely get away, which he did. From Bagoa we crossed to Góga.

At Góga we stayed for a whole month because the land route was infested by brigand Resbutos.[3] We waited for the fleet and in it we reached Dio two months after we had left Baçaim. At Dio there was plenty of trouble with the Captain and the Factor who helped us very little. At last, having prepared ourselves as best we could, we embarked for Suaqhem, Father Manoel Barradas, Father Francisco Carvalho, Father Luis Cardeira and I. Father Jorge D'Almeida returned to Baçaim again by the Father Rector's order, because he was not considered fit for the journey; as soon as he had arrived there he had again begun to vomit so much blood that he became very weak. We left on the 24th of March of 1623, the eve of the Annunciation of Our Lady the Virgin. We hoped for favours similar to those she had granted us on the vespers of her own feast in the river Naçavrim. Such we did experience, for this Lady defended and protected us from plentiful, very evident dangers, from storms, pirates, English and Dutch, Moors from Dofar,[4] galleys and *gelvas*[5] of the Turks on the coast of Xaer[6] and Aden, at the entrance to the Strait and throughout it, and in Suaqhem and Macuá from the Turkish Bâxâ and his ministers, till she made our way clear for us and placed us in Ethiopia.

The ship in which we came was a pinnace of Lucas de Souza chartered by Lalegy Dossy, captain Rapogy Sangvy. It had in tow a boat[7] as big as a ship[8] and so loaded with goods that the ship could barely haul it. It was so badly stowed and had such high side-planks that when the cable was cut it heeled over and nearly went to the bottom. Because of this and the feebleness of the monsoon, we were late in sighting Socotorâ. It distressed us not a little to see that

---

[1] Bhagwa, a small harbour about 4 miles from the coast, on the Sina river, in the northern part of the Surat district.

[2] A long, narrow boat, propelled by both sails and oars (*Hobson-Jobson*).

[3] Rajputs.   [4] Dhufar, on the south coast of Arabia.

[5] Arabic *jalba*, a skiff made of planks sewn together with coir.

[6] Shihr, now in the eastern part of the Aden Protectorate.

[7] *batel*, a ship's boat.   [8] *navio*, a full sized ship.

S

we could not stop the incessant heathen and Mahometan rites which the Baneanes performed on the poop, offering sundry essences and perfumes to their idols. On the prow the Moorish sailors, in asking their false prophet to give them a favourable wind, even made and offered to him a thing like a little horse of bamboo with a number of streamers.[1] They also pretended that his heel-bone had entered into an old Moor, who played his part by pretending to be mad and lashing out at everyone he met. In this frenzy he answered the questions they put to him about when they would catch sight of Cape Goardafui, when they would pass the entrance to the Strait, when they would reach Suaqhem. The replies were as false as the prophet who gave them, but in spite of all, they were very credulous and were well satisfied. Nor were they abashed afterwards when everything happened contrary to what their prophet had said.

The fact of the matter was that the lack of wind compelled us, since we could not anchor at Socotorâ, though we sighted it, nor at Caixem,[2] towards which we navigated for some days, to winter in Dofar bay. The ship was anchored there from the 18th of May to the 16th of October. We were in the ship without ever going on land and in constant alarm. There were few days when we did not receive reports, some-

[1] Such practices would be abhorrent to orthodox Moslems and we have not been able to find an exact parallel. Dr L. D. Barnett remarks that 'figures of horses . . . are very frequent in Southern India; they represent the horse on which the god Aiyanar . . . rides to perform his rounds for the protection of the villages. He is of course a Hindu god; but the Moors (i.e. Indian Muslims) are often inclined to assimilation, and it is possible that some of them might have adopted Aiyanar's horse as a symbol of a protecting power without realising that it is the vehicle of a Hindu god.' Ja'far Sharif, *Islam in India* (1921), pp. 139–140, states that in southern India, where the Moslems are mostly converts from Hinduism, little pottery horses and riders are offered at the shrines of Zul-qarnain (Alexander the Great); he remarks that it is often difficult to know whether such shrines are Moslem or Hindu. Judging by wind-raising rites elsewhere (e.g. Westermarck, *Ritual and Belief in Morocco*, p. 231) the streamers that Almeida saw were intended to catch any breeze there might be.

[2] Qishn, on the south coast of Arabia. The same Sultan ruled Qishn and Socotra, as he still does; he was usually friendly to the Portuguese, his territories on the mainland forming an enclave in the possessions of the Sultan of Shihr, who ruled Dhufar, to the east of Qishn. Mr Alan Villiers, who has very kindly placed at our disposal his wide experience of sailing in this region, considers the failure of the monsoon and the inability of the crew to anchor at either Socotra or Qishn to be very strange.

times that they knew about us on shore, at other times that the kinglet was coming or sending to look for us, or again that Dutch ships were passing along the coast and would not pass without seeing us, or again that Turkish galleys or ships had left Moqhâ and would probably reach Dofar and that, even if they did not, they would undoubtedly meet us on the way. Besides this there was the discomfort of hiding ourselves in the empty spaces on the ship whenever any people from land came on to her, and the lack of provisions, because of which we had to make do with rice and a little fish when it could be had. The water gave us much trouble, for it was so brackish as to be almost brine. As a result we all came to be covered with dense and very thick scabies. Though we were bled several times it lasted as far as Suaqhem and some persons had it as far as Ethiopia. The crew of the ship suffered much too, although they were on land most of the time, for many of them fell ill of fevers and scabies,[1] but what they regretted more was the sum taken from them for anchorage (it was over two thousand patacas), besides the loss of much cloth which was wetted by the rain and nearly all lost.

I shall say little about Dofar because I saw it only from the ship. It is known to be on the coast of Arabia, at an elevation of 15 to 16 degrees, between Caixem and Curiamuria. The town is small, the people are poor, the kinglet is a brother and vassal of the King of Xaer, who is master of much territory in Arabia, though as it is sparsely populated on this side he has not many people or much wealth. The town and Kingdom of Caxem are in the middle, along the coast between Xaer and Dofar. However, the King of Xaer and Dofar is master of most of the incense there is in the world. It is found in some very high and barren mountains extending for 40 or 50 leagues from Dofar to Caxem, and comes from little trees which have few leaves and no fruit other than the incense which is their resin. Dofar also has a very beautiful shore, many palms, arecas, Indian fig trees, betels and grapes in plenty for the country. This verdure comes from the fact that it enjoys two winters, the Indian, which arrives there laden with clouds though it does not discharge them in

---

[1] *Sarna*; it may have been prickly heat, but the circumstances were propitious for a number of skin diseases.

heavy, but in gentle and very steady rains for a duration of over three and a half months, and the winter of the Strait of Arabia, which comes at the same time as ours in Portugal. It has many wells and the country is so humid that most of the men and women, so I was told, have their feet and legs as much swollen by deformity as the *pericals* or *panicals*[1] of the Malavar coast in India.

CHAPTER 2

How we left Dofar, reached Suaqhem and Macuâ, and from there went into Ethiopia as far as Debaroâ

On the 16th of October we raised anchor and left Dofar and on the 4th of December we reached Suaqhem and anchored there. The voyage was slow, because the monsoon started feebly and so we lost many days before reaching Adem. Thereafter, in the most dangerous part of the passage, God favoured us so that we passed the entrance with a fresh wind. We passed through at night so as not to be seen by any of the Turkish *galvas* which are usually there to carry off ships to Moqhâ. We passed through on the Ethiopian side, I mean between the islet that lies in the opening[2] and the land of Ethiopia, not between the islet and the land of Arabia. Though the latter channel is deeper and a safer passage, yet the Turkish boats that watch the entrance are usually anchored behind certain promontories thrown out by Arabia. That morning we went along in sight of the mountains above Moqhâ and those of Ethiopia which correspond to them on the left. At midday we passed near to the island of Iabel Iaquer,[3] which is between one and the other coast, in the Red Sea, almost in the centre. The Baneanes and Moors saluted it, as is their custom, with various superstitious rites, offer-

---

[1] Two Malayalam words, confused by the Portuguese and treated as synonymous. The former means 'big leg', hence 'elephantiasis', the latter, 'fencing master,' then 'astrologer' (Dalgado).

[2] Perim.

[3] The island of Jebel Zuqur in lat. 14° N., 20 miles from the coast of Arabia and 70 from Africa.

ing it things to eat and speaking to it, asking it questions and answering as they liked. A little further begins a string of islands so close to each other that we often saw six or seven all in a row, while some of them, which are further apart, are so widely separated that those behind us were lost to sight. This string of islands is something like a spine in the Red Sea, which it divides along its whole length as the Apennines do Italy. The course to Suaqhem is between these islets and the coast of Arabia for the first three or four days' sail, then the Strait is crossed to the African side in another three or four days, cutting across to the north-west and trying to sight land in front of some islets called Aquico, where pilots from the land are taken on. Without them it is impossible to navigate the strip of coast that extends from there to Suaq-hem, as it is all full of islands and sandbanks, some under water and some above. We made land much below this point and for those days we were troubled by very strong head-winds. However, we took on a pilot and went on following our course through that network or labyrinth of islets and shallows till we almost arrived within sight of Suaqhem. There the wind failed us so that we spent ten or twelve days in going less than eight leagues until we succeeded in casting anchor on the 4th of December, fifty days after we had left Dofar.

Next day we left the ship, eight months and twelve days after we had embarked in her at Dio. Then we went to visit the Bâxâ with the captain, pilot and chief merchants. He received us with honour and affability. He said he would let us go to Ethiopia in peace because he was a friend of the Emperor and wished to have sincerely peaceful and friendly relations with him, and because the Emperor had sent to him asking him to treat well and send on safely the Fathers who would be coming there. He ordered *cabayas* to be put on all four of us (the honour he usually shows to those whom he honours most). We, however, knowing how little it matters and how much it generally costs, excused ourselves and I alone put one on, so that we should not appear to make light of his good will. I went out with the *cabaya*, I, the captain and the pilot, to our houses, all on horseback. When we arrived there we shed them, which is the custom, and at the same time one's purse sheds fifty or sixty patacas for the benefit of the Bâxâ's servants, who invented the custom for their own advantage. That is what each of theirs cost the captain and the pilot. Because I had excused myself and protested that I was a poor religious who neither aspired to nor wanted such heavily charged honours, the Bâxâ ordered that they should not ask me for the customary dues. The figure I cut cost me six or seven patacas even so.

Next day we took to the Bâxâ the *sagoate*[1] we brought for him because its price pays for the licence for us to pass through his harbours. The principal items were a coverlet from China, a counterpane of finely worked cotton silk, a velvet carpet, an inlaid Dio writing desk, half a dozen very fine *bofetás*, some trays and wash-basins from China and other pretty things, consisting of some scores of teacups. After the Baxâ's, we took another present to his Quequeâ, the man who, under him, gives orders and controls everything, and another to the Amym, the president and a kind of judge of the customs.[2] Nor was this the end of the matter for there are many who pluck and snatch, clerks, commanders of various degrees, porters, guards, everybody, in fact, sucks, bleeds and stings as much as he can. The duties on the baggage, especially, were very heavy, for they rated the cloth at half as much again as it was worth, and levied sixteen per cent of its valuation, besides the five pieces per cent that they exacted on any kind of cloth.

He despatched us to Maçuâ, fleeced in this way, but yet with honour and letters of recommendation in which he ordered the Quequeâ and Amin to let us pass on our way without meddling with our baggage, opening our bundles or taking any further duty from us, and to give us a strong guard for the first stages.

We were at Suaqhem for sixteen days, which we spent in unpacking the cloth we were carrying as alms for the Christians. We rested and partly recovered from scabies and the fatigues of the sea voyage in the healthy air on land, for it was then winter and a very mild one, and we were well sup-

---

[1] A present, especially on a festival or as a sign of homage (Dalgado).
[2] Turkish *kaimakam*, 'lieutenant-governor' and *emin*, for *gümrük emini*, 'superintendent of customs.'

plied with beef, mutton, fish, fresh cheese and some fruit like melons and water-melons, all of them very good of their kind and all cheap. It all comes from the mainland which is inhabited by Moorish Funchos.[1] They are usually tall men, thin and with tiny little eyes. The King of the Funchos shares in the revenues of the custom-house, which the Turks give him so that he should help them with caravans and provisions from land. Suaqhem is a very small islet. It is probably two musket shots long and one and a half wide. The arm of the sea or creek that divides it from the mainland is probably about the same. The houses are some of them of stone and mud, others of wood, and are roofed with matting.

We left Suaqhem on the 21st of December in a *gelva* that we hired for thirty crusados. We reached Macuâ in sixteen days, after going along the coast all the time, moving by day and spending the nights at anchor. Maçuâ is like Suaqhem an islet, a little bigger than the latter, next to the coast of Africa. The houses are partly of stone and mud, though some of them are covered over with lime and whitewash, and partly of wood and matting. It has some cisterns and a bastion at the entrance to the bar with a few guns. The river is not deep and can take only Dio small craft. Opposite, between Macuâ and Arquico or Dequeno (for so the natives call it) are two uninhabited islets.[2] Deqhono or Arquico is a town by the shore. There are many wells there that have been dug in the sand, from which the drinking water is drawn; it is carried to Macuâ every day in three or four *gelvas*. With it are watered some small gardens of different kinds of green vegetables, lemons and pomegranates which take well in the soil. When I arrived on this occasion it had no fort except an enclosure of stone and mud ten palms high. On the headland were a few, very flimsy, storeyed houses where the Quequeâ lived. Now, however, in the year 1633, when I returned there in July, I saw that a square fort had been built, apparently of stone and lime, some say of stone and mud. It adjoins the

[1] Supposed to be the same as the Fung of Sennar (Crawford, p. 116). The expression 'Moorish Funchos', however, suggests that the Portuguese may have distinguished between the Fung of Sennar and the so-called Fung of Suakin. Crawford has a good chapter on Suakin and Massawa. (*Fung Kingdom*, pp, 118-133.)

[2] Possibly the Sheikh Said Is.

Quequeâ's houses and has four bastions on its four sides. They and the wall are twenty to 25 palms high.

After we had given our presents to the Quequeâ, Amin and other officials and shown the Bâxâ's firmans, (though they did some spiteful things to us), we left on the 16th of January, accompanied by almost all the soldiery of Arquico, which would then have been some 70 musketeers, though there are over two hundred now. They went with us for a day and a half on the journey till we met the people of Zalot, a village the Emperor had given to the Fathers, chiefly in order that its inhabitants, who were over 300 men with *zargunchos* and shields, should go to meet them when they arrived, and also meet the goods they brought as alms, and give them protection as far as Debaroâ. Usually all along that route there are big bands of robbers, which is what nearly all the inhabitants of the neighbouring places are. Because the country is all big and high mountains and is in many parts uninhabited, and above all because it is so far from the court, they accord very little obedience to the Emperor and are hardly subjects in more than name. Besides the people of our village the Viceroy Keba Christôs, a strong Catholic who was encamped near Debaroâ at this juncture, sent a brother of his called Asma Guirguis and the Barnagaes Acabâ Christôs with many armed men to come and protect us. It was all necessary, for when it was reported that we had come and that the caravan travelling with us was a big one, there were innumerable robbers who held themselves called upon to attack us.

In four or five days we passed the dangerous places. During most of them we were climbing very high mountains among which were some cultivated fields and others of tall grass in which herds of horned cattle were grazing in great numbers, oxen and cows, amazingly fat and handsome. They go about in the same way all the year. In the months of December, January and February they graze these fields and the country near the sea where it is then winter. In June, July, August and September they go to the interior and enjoy its winter. Asmarâ is the name of a high but already a less mountainous place, eight or nine leagues before Debaroâ. There the winter of the interior of Ethiopia ends. From there we saw the clouds and showers of the maritime winter among the very lofty mountains and very deep valleys towards the sea without being afraid that they might make us wet for the natives of the country told us that it never reached so far.

A little way beyond Asmarâ we met with a troop of Portuguese from Maegogâ, among them João Gabriel, a highly esteemed man who had for many years been Captain of all the Portuguese in Ethiopia. This meeting cheered us greatly. Some servants of the Viceroy Kebâ Christôs came with them and brought us five mules that the Viceroy was sending us for the road, one for each of the four Fathers and a fifth for Manoel Magro, a man from India, who had accompanied us on the whole of this journey. They were very good mules and served us for many years. To show this prince's feelings, in the same year he sent another four mules to four more Fathers who entered in July, and the next year he sent seven to the Patriarch and the Fathers who entered with him. These were not small gifts in a country where wealth is not great.

Next day we reached the Viceroy's camp, the whole of which he ordered out to receive us in a beautiful meadow. There were probably as many as one thousand five hundred armed men, three hundred on mules, many of whom led handsome genets in their right hands. The Viceroy received us with such warmth and pleasure that the rejoicing of his heart was clearly seen in his face, eyes and whole bearing. He could not thank God enough for bringing us four Fathers to Ethiopia together at the same time when there were only four others there; for this reason many heretics were hoping that the teachers and preachers of the faith of Rome would soon be eliminated by death. However, when they saw that God brought four of us together, not in the monsoon, and delivered us from such perils, their hearts were softened and they said they could resist no more, and that this faith could not fail to be true seeing that God showed such favour to it and to its ministers. We were superbly feasted by the Viceroy and then went a league and a half away to sleep at a village of ours called Adegada. Early in the morning the Viceroy arrived there on a visit to us all but chiefly to Father Luis Cardeira who had not been able to reach the camp the prefor that country. It has seven or eight bastions with high curtain walls, two courtyards, one of which adjoins the houses, where a good stone tank has been made, and another where a beautiful church was now being built of stone and lime. Here there was a curtain wall and a very high bastion, which was needed as it had in front of it the third crest of the mountain which I said lay to the south-west. This is a big commanding position, for it is so much higher that it exposes the greater part of the fort to musketry fire. In Ethiopia, however, guns have not been much used hitherto and, although they have a good number of muskets, they handle them so badly that they do not fight much with them. So this small fortification, with twenty or thirty muskets, a small cannon and the sons of the Portuguese manning them, was held in Ethiopia to be a unique and impregnable place. The town is scattered all over the hill and has many houses of stone and mud with their enclosures built of the same material. Stone is plentiful there and very suitable for any kind of building, as it all comes out in slabs three or four inches thick and as broad and long as you want. It is extracted from the mountain without a pick. It is merely dug and one slab is separated from another with light, thin levers. The mud is all red and sticks in a way that makes lime unnecessary.

When we entered Fremonâ, then, we went straight to the church to give thanks to Our Lord for having brought us to it and to the mission we so greatly desired, and at the same time to visit the tomb and sacred relics of the holy Patriarch Dom Andre de Oviedo and the Fathers his companions who rest there in the Lord with him, and who are a constant workshop of miracles and the chief protection of the Portuguese and Catholics whom God preserved there for so many years. We then retired to our house, where we rested for some days while we awaited the Emperor's summons and command to go to Dambea. This summons was not slow in arriving, along with a letter from His Highness ordering that we should be informed that he awaited us with great joy. He charged the Viceroy to give us a strong guard for the road, a thing he did with great pleasure, ordering the Nebret[1] of Acçum to accom-

---

[1] *nebura 'ed*, the title of the Governor of Aksum.

pany us with his people as far as Syrê, and the Xumo of Syre to go and provide a guard for us till we had crossed the desert. They did this very punctiliously.

CHAPTER 4

How we arrived at the Emperor's court and camp and how we were received by him

At the beginning of February 1624 we reached Fremoná and at the end of the same month three of us, from among those Fathers who had just come, left there again. Father Manoel Barradas remained with Father Diogo de Mattos, both for their mutual comfort and so that they could assist at the Viceroy's camp and in the whole Kingdom of Tigrê, where many doors were opening to the preaching and acceptance of the holy Roman faith. Many lords of the country asked that the Fathers should go and teach their subjects, as they did to the great harvest and profit of many souls.

We spent twenty days on the way to Ganeta Jesus, our residency, where Father Luis d'Azevedo was, as I shall soon relate more fully. This place lies over against Dancaz to the north at a distance of four leagues. Here we awaited for one day the Emperor's order for us to come to the court. I say nothing about the route from Tigrê to this place now, because an opportunity will come later to speak of it more at leisure, for it is the most travelled route there is in Ethiopia and I went along it many times. As soon as the Emperor knew that we had reached Ganet he sent someone to us with a message that we should not delay. We left at dawn and towards midday we reached the top of a long, very steep ascent, for the district of Dancâz is something like a platform of land a little over a league long and a little less wide. The whole of this expanse is very high ground which can nowhere be reached without three or four hours spent in climbing the high mountains to which it rises on all sides. They are in a ring and are almost cut away perpendicularly.

served. He received the letter and then gave it to Father Antonio Fernandez, Superior of the mission, who was present, to read and interpret. After hearing it with great pleasure he delivered it to the secretary of the empire, who was at the same time his chronicler, for him to keep and later to include in his history. Soon afterwards I gave him the letters of the Father Assistant Nuno Mascarenhas, and of the Father Visitor of India Andre Palmeiro. These too he had read and heard with great pleasure. With that he sent us away to go and rest from the labours of the journey and sent after us a very splendid dinner, of many beeves, *calões* of wine, honey, *apas* and various dishes.

Next day I took him a *sagoate* of some pieces that we brought from India for him. Among other things there were a painting of the Nativity sent him by the Archbishop Primate D. Fr. Christovão,[1] who is in glory, a beautiful reliquary sent him by the Father Assistant Nuno Mascarenhas, an amber rosary sent him by the Father Visitor Andre Palmeiro and a coverlet embroidered on a frame from China sent him by the Father Provincial Luis Cardoso. He showed himself very much obliged and grateful to everyone. We then showed him the organs, which Father Luis Cardeira played skilfully, then the harp, harpsichord and other musical instruments, which he greatly applauded. He strongly enjoined upon the Father to teach them well to the children, because they were all heavenly things. What comforted me above all was the great piety, reverence and devotion with which he received a beautiful crucifix, that I presented to him in a rich casket from China. As soon as he saw it his eyes swam, not only the first time, but every time he saw it, and when he showed it to various ladies he could not keep back his tears. We were at Dancaz for eight days, which we spent in visiting the chief men and greatest lords and ladies of the court. Because he saw we needed to go and rest for some days from such long journeys, for it was a year since we left Dio, the Emperor was forced to permit us to withdraw to Gorgorrâ, a former residence of ours, where Father Pero Paez was buried, situated ten leagues from Dancâz in the centre of Dambeâ, near the great lake which these people call a sea.

[1] Cristovão da Sa e Lisboa, Archbishop of Goa, 1616-1625.

(3) THE JOURNEY OF FRANCISCO MACHADO AND BERNARDO PEREIRA, 1623–24

(Almeida, Book VIII, Chapters 8–9)

BOOK VIII

CHAPTER 8

How eight of our Fathers were sent to Ethiopia by different routes, and what happened on their journeys.

In the ships from the Kingdom which reached Goa in the monsoon of the year 1623 there came a letter from our Most Reverend Father Mucio Vitteleschi to Father Andre Palmeiro, Visitor of India, ordering him to despatch that year twelve Fathers of our Society on this mission. It was the time when, as I said above, we four Fathers were in Dofar where we spent the winter. The Father Visitor knew from our letters that we had stayed in the hope of entering the Straits in the next monsoon and we had warned him in them that it was not safe to send any more Fathers for the time being, for fear the Turks would be displeased and not be willing to grant permission to so many in the same year. All the same the Father Visitor decided to comply with our Father General's order, but he included the four who were in Dofar and added only eight of those in India. For greater safety and ease of entry he ordered that only 4 should come by way of Maçuâ, and assigned the other four to new routes, two to the Milinde coast and two to Zeila. The reason for sending some by the Milinde coast was that information had been received from men with experience of that coast claiming that one could enter Ethiopia from there, because Moors came who traded with the Christian Abyssinians and could act as guides and as a guard to the Fathers who were willing to go into the country with them. The Father Visitor was persuaded to send some by Zeila by a letter from the Emperor

Seltan Çagued in which he wrote to the Father Provincial asking him to send many Fathers, and saying that they could come through Zeila as the king of that country was his friend. He should have written Dancaly and he wrote Zeila.

The Father Visitor then designated Fathers Manoel Lameira, a native of Estremos, Thome Barneto, a native of Evora, Gaspar Paez, a native of Covilhã, and Jacinto Francisco, a native of Florença, to come by way of Macuâ, Fathers João de Velasco, a Castilian by nationality who had been received into the Society and trained in Portugal, and Jeronymo Lobo, a native of Lisbon, to open the new route from the Melinde coast, and Fathers Francisco Machado, a native of Villa Real, and Bernardo Pereira, a native of Vizeo, to come by way of Zeila. To begin with the first of them who made the usual journey, they made it very well and successfully as far as Maçuâ, for they left Dio at the end of March and reached that port on the second of May. There, however, they stayed for two and a half months, while the present they brought was taken to the Baxa of Suaqhem and his permission to go inland was awaited. This he delayed giving until a wild donkey or zebra, that he was expecting from the Emperor, reached Macuâ. He had asked us to procure it for him when we passed through. I spoke to the Emperor about it as soon as I reached Dancaz. He at once ordered it to be fetched and sent to Tigrê, but it could not reach the sea so soon. This was the reason for the Fathers' long delay and occasioned them intolerable hardship, for the heat at Macuâ was such during those months that some of the Fathers' bodies peeled all over and they changed their skins. At last their labours on sea and land were finished and they reached Fremonâ safely on St Mary Magdalene's day. Then, as we shall say later, they dispersed to different parts of the Kingdom of Tigrê to preach and teach, gathering ample fruit from their holy labours.

Fathers João de Velasco and Jeronimo Lobo, the pioneers of the new route by the Milinde coast, left Goa and reached the coast with a favourable wind. They passed through many harbours along it from Pate to Magadoxó, without finding in any of them anyone who dared to guide them inland or who could give them news of a possible chance to go in the future and reach the territories of the Abyssinian Empire. After many toils and all their assiduous efforts, they realised that they were labouring in vain and wasting their time.

They returned to India in order to enter by the usual route through the Straits and reach their coveted mission. In this they succeeded so well that the next year they entered in company with the Patriarch D. Afonso Mendez, as we shall relate in the proper place. Indeed, there is no route that way. Although there is continuous land, (for Melinde is the coast and the interior is Abyssinian) yet the distance is so great and the country inhabited by such savage people that I consider it to be impossible to break through.

The reason is that, as we have said already in the 1st book of this history (and as can be seen on a map of the territories belonging to the Abyssinian Empire which I have made) the most southerly parts of it that there are lie eight degrees north of the Equator,[1] or at least seven, as will be seen in the Kingdom of Nareâ (which still gives some recognition to the Emperor and pays tribute to him from time to time, although refusing it in most years) and in those of Combate and Bally, which have for many years been under the domination of Moors and Gallas and are not subject to the Empire at all. These are the Kingdoms which extend furthest to the south, Nareá to the south-west, Cambate to the south and Bally to the south-east. As I say they are all seven or eight degrees north of the line. The harbours of Magadaxó, Iugo and Pate lie as appears on the map, Pate beyond the line to the south, Iugo under the line and Magadaxo two degrees to the north of it. It follows from this that anyone who entered through Pate or Magadaxô would have at least five or six degrees to traverse going northwards. If careful attention is paid to the map, these must be traversed on a line to the quarter point north-west of north if going from Magadaxô towards Bally, or more or less west-north-west if wanting to go towards Nareâ. It is therefore apparent that, besides the windings of the routes through the country, in order to traverse six or seven degrees in the directions I have indicated, at

[1] Almeida's maps, accompanying the two MSS of the 'History', both show the southern states between 7° and 8° N., lat. 8° passing through Enarya. This displays a considerable amount of accuracy, for Sarka, the capital of Enarya, is 8° 12' N.

least 150 leagues must be travelled.[1] Anyone interested and all who suppose it to be possible to open up such a route should notice that Father Antonio Fernandez, as we have previously related, endeavoured to come from Ethiopia to this same Melinde coast. He travelled in company with the Emperor's Ambassador, a very courageous man, who brought with him twenty valiant soldiers. They hardly went outside territories which were then subject to the Emperor and they took with them letters from His Highness to all their rulers, commanding them to give all the help they could to the Father and Ambassador to enable them to accomplish their journey safely. Nevertheless they underwent great hardships, obviously risked their lives and returned to court without being able to achieve the object for which they had gone. From this any sensible person can judge how impossible it would be to break through and cross one hundred and fifty or two hundred leagues, through the countries of Cafres, Moors, Zimbas[2] and Gallas, where the petty kings and rulers are as numerous as the days of travelling, and you sometimes meet many in a single day; they are constantly at war with each other; they do not keep faith with those of their own race and nation and they rob, capture and kill all whom they can, for no other reason or purpose than the blind fury of their greed. I could prove this by many instances that I saw and experienced in the numerous journeys that I made through savage country, but there is proof enough of what I say in what happened to two other discoverers of new routes which I shall recount at greater length in a special chapter, as the occasion of such great glory to God and honour to the Society requires.

[1] From Mogadishu in a straight line to the source of the Webi Shabelle is about 600 miles.

[2] The WaZimba appeared on the Zambesi in 1542. They went north and reached Mombasa during a Portuguese attack. They helped to reduce the town, and went on to attack the people of Malindi, who destroyed them with the aid of the Segeju. After this their name is heard no more. Their origin is uncertain, but it is possible that they were members of the Jaga group of Bantu in the southern Belgian Congo, who broke out in the sixteenth century and began a career of devastation.

CHAPTER 9

Martyrdom of Fathers Francisco Machado and Bernardo Pereira

Father Francisco Machado was at the time Professor of Theology in the College of S. Paulo de Goa, where he had first read the course in Arts; he always asked for this mission with extraordinary fervour. Bernardo Pereira had then just completed his studies in theology and he too asked for it with great insistence. The Father Visitor notified and ordered them to enter by way of Zeila. With this object they embarked at Goa in a ship that was there belonging to the King of Caxem. The captain and merchants of the ship promised him [sic] that, as soon as they arrived there, the said King would certainly send them to Zeila, since he traded with that country and navigation from Caxem to Zeila was very easy, as indeed it is. The Fartâques and their King fulfilled all they had promised at Goa. The Fathers reached Caxem, without danger or extraordinary trouble, and they soon passed them on to Zeila. There, with the numerous recommendations that they had from the King and Moors of Caxem, they were well received at first. Since they were determined and eager to enter Abyssinian territory from there, they took them ten days' journey inland to the city of Aucâ Gurrelê, the usual court of the Kings, whom we call Kings of Zeila, giving them the name of their harbour and place on the sea-coast. This is what they should be called; they are properly called Kings of Adel, for that is the name of the Kingdom they have possessed and governed for many centuries, to which many extensive territories belong, as may be seen on the map, for he is lord of all that extends from Cape Darfuy and Guardafuy to Mount Felix and Zeila as far as the gates of the Red Sea, and all that we pass when we enter up to Dancaly or Baylur. In former times the empire of this King of Adel also extended far into the interior. In the time of its Vazir and Captain Major Hamed, nicknamed Granhe, which means left-handed, it reached so far that it controlled nearly the whole Abyssinian Empire which, however, was recovered by Portuguese arms as has been said above. All the same the Kingdom of Adel was always powerful and inhabited by Moors who were good horsemen, although just as some years ago the Gallas defeated and won many kingdoms from the Abyssinians, so today they defeat and win much territory from the Moors of Adel.

When the Fathers reached his court the King of Adel had sent some of his men as ambassadors to the Emperor with a musket and a big well-bred donkey as presents, hoping for a profitable return. So until these people returned safely he concealed the poison and hatred he bore in his depraved heart for a period of nearly two months and did no harm to the Fathers. On the contrary he detained them with promises of soon sending them where they wanted to go but yet he did not allow them to write or send news to the Emperor of their arrival and presence in Adel. As soon as the aforesaid ambassadors reached Auçâ, on the very same day, (which was the second of August of the year 1624) he ordered that they should be put in a dark shed and that a fetter should be fixed on them, taking the leg of one of them in one and the other's in the other. To give some colour to this tyrannical act he sent to tell the Fathers that the Emperor had treated his ambassadors very badly, that he had killed one of them, that he had taken little notice of the others, or of him himself, and that he had not sent anything of value in return for his present; they should, therefore, write to him saying that if he wanted to see them alive, he should give him proper satisfaction in gold and pieces of great value, and if not, then let him know that they would not leave that prison alive.

The Fathers then understood the Moor's evil heart, the happy lot that awaited them and the crown that God was making for them by the hands of that tyrant. They gave all possible thanks to the divine goodness, offering to it their blood and life in the utmost readiness to lose them for its love, well knowing the incomparable gains and rewards of so slight a loss. Rather to comply with the order given them than because they expected an answer, they wrote to the Emperor and the superiors of the Society in Ethiopia, giving them a short account of what had happened to them hitherto and of their present condition, showing themselves very submissive to God's will and ready to shed their blood for the lord whose holy faith they came to preach and teach in Ethiopia. The savage King too sent a letter of his own to the Emperor, as insulting as the pride and vileness of his breast could dictate. Among other things he abused him as an apostate, for having changed the Alexandrian errors, which he called the faith of his ancestors, for the holy faith of Rome, which he called the faith of the Portuguese.

These letters reached Dancaz in the middle of September. When the Emperor saw in the King of Adel's letter the insolence with which he wrote, and in the Fathers' the danger in which they stood, I cannot say which was greater, the compassion he felt for the Fathers or the wrath and anger he conceived against the savage Moor. He said he thought it certain that the Moor would already have killed the Fathers, for if that had not been his intention, he would not have been so abusive in the letter he had written him. Nevertheless, so that no one should think he valued the Fathers' lives lightly and did not do what he could to free them from captivity, he concealed for the time being the righteous anger he felt against the insolent Moor, and sent him a message full of affability, promising him everything he wanted in return for the release of the Fathers. Ras Cellâ Christôs too sent promising him a fine horse and trappings of great value, and wrote to the King begging him to send them soon, and saying that he would then send him other very rich pieces and jewels.

But they were working and toiling in vain, for hatred of the faith of Christ was more powerful in the Moor's heart than greed for all the things he could expect from the Emperor and his brothers if he sent away in safety the teachers and preachers of that faith. So, ten or twelve days after he had seized them, he ordered them to be killed by the sword in the same prison. From the great desire for martyrdom which they always showed in their lives and from what was expected of their great virtue, we can infer with how much pleasure and joy these lambs of God offered their necks to the knife and their lives in so sweet a sacrifice. The angels who accompanied and strengthened them, and all Heaven which assuredly opened to receive and welcome those victorious spirits who ascended thither in triumph, were witnesses of their glorious agony. Human witnesses there were not, for the savage willed that only the public executioner, at night, in the dark shed where they were, should carry out the cruel sentence he had pronounced against the saints. Next day many of the people then in Auçâ Gurrêlê related that the holy bodies were thrown into a courtyard outside the buildings in which they had died.

I shall now recount the evidence which makes it certain that their death was given them out of hatred for our holy faith. The Moorish King could have been moved to kill the Fathers for three reasons: first, out of hatred for their nation, because they were Portuguese; second, out of a desire to take from them the baggage they were carrying with them; third, out of hatred for the holy faith, knowing that they were going to Ethiopia to teach and preach it in that Empire. It cannot be believed that it was pure hatred of the Portuguese nation that moved him, as the Fathers were travelling with recommendations from the King of Caxem to the King of Adel, and as they were not soldiers or men that professed arms. This is plainly proved, since a Portuguese soldier was travelling with the Fathers, whom he had accompanied from Caxem. The King and Moors of Adel did not kill him and he still lives among them today. Two years ago in Ethiopia I saw letters written in his hand a few months previously and sent to Ras Cella Christôs and to our Fathers. If someone says that they spared this man's life because he became a Moor, at least to outward appearance, such a statement will be strong evidence in support of my argument which is that because they did not get, and did not even hope to get from the Fathers such a deviation from the holy faith they professed, therefore they killed them, and not because they were Portuguese. Still less can it be said that a desire to take from them the belongings they were carrying moved the Moor to put them to death. First, the Fathers did not carry gold, silver or pieces of great value, much less merchandise or cloth to buy and sell. They travelled as poor priests, even having much less than is usually carried on such missions, for they knew that the route was new and dangerous. Each one carried only his little basket with some church ornaments and devotional objects like beads, reliquaries and vernicles, Agnus Dei and similar things, which we are in the habit of giving to Christians to attach them to our holy faith and to the cult of Our Lady the Virgin. All these would have been in the King's hands, at least after he had arrested them. It would have been very easy for him, had he so wished, to take them and grant their lives and unhindered passages to Ethiopia, especially as he knew for certain that, if he had been willing to offer them for ransom, the Emperor and his brother Ras Cellâ Christôs would have sent him all that he asked and wished for in exchange for the Fathers. It was not the prompting of greed, for the Moor knew for certain that he was losing much gold and gaining nothing. It follows that hatred for our holy faith was the only thing that aroused such cruelty and so blinded this savage that, to satiate himself with the innocent blood of those lambs, he cut through all worldly considerations, ignoring what he owed to the King of Caixem, who had recommended them to him, what he could have gained from the Abyssinians, if he had sent them to them in safety, and what he might have to fear from that same people and their power and the Emperor, for having withheld their teachers from them. He did not think he did any wrong to God and to Heaven, but it rather seemed to him that he was rendering Him a signal service and making a most acceptable offering. Lest we should be in doubt that such was his intention, the savage King declared it to be so in a letter that he wrote a few days after killing the Fathers, to the rebel son of Cabreel, who was then in Amharâ country not very far from the borders of Adel. He exhorted him to fight bravely for the faith and religion of his predecessors and informed him that it was in order to destroy the faith of the Portuguese that he had killed those two men who had come to Ethiopia to preach it. As evidence of what he said he sent him as a present a handsome knife which he had found among the Fathers' belongings, because it was a fine piece.

For all these reasons I have always held these holy Fathers to be glorious martyrs, but I have been much more sure of the truth of this since I came to Aden in 1633 in company with three of our Fathers and two priests who were natives of aground on the coast; the boats were wrecked but the people in them were saved. Thence the Father went to Damão. This captivity lasted nearly a year during which, though he was well treated by some of the Dutch, most of them treated him very badly. He was in irons for many months and had very little to eat. He suffered many insults and blows on the neck and two or three times some of the more cruel heretics and enemies of the Catholic faith drew their swords and not only threatened him with death as a Papist and a Jesuit but were strongly determined to inflict it upon him. However the Lord pleased that the glory of martyrdom which was then postponed, should be given him in the Kingdom of Adel for the honour of our Ethiopian mission and so that we should all have him and his companion Father Francisco Machado as its particular protectors and patrons.

APPENDICES

might be supposed that these names were derived from the first person in each who held the office of Abba Boku. But in other societies which have age-sets there is little or no indication that this was ever the case; and in fact we are told by Bahrey himself that the Bareituma set Robale was called Ambisa or 'lion' by the Borana. The suggestion is that the *luba* names were originally taken from topical events or names and eventually became fixed and recurring; they vary moreover from tribe to tribe. Antoine d'Abbadie described the *luba* as being in pairs, and gave the following arrangement:

Birmaji	Malba	Mudana	Robale	Dulo
Aldada	Horata	Bifole	Sabaqa	Kirole[1]

Bahrey, it will be noted, divides his *luba* into two groups, first those of the 'fathers', *luba* 1 to 5, then those of the 'sons', *luba* 6 to 9 (the tenth of this cycle not having been formed at the time when he wrote), his arrangement being:

1 Melbah: his son 6. Harmufah.
2 Mudana: his son 7. Robale.
3 Kilole: his son 8. Birmaje.
4 Bifole: his son 9. Mul'ata.
5 Mesle: his son 10. not named.

This explains d'Abbadie's statement, for, as Cerulli puts it, the length of the *gada* grades means that the *luba* of a man's son goes into power forty years after his own *luba*: the complete cycle is therefore made up of two sets of *gada* grades, that of a man and that of his son. The *gada* grades, it should be noted, are periods through which a man must pass before reaching *luba*; whereas his *luba* set is one into which he is born and in which he remains all his life.

The following *luba* set names have been recorded, the order being that given by the authorities who have named them:

1593 Bahrey	1773 Bruce[2]	1880 d'Abbadie[3]	1901 de Salviac[4]	1914 Werner[5]
1. Melbah	Kilelloo	Malba	Badada	Imelba
2. Mudana	Gooderoo	Birmaji	Bultuma	Robale
3. Kilole	Robali	Kirole	Mardida	Indalana
4. Bifole	Dooloo	Sabaqa	Orota	Imarmufa I

[1] *Ann. Soc. Scient. de Bruxelles*, IV (1880), p. 175.
[2] Bruce (ed. 1813), vol. III, p. 247, calls these the 'seven southern nations' of the Galla; but though he prefixes the word *elma*, 'sons,' to each, some of them are obviously *luba* names, though *Gooderoo* suggests the Gudru tribe of the nothern Borana.
[3] *loc. cit.*, p. 175.   [4] *Les Galla*, pp. 193–194.
[5] *Journ. African Soc..* XIII (1914), pp. 263–264.

1593 Bahrey	1773 Bruce	1880 d'Abbadie	1901 de Salviac	1914 Werner
5. Mesle	Bodena	Bifole	Fadata	Imarmufa II
6. Harmufah	Horreta	Horata	Wabassa	Imalchisa I
8. Robale	Michaeli	Aldada	Bassira	Imalchisa II
8. Birmaje		Dulo	Daibassa	Buno
9. Mul'ata		Robale	Niukussa	Imbirmeji I
10.		Mudana	Daimoa	Imbirmeji II

From western and central Abyssinia come the following six, all recorded by Cerulli:[1]

Jida	Gombichu	Leka	Meta	Gulale	Obora
Horata	Robale	Robale	Dulo	Dulo	Robale
Mikile	Birmaji	Mikile	Birmaji	Birmaji	Dulo
Dulo[2]	Horata	Dulo	Robale	Mikile	Birmaji
Robale	Mudana	Mudana	Mikile	Robale	Melba
Birmaji	Dulo	Halchisa	Horata	Horata	Halchisa
Bifole*	Bifole*	Horata			
	Melba*	Birmaji*			
	Mikile*	Melba*			

Those marked * are 'considered as being in reserve', Cerulli, *loc. cit.*, I, 40, Bifole of the Jida being 'obsolete'. Since the number of *luba* must, it seems, be either ten or five, another *luba* (Horata) should perhaps be 'in reserve' in the Leka list.

Each *gada* grade lasts for 8 years, except those marked *, which last for 4 years only, two grades together being taken for time-reckoning as equivalent to one; there are thus 'six-*gada* tribes' and 'five-*gada* tribes':

Six-*gada* tribes

Leka	Jida	Gombichu	Meta	Gulale
Dobole I	Dabale	Dabale	Dabale	Dabale
Dobole II	Fole	Fole	Fole	Fole
Dobole III	Qondala	Qondala	Qondala	Qondala
Qondala	Dori ⎱ =	Dori ⎱ =	Dori ⎱ =	Dori ⎱ =
Raba⎱ =	Luba ⎰ Luba	Luba ⎰ Luba	Luba ⎰ Luba	Luba ⎰ Luba
Gula ⎰Luba	Yuba	Yuba	Yuba	Yuba

Five-*gada* tribes

Abichu	Obora
Dabale	Dabale
Fole	Fole
Qondala	Qondala
Luba	Luba
Yuba	Yuba

---

[1] *Etiopia Occidentale*, vol. I, c. 3.
[2] *dulu* (cf. Bahrey, chap. xi) = 'fight'.

u

The interaction of *gada* and *luba* may be represented schematically thus:

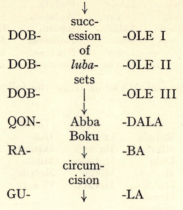

	↓	
	succ-	
DOB-	ession	-OLE I
	of	
DOB-	*luba-*	-OLE II
	sets	
DOB-			-OLE III
	↓	
QON-	Abba	-DALA
	Boku	
RA-	↓	-BA
	circum-	
	cision	
GU-	↓	-LA

2

Schleicher, working back in 8-year periods from 1846 when d'Abbadie said the Borana made their *luba*, arrived at the period 1582–1590 for Bahrey's Robale.[1] But this does not fit in with the regnal years of the Ethiopian kings as given in such works as the *Paris Chronicle* and the *History of Sarṣa Dengel*; and it is clear that these documents must be accepted in preference to Schleicher's method, for obviously in a period of three hundred years a slight error in reckoning the age-set lengths can easily occur among people who have no writing and no accurate method of time-keeping. On the evidence of the Ethiopian records, therefore, the date of Bahrey's book may be put at 1593 rather than 1582 as Wright suggested; and certain other dates may be established in the following way:

	Luba of	
Year	*Bahrey:*	*Events: Reign of Lebna Dengel,* 1508–1540
1522	Melbah	'He who was circumcised when the Galla began to invade Bali was called Melbah,' Bahrey, chap. V. 'The Galla came from the west and crossed the river of their country, which is called Galana, in the time of the *haṣe* Wanag Sagad,' Bahrey, chap. I. Wanag Sagad is Lebna Dengel.
		Reign of Galawdewos, 1540–1559
1559	Mesle	This *luba* defeated Nur Ibn Mujahid of Harar after he had killed Galawdewos, Bahrey, chap. IX.

[1] *Geschichte der Galla*, p. 10, n. 1.

Reign of Sarṣa Dengel, 1563–1595

1573   Robale   The king of Ethiopia gave battle to Robale near Lake Zeway, Bahrey, chap. XII. In his 10th year (1573) Sarsa Dengel attacked the Borana, whose *luba* was Ambisa (= Robale, Bahrey, chap. I) in the region of Lake Zeway (*PC*, p. 117).

1578   Robale   The *haṣe* attacked Robale of the Abati at Wayna Dag'a and not more than ten were left alive,' Bahrey, chap. XII. In his 15th year (1578) Sarṣa Dengel fought the Abati at Wayna Dag'a and killed all but one (*PC*, p. 117).

1585   Birmaje   The Galla killed Aboli of the royal family, and others, Bahrey, chap. XIII. In the 22nd year of Sarṣa Dengel (1585) the Galla killed Aboli (*PC*, p. 118).

1588   Mul'ata   Mul'ata made war on Gojam, Bahrey, chap. XV. In his 25th year (1588) Sarṣa Dengel defeated the Galla in Gojam (*PC*, p. 118).

1593   Mul'ata   'When this book was written it was the seventh year of the government of Mul'ata' (Bahrey, chap. XVIII).

The dates of Bahrey's *luba* periods, as suggested by his text and by the chronology of the kings of Ethiopia, may therefore be amended as follows:

1522	Beginning of Melbah	Lebna Dengel (Wanag Sagad),
1530	End of Melbah	1508–40
1530	Beginning of Mudana	
1538	End of Mudana	
1538	Beginning of Kilole	Galawdewos (Aṣnaf Sagad),
1546	End of Kilole	1540–59
1546	Beginning of Bifole	
1554	End of Bifole	
1554	Beginning of Mesle	Minas (Admas Sagad), 1559–63
1562	End of Mesle	
1562	Beginning of Harmufah	Sarṣa Dengel (Malak Sagad),
1570	End of Harmufah	1563–95
1570	Beginning of Robale	
1578	End of Robale	

1578   Beginning of Birmaje
1586   End of Birmaje

1586   Beginning of Mul'ata
1594   End of Mul'ata

1594   Beginning of next *luba*, not named by Bahrey, because his
       book ended with the seventh year of Mul'ata.

3

Systems similar to that of the Galla, using Galla terms, occur
among the Sidama (Darasa next to the Sidamo) who are in contact
with the Arusi Galla, and among negro peoples (Konso south of
Lake Chamo) who are in contact with the Borana. The Darasa
have seven *gada* grades with a 10-year duration, giving a cycle of
70 years. The names of the grades are, in Jensen's spelling:[1]

1. Lumassa
2. Raba
3. Luba
4. Juba (= Yuba)
5. Kolulu
6. Guduru
7. Tschowodji

At birth a child is assigned to the grade two places below that
of his father, i.e. a son of Lumassa would be Luba. Circumcision is
the last ceremony in the Luba grade. But no further information
seems available, and there is plainly a good deal of detail missed
out.

The Konso have a system of five grades[2] which are entered
successively at 18-year intervals; the names of the grades are:

1. Fareita
2. Khela
3. Gada
4. Orshada
5. Gura

Sons are always two grades behind those of their fathers; when
the father enters grade 3 Gada, all his sons irrespective of age
enter grade 1 Fareita; after 18 years the father enters grade 4
Orshada, and at the same time all his sons enter grade 2 Khela,
after which (and not before) they may marry. Thus, A marries

---

[1] Cerulli, *Studi Etiopici*, vol. II, pp. 38–42, sect. 17, quoting Jensen, *Im
Lande des Gada* (1936).
[2] Jensen, *Im Lande des Gada*.

soon after entering grade 2, and a year after marriage a son B is born to him. After 18 years A enters grade 3, and B, now aged 17, enters grade 1. After another 18 years A enters grade 4, and B, by this time aged 35, enters grade 2 and may marry. Together with B his younger brothers enter grade 1, and as some of them may be only 12 or thereabouts, grade 1 may contain men whose ages actually range from 35 to less than 10, since all sons enter the first and subsequent grades together. It is not certain to what extent the Konso practise circumcision, and how deeply this is connected with the age-grades. Jensen (1936) says they circumcise; but Azaïs, who visited them in 1926, says 'les Konso ne sont pas circoncis'.[1]

As to the origin of this system among the Galla, Antoine d'Abbadie assigned it to a supposed 'law-giver' named Maqo Bili,[2] in 1589, a date much too late to fit in with the ascertainable dates of Galla history in the sixteenth century. It is by no means entirely fanciful to suppose that one man invented such an institution, though d'Abbadie's date is obviously much too late. It is, in fact, hard to believe that so complex a system can have arisen quite spontaneously and without guidance. Cerulli believes that the *gada* system is an ancient Hamitic system once spread over Ethiopia, not necessarily brought in by the Galla, but maintained in certain areas by their influence, for they kept it while other peoples gave it up. It is not found among the Somali, except fairly recently among some Darod who adopted a class-system from the Galla. He adds that it is recognized that the grade system of the Nyika of the Kenya coast has been derived from the Galla.[3]

Whatever the precise origin of this custom, there seems no warrant for believing that its *transmission* to other African peoples such as the Nilo-Hamites and the Bantu Nyika of Kenya is due to any agency but the Galla.[4] It seems to be the fashion now to look elsewhere for the ultimate source of this system. Jensen believes that it came to the Galla from the Konso.[5] But a great deal more research into the political organization of the Konso is

---

[1] Azaïs et Chambard, *Cinq années de recherches archéologiques en Éthiopie* (1932), p. 253.

[2] *loc. cit.*, p. 174.

[3] *La lingua e la storia dei Sidamo* (*Studi Etiopici*, II, 1938), pp. 38–40.

[4] The remarks in Huntingford's *Nandi Work and Culture* (1950) that 'the age-sets of the Nandi and Masae are without doubt of Hamitic origin and derived direct from the *gada* system of the Gala' (p. 104) are not in themselves inconsistent with an ultimate non-Hamitic source. All that is said is that the Nandi got them from the Galla, who are Hamites.

[5] This seems acceptable to Fr. Bernardi, *Africa* (1952), vol. XIII, p. 316.

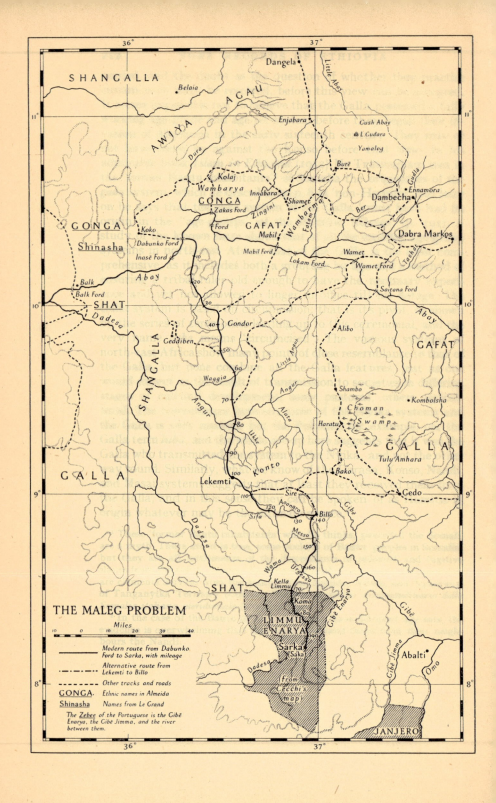

THE MALEG PROBLEM

Miles
10   0   10   20   30   40

————— Modern route from Dabunko
        Ford to Sarka, with mileage

—·—·—· Alternative route from
        Lekemti to Billo

– – – – Other tracks and roads

GONGA. Ethnic names in Almeida

Shinasha Names from Le Grand

The Zebee of the Portuguese is the Gibē
Enarya, the Gibē Jimma, and the river
between them.

APPENDIX II

THE 'MALÊG' PROBLEM

It is extremely difficult, if indeed in the present state of our knowledge of the topography and toponymy of Ethiopia it is possible, to determine precisely the route followed by Fernandes and his companions on their journey from Gojam to Enarya. The chief problem is presented by the 'Malêg', the 'big river' that they crossed before reaching the Enaryan frontier, but it is also pertinent to identify 'Minê', where they crossed the Nile, the 'Anquêr', a river they crossed the day before the 'Malêg', and 'Gancâ', the 'steep mountain' where they met the frontier guards.

Their journey was also described by Páez, who knew Fernandes personally, as Almeida did, and was in the country at the time, as Almeida was not. There is no important difference between the two accounts though there is enough variation to show that Almeida had access to some source of information other than Páez's MS. This source may well have been Fernandes himself. Telles merely summarises what Almeida tells us. Several later writers, Bruce, Sir Charles Rey and Miss Sanceau among them, have described the journey briefly but little attempt has been made to solve the difficulties of the story.

Fernandes went first to 'Collelâ' (Kollela) and then to 'Ombramâ' (Wambarma). From Wambarma to the Gonga settlement which Almeida calls 'Sinassê' was two or three days' travel; from there to 'Minê' took three days, and there they crossed the Nile. This can be done only at certain places and these are not likely to have changed since 1613. Indeed, the river can only be reached at all at specific points, for it runs through steep gorges and the traveller must use one of the paths down the cliffs. Now Fernandes is said to have crossed at a point 'opposite' the river's source on a line running east and west. This implies a ford near the confluence of the Nile and the Balas, and such a ford does exist at Beri and is marked on Cheesman's map. It is not, however, possible that Beri should be Mine. Fernandes would have had to travel very far off his route to go there and could not possibly have made the journey in five or six days. He would have been lucky to reach Beri at all after travelling for so long through the hot, unhealthy, swampy country of the pagan Nilotic tribes and it is most unlikely that neither Almeida nor Páez should have said anything of the changed character of the country and its inhabitants. A glance at the map will show the improbability of Almeida's statement. It is, however, possible to suggest why it should have been made. The Jesuits greatly oversimplified the course of the Nile. They knew, of course, that it curved round Gojam, making it, in Almeida's words, 'like a peninsula,' and then flowed northwards to Egypt. Neither their writings nor their maps, nor for that matter Bruce's, show any realisation of the important bend to the south that it makes near the Zakas ford. The result was that once they knew that a given place was on the Nile below the point at which it begins to turn northwards, they assumed that its latitude was somewhere to the north of that point, and if the place in question was below the Zakas ford its position was seriously distorted.

Mine, then, cannot be Beri and must be sought much higher up the river. It is evident from Almeida's narrative that the journey from the Nile to Enarya was known to be dangerous; the intervening territory was no longer subject to the Emperor and was exposed to Galla raids, even where it was not wholly subdued by them. It is reasonable to suppose that Fernandes would take the shortest route across this savage region. Mine is therefore likely to be fairly near the point where the Nile approaches closest to Enarya. It is not likely to be a crossing east of Mabil nor west of Inase. The river itself was a barrier to raiders and it is likely that the caravan route would have come as far south as it could before making the crossing. Caravans are therefore more likely to have used Mabil or Inase than Zakas or any ford to the west of Inase. Cheesman visited the ford at Zakas and his account of it does not accord with what we are told of Mine. He was there at the end of March, which had been unusually rainy that year, but he describes the flow of water as 'tranquil' and says that in the dry season it could be crossed on foot. Fernandes was at Mine in April; the current was very fast and he made the crossing on a raft guided by swimmers.

Mine cannot be Zakas but we do not possess sufficiently detailed descriptions of the other fords in this stretch of the Nile to say which of them it could be. That most frequently used now is the ford of Saytana (Saitana), from which the route[1] follows the high ground west of the Choman marshes through Shambo and Haratu to Bako, where it turns westward to Lekemti. Fernandes, however, travelled 'due south' from Mine to Enarya (p. 146). Mine is

[1] We are indebted to the Rev. A. F. Matthew for making inquiries on our behalf about this route from Colonel Hodder, the Chief of Police in Wallaga. It is now more frequented than the Mabil route.

more likely to be Mabil,[1] whence a well-established caravan route leads almost direct to Lekemti and Sarka, the capital of Enarya. It is strange that Fernandes should have spent five or six days in travelling from Wambarma to Mabil, but travel time is a most unreliable indication of distance, being influenced by numerous factors, such as the weather, the terrain, the competence of guides, etc.

From Mine Fernandes reached the 'Ganca' mountain, the northern frontier of Enarya, in about a week and after crossing two rivers, the 'Anquer' and the 'Maleg', of which the latter is called 'big'. The name Ganca is not found on modern maps but it occurs in the early eighteenth century chronicle in the phrase 'frontiers of Enarya and Ganqa' (AJIB, p. 246). Six days of travel brought him from Ganca to the court, presumably at or near Sarka. Almeida gives the total distance as 50 leagues, i.e. 200 miles, which is approximately correct.

The maps accompanying the two manuscripts of Almeida show two large rivers south of the Nile, the Anquer and the Maleg, which unite and continue under the name of Maleg until they join the Nile north of Fascalo. The Maleg is shown as the larger of the two, rising about 15 leagues east of the source of the Anquer. In reality there are no rivers which conform to this, and we are forced to consider as candidates a number of much smaller rivers which Fernandes must have crossed.

The Anquer, which Páez calls the Manquer, recalls the Angur, the principal right bank tributary of the Dadesa; it flows from east to west roughly half way between the Nile and Saka, a little north of Lekemti. There is no name anything like Maleg on any map that does not derive at least in part from Jesuit sources, and no later traveller has recorded it; it was unknown to d'Abbadie's native servant. It is, however, clearly written in both manuscripts of Almeida's work, is spelt in the same way by Páez and is legibly marked on both versions of Almeida's map. That such a name could have existed is shown by the occurrence of the place name Yamālog,[2] or Yamālogue, in Gojam (AJIB, pp. 65, 618; Royal Chronicle, p. 543; Guida, p. 373), which Cecchi's map gives as Malog. It seems incontestable that the name has disappeared since Almeida's time and been replaced by another, most likely one given by the Galla.[3] Weld Blundell, however, suggested (GJ,

---

[1] Harris's map certainly suggests that what he calls Mine is the Mabil ford.

[2] Possibly Ya-Mālog, 'of Malog'; malog may be Agau 'he swore'.

[3] The whole of this region has been inhabited by Galla since the sixteenth century, and most of the place names are therefore Galla.

APPENDIX III

KINGS OF ABYSSINIA FROM 1268 TO 1769

	Name	Throne-name
1268–1283	"Yekuno Amlāk"	Tasfā Iyasus
1283–1292	'Yāgbe'a Ṣyon"	Salomon
1292	Ṣēnfa Ar'ēd	
1293	Hezba Asgad	
1294	Qedma Asgad	sons of Yāgbe'a Ṣyon
1295	Jin Asgad	
1295 ?	Sab'a Asgad	
1297–1312	Wedem Ar'ād	
1312–1342	'Amda Ṣyon I	Gabra Masqal
1342–1370	Newāya Krestos	Sayfa Ar'ēd
1370–1380	Newāya Māryām	Wedem Asfarē or Germa Asfarē
1380–1409	Dāwit I	
1409–1412	Tēwodros	Walda Anbasa
1412–1427	Yeshāq	Gabra Masqal
1427	Endreyās	
1427–1433	Takla Māryām	Hezba Nāñ
1433	Sarwē Iyasus	Mehreka [Meherka] Nāñ
1433–1434	'Amda Iyasus	Badel Nāñ
1434–1468	Zar'a Yā'qob	Kuesṭanṭinos I
1468–1478	Ba'eda Māryām	
1478–1495	Eskender	Kuesṭanṭinos II
1495	'Amda Ṣyon II	
1495–1508	Nā'od	'Anbasā Baṣar
1508–1540	{ Lebna Dengel (Dawit II)	Wanāg Sagad
[1528	Invasion of Grañ]	
1540–1559	Galāwdēwos	Aṣnāf Sagad I
1559–1563	Minās	Admās Sagad I
1563–1595	Sarṣa Dengel	Malak Sagad I
1595–1604	Za Dengel	Aṣnāf Sagad II
1604	Yā'qob	Malak Sagad II
1604–1632	Susneyos	{ Malak Sagad III Selṭān Sagad I
1632–1667	Fāsiladas	'Ālam Sagad Selṭān Sagad II
1667–1681	Yohannes I	Al'āf Sagad

Name	Throne-name
1681–1704 Iyāsu I	Adyām Sagad I
1704–1706 Takla Hāymānot I	Le'ul Sagad
1706–1709 Tēwoflos	Aṣrār Sagad
1709–1714 Yosṭos	Ṣahay Sagad
1714–1719 Dāwit II (III)	Adabār Sagad
1719–1730 Bakāffā	Aṣma Sagad or Masih Sagad
1730–1755 Iyāsu II	Adyām Sagad II
1755–1769 Iyoas I	Adyām Sagad III

Ludolf and Le Grand's Hanazo, which he shows as leaving the mountains of Angot and entering the sea at Zeila: there is no such river.

Bruce's map is an improvement in that his latitudes and longitudes are much more correct: Lake Tana is now placed, as it should be, between long. 37° and 38°, and the southern part of Gojam is crossed by lat. 10°. But the shape of Lake Tana is wrong, though its size is brought nearer to actuality. As a means of identifying place-names, Bruce's map is less useful than its predecessors.

19TH CENTURY

The map by James McQueen illustrating Harris's *Highlands of Aethiopia*, 1843 (vol. i), 'compiled from the latest and best authorities,' though full of errors, has a number of major improvements, especially in the north and centre. The course of the Awash is approximately correct, and an attempt is made to show part of the hitherto utterly unknown southern Ethiopia. The delineation of Gojam is much more correct than on the older maps. These improvements seem to be due to Beke,[1] whose maps are to be considered as the first approximately correct surveys of Abyssinia; but though Beke spent some time in Gojam, he did not discover the Ebantu peninsula. Nevertheless his maps (especially that in *JRGS*, vol. xiv, 1844, p. 2) and even more his descriptions, are full of important information which anyone working on the historical topography of Ethiopia cannot neglect. Our debt to Beke is greater than might appear from our mention of him, and as far as Gojam, Damot, and Agaumeder are concerned his map is most valuable; yet he himself made the Little Abay enter the lake from the west instead of from the south.

This error persists in Keith Johnston's outline map of Abyssinia, 1867 (*Routes*, p. 109), which is, however, one of the first maps to show the proper proportions of the country and to give a correct idea of the coast-line. Where Johnston has got his distances wrong is from Lake Tana to the coast, and even here it is only some 30 miles in excess; his distance from Aksum to the coast on the other hand is 10 miles too little. Other measurements agree either wholly or to within a mile or two with the EAF map (1/1 million) of 1942. The measurements on his larger map of 'Part

---

[1] See his *Statement of facts relative to the transactions between the writer and the late British Political Mission to the Court of Shoa* (1845; ed. 2, 1846). Beke is on the whole a fairly reliable authority for the parts which he visited; for the regions south of Gojam his material is mainly derived from native statements.

of Abyssinia' at the end of *Routes* agree substantially with the outline map. On both the rivers are not all quite accurate, but much
more so than on previous maps. On the larger map is printed the
note 'no map of this country can be depended upon in all its details,[1] and the journeys made this year [1867] by M. Munzinger
and Col. Merewether near Massua ... have already rendered a
portion of this map obsolete'. [These journeys and Merewether's
map are included in *Routes*.]

The official record of the Abyssinian Expedition of 1867–8, by
Major Holland and Captain Hozier, contains a number of maps,
among them one of Abyssinia between lat. 16° 30′ N. and 9° S.,
and long. 35° and 44° E., compiled by E. G. Ravenstein on a
scale of approximately 1/1,584,000. It gives the provinces, with a
fair amount of detail and a large number of place-names. In its
framework of degrees this map is reasonably close to the modern
1/1 million map; in its measurements it is on the whole nearer to
the 1/1 million than to Keith Johnston's large map in *Routes*.
The topography is about equal to Johnston's; but Gojam and the
southern part are still full of errors. [Referred to as *AE* in
Gazetteer].

Mansfield Parkyns' map (1853) covers the country between the
south end of Lake Tana and Massawa. The distances are often less
than reality, and the courses of the rivers are somewhat distorted.
The map is useful because it gives clues to some names not marked
on all modern maps. The 'Carte d'une portion de l'Abyssinie' of
Ferret and Galinier (1841–2), given in *Routes*, p. 19, takes in the
country from Gondar to Massawa. The measurements are reasonably accurate, and owing to the large scale it has much topographical detail. The map made by Cecchi, and included as *foglio*
III in vol. ii of his *Da Zeila etc.* (1885), which shows the kingdoms
of the Gibē region as they were before the conquest by Menilek
(and is thus of special value), is reproduced in this volume. His
map of Gojam (vol. ii, *foglio* I) is the first to show approximately
the correct course of the Little Abay, but it does not show the
Ebantu peninsula. Both maps are of commendable accuracy, but
foglio III has a rather confused picture of the Omo and Gibē
rivers.

20TH CENTURY

The maps of H. Weld Blundell (*GJ*, vol. xxvii, 1906) and R. E.
Cheesman (*Lake Tana and the Blue Nile*, 1936) show the course of
the Abay in some detail, the former only the southern part, the
latter the whole course as far as long. 35°, and the whole of Lake

---

[1] This caution still holds good.

x

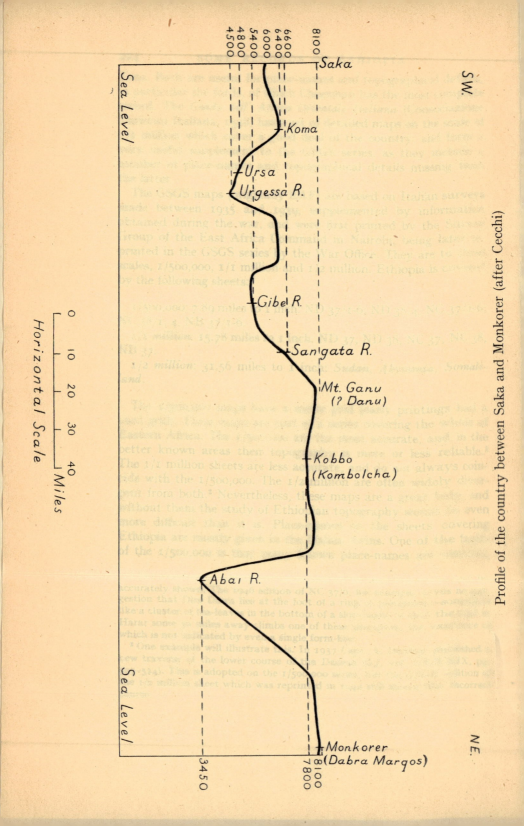

Profile of the country between Saka and Monkorer (after Cecchi)

some of those missing occur on the 1/1 million, and some on the 1/2 million sheets.[1]

Scales of the maps referred to:

Almeida, B.M. Add. MS 9861. 25 Portuguese leagues to 1 inch (100 miles to 1 inch).
Almeida, S.O.A.S. MS 11966. 25 Portuguese leagues to 1 inch.
Ludolf. 1° lat. = 1.8 inches.
Le Grand. 1° lat. = 1.1 inches.
D'Anville. 1° lat. = 0.5 inch.
Bruce. 1° lat. = 0.9 inch.
Harris. 60 miles to 1 inch.
Beke. 45 miles to 1 inch.
Keith Johnston, *Outline*. 45 miles to 1 inch.
Keith Johnston, *Large map*. 10 miles to 1 inch.
Abyssinian Expedition. 25 miles to 1 inch.
Parkyns. 25 miles to 1 inch.
Ferret and Galinier. 6.314 miles to 1 inch.
Cecchi. 15.78 miles to 1 inch.

COMPARATIVE TABLE OF DISTANCES (MILES)

	Johnston		Abyssin-ian Expedition	Parkyns	Ferret and Galinier	EAF 1/1 million
	Outline	Large				
Massawa–Dahlak	35	—	30	—	—	34
Massawa–Adigrat	90	93	92	82	97	92
Adigrat–Adua -	40	39	37	32	40	40
Adua–Aksum -	11	13	12	10	11	12
Aksum–Gondar -	135	133	142	119	147	135
Gondar–Sokota -	110	110	102	95	—	107
Sokota–Ashangi -	42	45	40	36	—	32
Ashangi–L. Tana	150	150	140	136	—	130
Ashangi–Gondar	150	154	145	—	—	138
L. Tana–L. Hayq	160	166	167	—	—	155
Gondar–L. Tana	25	25	20	25	25	19
L. Hayq–Gulf of Tajurra - -	172	—	175	—	—	145
Aksum–coast -	185	—	183	—	—	194

[1] To give some idea of the sort of country that is found in southern Ethiopia, we append a profile of a route from Sarka to Monkorer (Dabra Markos) in Gojam, based on Cecchi, vol. III, plate viii, and checked with the 1/1 million and 1/500,000 *GSGS* maps.

APPENDIX V

GAZETTEER OF PLACE-NAMES

Note.—This Gazetteer includes all place names in North-East Africa mentioned in our texts, together with such identifications as we can suggest and with examples of the forms of the names found in classical sources and in the Ethiopic inscriptions and chronicles. For the abbreviations used in referring to these chronicles see p. xix. Roman numerals are used to indicate the century to which each source belongs. In arranging these names *Ç* has been given the same place as *S*.

ABARGALE. The Avergalle of modern maps, 95 miles NE of Gondar. [XVI *CS* 151 Abārgalē.]

ABAVJ. The Abay or Blue Nile. [XV *CZ* 158, *CB* 169, XVI *CS* 9 'Abāwi; XV *CB* 158 Abāwi; XVIII *AJIB* 37 Abay.]

ABEXGAJ. 'The Gibbe, rising in the mountains of Agabdjai (Abeze-gaye), a district adjoining Guragie.' (Beke, 'The Nile and its tributaries,' *JRGS*, xvii, 1847; p. 54 of reprint.) Soleillet has Agabdja, a village on the way from the Awash to Gurage; so far as it is possible to measure his itinerary it was about 11 or 12 hours' march from Abalti, which is 25 miles WNW of Endeber in Guragē (*Voyages en Éthiopie*, p. 157). [XVI *HSD* 60 Abazagāy, 143 Abajagāy; *CS* 194 Abajagāy.]

ACHEFER. A district immediately SW of Lake Tana, marked Acefer on NC 37/1. [XVI *HSD* 131 Ačefer; *CS* 143 Ačafar, 138 Ančafar; XVIII *RC* 335 Ačafar.]

ACÇUM. Aksum, the ancient capital of Abyssinia, 12 miles WSW of Adua. [II Ptolemy Axúmē; IV *DAE* 11 Aksum; XV-XVI *CZ* 49, *CS* 123 Aksum.]

ADAXA. Written Hadasha by Beke, and situated east of Keranio between the rivers Saday (NC 37/2 Sede) and Tammi (NC 37/2 Tummi), and between Mota and the Abay. [XVI. *CS* 130 Hadāšā.]

ADEGADA. The site of this place is doubtful. Using Almeida's map as a guide, it may be identified with the place given in the *Guida* as Adi Gheda (Adi Geda) about 3½ miles SW of Debarwa.

AFA. Perhaps a mis-writing for Aça.

AGAMEA. The district round Adigrat, spelt Agame on NC 37/2. [II Cosmas, Mon. Agame; XVIII *AII* 234 Agāmyā; *RC* Agamēyā.]

ALABA. A district which was once a small state immediately E of Tambaro and SW of Lake Shala. [XV *CGA* 2, 59 Halabā; *CZ* 18 Halab.]

ALAMALE. This seems to refer to the Gurage tribal division called Aymallal, north of the river Maki. [XV *CA* 10 Alāmālē; *CB* 159 Elamālē.]

ALATA. A stream which enters the Abay from the north about 19 miles from Lake Tana; in Bruce's day it was also a village. [XVIII *RC* 538 Alatā.]

ALDOBA. The district of Waldeba, immediately W of Sokota (in Semen), and S of the Takaze. [XV *CZ* 28, XVI *CS* 123, XVIII *AJIB* 142 Wāldebā.]

ALLELUIA MONASTERY. This was at Hallelo, N of Aksum and S of the Mareb. The map of Ferret and Galinier shows Allelo about 20 miles NW of Aksum (*Routes*, opp. p. 19) in a hilly region called Torat. The place was called Dabra Hālolē in the time of Zar'a Ya'qob, and was burnt by Grañ in 1535. It received its name from a story that a monk there heard angels singing Alleluia (Basset, *Conquête*, p. 445). [XV *CZ* 28 Hālolē, Hālēlo; XVIII *AJIB* 160 Alēlo.]

AMACEM. The district of Hamasen, N of Asmara. [IV *DAE* 8 HSM XV *CZ* 48 Hasēmēn; XVI *CS* 99, *HSD* 146 Hamāsēn; XVIII *PC* 42, *RC* 469 Hamāsēn.]

AMBA GUEXEN. Amba Geshen in Amhara, to the NW of Amba Sel. This is not marked on modern maps, except those of Sir Clements Markham, who places it 10 miles NE of Magdala (a position where NC 37/2 has Amba Moka), and *AE* which shows it 20 miles NE of Magdala. Markham apparently did not actually go there, but saw it through glasses (*History of the Abyssinian Expedition*, p. 288). [XVI *CS* 243 Ambā Gāšanā, other variants being Gešēn, Gešan, Gešēnā, Gešē; XVIII *PC* 100 Gečena.]

AMBAÇANET. Somewhere in Tigre, perhaps in Temben or Haramat districts. In the latter Pearce has a place called Basanate. Alvares names Abacinete a few leagues from Aksum which may be the same place. Sapeto gives it as Ambā sanēti near Adua (*Viaggio*, p. 428). [XV *CB* 129 Ambā sānēt, 142 Ambā sanāyt.]

AMBACEL. Amba Sel, about 20 miles N of Dessie, the modern village of Amba Sel being 28 miles from Dessie. (NC 37/2.) [XVI *CS* 83 Ambāsal; XVIII *RC* Ambāsal, Ambasāl, Ambā sa'al, Amba sel.]

ANDERTA. Enderta, 25 miles NE of Makalle. [XVI *CS* 296 Endartā; XVIII *AJIB* 26, *AII* 144 Endartā.]

ANFRAS. Not shown on modern maps, but appears on Bruce's map between two rivers which he writes Corno and Arno almost due E of Meṣraha Island in Lake Tana; ND 37/4 marks 'Portuguese castle' about 6 miles from the lake shore. *AE* shows Emfras district here. The town was built on a 'high mountain' overlooking the lake, and was at one time a residence of the kings of Abyssinia. Poncet describes it as smaller than Gondar, though better sited and better built. (*Voyage*, Hakluyt Soc., ser. II, vol. 100, p. 136.) [XVI *CM* 28, *HSD* 95, *CS* 95 Emfrāz, 'Emfraz, Enfrāz; XVIII *RC* 213 Enfrāz.]

ANGOT. The province which lies E. of Amhara. [XIV *CGA* 8, 17 Angot; XV *CZ* 40 Angot; XVI *HSD* 8, *CS* 150 Angot; *HGG* 200 Anguat.]

ANQUER. The Angur (NC 37/4 Angar) a tributary of the Dadesa. See Appendix II: The 'Malêg' Problem.

AOAGE. There seem to have been two districts called Waj or Wag: (1) N of Lasta, E of Semen, and S of Abargale, a district of the Agau, chief town Sokota; (2) in Shoa near Dabra Berhan, called Waj in the *Futuh*. It is evident that Almeida refers to the first of these, for he puts it on the right bank of the Takaze. [XV *CZ* 15 Waj; XVI *HSD* 46, *HGG* 197 Waj; *CS* 151 Waj, Wāg.]

AQUICO. Possibly Akik.

ARAR. Harar. See Auça Gurrele. [*CA* 52 Harar.]

AR'EÑA. Possibly the same as the Ar'an of the *Futuh*, which Basset (*Conquête*, p. 83) places between Faṭagar and the land of the El Maya (? those of Arho in the Danakil country; see note on p. 120).

ARQUICO. The modern Arkiko, Arqiqo (Archico of Italian maps), about 6 miles S of Massawa. It was also called Dequeno or Deqheno (in Portuguese spelling). [*HSD* 130 Dakano, a name seemingly derived from the Saho word *dakono*, 'elephant'; *AII* 125 Dahono.].

AÇA. Bruce (bk V, chap. 5) mentions a stream in the plain of Adua which flows into the Mareb. This is the Hassam, of which Beke says that the name is 'not Assa nor Assam' and that it really joins the Takaze towards the SW, adding that the name should be Hassam. ('The Nile and its tributaries,' *JRGS*, vol. xvii; p. 5 of reprint.) The existence of a river Assam is confirmed by Keith Johnston's map (*Routes*, end); but Ferret and Galinier show a stream or perhaps a district (for the marking is not clear) flowing into the Mareb NW of Adua (*Routes*, opp. p. 19). Almeida refers by this name to a place; and Parkyns marks a district of Assa *east* of Adua; Salt also crossed a stream called Assa between Fremona and Adua (*Valentia*, vol. iii, p. 74). [Perhaps the Ah'sa of the *Kebra Nagast*.]

'Āsā Zanab. 'Fish's tail,' a place somewhere in Southern Ethiopia. [XVI *HGG* 199.]

Asmara. The modern Asmara.

Auça Gurrele. The modern Aussa, this particular place being perhaps represented by the Gurrale of NC 37, a hill-feature (5141 ft.) 90 miles NW of Lake Abbe or Abhebad. In modern times the Sultans of Aussa appear to have had no fixed residence (Thesiger in *GJ*, vol. lxxxv, 1935, p. 15), but in the sixteenth and seventeenth centuries they evidently had at least semi-permanent capitals, for the capital of the emirate of Harar was transferred from Harar to Aussa in 1577 and remained there till about 1647 (Cerulli, *La lingua e la storia di Harar*, p. 38). It is therefore to be supposed that Almeida meant Gurrale, though its position on his maps is rather that of Harar itself. Indeed, Le Grand speaks of 'Auca, que le Pere Jean dos Santos appelle mal-à-propos Arar' (*Voyage*, p. 224). [XVI *HGG* 199 Awsā.]

Axguagua. This is perhaps what *RC* calls 'the land of Šaguā of Dāwnt'. NC 37/2 places *Daunt*, with a village *Daont* to the north of the Bashilo river and W of Magdala. Almeida's Axguagua (Ašguagua) must be somewhere E or NE of Dabra Zebit (NC 37/2) where the Takaze rises, an area which may fairly be described as 'the beginning of Angot'. The mention of Mazalā below the summit of Ašguagua in *AJIB* 44 suggests the mountain mass in Santara district (10,499 ft and 40 miles NNW of Lake Hayq) where the village of Madscel (thus NC 37/2) may represent Mazalā. [XVI *CS* 246 Ašguāguā; XVIII *AJIB* 44, *RC* 279 Ašguāguā.]

Auzen. Now represented by Hausien (Hausen), 20 miles S of Adigrat. [Perhaps the Hawzaña of *CGA* 2, 47.]

Badões, The. This is evidently the place on the coast of Italian Somaliland called Baduis on Linschoten's map, and Os Bodios on a map ascribed to the seventeenth century cartographer Pierre Berthelot, cited in Vincent's edition of the *Periplus* (p. 141). We have not been able to trace the name on any modern map.

Bahargamo and Sufgamo. The former is described by Almeida as the southern limit of the empire of Ethiopia; and both names occur in hymns of Yeshaq (1412–1427; Guidi, *Canzoni*, 2, 56). It is quite clear that these districts were in the south of the Sidama region near a lake or lakes; it is equally clear that Almeida places them too far north on his maps. Cecchi suggested Lake 'Abba' for the lake, by which he probably meant Abaya (the local name of the lake called Margherita by the Italians), at the SW end of which lies the country of Gamo, a name that may form the second element of both these names. (The Galla *gama*, 'beyond,' which has been suggested, must be ruled out, for the names existed a hundred years before the Galla invasion.) Basset suggested Lakes Abaya and Chamo (*Conquête*, p. 396), adding that these are also called Basso Narok and Basso Naebor; the latter however are Masai words, which according to von Hohnel refer to lakes Rudolf and Stefanie. (*Basso* seems to be a corruption of the Masai *e-wuaso*, 'river'; *na-rok* = 'black,' and *na-ibor* = 'white' [XV *CGA* 2, 56 Bāhr gamo; 2, 57 Suf gamo].

BALY, BALLI. The Moslem state of Bali, a member of the 'empire of Zeila', was south of Hadya and stretched approximately from the Webi Shabelle in the E (where it bordered on Ifat and Dawaro) to the Omo in the W. Al 'Umari describes it as the most fertile of all the Moslem states. (*Masalik al absar*, ed. Gaudefroy-Demombynes, chap. 8.) [XV *CZ* 17; XVI *CG* 28, *CS* 15 Bali, Bali.]

BATERAT. A mountain between Enarya and Janjero. Not identified.

BAXILO. The river Bashilo, which rises E of Magdala and flows into the Abay from the east. [XVI *CS* 141; XVIII *AJIB* 78 Bašelo.]

BAYLUR. The modern Beilul, a village about a mile from the sea, and 26 miles NW of Assab, which has succeeded it as the port for this part of the Red Sea coast.

BED. In Agaumeder S of Lake Tana; shown as Bad by *AE*. [XVI, XVIII *CS* 102, *AJIB* 12, *PC* 24 Bad; and perhaps the Wedo of *HSD* 134, though this last is doubtful.]

BEGAMEDER. The name of this province, which extends from the Ethiopia-Sudan frontier to Lasta and includes the country on the north side of Lake Tana, has been variously derived from Ethiopic *bagge*, 'sheep,' and from *Bega*, 'the Beja people.' The Portuguese maps confirm the possibility that in earlier times the use of the name was restricted to the country E of Lake Tana, and Beke remarks on the scarcity of water in 'Biegemider', adding that 'in Europe, Biegemider is said to be noted for its fine flocks of sheep . . . but it is only necessary to see the country to be satisfied that it never was and never can be a sheep country' (*JRGS*, vol. xiv, p. 53). As to a derivation from Beja, it is too far south for a reasonable connexion with that people to be easily established. The allusion to lack of water suggests Amharic *bagā*, 'dry season,' as a possible source of the name. [XV *CZ* 14; XVI *CS* 20 Begameder; *HSD* 50 Bēgameder; *HGG* 200 Bagēmeder; Ludolf in XVII writes Bagēmeder; XVIII *AJIB* 6, *AII* 40 Bēgameder.]

BELENÊ, 'which is the country of Amacem,' is perhaps the land of the Bilen or Bilin (Bogos), N of Hamasen, the most northerly of the Agau-speaking peoples. [*KN* Belēn.]

BETERAMORA. Perhaps S of Shoa, as it is mentioned in the *Futuh* in connexion with Ganz, *q.v.* [XIV *CGA* 9, 2 Baṭer 'amorā; XVI *HSD* 144 Baṭer'āmorā, *HGG* 196 Baṭera 'Amorā. Amharic *āmorā* = 'vulture'.]

BIZAMO. Formerly a district between the Abay and Lekemti, and in pre-Galla days part of Damot: 'The Nile [Abay] passes between Bezamo, which is a part of the kingdom of Damot, and Gamarcansa, which belongs to the kingdom of Goiam.' (Le Grand, *Voyage*, p. 109.) [XV *CGA* 2, 15; XVI *CS* 26, *HSD* 52 Bizāmo; *CS* 26 Bizāmā.]

BORA. Bora, 25 miles NE of Sokota. (Perruchan's copy of B.M. Add. MS 9861 has Bota in error.) [XVI *CS* 4 Borā.]

BOXA. The Bosha of Garo in SE Jimma. [XV *CGA* 2, 40; XVI *HSD* 44, *HGG* 204 Bošā.]

BRANTY. The Branti is a tributary of the Kilti, which it joins not far from the junction of the Kilti with the Little Abay. It is shown on Ludolf's map, but not in such a way that it can be identified with any existing river. *AE* shows the Branti joining the Kelti about 20 miles SSW of the mouth of the Little Abay. [Awiya Agau *beranti*, 'rapid.']

BRABA. The town of Brava on the eastern Somali coast, 110 miles S of Mogadishu. [Swahili, Barawa.]

BUR. In Tigre. Bruce speaks of Lower Bur NW of Assab in the Lowlands, and Higher Bur to the NE of Agamer. *HSD* says that when Yeshaq went to Debārwā the peasants of Bur and Sarāwē (Serae) raided his stock (p. 74). [XV *CZ* 48 Bur; XVI *HSD* 74, *CS* 128, *AII* 38, Bur. To be distinguished from Burē in Damot, *CS* 107.]

BUZANA. Placed by Mendes' and Almeida's maps between Sugamo (Sufgamo) and Cambat (Kambatta); the latter call it Buzama.

CAFA. The kingdom of Kafa (Kaffa).

CAGMA. The *Futuh* has Qāqma, which is evidently a district, for it speaks of Upper and Lower Qāqma. It seems to have been within the Abyssinian sphere, for the king of Abyssinia made one Takla Haymanot, a moslem, *garad* (chief) of Qaqma; it lay in the direction of a place which the *Futuh* calls Serjedda

Crawford, on the strength of Mendes' spelling *Adefali*, with Arafali at the south end of the Gulf of Zula (*Fung Kingdom*, p. 129). Ludolf's map (1683) somewhat inexplicably shows it as an island in the Gulf of Zula, as also does Le Grand's. [XVIII *AII* 134 The *Defala* people in Tigre.]

DEK. Deq or Dek is the larger of two islands near the south end of Lake Tana (the other is called Daga). [XV *CB* 168 Daq; XVI *HSD* 43 Deq; XVI *CS* 132, XVIII *AII* 151, *RC* 484 Daq.]

DEQHANA. See Quinfaz.

DEQUENO. The Saho name for Arkiko, *q.v* [XVI *HSD* 145 Dakano, Dakono; XVIII *AII* 125 Dahono.]

DEQUIM. The 'Kingdom of Dequin' is marked on Le Grand's map between Sennar and the region where the Mareb disappears in the sand. Crawford identifies it with the country round Kassala, where there is a place or district called Duqein (*Fung Kingdom*, p. 115). He also suggests that this is another of the 'elephant' names, quoting the Saho and Afar words for 'elephant'; but this is out of the area where DKN is the Hamitic root for 'elephant', the nearest Hamitic language-groups being Agau, which has ZHN and JN (for JHN = ZHN), and Beja and Kunama, which have KRB. Crawford, however, quotes from Ibn Hawqal a river called Al Dujn, and a 'neighbourhood and fields of Dujn', which suggest that the name may really be derived from dukn (Arabic *dukhn*, 'millet').

DOARO. The Moslem state of Dawaro, in which was situated Harar, lay alongside Ifat according to the descriptions of Maqrizi and Al 'Umari. There was also an area in the Sidama country known locally as Dawaro by the Kullo because it was colonized by refugees from Dawaro proper during the war with Grañ. It is of course to Dawaro proper that Al-meida refers. [XIV *CGA* 8, 13; 10, 34 Dawāro; XVI *HGG* 198 Dawaro; *CS* 185 Dawāro.]

DOBA. This appears to have been the name of a people, the Dob'ā, rather than a region. Almeida's map (B.M. Add. MS 9861) puts them NW of Senafe in Tigre, and Bruce puts them between Bur and Temben. But it seems possible that they may have extended further south towards Lake Ashangi, 18 miles N of which is a mountain called Dubbai on ND 37/5 which may preserve their name. Trimingham suggests that they may have been of Afar stock (*Islam in Ethiopia*, p. 81). [XV *CB* 138 Dobe'a, 143 Dabyā; XV, XVI *CZ*, *CM* Dob'ā, Dob'ā, Dobāya, Dobya, Dab'a, Deb'ā.]

EBENAT. ND 37/5 has Ebbenat, 25 miles E of Lake Tana, between the lake and Mechetoa. [XVI *CM* 29 Hebnāt; XVIII *AJIB* 61 Ebnāt; *RC* 428 'Ebnāt.]

ENARYA. See Narea. [XV *CGA* 2, 29 Ēnaryā; XVI *HGG* 204 Enaryā, *CS* 46 Enāryā.]

FATEGAR. One of the Moslem states, originally on both sides of the Awash, but latterly on the right bank, SE of Shoa and lying between Ifat and Dawaro. [XIV *CGA* 8, 14; 10, 32; XV, XVI *CZ* 15, *HGG* 198, *HSD*, *CS* 285 Faṭagar, Faṭagār.]

FAXCALO. Written Fascalo in B.M. Add. MS 9861. Fazogli, Fazuqli, on the Blue Nile about 180 miles S of Sennar. [XVI *CS* 206 Fāzqulo, Fāzqelo.]

FELIX, Mount. The modern Ras al Fil, 10 miles west of Alula on the north Somali coast. Ras al Fil is the Arabic equivalent of the Mount Elephas of Strabo (XVI § 4, 14), the *Periplus* (§ 11) and Ptolemy (IV § 7, 10). It also occurs in 1611 (*Purchas his Pilgrimes*, bk IV, ch. 1 § 2) as Feluke, of which Almeida's Felix is evidently another form. Modern maps also give Ras Filuk.

FOCAJ. Almeida seems to have taken this name from Páez (bk 1 c. 1, Beccari vol. ii p. 14) where it is spelt Focâi. It may perhaps be a mistake for Tokar, a place some 55 miles SE of Suakin. Capital T and F are very similar in some MSS, including S.O.A.S. 11966.

FREMONA. According to Lobo (Le Grand, p. 202) this place was 3 leagues from Aksum, and the maps place it to the east. Almeida's map in B.M. Add. MS 9861 makes the distance about 10 leagues (though S.O.A.S. MS 11966 makes it only half this). The proper name for the place is Maegoga (in Almeida's spelling), from *may* = 'water', *guagua* = 'rushing'. Ferret and Galinier show a district of Maigogua about 10 miles east of Aksum; *AE* marks Fremona at the same distance. Salt says that the name Fremona 'if ever adopted by the inhabitants is now wholly unknown' (Valentia, vol. iii p. 74).

GADANCHO. Evidently one of the provinces lost to the Abyssinian empire by Almeida's time; its position is unknown. [Perhaps the Gadāyčo or Gadāyto of *CZ* 17.]

GAFATES. The people of Gafat, a country originally south of Abay, adjoining Damot. The inhabitants were driven across the river by the invading Galla in the sixteenth century. Their language, which became extinct towards the end of the nineteenth century, is Semitic, not Hamitic. Beke reported that in his day 'it appears to be spoken in only a small portion of

HADEA. The Moslem state of Hadya stretched roughly from lat. 39° westwards beyond the area later occupied by the Galla monarchies of the Gibē. But it is probable that Almeida refers to the smaller kingdom of Hadya that grew up within the limits of the larger state, and submitted to Grañ in 1532. (See p. lxiii.) The people call themselves Gudela. [XV, XVI *CZ* 16, *HSD passim, CS* 32 Hādyā, Hadyā. XV, XVI *CZ*, *CS passim* Gudelā, Gudolā, Guedalā, Guedēla.]

HAOAX. The river Awash or Hawash. [XV *CZ* 63 Hawāš.] (On the end of this river in Aussa, see Thesiger in *GJ*, vol. lxxxv, 1935, pp. 1 *seq.*)

HARICE. Placed by Almeida, together with Aça, Torat, and Sire, south and SE of the Mareb. No such name appears on either ND 37/2 or ND 37; but Mansfield Parkyns' map shows a place which he writes Addy Harisho, 6 miles from Mai Chena and 6 miles from the Mareb, in the district of Rocabaita. The place called Adi Agghera on ND 37/2 may represent Almeida's Harice, for it is 6 miles from Chena, 6 miles from the Mareb, and NE of the village of Rocabaita. See Torat. Crawford identifies it with Arresa (*Fung Kingdom*, p. 144), but this is on the wrong side of the Mareb. The Jesuits knew this part of Abyssinia well, and are not likely to have made such a mistake.

HAZALO. A place in southern Ethiopia, not identified. [XVI *HGG* 199 Hazalo.]

HOLCAIT. Almeida's maps have Olcait. The province of Walqayt is NW of Semen and N of Gondar. [IV perhaps the WLQ of *DAE* 8; *AJIB* 307, *AII* 135, XVIII *PC* 79, *RC* 252 Wālqāyt.]

IANGARA. This is said to be in Kambatta; but the name suggests confusion with Yangaro or Janjero. Páez writes it Jangrâ; Bruce, after the English Telles, has Sangara.

JAN AMORA. Ferret and Galinier mark Jannamora SSW of Mai Talo; ND 37/5 has Genemora 30 miles SSW of Mai Tsalo. [XVI *HGG* 199, *CS* 151 Jan'amorā.]

JEBALA. Jebala or Jibala is about 15 miles north of Dabra Marko in Gojam. It is one of two 'fortress-like stone pinnacles [the other is called Mutara] . . . famous as prisons for political offenders of high degree' which rise from the great ravine of the Chamwaga river [*AJIB* 49 Čamogā], a tributary of the Abay (Cheesman, *Lake Tana*, p. 315). [XVI *HGG* 203 Jebalā. Perhaps Agau *jiba-lā*, 'uninhabited place,' since Mutara seems to be Agau *mutar-ā*, 'raised to a point.']

IUGO. The river Juba in Somalia. In Jesuit documents this word appears sometimes as the name of a river, and sometimes as the name of a place; cf. letters in Beccari, vol. xii, pp. 37, 86, 89, 126.

KELTY. Written Kilti on the 2-million map; Cheesman shows it as joining the Little Abay about 30 miles south of Lake Tana. [XVIII *AII* 169 Kilti. Agau, Kialti.]

LAMALMON. This is the western extension of the Semen range. The road to Aksum ran through the Lamalmo Pass, which is called Lemalemo on Italian maps (ND 37, Malo), about 25 miles NW of the summit of Buahit, the second highest peak of the Semen range. [XVI *CS* 123 Lamalmo; XVIII *AJIB* 158 Lamālmo; *AII* 22 Lamalmo; *RC* 343 Lamālamo.]

LASTA. The province of Lasta is east of Begameder. [XVI *CS* 298 Lāstā; XVIII *AII passim*, Lastā.]

MACARAQUER. The position of this is not yet identified, but it was somewhere on Amba Geshen. [Perhaps the same as the Manquarquaryā enqorā (= pass of M.) of *CS* 224.]

MACHY. The river Maki. See note on p. 30.

MAEGOGA. See Fremona.

MAGADAXO. Mogadishu or Mukadisha on the coast of Somalia.

MAGAZA or MAZAGA. Basset (*Conquête*, p. 426) identifies Magaza with Ras el fil, about 10 miles NW of Gallabat (ND 37/4), and the text of the *Futuh* certainly suggests that the place to which Grañ went from Aksum was not between the Takaze and Mareb rivers. But such an identification does not agree at all with its position on Almeida's maps. It is possible that there has been confusion here between a general term and a place-name proper. Bruce, who claimed to have been made governor of Ras el fil, says 'the country from Tcherkin [ND 37/4 Chirchin?] to Ras el Feel, or Hor Cacamoot, is all a black earth, called Mazaga, which some authors have taken for the name of a province. However the word Mazaga, in the language of the country, signifies fat, loose black earth or mould' (bk. VIII, chap. 3), i.e. Amharic *mazagā*, 'black cotton soil.' This is borne out by Parkyns, who speaks of 'mazzagas, that is, the low flats of dark soil which the people cultivate though they live on the neighbouring hills' (vol. ii, p. 340). On his map he marks 'Mazaga or Low Plains' along the left bank of the Takaze in Waldeba and Walqayt. Bruce adds that as a specific name the word is applied to the 'hot, unwholesome, low stripe of country' on the frontier of Sennar (bk. VI, chap. 1). This is confirmed by the existence of a line of '*Mazaga*-names' stretching from the Takaze to Gallabat: *Mezzega* (ND 37/1), lat. 14° 30', long. 38° 55'; *Mezzaga Romodan* (ND 37/4), lat. 13° 40', long. 36° 55'; and *Messega Ghirmai*

(ND 37/4), 15 miles south of the last. (Spelling as on the map.)
It is thus possible that Almeida really did make a mistake in
regarding Mazaga as a 'province less than a kingdom'; his
location of it between the Takaze and Mareb does however
agree with the sites of the Mezzega names. [XVI CG 77,
CS 162 Mazagā.]

MALEG. The name of a river. See Appendix II: The 'Malêg'
Problem.

MAREBO. The river Mareb or Marab. [XVI HSD, CS 128; XVIII
AJIB 165, AII 228, PC 40 Marab.]

MARGAY. Possibly the Merdjai of the Futuh (Basset, Conquête,
p. 95), the text of which shows it to have been somewhere near
the Awash.

MARRABET. A district between the Abay and Wanchit (Wachit)
rivers in Shoa, north of Addis Ababa. [XV CB 127 Mahra-
bētē, Mahrabēt; XVI CS 274 Marahbētē; XVIII AJIB 190
Marābētē. XVI CS 274, AJIB 189 Wančet.]

MAÇUA. Massawa. [XVI CM 22 Meṣwā; XVIII PC 17 Maṣwā',
Meṣwā', Meṣwā.]

MAUZ. Beyond doubt a misspelling of Mans or Mens, a district between Marrabet and Gedem, lying between the rivers Kashem
and Mofer (NC 37/2 and 1/2 million maps). [XV CB 116
Manzh, Menzhel.]

MELINDE. Malindi on the Kenya coast.

MEROE. The ancient city of Meroe in the Sudan.

MINE. See Appendix II: The 'Malêg' Problem.

MOTA. Now Mota in Gojam. NC 37/1, 50 miles NNE of Dabra
Markos.

NAREA. The kingdom of Enarya. [XVI HGG 204, CS 46 Enāryā.]

NEBESSE. Now the district of Ennebse between Mota and the
Abay, NS 37/1. Beke says that Enabsie, though under the
ruler of the peninsula, was not strictly part of Gojam proper.
(JRGS, vol. xiv, p. 26). [XVI CS 58, XVIII AII 49 En-
nabe'esē; XVIII AJIB 78, RC 210 Ennābesē.]

OBE. The Webi Shabelle. See Wabi.

OGARA. The district of Wagara. Marked on Ferret and Galinier's
map between Gondar and Semen, with 'Colla Waggara'
(quallā Wagarā, 'the lowland of Wagara') immediately to the
north. Bruce describes it as Woggora, a plain lying to the
south of Lamalmon and divided from the mountain by the
'Macara' (bk. V, chap. 7). It was in Wagara that Galāwdēwos
defeated the Moslems in 1542. [XVI CG 21, HSD 97, CS 52;
XVIII AJIB 142, RC 348 Wagarā.]

OGGE. Almeida's maps show a 'kingdom of Oge' south of Lake

Zway (his text says south of Shoa). Unless his geography is at fault, Oge cannot therefore be the Waj of the *Futuh*, if that was near Dabra Berhan (see Aoage); but it might be Bruce's 'Wadge' (bk. III, 'Baeda Mariam'). It is in any case to be distinguished from Waj in Lasta, and is perhaps the Wagē of *CA* 10, whereas the Lasta Waj (Almeida's Aoage) is Waj or Wāg in the Abyssinian records.

OIFAT. The Moslem state of Ifat or Wifat. [XV, XVI *CZ* 16, *CG* 14 Ifāt; XVIII *PC* 12 Wifāt.]

OINADEGA. This is a geographical term, descriptive of the temperate regions of Abyssinia, and meaning literally 'the highlands of the grape' (*wayna*). It is applied to various localities in this temperate zone; the area referred to by Almeida was to the west of Lake Tana; there is another in Fogara on the eastern side of the lake. [XVI *HSD* 62, *HGG* 201, *CS* 101 Wayna dag'ā; variant in *CS* -dagā.]

OLECA, HOLECA. This 'province' seems to be represented now by the river Wolaka (Walaqa), a tributary of the Abay north of the Jamma. The district is referred to in *CS* and *HSD*, the river is named in *CS*. [XVI *CS* 15, 18, *HSD* 32; XVIII *AII* 82 Walaqā.]

OMBAREA. The facts concerning this district are: (1) In *HSD* 132 we are told that the king reached Wambaryā from Ačafar; from Wambaryā he crossed the river Durā and thence, passing through Hankāšā district, arrived at Gubā'ē. (2) In *HSD* 176 Wambaryā is called the country of the Gafat. (3) In *PC* 24 the king went to the country of the Wambaryā from Balyā. These facts suggest that (*a*) Wambarya cannot be Wanbera, which is some way west of the Dura, and (*b*) it is the name of the district south of Askuna, close to, and west of, the Sori river, between that and the Dura; the name perhaps survives in Inabara east of the Sori. The Jesuits used the name Ombarea for a large area on the right bank of the Abay which was conquered by Se'ela Krestos in 1615; Páez calls it a 'kingdom opposite the kingdom of Fazcolo', a statement due to the distortion of Almeida's maps. (Beccari, vol. ii, p. 258).

OMBRAMA. This was the starting point of Fernandes' journey to Enarya, and seems to be the district of Wambarma between the rivers Zingini and Faṭam [*AJIB* 38 Faṣam] 30 miles WSW of Dembecha. [XVI *CS* 26 Wambarmā; XVIII *AJIB* 185 Wambarma, var. Wabarmā.]

ORIJA. In the list of kingdoms and provinces given by Páez this name appears as Orgâr, which is perhaps the Wārgār of *CA*. Cerulli has identified this with Warijhe, another name occuring in the Chronicles; this variant may account for Almeida's Orija. It is also conceivable that Almeida confused the Orgâr of Páez with the Orgabija of Alvares (p. 330); the latter however is probably Argobba. The position of Wārgār is not known. (Cf. Trimingham, *Islam in Ethiopia*, p. 72.)

OXELO. A place called Wašluh is described in the *Futuh* as being at the extremity of Ganz (*Conquête*, p. 201). If Ganz is south of Shoa, Oxelo cannot be the Wāsl of *CB* 151, for there the king is said to have gone from the Dobe'a country towards Angot, to have reached Wāsl, and thence gone towards Gedem. In *CZ* 65 it is said that pieces of the body of Arwē Badlāy were sent to Aksum, Manhadbē, Wāšl, Jejeno, Lawo, and Wiz. If Manhadbē = Madabāy, this too suggests that Wāsl was at any rate north of Shoa. We should perhaps identify Oxelo with the Wasel of the *Futuh*, which Basset suggests is the Acel of Alvares; but it cannot be Ambasel, as he suggests (*Conquête*, p. 283), for Almeida writes this Ambacel (see above). Moreover it was evidently one of the provinces lost to the empire by Almeida's time, and this was certainly not true of Amba Sel.

PATE. The island of Pate near Lamu off the Kenya coast.

QAČENO. In Ifat, but otherwise unknown. [XV *CB* 151 Qačeho, Qačēno; XVI *HGG* 200, *CS* 45 Qačeno.]

QUESSAN. There seems to be some confusion here between names and rivers. The *name* seems to be the Kashem of NC 37/2, one of the streams which unite south of Wara Ilu to form the Wanchit; this enters the Jamma 20 miles from its junction with the Abay. Bruce calls it Geshen; and there may be a connexion with the district name Geshe or Gishe north of Mans (Mens). [XVI *CS* 219 Qačam; *CB* 116 Gešē, Gesē.]

QUINFAZ. Described by Almeida as being, with Ebenat, on the south of the Takaze, which separates them from the districts of Deqhana and Aoage (Waj). Bruce says that Dehaanah and Waag are among the five 'clans' of the Lasta Agau. The place is so far unidentified. Deqhana [XVI *CS* 132 Dāḳanā], however, may be the Dahana of Keith Johnston's map, between the Tella and Meri rivers east of the Takaze, in an area where ND 37/5 has a river Daama, which may stand for Da'ana representing Dahana. Beke also has Dahana here (*JRGS*, vol. xiv, p. 57). [XVI *CS* 155 Kinfaz; *Futuh*, K-nfāt (first vowel uncertain).]

SACAHALA. Sakala, a district about 40 miles west of Dembecha, in which the Little Abay rises, south of Lake Tana. [XVI *CS*

105 Sākala, Sakala; XVIII *AII* 54 Sakalā.]

ÇALAOÂ. A province marked south of Abargale and written Salaoa on Almeida's maps. The district of Seloa (ND 37/5) or Salawa is some 10 miles east of Abargale. [XVI *CS* 151, *CG* 77; XVIII *PC* 16, *AII* 262 Salawā.]

SALEMT. ND 37/5 has Tzellemti north of Sokota in Semen, on the south side of the Takaze. [XVI *CS* 247 Ṣalāmāt; XVIII *AJIB* 207, *RC* 469 Ṣalamt; *KN* Zalamt.]

ÇAMA. This is shown south of the Mareb on Almeida's map in S.O.A.S. MS 11966; and according to Ludolf, who writes it Samʿā, was a province of Tigre. It may be the place shown on Bent's map as Zama (*Sacred City of the Ethiopians*). [*AJIB* 207 has Čama at the entry of Tamben, but this may refer to another place, though it agrees more or less with the position of Cama on Almeida's map.]

ÇANA. ND 37/5 has a district of Zana on the north bank of the Takaze and SW of Sksum. [XVI *CS* 212, XVIII *PC* 17, *AII* 128 Zānā may refer to this place.]

SEGADE. A district of Walqayt SW of Mesfinto (ND 37/4 Tzeghede). Possibly the Takade of Rüppel (*Reise*, vol. ii, p. 151). [XVI, XVIII *CS* 166, *AJIB* 18, *AII* 243 Ṣagade; *KN* Zagadē.]

ÇEMEN. See Cemen.

SENAFEE. Now Senafe in Tigre, 30 miles north of Adigrat.

SERAOE. The province of Serae or Sarawe on the north side of the Mareb. [XV, XVI, XVIII *CZ* 47, *HSD* 74, *AJIB* 63, *AII* 227 Sarawē; *PC* 14 Sarawe, Sarāwē.]

SERCA. See Cerca.

SHOA. The southern part of Abyssinia proper, formerly a kingdom. [XV, XVI *CZ* 14, *CM* 23, *CS* 17, Šawā, Šewā; XV *CA* Sawā.]

SUAQHEM. Suakin on the Red Sea coast north of Massawa. [XVI *CS* 206 Sewākēn; XVI *HSD* 64 Sawāken; XVIII *PC* 48 Sawākin.]

SUFGAMO. See Bahargamo.

SYRE. The district of Sire in Tigre, west of Aksum and south of the Mareb. [XV *CZ* 47; XVI *HSD* 68, *CS* 111 Sirē.]

TACAZEE. The river Takaze. [IV *DAE* 11 Takaze; XVI, XVIII *CS* 120, *PC* 16 Takazē, Takazi; *AJIB* 20, *AII* 22 Takazē.]

TACUÇA. *AJIB* 165 mentions a place called Taqusa (*AE* Dagosa) north of Dangal bar on a route to Gondar. The *RC* however has a place of the same name between Gondar and Semen. Lobo (Le Grand, p. 205) has Guca, 'the base of Lamalmon' (almost the words of Almeida). It is clear that there were two places of this name, and that Almeida refers to that on Lamalmo on p. 45, while on p. 43 he seems to refer to a place on the west of the lake. [XVIII *AJIB* 165 Ṭāqusā; *RC* 232 Ṭaqusa, 228 Daguasa.]

TALACEON. Evidently a province that by the seventeenth century had been lost to the empire. Unidentified.

TANQHA. The reference of Almeida to this, its position on Le Grand's map (where it is called Tancoa), and the sequence of forms of the name show that it is the modern Tumha (NC 37/1) 5 miles NW of Dangela. [XVI *CS* 163 Tankuā; XVIII *AJIB* 12 Temkua; *AII* 169 Tumhā.]

TEMBEM. Temben, the district round Abbi Addi, north of Makalle. Italian maps have Tembien. [XVI *HSD* 69, *CS* 169 Tambēn; XVIII *AJIB* 79, *AII* 156 Tambēn.]

TIGRE. The northern part of Abyssinia. [X Schol. on Cosmas, Tigrētai, Tigrētanes; XV *CZ* 49 Tegre, Tegre'y, XVI *CS* 77; XVIII *PC* 10 Tegrē.

TORAT. Associated by Almeida with Aça, Harice, and Sire, on the south side of the Mareb. The mention of the people called 'the Madabāy of Torāt' in *HSD* shows that it was the district 35 miles NW of Aksum called Medebai on the maps (e.g. ND 37/2), between Addi Harisho and Sire. [XVI *HSD* 146, *CS* 129 Torāt.Medebai: *HSD* 146 Madabāy; Conti Rossini, *Catalogo dei nomi propri di luogo*, quotes from the *Catalogue raisonné des MSS. éthiopiennes appartenant à Antoine d'Abbadie*, 1859, p. 151, the form Madabāy; *CZ* 65 has Manhadbē, which seems to be another form of it.]

XERCA. In Waj; to be distinguished from Sarkā in Gojam, the Cerca of Almeida, and from Sarkā (Saka) in Enarya. [XVI *HSD* 57 Šerka.]

WABI. The Webi Shabelle, 'leopard river,' commonly called, as in the Abyssinian Chronicles and the *Futuh*, simply Wabi, Webi, 'the river.' Somali *webi*, 'river'; *shabel*, 'leopard.' It rises near Lake Awasa, crosses Somaliland, and loses itself in the sand a few miles before it reaches the Juba south of Mogadishu. [XVI *HGG* 198, *HSD* 57; XVIII *PC* 24 Wabi. Written Obe by Almeida in bk IV, chap. 25.]

WAJ, WAG. See Aoage.

ZALOT. Keith Johnston's map shows Zalot 5 miles SSE of Asmara; Ferret and Galinier call it Tsalot. [Perhaps the same as Za'lat Mikā'ēl of *CB* 157.]

ZARIMA. The Zarima (ND 37/4 Zerima; Keith Johnston, Sarima) rises at an altitude of about 10,000 ft. above Wolchefit, and runs down towards the NNW. Keith Johnston shows it as joining the Qollima, a tributary of the Takaze, though ND 37/4 shows it as disappearing about 25 miles before its supposed junction with the Qollima; Parkyns gives it as a tributary of the Takaze.

ZARMAT. NC 37/1 has a place called Sharmut on the shore of Lake Tana about 7 miles NNE of the point where the Abay leaves the lake. But both Almeida and Páez say that it was in Shoa; if so, it cannot be beside Lake Tana. Moreover, Fernandes took about 14 days to reach the Nile crossing 'near Nebesse' after leaving Zarmat, which also rules out an identification with Sharmut. And since in *CB* 154 the king is said to have gone from Dabra Berhan to Sarmat, it is clear that the place was in Shoa, and a long way from Lake Tana; we have not however been able to locate it on any map. [XV, XVI *CB* 154, *CS* 18 Sarmāt.]

ZEBEE. The Gibē river-system. (Italian maps, Ghibie.) The geography of this river-system is somewhat complex. The main stream or Great Gibē rises near Haratu on the western edge of the Choman swamp, about 100 miles NW of Abalti. Near Sogido, 55 miles south of Haratu, it is joined by the Gibē Enarya, which rises SE of Sarka and flowing northwards bounds Enarya on the east. About 30 miles SE from Sogido the Gibē Jimma, also from the south, enters the main stream at a point 7 miles NW of Abalti; and 10 miles from here the river thus augmented joins the Omo. [XVI *HSD* 38 Zebē; XVIII *PC* 55, *AJIB* 261 Gibē. Beke regarded *Zebee* and *Gibbe* (in his spelling) as distinct names, the former of Gonga, the latter of Galla origin. The Galla name, he suggested, meant 'lake' or 'standing water', while *zebee* he believed to be a dialect form of the *Swahili* word *ziwa*, 'lake' (though which dialect he did not specify). He also derived the name of Lake *Zwai* from *ziwa* ('The Nile and its tributaries,' pp. 62, 63). The change from *zebee* to *gibbe* he believed to be due to the Galla invasion. It is true that the occurrence of *zebe* in the sixteenth century *HSD* lends some colour to this, though the Kafa *gibe* (in the phrase *gibē ašō*, 'foreign man,' i.e. 'man from the Gibē') suggests that the words are really the same. The equation of *zebe* with *ziwa* is merely fanciful, as also seems to be the derivation which has been suggested from *qibe*, 'butter,' on account of the colour of the water.]

ZEILA. The roadstead of Zeila, formerly the principal harbour of Somaliland and southern Ethiopia. [I *PME* 7 Aualītēs; XIV Al 'Umari, *Masalik al absar*, 4, Zaila'.]

ZOAJ. Lake Zway or Zeway, the largest and most northerly of the

south Ethiopian chain of lakes. It is said to be called Jilalu
in Guragē and Lagi in Galla. According to a local tradition it
occupies the site of a territory once ruled by seven chiefs
which was covered by water in one night, 'so long ago that no
one knows when' (Basset, *Conquête*, p. 371). [XVI *HGG*
200 Zewāy; XVIII *PC* 23 Zeway.]

INDEX

(Foreign, i.e. not English, words and titles are given in italics. When such words are not Portuguese, Ethiopic or Amharic, the language to which they belong is shown in brackets. The cedilla is retained only where it is correctly used. In the text it is often inserted when superfluous and omitted when necessary. The accents used by Almeida in writing African and oriental names are ignored, his practice in this respect being hopelessly erratic.)

Gum, civet in, 52; economy of, lxxix, lxxx; history of, lxxxvi–lxxxix; list of kings of, lxxxvi, lxxxvii; other references, lxxvi, lxxvii
Gumar (Gomar), 10, 11, 124, 237
Gundeira, 48
Gunpowder, 48
Guns in Ethiopia, 186
Gura, lxix
Gur'a, lxix
Gurabo, lv
Guragē, situation of, 11, 19; dialects, 56; history, lxviii–lxx; other references, lxii, lxvii, lxxxiv–lxxxvi, 10, 47, 162, 163, 237
Guragues, 237; and see Guragē
Gurguto, lix
Gush Abay. See Nile, source of
Gushi rasho (Kafa), lv
Guzarate. See Gujerat

Habaš, 7
Habashat, 7, 8
Habela, 97, 237
Habeto, 7
Habex, 7, 8
Hadea, 237; and see Hadya
Hadiya (Gudela), li, lxii, lxv
Hadya (Hadea), lii, lxii, lxiii, 10, 11, 69
Hafun, 233
Hagalababo, Galla tribe, 113
Hagenia abyssinica, 98; see also Kosso
Hail, 21
Hairdressing, 61, 127, 138
Hakāko, Galla tribe, 112, 113
Halabdo (Galla), 128
Halchisa, luba, 207
Halmam Gama, lxviii
Hamalmal, grandson of Lebna Dengel, 116, 117
Hamasen (Amacem), 72, 94, 227
Hamed. See Grañ
Hamelmal, governor of Kambatta, 162 seq., 171
Hamites, l, li, 54, 55
Hana, lxxxvii
Hana Gafare, lxxxviii
Hanazo, 222
Haoax, river, 238; and see Awash
Haramaya, Lake, 120

Harar (Arar), lii, lxvi, lxvii, lxix, lxxii, lxxv, xcv, 43 228, 229; language of, 56
Harbo, 118
Hare, 52
Harice, 32, 238
Harir, 93
Harmufāh, luba, lxxv, 118
Harrier, 53
Harsu, Galla tribe, 113
Haruro, li
Haṣē, 7, 111
Haṣēgē, 7
Hayal (*Hayel*), 94
Hazalo, 117
Hebrew language, 55
Helena, Queen, xxxvii, 103, 107
Henry VIII, King of England, 69
Heqo, lvi
Hezabay, 94
Hezba Nañ (Hezbinanho), King, 101
Hine, Galla tribe, lxii
Hinnakaro, lv
Hinnari, lv
Hinnimacho, lv
Hinnucho, lv
Hippopotamus, 31, 35, 58
Hiyo, 55
Hodder, Col., 214
Hodeida (Odida), 55
Hoko, Galla tribe, 112, 113
Holcait, 238; and see Walqayt
Holeca, 241; and see Walaqa
Homerites, 8
Hondius, xciii, xciv, xcvi, 12
Honey, lxxix, 64, 65, 78, 94, 95
Hopper (Anglo-Indian), see *Apa*
Horata (Horreta), luba, 206, 207
Horn (musical instrument), 96
Horo, Galla tribe, lxii
Horreta, luba, 207
Horse, bamboo, 176; harness, 50, 51; in army, 77, 81; trade in, 43, 50; Galla ride, 117, 137, 139
Hortelio. See Ortelius
Houses, Abyssinian, 20, 83, 84; Janjero, 161; Kafa, 161
Hoy, 6
Humbanā, Galla tribe, 112
Husain, Sheikh, lii, lxxxix
Hyaena, 44, 51

Iabeddu, 94